Generative AI Applications and Intelligent Systems:

From Chatbots to Cybersecurity

Bahaa Eddine Elbaghazaoui
https://orcid.org/0000-0002-3206-5162
Sultan Moulay Slimane University, Morocco

Mohamed Amnai
Ibn Tofail University, Morocco

Noreddine Gherabi
https://orcid.org/0000-0002-2020-249X
Sultan Moulay Slimane University, Morocco

IGI Global
Scientific Publishing
Publishing Tomorrow's Research Today

Vice President of Editorial	Melissa Wagner
Director of Acquisitions	Mikaela Felty
Director of Book Development	Jocelynn Hessler
Production Manager	Mike Brehm
Cover Design	Jose Rosado

Published in the United States of America by
IGI Global Scientific Publishing
701 East Chocolate Avenue
Hershey, PA, 17033, USA
Tel: 717-533-8845 | Fax: 717-533-7115
Website: https://www.igi-global.com E-mail: cust@igi-global.com

Library of Congress Cataloging-in-Publication Data

No LCCN (CIP Data Pending)
ISBN13: 9798337380117
Isbn13Softcover: 9798337380124
EISBN13: 9798337380131

British Cataloguing in Publication Data
A Cataloguing in Publication record for this book is available from the British Library.

Table of Contents

Detailed Table of Contents

Generative AI has revolutionized text and language processing, offering transformative competencies that redefine how virtual media is created, personalized, and ate up. This period employs advanced neural networks, along with transformers and generative pre-educated fashions, to deliver coherent, contextually relevant, and human-like textual content. Within the realm of digital media, generative AI allows numerous programs, along with computerized content material advent, sentiment evaluation, actual-time translation, conversational dealers, and personalized marketing campaigns. The mixing of generative AI into digital media workflows has brought about improved performance and creativity, allowing content material creators to generate amazing outputs with minimal attempt. Moreover, it empowers corporations to deliver hyper-customized man or woman tales with the aid of tailoring content material material based totally on individual possibilities and consumption styles.

The ambiguity and gradience of natural human language are frequently difficult for conventional sentiment analysis models to capture, particularly in crucial situations like false information pertaining to health. This chapter explores how fuzzy linguistic

This chapter discusses how chatbots have changed, where they are used and the ethical questions they raise, focusing on their roles in healthcare, education and helping customers. Earlier, they only responded through rules, but now, thanks to AI and natural language processing, chatbots can engage in complicated, talking-like discussions with people. According to the analysis, there is a clear increase in studies about big artificial intelligence models such as ChatGPT and their effect on mental health, education and public health. Yet, the presence of biased content, privacy risks, false information and emotional dependency in digital platforms calls for careful thought. At the end of the chapter, it is recommended that disciplines collaborate to face these issues and that a balance of good design and regulations is important. As chatbots are designed for the future, enhancing transparency, improving user trust and following ethical guidelines are all important.

The rapid advancement of artificial intelligence has catalyzed the emergence of intelligent chatbots as pivotal tools in higher education. Initially deployed for administrative tasks, these conversational agents have evolved into sophisticated virtual advisors that support personalized learning by adapting to individual student needs. This chapter examines the role of chatbots as intelligent advisors, highlighting their capabilities to provide context-aware guidance, real-time feedback, and motivational support. It explores the pedagogical benefits of integrating chatbots into academic environments, including enhanced learner autonomy, inclusivity, and scalability. The discussion also addresses key challenges such as data privacy,

examining how AI improves recommendation quality and where challenges remain. Using the MovieLens 10K dataset, we conduct a comparative analysis of widely used algorithms. The performance of RS algorithms is assessed both as a machine learning problem, through collaborative and content-based filtering, and as a deep learning problem, by evaluating recent neural models. We also discuss evaluation methodologies, data types, and the potential of combining algorithms to enhance performance. The findings provide a clearer view of AI's role in RS, highlighting strengths, limitations, and future research opportunities.

Weight initialization is a critical factor in training convolutional neural networks (CNNs), particularly in remote sensing (RS) applications where data is often high-dimensional, imbalanced, and noisy. This review explores traditional methods such as Random, Xavier, and He initialization, as well as modern strategies like MetaInit, GradInit, RGB-based, Laor, and convergence-aware approaches. These techniques are evaluated in the context of RS-specific challenges and benchmarked across architectures like VGG, ResNet, and DenseNet. Case studies in urban segmentation, SAR target recognition, and infrastructure quality assessment show that domain-sensitive initialization improves convergence speed, training stability, and classification accuracy. The review emphasizes the importance of selecting adaptive and data-aware initialization schemes that align with RS data characteristics. Overall, weight initialization should be treated not as a fixed preprocessing step but as a key design element for building robust, accurate, and scalable deep learning models in RS.

Large language models (LLMs), such as GPT-4 or BioGPT, offer us attractive prospects for automatic natural language processing in the medical field, particularly in the field of radiology. However, their use raises important questions regarding the reliability of the results they provide us. This study comprehensively examines the errors generated by these models in simulated radiological scenarios, analyzing their types, origins, and potential clinical repercussions. To reduce these errors, we explored strategies such as prompt reformulation and the addition of clinical context. Our initial results show that structured approaches can significantly reduce factual errors and hallucinations. Two scientific articles resulting from this work are currently being submitted.

The convergence of Digital Twins and the Internet of Things (IoT) is transforming industrial ecosystems by facilitating real-time intelligence, predictive analytics, and data-driven decision-making. However, this integration also amplifies cybersecurity vulnerabilities, necessitating robust and adaptive security frameworks. This chapter critically examines the cybersecurity imperatives associated with Digital Twin–IoT environments, highlighting threats such as ransomware, data breaches, and supply chain attacks. It underscores the role of secure communication protocols, identity and access management, and blockchain-based solutions in mitigating risks. Regulatory frameworks—including GDPR, NIST, and ISO/IEC 27001—are analyzed to elucidate compliance complexities in transnational contexts. Through empirical case studies, the chapter illustrates past cyber incidents and identifies strategic mitigation practices. Finally, it explores emerging challenges posed by quantum computing and edge security, advocating for dynamic, future-ready cybersecurity architectures.

This study presents an AI-powered solution addressing three critical challenges in IoT security: Class imbalance in intrusion datasets, limited diversity in attack patterns, and the need for real-time analysis of network traffic. Our hybrid approach combines optimized machine learning models (Logistic Regression, Random Forest with One-vs-Rest strategy) with advanced deep learning architectures (FNN, LSTM, GRU) to handle complex multi-class classification of network intrusions. We developed an end-to-end detection system featuring a user-friendly Streamlit interface that supports PCAP file analysis, real-time traffic visualization, and interactive threat reporting. The system achieved 98.56% detection accuracy in our evaluations, significantly outperforming conventional methods. Practical implementation features include automated firewall configuration recommendations and dynamic IP blocking for high-risk threats. This research demonstrates how AI-driven security solutions can provide adaptive protection for IoT ecosystems, offering both technical innovation and practical utility.

Preface

OVERVIEW OF THE SUBJECT MATTER

The ongoing evolution of **Generative Artificial Intelligence (GenAI)** is reshaping the foundations of intelligent systems. Once limited to analytical prediction and pattern recognition, artificial intelligence now creates, reasons, and interacts in ways that mirror human cognition. GenAI has moved beyond algorithms that simply learn from data to those that can produce new, coherent, and context-aware information across text, audio, imagery, and decision processes.

This book, ***Generative AI Applications and Intelligent Systems: From Chatbots to Cybersecurity***, explores the practical dimensions of this transformation. It examines how generative models are being integrated into real-world systems that enhance communication, learning, creativity, and digital protection. Through eleven chapters, the volume presents a balanced blend of conceptual insight, applied research, and engineering practice, illustrating how GenAI is enabling a new generation of intelligent, ethical, and secure digital ecosystems.

RELEVANCE AND CONTEXT IN THE MODERN WORLD

Artificial intelligence has entered a decisive phase where creativity and reasoning converge. The rise of large language models and multimodal architectures has empowered developers and researchers to design systems capable of adaptive dialogue, automatic content generation, and self-improving decision-making. These advances have changed how organizations communicate, educate, and protect digital assets.

However, the same capabilities that enable innovation also introduce new challenges related to misinformation, bias, and cybersecurity. The responsible integration of GenAI into education, healthcare, media, and industrial infrastructures is therefore essential. This book positions itself within that responsibility: it provides the reader with analytical and technical foundations to design intelligent systems that are both powerful and trustworthy.

TARGET AUDIENCE

The content of this book is aimed at:

- **Researchers and practitioners** who seek to deepen their understanding of generative architectures and applied AI.
- **Educators and instructional designers** interested in adaptive and personalized learning systems.
- **Developers and engineers** building conversational agents, recommender systems, and domain-specific AI applications.
- **Healthcare and cybersecurity professionals** exploring GenAI for reliability, risk detection, and system resilience.
- **Policy makers and innovators** developing frameworks for responsible and secure AI deployment.

Each chapter provides clear objectives, real-world examples, and discussion of ethical considerations, offering a multidimensional view of intelligent system design in the era of generative technologies.

CHAPTER SUMMARIES AND CONTRIBUTIONS

1. Generative AI in Text and Language Processing for Digital Media

This chapter presents the foundations of text-based GenAI applications, including automated summarization, translation, and narrative generation. It highlights how these tools are reshaping journalism, marketing, and creative industries by combining linguistic fluency with computational precision.

2. Beyond Binary Sentiment – Leveraging Fuzzy Linguistic Hedges to Enhance NLP-Based Fake News Detection

The authors introduce fuzzy linguistic modeling to move sentiment analysis beyond simple polarity. By refining nuance and intensity of expression, the chapter provides a more sophisticated mechanism for identifying misinformation and emotional manipulation in online communication.

3. Artificial Intelligence and the Didactics of Mathematics in Secondary Education – Transforming Teaching and Learning Practices

This contribution explores the impact of AI on mathematics education. It demonstrates how adaptive tutoring systems generate personalized exercises, explain problem-solving steps, and provide immediate feedback, leading to more inclusive and data-driven teaching strategies.

4. Chatbots – Evolution, Technologies and Applications

A historical and technical overview of conversational agents, covering rule-based chatbots, retrieval-based models, and generative systems built on transformers. The chapter emphasizes design principles for natural interaction, contextual understanding, and user experience optimization.

5. Chatbots as Intelligent Advisors – Transforming Personalized Learning in Higher Education

This chapter extends the discussion to higher education, showing how intelligent chatbots act as mentors and learning companions. Real case studies illustrate how they support academic advising, feedback collection, and self-regulated learning.

6. Design and Evaluation of a Personalized AI Tutoring System Using ChatGPT

The authors detail the design of a personalized tutoring platform powered by ChatGPT. They examine dialogue adaptation, learner modeling, and performance evaluation, demonstrating how generative dialogue can replicate aspects of human tutoring at scale.

7. Navigating Preferences with Artificial Intelligence – A Spotlight on Recommender System Innovations

Focusing on personalization beyond conversation, this chapter reviews the evolution of recommender systems. It describes how generative reasoning enhances hybrid approaches, producing recommendations that are contextual, explainable, and user-centric.

8. A Comprehensive Review of Weight Initialization Strategies for CNNs in Remote Sensing

This technical review analyzes how weight initialization influences the learning stability of convolutional neural networks in remote-sensing applications. It explores generative pretraining strategies that improve accuracy in environmental and geospatial analytics.

9. Assessing the Reliability of Large Language Models in Radiological Scenarios – Error Typology and Mitigation Strategies

The chapter investigates how GenAI can assist in radiology interpretation while ensuring reliability and safety. It categorizes common error types and proposes validation protocols to minimize diagnostic risks and enhance model accountability in medical contexts.

10. Safeguarding Digital Transformation – Cybersecurity for Digital Twin and IoT Ecosystems

This contribution links generative intelligence with cybersecurity engineering. It presents architectures for protecting digital twins and IoT networks through threat simulation, anomaly detection, and adaptive defense, reinforcing the concept of proactive digital resilience.

11. Securing IoT with Advanced Machine and Deep Learning for Multi-Class Intrusion Detection

The final chapter focuses on defending connected environments. It introduces advanced deep-learning models capable of detecting and classifying multiple intrusion types in real time, showing how generative algorithms contribute to robust IoT protection frameworks.

CONCLUSION – IMPACT AND CONTRIBUTION TO THE FIELD

This book demonstrates how **Generative AI** can be effectively applied across education, communication, and cybersecurity to create systems that are not only intelligent but also adaptable and transparent. It emphasizes the convergence of creativity, automation, and protection as the foundation of the next generation of intelligent systems.

By uniting diverse academic and professional perspectives, the volume highlights a future where generative intelligence enhances human expertise rather than replacing it. It offers a comprehensive reference for researchers, practitioners, and decision-makers dedicated to designing AI applications that promote innovation, trust, and resilience in the digital era.

Chapter 1
Generative AI in Text and Language Processing for Digital Media

N. Rajkumar
https://orcid.org/0000-0001-7857-9452
Alliance School of Advanced Computing, Alliance University, India

G. Nagarajan
https://orcid.org/0000-0003-3278-1326
Department of Computer Science and Engineering, Saveetha School of Engineering, SIMATS, Chennai, India

C. Viji
https://orcid.org/0000-0002-2759-8896
Alliance School of Advanced Computing, Alliance University, India

A. Mohanraj
Sri Eshwar College of Engineering, India

Balusamy Nachiappan
https://orcid.org/0009-0006-0951-8078
Prologis, India

Judeson Antony Kovilpillai
Amity University, India

Prabhu Shankar B.
https://orcid.org/0000-0003-4394-9171
Vel Tech Rangarajan Dr.Sagunthala R&D Institute of Science and Technology, India

ABSTRACT

Generative AI has revolutionized text and language processing, offering transformative competencies that redefine how virtual media is created, personalized, and ate up. This period employs advanced neural networks, along with transformers and generative pre-educated fashions, to deliver coherent, contextually relevant, and human-like textual content. Within the realm of digital media, generative AI allows numerous programs, along with computerized content material advent, sentiment

DOI: 10.4018/979-8-3373-8011-7.ch001

evaluation, actual-time translation, conversational dealers, and personalized marketing campaigns. The mixing of generative AI into digital media workflows has brought about improved performance and creativity, allowing content material creators to generate amazing outputs with minimal attempt. Moreover, it empowers corporations to deliver hyper-customized man or woman tales with the aid of tailoring content material material based totally on individual possibilities and consumption styles.

1. INTRODUCTION

Generative AI has emerged as a transformative force in modern-day technology, especially within the realm of text and language processing for digital media. This segment explores the definition, evolution, and importance of generative AI from the aspect of its large scope and packages in the digital media landscape.

1.1 Definition and Evolution of Generative AI

Generative artificial Intelligence (AI) refers to a category of AI models designed to produce new content material, together with text, pictures, audio, and video, by getting to know patterns and systems from present data. Unlike traditional AI structures, which are focused on category or choice-making, generative AI creates outputs that mimic human creativity.

The evolution of generative AI has been pushed by improvements in deep learning, in particular with the development of models like Generative Adversarial Networks (GANs) for pictures and transformer-based architectures like GPT (Generative Pre-trained Transformer) for textual content. The ones models leverage substantial datasets and powerful computing to supply awesome, coherent content.

Historical Perspective: From Rule-Based Systems to Neural Networks

The journey of generative AI can be divided into three distinct phases:

1. **Rule-Based Systems (1950s–1980s):**

Early AI systems were primarily based on predefined guidelines and logic, offering constrained flexibility and creativity. Language processing relied on syntactic parsing and rule-based grammars.

2. **Statistical Approaches (1990s–2000s):**

The emergence of statistical techniques, which include Hidden Markov models (HMMs) and N-grams, delivered probabilistic reasoning to language modeling. Those strategies laid the idea for extra sophisticated AI models.

3. **Deep Learning Era (2010s–Present):**

The arrival of neural networks, particularly recurrent neural networks (RNNs) and long-term short-term memory (LSTM) models, revolutionized series modeling. The development of transformers has similarly superior the field, permitting generative models like GPT, BERT, and T5 to handle complex language responsibilities with first-rate accuracy.

Importance of Text and Language Processing in Digital Media

Text and language processing lie at the heart of digital media, shaping how information is generated, consumed, and communicated. It enables a range of applications that have redefined industries:

- **Content Generation:** From computerized information articles to innovative writing, generative AI is a cornerstone of cutting-edge content material cloth manufacturing.
- **Customer Interaction:** AI-driven chatbots and digital assistants enhance patron reports via the usage of providing short and accurate responses.
- **Information Access:** Summarization and translation tools enhance the accessibility of records for international audiences(Pamudhurthy et al., n.d.).

As virtual media continues to extend, the role of text and language processing will only grow, driving performance and innovation in content material creation and shipping.

1.2 Scope of Generative AI in Digital Media

Generative AI's capability in digital media extends beyond conventional packages, imparting groundbreaking equipment and answers at some point of industries.

Role in Content Creation, Sentiment Analysis, Chatbots, etc.

1. **Content Creation:**

Generative AI enables the fast manufacturing of super content, which encompasses articles, blogs, and social media posts. Tools like OpenAI's GPT models can generate contextually accurate and stylistically appropriate text, saving effort and time for content material fabric creators(Chumakov et al., 2023).

2. **Sentiment Analysis:**

With the aid of reading customer-generated content along with opinions, tweets, and remarks, generative AI allows groups to understand public sentiment. This insight drives advertising and marketing strategies and brand management.

3. **Chatbots and Virtual Assistants:**

AI-powered conversational marketers like ChatGPT, Google Assistant, and Amazon Alexa offer seamless customer service and private assistance, enhancing individual engagement and pleasure.

4. **Personalized Recommendations:**

Generative AI tailors content to male or woman possibilities, enhancing the user experience on systems like Netflix, Spotify, and Amazon.

5. **Text-to-Image or Video Synthesis:**

By way of transforming textual descriptions into seen content, tools like DALL-E permit new possibilities in advertising and advertising and marketing, gaming, and innovative industries.

Importance for Businesses, Consumers, and Researchers

1. **For Businesses:**
    - o **Enhanced Productivity:** Automating repetitive responsibilities like drafting emails or growing advertising and advertising and marketing reproduction permits companies to awareness on strategic tasks.
    - o **Improved Customer Experience:** AI-powered personalization and chatbots make sure customers attain a tailored and at once guide.
2. **For Consumers:**
    - o **Ease of Access:** Ease of get right of entry to: Summarization, translation, and recommendation structures simplify facts get admission to and consumption.
    - o **Engaging Experiences:** Interactive AI, along with voice assistants and AI-generated media, enriches consumer reports.
3. **For Researchers:**
    - o **Accelerated Discoveries:** AI-generated summaries and literature opinions accelerate study workflows.

- o **Cross-Disciplinary Applications:** Generative AI allows studies in linguistics, cognitive technological know-how, and computer technology.

Generative AI isn't just reshaping digital media but also fostering collaboration and creativity throughout industries. Its potential to automate, customize, and innovate is ushering in a brand new generation of content material-driven generation.

2. CORE TECHNOLOGIES IN GENERATIVE AI FOR LANGUAGE PROCESSING

The technological underpinnings of generative AI in language processing are rooted in advanced systems that use techniques and models. This segment delves into the fundamental technologies that allow generative AI to method, understand, and generate human-like text.

2.1 Natural Language Processing (NLP)

Natural Language Processing (NLP) is a subfield of AI that specializes in permitting machines to recognize and device human language. It includes the improvement of algorithms and models that could interpret linguistic systems, derive the meaning from text, and generate coherent responses. NLP is the foundation of generative AI programs in language processing and has numerous key components that facilitate those responsibilities.

Tokenization is a vital step in NLP, in which textual content is broken down into smaller units, inclusive of terms or subwords, to simplify evaluation. As an instance, the sentence "The AI revolution" may be cut up into tokens like "The," "AI," and "revolution." Parsing follows, which entails reading the grammatical form of a sentence to apprehend how its components relate to each other. This will be finished through dependency parsing, which identifies difficulty-verb-item relationships, or constituency parsing, which breaks sentences into hierarchical phrases. Semantic analysis is every other critical aspect, focusing on the know-how the means of phrases and sentences. Techniques, inclusive of word feel disambiguation and named entity recognition (NER), assist the version to pick out particular entities like people, groups, or places in a text.

Part-of-speech (POS) tagging is used to assign grammatical roles, in conjunction with nouns or verbs, to every phrase in a sentence. That is essential for syntactic and semantic understanding. In the long run, language modeling predicts the risk of word sequences, allowing the era of coherent sentences. The components work together to allow machines to technique and generate human-like textual content successfully.

Examples of outstanding NLP models include BERT (Bidirectional Encoder Representations from Transformers), developed through Google, which techniques textual content bidirectionally and improves tasks which including sentiment assessment and query answering. Every other key model is GPT (Generative Pre-trained Transformer) by using OpenAI, designed for textual content technology through predicting the subsequent phrase in a chain. T5 (textual content-to-text content switch Transformer) is each other versatile model by Google, capable of managing duties which consist of translation, summarization, and sort with the aid of the use of converting them into a textual content-to-text format(Singla et al., 2024).

Figure 1. NLP pipeline diagram

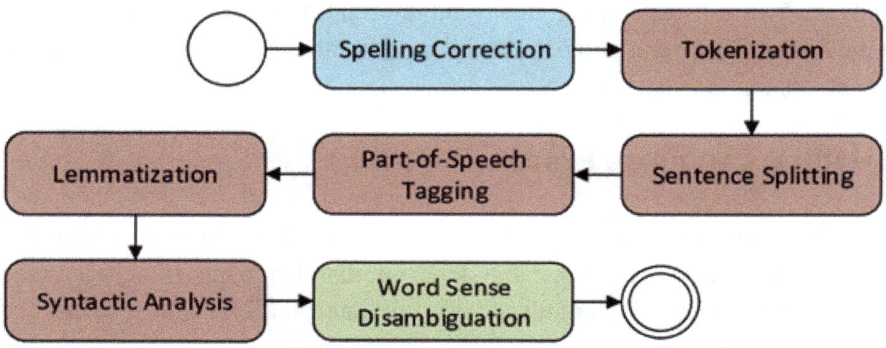

2.2 Transformer Models and Language Generation

Transformers are a pivotal innovation in present-day NLP, revolutionizing language processing through overcoming the constraints of earlier sequential fashions like RNNs and LSTMs. Introduced inside the seminal paper "Attention is All You Need" by Vaswani et al. In 2017, transformers leveraged the self-hobby mechanism to procedure whole sequences of textual content simultaneously, making them pretty green and scalable.

The self-attention mechanism enables transformers to recognize relevant phrases internal a sequence, even if they may be far apart. This functionality is especially essential for knowledge context in prolonged texts, permitting the technology of coherent and contextually appropriate responses. Moreover, transformers' capacity to manner sequences in parallel drastically improves computational efficiency compared to earlier models that processed data sequentially.

Generative models like GPT are built on a transformer shape. Those models generate human-like textual content by predicting the subsequent word in a sequence primarily based on the context provided. The method starts with pre-schooling, where the model learns language patterns from large datasets, which encompass books, articles, and internet websites. This is determined via quality-tuning, in which the model is customized for unique obligations, consisting of summarization or the talk era. While producing text, the model makes use of its pre-trained statistics to provide coherent and contextually relevant sentences, phrase by phrase.

Figure 2. Transformer model Architecture

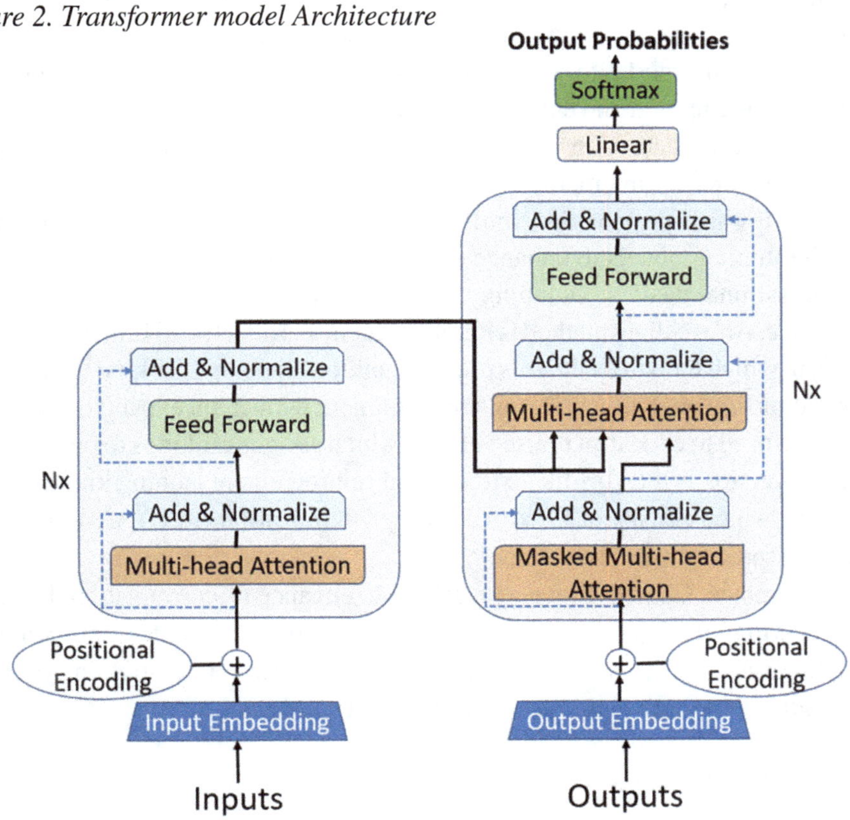

2.3 Reinforcement Learning in Text Generation

Reinforcement Learning (RL) is a machine learning approach where models learn to make decisions by interacting with an environment and receiving feedback in the form of rewards or penalties. In text generation, RL plays a critical role in fine-tuning models to improve the quality and relevance of their outputs(Saha, 2025).

Conversational agents, such as ChatGPT, rely on RL to enhance their performance. A notable technique is Reinforcement Learning from Human Feedback (RLHF), where human evaluators provide rankings for different model outputs based on their quality and alignment with user expectations. This feedback is used to train a reward model, which assigns scores to outputs. The generative model is then fine-tuned using reinforcement learning algorithms, such as Proximal Policy Optimization (PPO), to optimize its behavior based on the reward model.

For instance, ChatGPT leverages RLHF to improve its conversational abilities, ensuring that responses are helpful, accurate, and contextually appropriate. This process allows the model to adapt and align with human preferences over time, resulting in more natural and engaging interactions. Reinforcement learning (RL) is a decision-making method in which models discover ways to make decisions with the useful resource of interacting with an environment and receiving feedback in the form of rewards or penalties. In the textual content era, RL performs a crucial role in fine-tuning models to enhance the excellent and relevance of their outputs.

Conversational dealers, including ChatGPT, depend upon RL to enhance their performance. An excellent method is Reinforcement learning from Human comments (RLHF), in which human evaluators provide rankings for one-of-a-kind version outputs based mostly on their wonderful and alignment with client expectations. These remarks are used to educate a praise version, which assigns rankings to outputs. The generative version is then brilliantly the use of reinforcement gaining knowledge of algorithms, which consist of Proximal Policy Optimization (PPO), to optimize its behavior based on the praise version.

As an instance, ChatGPT leverages RLHF to enhance its conversational competencies, making sure that responses are beneficial, correct, and contextually suitable. This manner allows the model to evolve and align with human options over the years, resulting in more natural and attractive interactions.

2.4 Neural Networks in Text Synthesis

In advance of the appearance of transformers, neural networks alongside Recurrent Neural Networks (RNNs), Long Short-Term Memory networks (LSTMs), and Gated Recurrent Units (GRUs) were the dominant fashions for text synthesis. Those models have been designed to deal with sequential records and have performed a big function in advancing language modeling and textual content technology.

RNNs were the earliest neural architectures for sequential information. They maintained a hidden nation that captured statistics about previous inputs, permitting the version to generate text by predicting the following phrase in a sequence. But,

RNNs struggled with long-term dependencies due to vanishing gradient issues, limiting their effectiveness for longer texts. LSTMs addressed this challenge by introducing a memory cell that would keep statistics over longer sequences, making them extra effective for managing context. GRUs, a simplified model of LSTMs, supplied similar skills with fewer parameters, making them computationally green.

No matter their improvements, RNNs, LSTMs, and GRUs confronted scalability issues at the same time as handling big datasets and complicated obligations. Transformers resolved these challenges with the resource of having rid of the need for sequential data processing. Not like their predecessors, transformers process complete sequences in parallel, taking into consideration extra overall performance and scalability. This transition marked a turning point in NLP, allowing the development of massive-scale fashions like GPT-4 that would generate great, human-like textual content all through various domains.

3. APPLICATIONS OF GENERATIVE AI IN DIGITAL MEDIA

3.1 Automated Content Creation

One of the maximum terrific applications of generative AI in digital media is automated content material cloth advent. Equipment like OpenAI's ChatGPT has enabled the generation of blogs, articles, and innovative writing with exceptional ease and overall performance. The one tool can analyze a given set of data, understand its context, and produce coherent, nicely-based content material in a matter of seconds. That is specifically useful for digital marketers and publishers who require a high volume of content on a ordinary basis. In preference to relying on human writers, which can be time-consuming and expensive, AI-generated content gives a greater scalable and cost-effective answer. AI structures can also optimize the content material for search engine optimization, ensuring that it ranks well on search engines like Google and reaches a broader audience. For virtual marketers, this no longer handiest saves time but also allows for a more targeted method to content introduction, as AI can tailor its output primarily based on particular target audience options or inclinations(Gujar, 2024).

3.2 Chatbots and Virtual Assistants

Some other important software of generative AI in digital media is the improvement of chatbots and virtual assistants. Those AI-pushed equipment are designed to interact with customers, offering assistance in diverse domains, which include customer service, e-commerce, and healthcare. Generative AI powers these chatbots, permitting them to comprehend natural language, respond contextually, and even maintain complex conversations. In customer support, for example, chatbots can manage queries, clear up problems, or maybe offer customized recommendations based on a consumer's records. That is especially valuable for groups working in industries like e-trade, in which supplying properly timed responses to purchaser inquiries can significantly impact earnings and client satisfaction. Healthcare, moreover, benefits from AI-powered virtual assistants that may offer scientific records, help with appointment scheduling, and offer customized health recommendations. Popular examples of generative AI-driven virtual assistants include OpenAI's ChatGPT, Google's Bard, and Amazon Alexa. Those systems have made it less complicated for clients to get proper access to information, perform obligations, and enhance their everyday experience in a wide variety of programs.

3.3 Sentiment Analysis and Social Media Monitoring

Generative AI has made massive strides in the location of sentiment assessment and social media monitoring. In these days' fast-paced digital world, real-time monitoring of customer sentiment has turned out to be crucial for organizations, public relations teams, and crisis management professionals. Sentiment assessment equipment powered by manner of generative AI can examine tremendous amounts of social media information to gauge public opinion, pick out developments, and stumble upon emerging issues. For example, organizations can use AI to track customer reviews on sites like Twitter, Facebook, or Instagram to recognize how their services or products are being received. This permits companies to adjust their strategies, address horrible remarks, and engage with their audiences greater successfully. Additionally, sentiment evaluation is essential in PR and disaster control because it lets corporations show the general public's perception of their logo, merchandise, or services in real-time. With the aid of analyzing social media conversations, generative AI can hit upon potential PR crises and alert businesses to take corrective action earlier than issues become severe (Medhat et al., 2025).

3.4 Personalized Content Recommendations

Generative AI also performs a crucial function in delivering personalised content pointers, a key feature of structures like Netflix and Spotify. These systems rely upon AI to research consumer options, past interactions, and behavior to advocate films, TV indicates, track, and special kinds of content material which may be tailor-made to individual tastes. By leveraging AI algorithms, those systems can constantly refine and update their pointers, making sure that customers are furnished with content they may possibly experience. This is not the simplest complement the man or woman experiences, however additionally boosts engagement. Customized content recommendations help customers find new content material fabric they might not have come across otherwise, leading to accelerated time spent on the platform. For companies, this may translate into better person retention, extended engagement costs, and in the end, more revenue. The fulfillment of advice structures on systems like Netflix and Spotify demonstrates the power of generative AI in driving consumer delight and engagement.

3.5 Text Summarization for News and Research

Textual content summarization is each other crucial software program of generative AI in digital media, specifically in the fields of journalism and academia. With the sheer quantity of facts being produced day by day, it could be overwhelming for people to sift through lengthy files, articles, or study papers to extract key insights. Generative AI-powered textual content summarization equipment can automatically generate concise summaries of prolonged content, presenting users with a brief assessment of the principal elements. That is specifically treasured in journalism, wherein newshounds can use an AI gadget to summarize fact articles or reports, letting them stay up to date on more than one tales without spending hours reading through large documents. In academia, AI-driven textual content summarization can help researchers quickly look at the relevance of a paper or look at, saving them treasured time while reviewing literature for their or her paintings. The one gear can also be used in numerous industries, together with regulation and finance, in which experts want to analyze large volumes of documents regularly. By means of decreasing the effort and time required to digest complex records, generative AI-powered textual content summarization is improving productivity and decision-making in many sectors.

Generative AI has proven to be a game-changer within the virtual media landscape, with its programs spanning computerized content creation, chatbots, sentiment analysis, customized pointers, and text summarization. Those generations not only most effectively decorate the performance and effectiveness of severa strategies but additionally decorate the consumer enjoy, making interactions more customized and meaningful. As AI continues to evolve, its impact on virtual media will most effectively expand, unlocking new possibilities for content material creation, customer engagement, and statistics processing.

As generative AI continues to reinforce and combine into diverse components of society, it brings with it extensive ethical implications and challenges that need to be addressed. Those issues span at some point areas such as bias in language models, plagiarism and authorship troubles, the advent of incorrect facts and deepfake texts, and the environmental expenses of large-scale AI fashions. Every one of these regions gives particular barriers that require careful consideration and innovative solutions to ensure that the AI era evolves and is deployed in an accountable and moral way.

4. ETHICAL IMPLICATIONS AND CHALLENGES

4.1 Bias in Language Models

One of the maximum urgent moral troubles surrounding generative AI is the presence of bias in language models. These biases can emerge from the information used to educate the models, which regularly mirror societal prejudices or stereotypes. As an example, a language model might likely generate outputs that reinforce harmful gender, racial, or cultural stereotypes. This could be seen in conditions in which AI-generated textual content assigns certain developments to people based on their gender or ethnicity, or even as it produces responses that can be discriminatory or offensive. Such biases in AI-generated content can have some distance-achieving outcomes, perpetuating inequality and reinforcing poor perceptions. To address these issues, it is crucial to put in force techniques which encompass fact augmentation, wherein training datasets are deliberately varied to embody a broader sort of views, and fairness auditing, in which models are often evaluated to perceive and accurate biases. Via actively using jogging to mitigate bias, developers can ensure that generative AI structures produce outputs that are honest, inclusive, and free from discrimination.

4.2 Plagiarism and Authorship Concerns

As AI technologies are increasingly used to generate content material, plagiarism and authorship concerns have end up primary ethical troubles. The capacity of generative AI to provide articles, essays, songs, and even code will raise questions about the ownership of such creations. If an AI version generates content material that carefully resembles or copies contemporary artwork, it may be visible as a violation of intellectual property rights, notwithstanding the reality that the AI itself does no longer have reason or recognition. The crooked implications of AI-generated content are nevertheless evolving; however, there must be clear guidelines across the attribution of authorship and the use of AI equipment in content creation. Transparency in AI systems is essential because it lets customers recognize how content material is generated and where it comes from. Moreover, clean attribution ought to be given to AI-generated works, ensuring that creators, whether or not or now not human or device, are well credited for his or her contributions. Without outright safeguards in place, the road between authentic artwork and AI-generated content material fabric ought to come to be increasingly blurred, major to capacity felony disputes and moral dilemmas.

4.3 Misinformation and Deepfake Texts

The danger of misinformation is another sizable ethical issue posed by generative AI. As AI structures come to be more state-of-the-art, they may be able to produce incredibly convincing faux records, manipulated texts, and deepfake content. Those AI-generated falsehoods can unfold throughout social media systems, deceptive the general public and distorting perceptions of truth. As an instance, AI can be used to generate fabricated statements or faux narratives that appear like legitimate information articles or social media posts, making it difficult for humans to distinguish between credible sources and unreliable ones. This trouble is compounded with the resource of the sheer amount of content material that may be created in a quick amount of time, overwhelming truth-checking efforts, and making it more difficult for people to confirm the authenticity of information. To combat this difficulty, the function of reality-checking and responsibility becomes increasingly important. Enforcing strong truth-checking structures, each automated and human-pushed, can help ensure that AI-generated content is very well vetted in advance before being shared publicly. Additionally, it is important for structures that host AI-generated content material to take responsibility for monitoring and curtailing the unfold of incorrect information, ensuring that duty lies with individuals who create, distribute, and expand false content fabric.

4.4 Environmental Costs of Training Models

Every different vital ethical attention of generative AI is the environmental cost associated with training massive AI models. The ones fashions, which require massive portions of computational energy, devour great power, and contribute to a high carbon footprint. Education modern-day fashions, inclusive of large language models, regularly includes running plenty of computations over prolonged intervals of time. This technique can be significantly resource-intensive, main to substantial power intake. The environmental effect of schooling AI models is a developing problem, especially as the call for more advanced AI technologies continues to upward thrust. The carbon emissions generated with the aid of these fashions are contributing to the broader trouble of climate change, and the development of AI must be balanced with efforts to lessen its ecological impact. To mitigate the environmental expenses, there are several strategies that can be implemented. One approach is the optimization of AI schooling techniques to make them more power-efficient, lowering the huge amount of computations required without compromising the general performance of the models. Furthermore, builders can explore using renewable energy assets for training AI models, minimizing the carbon footprint associated with their development. Every other approach is to popularity on growing more efficient algorithms that require much less computational energy, thereby reducing the power intake associated with training and deploying AI systems. By using the use of prioritizing sustainability in AI development, it is feasible to reduce the environmental impact of those technologies whilst despite the fact that advancing their abilities.

While generative AI can bring about transformative adjustments in numerous industries, it also offers numerous moral challenges that need to be addressed. Bias in language models, plagiarism and authorship issues, the unfolding of wrong facts, and the environmental expenses of schooling AI systems are all areas that require careful attention and motion. With the aid of enforcing techniques together with equity auditing, transparency, reality-checking, and sustainable development practices, we will assist in ensuring that the advantages of generative AI are found out while minimizing its negative effects. As AI technology continues to adapt, it's essential for developers, policymakers, and society at large to interact in ongoing discussions about a way to navigate these moral challenges and build a future in which AI serves the greater good.

Generative AI has made significant strides in numerous fields, with actual international programs transforming industries and creating new possibilities. In this section, we find numerous case studies of AI implementations across various domains. The examples spotlight the evolution of AI models and their programs in digital media, search engine optimization, journalism, and social media content moderation, presenting insights into the strength and capacity of AI technologies.

5. CASE STUDIES AND REAL-WORLD IMPLEMENTATIONS

5.1 Case Study: OpenAI's GPT Models

The evolution of OpenAI's Generative Pre-trained Transformers (GPT) fashions offers an outstanding example of the way AI can evolve to become even more state-of-the-art and successful. The adventure started with GPT-1, a modest model that laid the muse for future iterations. GPT-1 had 117 million parameters and grew to be skilled at predicting the subsequent word in a sentence through analyzing huge portions of textual content. Even though it became a step forward in the realm of natural language processing, it became constrained in its capability to generate coherent, lengthy-form text and recognize complex contexts.

With the release of GPT-2, OpenAI took a sizeable leap in advance. GPT-2 had 1.5 billion parameters, which enabled it to generate textual content that modified into not most effective greater coherent but also more contextually aware. It may produce whole paragraphs, articles, or maybe memories, making it a powerful device for content introduction in digital media. Its capacity to generate textual content in diverse writing patterns and adapt to important topics marked a crucial milestone in the development of generative AI models. The discharge of GPT-3-3 3 in addition pushed the limits, with one hundred seventy-five billion parameters, which allowed the version to comprehend and generate exceedingly nuanced and context-rich content. GPT-3 became able to engage in conversations, answering complicated questions, and generating human-like text, which garnered amazing interest and opened out new opportunities in fields like digital advertising, content introduction, and customer support.

By the time GPT-4 was delivered, the model became even more delicate, providing stepped forward language records, era, and accuracy. It may cope with responsibilities in conjunction with summarizing text, translating languages, developing code, or even imparting insights into complex topics. The GPT models have discovered programs in virtual media, which encompass automatic content generation, improving customer support via chatbots, generating creative writing, and supporting research. The key milestones executed with the resource of OpenAI's GPT models have not only best advanced the sector of natural language processing but moreover demonstrated the transformative ability of AI in normal packages(Wong et al., 2023).

5.2 Case Study: Google's BERT in Search Engine Optimization

Google's BERT (Bidirectional Encoder Representations from Transformers) version has had a huge effect on search engine optimization (search engine optimization) and content material rating. Delivered in 2019, BERT became an innovative leap forward for Google's search algorithms, as it allowed the search engine to better recognize the context of phrases in search queries. Unlike previous fashions that by and large focused on keyword matching, BERT enabled Google to research the relationship among phrases in a sentence, offering deeper data on patron cause.

For example, at the same time as a purchaser searches for a word like "2019 Brazil vacationer to united states of america of america need a visa," BERT allows Google to better understand that the man or woman is calling whether or not a traveler from Brazil to america desires a visa, in vicinity of truly matching key terms like "Brazil," "traveler," or "visa." This contextual expertise has appreciably progressed the accuracy of are looking for effects, providing customers extra relevant facts based on their specific queries. For content material creators and digital entrepreneurs, the implementation of BERT has reshaped search engine optimization strategies. Traditional search engine optimization strategies, which centered on keyword optimization, are not sufficient on their own. As an alternative, creating content material that aligns with the cause the return of are trying to find queries and gives extensive, contextually applicable records is now paramount.

The effect of BERT on user experience has been profound, as it has extensively progressed the excellence and relevance of are search for effects. Customers at the moment are capable of finding extra accurate solutions to their questions, with content fabric, this is more aligned with their dreams. For corporations, this shift manner that seo techniques should prioritize tremendous, informative content that addresses individual queries comprehensively. BERT has also emphasized the significance of herbal language processing in seek, because it brings AI's capability to recognize human language closer to human-like comprehension.

5.3 Case Study: AI in Journalism (The Washington Post's Heliograf)

In the vicinity of journalism, AI has all commenced to play a key function in automating content introduction, and one of the most notable implementations of that is The Washington Post's use of its AI-powered device, Heliograf. Heliograf grow to be launched in 2016 as a device designed to write down data articles autonomously, in particular for breaking news and sports events. This AI tool can look at uncooked facts and generate coherent, correct information reviews in a fragment of the time it'd take human reporters.

Heliograf makes use of natural language era (NLG) algorithms to write articles by pulling facts from numerous sources in conjunction with public databases, government reviews, and sports activities information. For instance, when covering election effects or sports activities scores, Heliograf can robotically generate reviews that may be accurate, timely, and regular. This capability has allowed The Washington positioned as much as increase its coverage of ordinary sports with out requiring reporters to manually write every tale. In doing so, Heliograf has freed up reporters to interest on extra in-depth reporting and investigative work.

But the upward thrust of AI-generated facts also raises essential implications. One of the concerns is the high-quality and accuracy of automatic content fabric, specifically in sensitive areas, which include politics and economics. At the same time as Heliograf can produce accurate evaluations primarily based on facts, it can not usually capture the nuances or offer the important evaluation that human newshounds provide. There is additionally the capability for moral concerns, together with the possibility of AI generating biased content or the risk of automation reducing job opportunities for journalists. Despite the reality that using AI in journalism represents a big shift in how records are produced and fed on, it highlights the developing function of AI in media industries.

5.4 Case Study: Social Media Content Moderation with AI

Social media structures have become breeding grounds for effective engagement and perilous content. The upward thrust of hate speech, harassment, and incorrect information on systems like Facebook and Twitter has triggered the ones corporations to discover the usage of AI for content moderation. AI-pushed content material moderation tools are designed to encounter and dispose of risky content, together with hate speech, photograph violence, and false facts, in real-time.

Facebook has applied AI systems that analyze posts, comments, and images to become aware of possibly dangerous content material. The platform makes use of tool mastering algorithms to find hate speech, threats, and picture violence, with the purpose of getting rid of harmful posts before they spread widely. In addition, Twitter makes use of AI to discover toxic language and block abusive users. These structures depend upon massive datasets of categorized content material to educate AI models, permitting them to recognize dangerous styles in textual content and images. AI has been proven to be powerful in filtering large volumes of content material, short and efficiently, something that might be almost not feasible for human moderators to do at scale.

But, the use of AI for content material moderation additionally affords demanding situations. One major problem is the ability for fake positives, wherein AI systems mistakenly take away valid content, which encompasses satire or essential speech. Moreover, AI systems may additionally struggle with detecting context, mainly with reference to nuanced language or cultural variations(An, 2023; Bhoyar, n.d.). While AI tools are usually enhancing, they may not be infallible and require human oversight to ensure fairness and accuracy. Furthermore, the deployment of AI in content moderation raises questions about freedom of speech and the extent to which tech corporations have to manage the content material shared on their platforms. The stability amongst moderating harmful content fabric and defensive customers proper to express themselves remains a complicated ethical dilemma.

The case research stated right here provides a glimpse into the numerous applications of AI in real-world situations, from content creation and seo to journalism and social media moderation. These implementations show off the large potential of AI to convert industries and enhance user studies. But, in addition, they highlight the ethical challenges and issues that have to be addressed to make sure that AI technology is used responsibly and for the advantage of society. As AI keeps to adapt, it's going to certainly cause further improvements in how we engage with information, media, and every extraordinary.

6. FUTURE DIRECTIONS AND EMERGING TRENDS

The future of generative AI in digital media is filled with interesting opportunities as the era continues to conform and redefine the manner we interact with statistics, create content material fabric, and devour media. As AI models emerge as more and more state-of-the-art, we're witnessing the emergence of recent traits as a good way to form the digital media landscape. Those developments encompass the development of next-generation language fashions, advancements in human-AI collaboration, the application of AI in multilingual and espresso-beneficial aid language processing, and the establishment of regulatory frameworks to manual the ethical use of AI era. In this segment, we discover those destiny instructions and their potential implications for the virtual media industry (Madaan et al., 2024; Rajkumar N et al., 2026).

6.1. Next-Generation Language Models

One of the biggest enhancements in AI research is the improvement of subsequent-generation language models that circulate beyond conventional text-based processing to include multimodal capabilities. A good example of this is the improvement towards multimodal AI, inclusive of GPT-4 vision, which combines text generation with the functionality to method and interpret pictures and movies. These models constitute a primary step ahead in artificial intelligence, as they permit machines to recognize and generate content material for the duration of special types of media. Through integrating multiple modalities, AI can create richer, dynamic, and tasty content, enhancing the customer experience throughout numerous virtual structures(Sharma et al., 2025).

Multimodal models like GPT-4 vision are designed to recognize the relationships amongst text, pixels, and movies, taking into consideration extra context-conscious and creative outputs. As an instance, a person should enter a picture and ask the AI to generate a descriptive paragraph or create an associated video script. Such models can also revolutionize industries like advertising and marketing, where AI may want to generate multimedia content fabric primarily based on character alternatives, demographic records, or real-time interactions. Similarly, the fusion of textual content and distinctive media formats needs to bring about new opportunities in storytelling, advertising, schooling, and leisure, supplying users a extra customized and immersive enjoy(AlAli & Wardat, 2024).

Those enhancements in multimodal AI no longer best improve the excellent of content creation but additionally growth the scope of what's possible with generative AI. AI's potential to seamlessly deal with a couple of sorts of media allows creators to supply richer, greater complex content material material that can be tailored to particular audiences. As AI continues to progress on this route, we are able to expect to see similar integration of textual content, pictures, motion pictures, or even audio in virtual media, permitting a more holistic approach to content introduction and consumption (Nachiappan, Rajkumar, et al., 2026).

6.2. Human-AI Collaboration in Content Creation

As AI continues to mature, one of the most promising tendencies inside the digital media enterprise is the growing emphasis on human-AI collaboration. In place of converting human creativity, AI is increasingly number of getting used as a device to decorate and assist innovative strategies. Hybrid fashions, where AI assists human creativity, are rising in the course of numerous domains, which include writing, image format, tune composition, and video manufacturing. These hybrid models allow human creators to paintings alongside AI structures to offer modern content that blends the strengths of each human imagination and tool efficiency.

As an example, inside the realm of content creation, AI-powered tools like ChatGPT can help writers brainstorm, generate drafts, or refine their prose. Through the use of dealing with repetitive responsibilities along with editing, proofreading, and generating preliminary drafts, AI permits writers to awareness on better aspects of their artwork, at the side to structuring narratives, adding emotional intensity, and ensuring originality. Similarly, in image layout and video production, AI can assist in responsibilities like colour correction, video editing, and photograph enhancement, permitting designers and filmmakers to experiment with new thoughts and iterate greater rapidly.

This collaboration amongst people and AI is not only remodeling innovative workflows but additionally enabling the democratization of content fabric creation. Tools that leverage AI's competencies have emerged as more accessible to individuals with varying levels of know-how, allowing all and sundry with a concept to create brilliant content. Whether or not it's through AI-powered video modifying software, design structures, or song manufacturing equipment, the ability to harness AI for progressive functions opens up new avenues for self-expression, entrepreneurship, and innovation.

The combination of AI in innovative fields will moreover raise important questions on authorship, originality, and the nature of creativity. As AI-generated content becomes greater sophisticated, it may end up increasingly hard to differentiate between human-made and tool-generated works. This shift in stressful conditions conventional notions of inventive ownership and raises important ethical concerns, in conjunction with the feature of AI in the innovative manner, and how credit is to be attributed.

6.3 AI in Multilingual and Low-Resource Language Processing

Every other growing fashion in AI is the utility of synthetic intelligence to multilingual and low-resource language processing. At the same time as most AI language models have been mainly skilled on languages like English, which have large portions of training data, many languages around the sector are underrepresented in AI education datasets. This creates a giant barrier to developing reality global digital content fabric, as AI-powered systems are frequently tons less effective at expertise and generating text in those low-useful aid languages.

In reaction to this challenge, researchers are developing new strategies to enhance AI's potential to manner and generate text in more than one language, alongside human beings with constrained virtual resources. One method is using transfer learning, wherein AI models knowledgeable on multilingual languages are fine-tuned to paintings with low-resource languages. Each different strategy is the introduction of multilingual models, which are designed to paintings across many one in all a kind languages concurrently, improving the accessibility of AI systems for customers in regions in which positive languages are less represented in virtual content.

The capacity to break down language boundaries is particularly crucial for international digital content. With the upward thrust of social media, e-alternate, and global communication, human beings spherical the world are interacting with digital systems of their local languages. AI-powered systems that aid multilingual verbal exchange enable organizations to acquire broader audiences and create content that resonates with humans in numerous linguistic and cultural contexts. Furthermore, AI's potential to understand and generate text in low-useful resource languages can help hold endangered languages and sell linguistic range, making sure that no language is left in the returned of within the digital age.

By means of manner of advancing multilingual and coffee-resource language processing, AI has the potential to bridge the digital divide and make content material material more inclusive and available for worldwide audiences. This development will not only empower people to talk at some stage in language boundaries but also create new possibilities for content creators, marketers, and companies to interact with a much wider and extra numerous purchaser base.

6.4. Regulatory Frameworks for AI in Digital Media

As AI continues to revolutionize the digital media landscape, there may be a developing need for regulatory frameworks that deal with the moral implications and capability risks associated with the ones generation. With the growing reliance on AI for content material introduction, statistics evaluation, and decision-making, governments and company stakeholders need to paintings together to establish moral guidelines and global requirements for AI development and deployment.

One of the key demanding situations in regulating AI is making sure that these generations are evolved and applied in strategies that align with societal values, which incorporates fairness, transparency, and responsibility. Ethical tips for AI in virtual media should address problems along with bias, misinformation, privateness, and transparency in algorithmic selection-making. As an example, AI systems used for content moderation on social media structures should be obvious in their selection-making strategies, with clear reasons for ways content is flagged or removed. Similarly, AI-pushed content material material introduction gear must provide transparency regarding their information resources and the strategies used to generate content.

In addition to addressing ethical concerns, regulatory frameworks must ensure that AI technology is utilized in approaches that sell innovation and financial growth while safeguarding public interests. This calls for a balance between encouraging technological improvements and shielding people's rights and freedoms. International requirements for AI in virtual media are vital for ensuring consistency and equity throughout various areas and industries. International collaboration on AI law can help prevent the misuse of that generation, guard client privacy, and ensure that AI is used to enhance, in preference to undermine, democratic values.

The destiny of generative AI in virtual media holds sizeable promise, with upgrades in subsequent-generation language models, human-AI collaboration, multilingual processing, and regulatory frameworks all playing an essential role in shaping the organisation. As AI keeps to adapt, it will carry new possibilities for content material fabric creators, businesses, and clients alike, while also raising essential moral questions that need to be addressed. The key to harnessing the total capacity of AI lies in making sure that this technology is advanced and used responsibly, with a focus on fairness, transparency, and inclusivity.

7. CONCLUSION

Generative AI has surely converted the digital media landscape, redefining how content is created, distributed, and consumed. Its capabilities span text technology, picture and video synthesis, customized pointers, and masses more. This splendid innovation has opened new avenues for creativity, performance, and interactivity, reaping rewards for people, companies, and society on a massive scale. But with such transformative strength comes the obligation to navigate its demanding situations thoughtfully and ethically.

7.1 A New Era of Creativity and Innovation

One of the maximum profound influences of generative AI is its capability to democratize content creation. Systems like GPT and DALL-E have made it possible for human beings, no matter their technical background, to supply extremely good textual content, visuals, or even tracks. This democratization fosters a state-of-the-art wave of creativity, empowering clients to hold their ideas to existence with unheard-of ease. For organizations, generative AI streamlines workflows, allowing fast content material cloth manufacturing at scale, optimizing advertising techniques, and improving client engagement via customized reports.

In industries like journalism, generative AI is augmenting conventional practices with the aid of automating repetitive responsibilities, which encompass summarizing reports and producing habitual fact stories. This lets journalists to consciousness on investigative and in-depth reporting. Further, in advertising and amusement, AI-pushed tools are allowing the creation of dynamic, centered campaigns and immersive storytelling reviews. The capability for innovation is large, with generative AI paving the way for truly new industrial agency fashions and ingenious expressions.

7.2 Addressing Ethical Challenges

Despite its benefits, generative AI raises large moral concerns that demand careful consideration. Bias in AI-generated outputs, as an example, remains a pressing issue. Models educated on biased datasets can also inadvertently perpetuate stereotypes or produce discriminatory content material. To mitigate this, builders want to prioritize fairness auditing, dataset diversification, and transparency in AI education techniques. Moral AI improvement should be a collaborative effort involving technologists, ethicists, policymakers, and numerous organizations to ensure inclusivity and fairness.

The ability for misinformation and deepfake content is every other essential assignment. Generative AI's ability to provide fairly convincing, however, faux records poses dangers to public accept as true with and societal harmony. Addressing this issue requires strong fact-checking mechanisms, both computerized and human-driven, alongside stricter guidelines for the dissemination of AI-generated content fabric. Social media platforms and content hosting offerings need to take responsibility for tracking and curtailing the spread of wrong statistics, leveraging AI tools to pick out and take away dangerous content material right away.

Plagiarism and authorship troubles additionally upward push up with the widespread use of generative AI. As AI-generated content turns into more contemporary, distinguishing between human-created and AI-generated paintings will become more and more difficult. Clear hints on attribution and the ethical use of AI tools are crucial to hold highbrow property rights and uphold creative integrity. Moreover, educational establishments and groups need to draw attention to these troubles, fostering a way of lifestyle of moral AI usage.

7.3 Environmental Considerations

The environmental charge of education, huge AI fashions are each different aspects of the problem. Schooling and deploying generative AI structures require vast computational resources, contributing to an immoderate carbon footprint. As AI adoption grows, so does its environmental impact. To deal with this, researchers and organizations are exploring methods to make AI development greater sustainable. Techniques encompass optimizing training algorithms for electricity performance, using renewable energy resources for statistics facilities, and growing light-weight models that maintain standard performance at the same time as decreasing beneficial resource intake. Balancing innovation with environmental responsibility is critical to make sure that generative AI improvement aligns with global sustainability goals.

7.4 Bridging the Gap: Accessibility and Inclusivity

Generative AI has the potential to bridge digital divides by way of manner of creating an era extra on hand and inclusive. As an instance, AI-driven tools can be a useful resource for multilingual verbal exchange, allowing agencies to reach global audiences and offering clients content in their preferred languages. In schooling, generative AI can create personalised studying reviews, adapting content material to character wishes and improving information acquisition.

Furthermore, generative AI gives possibilities to maintain and promote cultural diversity. Through supporting content material cloth advent in underrepresented languages and showcasing various cultural narratives, AI can foster more expertise and appreciation of worldwide perspectives. But, realizing this potential requires intentional efforts to include marginalized organizations in AI development and deployment approaches. Collaborative tasks amongst governments, academia, and organisation stakeholders can make certain that generative AI blessings everyone, regardless of their geographic or socioeconomic status.

7.5 The Road Ahead: Future Directions

Looking in advance, the destiny of generative AI in virtual media is very interesting and complex. Emerging tendencies, collectively with multimodal AI, which integrates textual content, pics, and films, promise to enhance user reports and expand creative possibilities. For instance, fashions like GPT-4 imagination and prescient show the method's capability and generate content throughout one-of-a-kind media formats, paving the way for richer, extra interactive programs in gaming, education, and digital reality.

Human-AI collaboration will continue to evolve, with AI augmenting rather than replacing human creativity. Hybrid workflows, wherein AI assists with ideation, improving, and execution, will enable creators to obtain more while retaining innovative control. This symbiotic dating can cause groundbreaking improvements, mixing the performance of machines with the ingenuity of people.

Any other critical place of recognition is the mixing of generative AI into low-useful resource language processing. Via prioritizing the improvement of AI fashions that help underrepresented languages, we are capable of celebrating linguistic variety and make certain that no network is left inside the back of in the digital revolution. This attempt could require a large investment in fact series, model training, and collaboration with neighborhood specialists to create AI structures that understand and understand cultural nuances.

In the long run, regulatory frameworks and moral pointers will play a pivotal role in shaping the destiny of generative AI. Governments, enterprise leaders, and global corporations must paintings together to establish requirements that promote transparency, accountability, and accountable innovation. These frameworks have to deal with problems collectively with information privacy, algorithmic bias, and the societal effects of AI, ensuring that the generation evolves and is deployed in strategies that align with human values.

7.6 Conclusion: A Balanced Approach

Generative AI represents an enormous leap ahead in the evolution of technology, imparting exceptional possibilities for creativity, performance, and inclusivity. But its transformative capability must be harnessed responsibly. With the aid of addressing moral demanding situations, prioritizing sustainability, and fostering collaboration throughout sectors, we are able to make certain that generative AI serves as a force for correct.

As we navigate this new generation, it's far crucial to strike a balance between innovation and ethical issues. Generative AI's fulfilment lies not only in its technical skills, but additionally in its capability to uplift humanity. By means of embracing transparency, inclusivity, and sustainability, we can unencumber the complete functionality of generative AI, shaping a destiny in which the era complements our collective well-being and drives improvement throughout all components of society.

REFERENCES

AlAli, R., & Wardat, Y. (2024, May). Opportunities and challenges of integrating generative artificial intelligence in education. *International Journal of Religion.*, *5*(7), 784–793. DOI: 10.61707/8y29gv34

An, B. (2023, June 20). AI-generated text detection: Challenges and future directions. *International Journal of Asian Language Processing.*, *33*(02), 2330002. DOI: 10.1142/S2717554523300025

Bhoyar M. (n.d.). Enhancing Conversational Agents with Generative AI: A Framework for Creating More Adaptive and Context-aware chatbots.

Chumakov, S., Kovantsev, A., & Surikov, A. (2023, January 1). Generative approach to aspect based sentiment analysis with GPT language models. *Procedia Computer Science*, *229*, 284–293. DOI: 10.1016/j.procs.2023.12.030

Gujar, V. (2024). New age marketing: AI personalization strategies in digital world. International Advanced Research Journal in Science, Engineering and Technology, 11(3).

Madaan, G., Asthana, S. K., & Kaur, J. (2024). Generative AI: Applications, models, challenges, opportunities, and future directions. Generative AI and implications for ethics, security, and data management, 88-121.

Medhat, M., Ayoub, L. W., Daher, M., & Mohamed, K. M. (2025). Ethical Considerations in AI-Generated Content on Social Media. In *Sustainable Data Management: Navigating Big Data, Communication Technology, and Business Digital Leadership* (Vol. 1, pp. 611–620). Springer Nature Switzerland. DOI: 10.1007/978-3-031-83911-5_52

Nachiappan B, Rajkumar N, Radha V, Kalpana C, Viji C, Nagarajan G, Mohanraj A. (2026). Fusion of Generative AI and Blockchain Conceptual Framework. In *Fusion of Multimodal Generative AI and Blockchain Technology in Digital Media* (pp. 57–86). IGI Global Scientific Publishing.

Pamudhurthy PS, Komali R, Panyam AB, Katarukonda A, Raithatha H. Real Time Language Translation Using AI and ML.

Rajkumar N, Viji C, Nachiappan B, Mohanraj A, Nagarajan G, Ravi J, et al. (2026). Generative AI in Virtual Media Image, Video, and Animation Generation. In *Fusion of Multimodal Generative AI and Blockchain Technology in Digital Media* (pp. 209–230). IGI Global Scientific Publishing.

Saha, B. (2025). Generative AI for Text Generation: Advances and Applications in Natural Language Processing. *Journal of Computer Allied Intelligence (JCAI, ISSN: 2584-2676), 3*(1), 77-91.

Sharma, C., Sharma, S., Bhardwaj, V., & Dhaliwal, B. K. (2025, June 4). Generative artificial intelligence for sustainable development: Predictive trend analysis in key sectors using natural language processing. *Discover Applied Sciences*, *7*(6), 596. DOI: 10.1007/s42452-025-07207-7

Singla, S., Thakur, A., Swami, A., Sawarn, U., & Singla, P. (2024, November). Advancements in Natural Language Processing: BERT and Transformer-Based Models for Text Understanding. In *2024 Second International Conference on Advanced Computing & Communication Technologies (ICACCTech)* (pp. 372-379). IEEE. DOI: 10.1109/ICACCTech65084.2024.00068

Wong, M. F., Guo, S., Hang, C. N., Ho, S. W., & Tan, C. W. (2023). Natural language generation and understanding of big code for AI-assisted programming: A review. *Entropy (Basel, Switzerland)*, *25*(6), 888. DOI: 10.3390/e25060888 PMID: 37372232

Chapter 2
Beyond Binary Sentiment:
Leveraging Fuzzy Linguistic Hedges to Enhance NLP-Based Fake News Detection

Mohamed Bahra
https://orcid.org/0000-0003-3305-5203
Abdelmalek Essaadi University, Morocco

Abdelhadi Fennan
Abdelmalek Essaadi University, Morocco

ABSTRACT

The ambiguity and gradience of natural human language are frequently difficult for conventional sentiment analysis models to capture, particularly in crucial situations like false information pertaining to health. This chapter explores how fuzzy linguistic hedges, like "somewhat," "extremely," and "not," can improve sentiment analysis's semantic depth. We present a sophisticated sentiment-aware classification pipeline designed for fake news detection by fusing fuzzy logic with contemporary deep learning architectures (LSTM). Our model, when applied to Covid-19 infodemic datasets, not only increases classification accuracy but also offers more comprehensible insights into the emotional tone of factual versus misleading content. We also go over how fuzzy sentiment scoring affects more general NLP uses like automated fact-checking systems, policy communication, and social media monitoring

DOI: 10.4018/979-8-3373-8011-7.ch002

1 INTRODUCTION

The COVID-19 pandemic, declared a global crisis in early 2020, dramatically transformed not only public health landscapes but also the ways in which people consume and interact with information. During periods of widespread confinement and social distancing, internet usage—and particularly social media activity—surged, creating a fertile environment for the rapid spread of fake news. This phenomenon, dubbed the "infodemic" by the World Health Organization, exacerbated the already complex challenges of managing public health, sowing confusion, fear, and distrust across societies. Among the many types of misinformation circulated, those related to COVID-19 posed immediate risks to human life by promoting false cures, anti-vaccine sentiments, and conspiracy theories.

In this digital landscape, traditional fake news detection methods, while effective in some contexts, revealed significant limitations. Standard sentiment analysis models (Dang, Moreno-García, & De la Prieta, 2020), for example, often treat language in binary terms—classifying expressions as either positive or negative—while ignoring the inherent ambiguity and gradience of natural language. Yet, the emotional tone embedded in misinformation often relies on nuanced expressions like "somewhat dangerous," "not entirely safe," or "extremely effective," which escape binary classification. These linguistic subtleties are crucial for understanding intent, emotional manipulation, and the psychological impact of false narratives.

To bridge this semantic gap, our research proposes a novel sentiment-aware classification pipeline that was grounded on our previous work (Mohamed, Abdelhadi, Adil, & Haytam, 2019) to which we integrates fuzzy logic with deep learning—specifically, Long Short-Term Memory (LSTM) networks. Fuzzy logic allows for a more flexible and human-like interpretation of language, accommodating degrees of truth and emotional intensity rather than rigid categorizations. By applying fuzzy linguistic hedges such as "very," "somewhat," and "not," our model assigns more refined sentiment scores to textual content. These scores are then used as enriched features within an LSTM-based classifier to differentiate between factual and misleading content more effectively.

Using a combination of COVID-19-related datasets—including the Infodemic dataset by Patwa et al. (Patwa et al., 2021) and the CoAID repository (Cui & Lee, 2020) —our experiments demonstrate that this hybrid model not only improves classification accuracy but also enhances interpretability. Furthermore, the proposed method offers promising applications in broader NLP tasks such as automated fact-checking, policy communication, and real-time social media monitoring, contributing to the development of more transparent and resilient information ecosystems in times of crisis.

2 RELATED WORK

The detection of fake news has emerged as a major research domain within natural language processing (NLP) (Oshikawa, Qian, & Wang, 2018), particularly due to its implications for public opinion, democratic integrity, and public health. The term "fake news" encompasses both *misinformation*, which is unintentionally false content, and *disinformation*, which is deliberately misleading information (Aïmeur, Amri, & Brassard, 2023). With the rise of digital communication technologies and social media platforms, the dissemination of such content has become more widespread, prompting the development of computational techniques to detect and mitigate its effects.

2.1 Early Approaches and Datasets

Initial research efforts in fake news detection focused on binary classification models that used surface-level textual features such as word counts (Günther & Quandt, 2018), term frequency-inverse document frequency (TF-IDF) (Havrlant & Kreinovich, 2017), and n-gram representations (Oriola, 2021). The release of datasets such as LIAR by William Wang (Wang, 2017), which contains manually labeled political statements, laid the foundation for training supervised models. Other datasets like FakeNewsNet (Shu, Mahudeswaran, Wang, Lee, & Liu, 2020), ISOT (Hakak et al., 2021), and CredBank (Mitra & Gilbert, 2015) enriched this field by introducing social, contextual, and temporal information to improve classification accuracy.

The COVID-19 pandemic introduced a new layer of urgency, as fake news transitioned from political propaganda to matters of public health. New datasets like the *Infodemic* dataset, curated from social media and news articles, and *CoAID*, which includes social engagements and user behavior data, allowed researchers to target health-related misinformation specifically. These datasets have enabled the training of models tailored to the vocabulary, sentiment, and thematic features specific to pandemic-era content.

2.2 Machine Learning and Deep Learning Models

Classical machine learning algorithms such as Naïve Bayes (NB) (Bayes, 1968), Support Vector Machines (SVM) (Mammone, Turchi, & Cristianini, 2009), and Random Forests (RF) (Breiman, 2001) were among the first tools used to classify fake news. These models rely heavily on handcrafted features and have shown decent performance when applied to well-structured data. For instance, Granik and Mesyura (Granik & Mesyura, 2017) applied Naïve Bayes for fake news classification and demonstrated that even simple probabilistic models can be effective under certain conditions.

With advancements in deep learning (Shone, Ngoc, Phai, & Shi, 2018), more sophisticated models such as Convolutional Neural Networks (CNNs) (Li, Liu, Yang, Peng, & Zhou, 2021) and Recurrent Neural Networks (RNNs) (Medsker & Jain, 2001), especially Long Short-Term Memory (LSTM) networks (Graves, 2012), have been introduced to handle complex language patterns and contextual dependencies. Thota et al. (2018) compared various neural architectures and showed that using pre-trained embeddings such as Word2Vec with dense neural layers outperformed traditional models (Thota, Tilak, Ahluwalia, & Lohia, 2018). Further, hybrid models combining CNN and bidirectional LSTM (BiLSTM), as explored by Balwant (Balwant, 2019), have been shown to capture both local and sequential features in text effectively.

However, these models often overlook the nuanced semantics inherent in human language—particularly the gradience and ambiguity introduced by sentiment. Sentiment analysis has emerged as a parallel line of inquiry, where researchers attempt to link emotional tone to the veracity of content. Zaeem et al. (Zaeem, Li, & Barber, 2020) and Ajao et al. (Ajao, Bhowmik, & Zargari, 2019) found statistical relationships between negative emotions and fake news, suggesting that sentiment can be an important feature in classification. These studies, however, typically treat sentiment as a binary or ternary classification (positive, negative, neutral), which fails to capture the intricacies of human expression.

2.3 Fuzzy Logic in NLP and Sentiment Analysis

Fuzzy logic, first proposed by Lotfi Zadeh (Lotfi Asker Zadeh, 1988), provides a mathematical framework for reasoning under uncertainty and imprecision—qualities inherent in natural language. Fuzzy sets allow for partial membership, enabling more granular representation of sentiment. Linguistic hedges (Zadeh, 1972) like "very", "somewhat", or "not" can significantly alter the perceived meaning of a statement. In this regard, fuzzy logic becomes a powerful complement to NLP tasks, especially those involving sentiment or opinion mining.

Few researchers have ventured into combining fuzzy logic with machine learning for fake news detection. In our prior work, we proposed a sentiment-aware system that utilized fuzzy linguistic variables to better understand user-generated content. Building upon this foundation, the current study integrates fuzzy logic-based sentiment scoring with LSTM to better capture both the semantic and emotional dimensions of fake news content.

This fusion addresses a gap in existing literature where the emotional tone is often oversimplified and treated as static. By incorporating fuzzy modifiers, our model can differentiate between "not dangerous" and "extremely dangerous", which might carry similar keywords but very different meanings. This level of granularity is particularly crucial in health-related misinformation where the stakes are high.

3 DATASET DESCRIPTION

To build a domain-specific model aligned with pandemic discourse, we used two labeled datasets:

3.1 Infodemic Dataset (Patwa et al.)

- 10,700 social media posts (Twitter and news articles)
- Labeled as **real** or **fake** by human annotators and verified accounts

Examples:

- **Real**: *"Current understanding is COVID-19 spreads through respiratory droplets..."*
- **Fake**: *"Leave objects in the sun to avoid catching the coronavirus."*

3.2 CoAID (Cui et al.)

- Contains fake/real Covid-19 news articles from news sites and user engagement on social platforms.

Examples:

- **Fake**: *"The WHO stated that asymptomatic spread is 'very rare', so masks aren't necessary."*
- **Real**: *"Going to movie theaters is still considered risky, say health experts."*

Together, we merged and balanced the two datasets to yield:

Table 1. Distribution of data splits used for training, validation and test of our proposed approach

Split	Real Samples	Fake Samples	Total
Training	4,018	3,718	7,736
Validation	1,369	1,269	2,638
Testing	1,369	1,269	2,638
Total	**6,756**	**6,256**	**13,012**

4 THEORY FOUNDATION

4.1 Fake news and Sentiment analysis

Fake news can be either misinformation (false, but not intentionally deceptive) or disinformation (deliberately misleading). Sentiment analysis has emerged as a valuable tool for fake news detection, premised on the assumption that false content often exhibits exaggerated emotional tone. However, typical sentiment classifiers categorize sentiment as binary (positive or negative), overlooking nuanced expressions that may signal deception.

In reality, misinformation often relies on emotionally charged yet subtly phrased language—using terms like "possibly harmful" or "not entirely safe"—which may not be captured by standard polarity-based models. These expressions fall into a gray area that traditional classifiers struggle to interpret accurately. As a result, important emotional and persuasive cues embedded in misleading content may go undetected, limiting the effectiveness of sentiment-based detection systems. This challenge motivates the need for more flexible and expressive approaches capable of capturing the gradience of sentiment in fake news discourse.

This table below (**Table 2**) shows how conventional binary sentiment analysis may fail to differentiate between subtly misleading and genuinely informative statements. While both "not entirely safe" and "not completely useless" might be labeled as neutral, their implied sentiment and psychological impact differ significantly

Table 2. Example of Sentiment Gradience in Fake News vs. Real News Statements

Statement	Sentiment Classification (Binary)	Nuanced Sentiment Interpretation
"COVID-19 vaccines are extremely dangerous and should be avoided."	Negative	Strong negative / Alarmist
"Some people say the vaccine might not be entirely safe."	Neutral	Mild negative / Doubt-inducing
"Health authorities confirm vaccines are safe and effective."	Positive	Strong positive / Reassuring
"Vaccines are not completely useless."	Neutral	Weak positive / Defensive

4.2 Fuzzy logic in NLP

In the context of sentiment analysis, fuzzy logic enables systems to represent emotional tone on a gradual scale, capturing nuances that are lost in binary or even ternary models. For instance, expressions such as *"not terrible"*, *"somewhat risky"*, or *"mildly effective"* fall between clearly positive or negative categories and require more flexible interpretation. Fuzzy logic thus provides the tools to assign graded sentiment scores, improving the model's ability to interpret subtle linguistic cues and ambiguous emotional signals that are common in fake news content.

4.3 Linguistic Hedges and Emotion Modifiers

Linguistic hedges —terms like *"very," "quite," "almost,"* or *"not"*—play a key role in expressing degrees of certainty, intensity, or polarity in human language. These modifiers adjust the strength or direction of a sentiment and are essential for understanding how meaning is shaped in context.

We classify hedges into the following categories:

- **Concentrators** (e.g., "very", "extremely"): Increase sentiment intensity.
- **Dilators** (e.g., "somewhat", "slightly"): Reduce sentiment intensity.
- **Negators** (e.g., "not"): Invert sentiment polarity.

These elements, when embedded in text, significantly influence the perceived emotional strength and factual credibility of information. In the realm of fake news, such hedges are frequently used to manipulate tone subtly, making false claims appear cautious, credible, or emotionally compelling—thus reinforcing the need for sentiment models that can interpret them effectively.

Figure 1. fuzzy logic and linguistic hedges representation

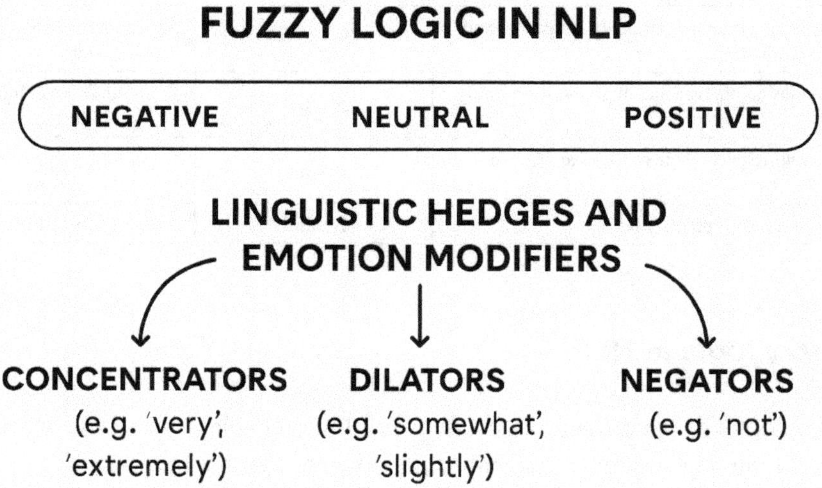

4.4 Long-Shirt-Term-Memory (LSTM)

Long Short-Term Memory (LSTM), a variant of Recurrent Neural Networks (RNNs), was designed to better capture long-term dependencies in sequential data. Unlike basic RNNs, LSTM introduces memory cells and gating mechanisms that help retain relevant information over time, making it particularly effective for tasks requiring context, such as sentiment analysis, text classification, and fake news detection. In our approach, LSTM enables the model to understand the sequence and emotional flow of a text, especially when combined with fuzzy sentiment features.

5 PROPOSED APPROACH

This section outlines the key components of our proposed approach, which integrates fuzzy sentiment enhancement into a deep learning pipeline for fake news detection. The overall architecture is structured into three sequential stages: linguistic preprocessing, semantic vectorization with fuzzy sentiment mapping, and classification via LSTM. The following subsections elaborate on the first two stages.

Figure 2. The architecture of our proposed approach

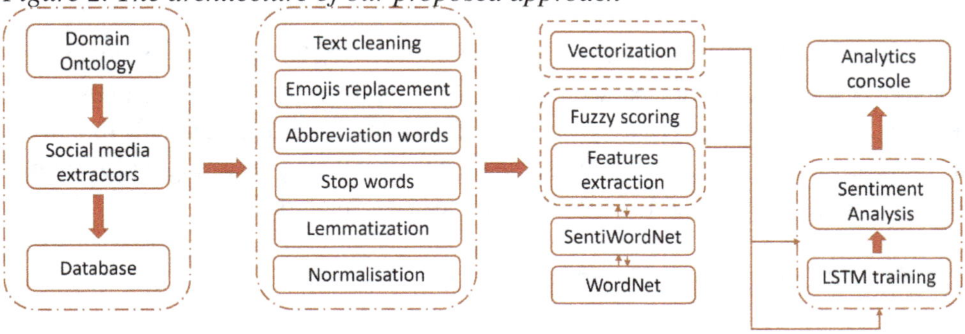

5.1 Text preprocessing

Prior to any modeling, the raw textual data undergoes a comprehensive preprocessing pipeline designed to normalize, standardize, and enrich the linguistic structure of the content. This ensures that downstream processes operate on clean and semantically consistent input.

Structural Cleaning: URLs, punctuation, and non-alphabetic characters are stripped from each sentence. All remaining text is converted to lowercase to reduce lexical variability.

Emoji Interpretation: Emojis—often used as proxies for emotional tone—are replaced with equivalent textual labels to preserve their affective content in a format compatible with natural language models.

Lexical Expansion: Abbreviations (e.g., “brb” → “be right back”) and contractions (e.g., “didn't” → “did not”) are systematically expanded. This step improves token consistency and aids in syntactic parsing.

Stop-word Pruning: High-frequency, low-information terms (e.g., “the”, “in”, “and”) are removed using the standard English stop word corpus provided by the NLTK toolkit (Bird, 2006).

Lemmatization: Tokens are reduced to their base forms using a lemmatizer (Khyani, Siddhartha, Niveditha, & Divya, 2021). This reduces inflectional variance and facilitates better alignment with semantic resources such as sentiment lexicons.

5.2 Vectorization and fuzzy sentiment scoring

Once preprocessed, the cleaned text is transformed into a numerical representation suitable for neural processing, and augmented with fuzzy logic-based sentiment scores that capture the emotional gradience embedded in natural language.

5.3 Word Embedding

We employ Word2Vec embeddings (Goldberg & Levy, 2014) to convert tokenized text into dense vector representations. These embeddings are trained to capture contextual similarity between terms, ensuring that words with similar semantic functions lie close in the vector space (Almeida & Xexéo, 2019). The resulting word vectors serve as the primary input to the sequential learning model.

5.4 Fuzzy Sentiment Mapping

To integrate emotional nuance into the model, we compute a fuzzy sentiment score for each sentence using the following process:

1. **Sentiment Term Identification**: Opinion-bearing words are identified using part-of-speech tagging, along with any surrounding linguistic hedges.
2. **Initial Polarity Retrieval**: Using lexical databases such as SentiWordNet (Baccianella, Esuli, & Sebastiani, 2010) and WordNet (Fellbaum, 2010), we retrieve polarity scores for these terms, representing the base sentiment.
3. **Hedge-Driven Adjustment**: The base sentiment score is modified based on the presence and type of hedge:
   - For **negators** (e.g., *not*), the score is inverted: $\boldsymbol{f}(\mathrm{s}) = \mathbf{1} - (\mathrm{s})$
   - For **intensifiers** (e.g., *extremely*), the emotional strength is amplified:

$$f(\mathrm{s}) = [\mathrm{s}]^2$$

   - For **attenuators** (e.g., *somewhat*), the intensity is softened:

$$f(\mathrm{s}) = [\mathrm{s}]^{1/2}$$

The final fuzzy sentiment score is then normalized and concatenated with the corresponding sentence embeddings, enhancing the input representation for downstream classification. This fusion allows the model to better interpret the emotional intent behind the text, which is often a subtle yet powerful signal in fake news content.

6 RESULTS AND DISCUSSIONS

To empirically assess whether the integration of fuzzy linguistic hedges into an LSTM-based classifier improves fake news detection performance, we compare three configurations:

Baseline A: LSTM with standard Word2Vec embeddings (no sentiment features).

Baseline B: LSTM with Word2Vec embeddings + traditional polarity sentiment score (binary/ternary).

Proposed Model: LSTM with Word2Vec embeddings + fuzzy sentiment scores influenced by linguistic hedges.

6.1 Experimental Setup

Datasets: Merged Infodemic + CoAID datasets (balanced, as detailed in **Table 1**).

Preprocessing: As described in Section 5.1.

Embeddings: Pre-trained Word2Vec (Google News, 300 dimensions).

Fuzzy Sentiment Scoring: Integrated as described in Section 5.2 using SentiWordNet and adjusted via linguistic hedge types.

Classifier: LSTM with 2 layers (128 hidden units), dropout = 0.3.

Evaluation Metrics: Accuracy, Precision, Recall, F1-Score, AUC.

Training: 10 epochs, Adam optimizer, batch size = 64.

6.2 Results

The table below (**Table 3**) describe the results of our proposed approach

Table 3. Results of our experiment

Model	Accuracy	Precision	Recall	F1-Score	AUC
Baseline A (LSTM only)	83.1%	82.6%	83.9%	83.2%	0.880
Baseline B (LSTM + binary sentiment)	84.7%	84.2%	85.1%	84.6%	0.895
Proposed (LSTM + fuzzy sentiment)	**87.9%**	**87.2%**	**88.4%**	**87.8%**	**0.921**

6.3 Discussion

The results clearly demonstrate the positive impact of integrating fuzzy sentiment features:

Higher F1-Score (+4.6%) compared to the plain LSTM, confirming that the emotional cues captured via linguistic hedges add discriminative power.

Improved AUC indicates that the model is more reliable at separating real and fake samples across various thresholds.

Traditional binary sentiment models fail to distinguish between subtly different expressions like "somewhat risky" and "not entirely safe", often labeling both as neutral or slightly negative. The fuzzy-enhanced model correctly interprets the intensifier or dilator impact, allowing for better contextual disambiguation. Hereafter in the **Table 4**, we showcase some of the output.

Table 4. Example of some classification output

Statement	Baseline Prediction	Fuzzy Model Prediction
"Vaccines might not be entirely safe."	**Real (False Negative)**	**Fake (Correct)**
"COVID-19 vaccines are very effective."	Real (Correct)	Real (Correct)
"Some say 5G causes coronavirus."	**Real (False Negative)**	**Fake (Correct)**

7 CONCLUSION AND FUTURE WORK

In this chapter, we introduced a hybrid model for fake news detection that combines fuzzy logic and deep learning to better capture the semantic and emotional subtleties of misinformation. Traditional sentiment analysis methods often overlook linguistic nuances expressed through modifiers like "somewhat," "very," or "not." By integrating fuzzy sentiment scoring based on these hedges into an LSTM classifier, our approach achieved superior performance in both accuracy and interpretability when tested on COVID-19-related datasets.

The results demonstrate that understanding emotional gradience is crucial for identifying manipulative language often used in misleading content, particularly in sensitive domains like public health. Beyond detection, our approach also enhances model explainability, which is essential for trust and transparency in AI-driven systems.

As future work, we aim to extend this framework by incorporating transformer-based architectures such as BERT or RoBERTa, enhanced with fuzzy-aware embeddings. Additionally, real-time deployment on social media streams, multilingual adaptation, and integration with explainable AI (XAI) techniques will be explored. These directions could further strengthen the model's utility in automated fact-checking systems, policy decision support, and digital media monitoring, especially during infodemics and crises requiring rapid, reliable information filtering.

8 REFERENCES

Aïmeur, E., Amri, S., & Brassard, G. (2023). Fake news, disinformation and misinformation in social media: A review. *Social Network Analysis and Mining*, *13*(1), 30. DOI: 10.1007/s13278-023-01028-5 PMID: 36789378

Ajao, O., Bhowmik, D., & Zargari, S. (2019). *Sentiment aware fake news detection on online social networks.* Paper presented at the ICASSP 2019-2019 IEEE International Conference on Acoustics, Speech and Signal Processing (ICASSP). DOI: 10.1109/ICASSP.2019.8683170

Almeida, F., & Xexéo, G. (2019). Word embeddings: A survey. *arXiv preprint arXiv:1901.09069.*

Baccianella, S., Esuli, A., & Sebastiani, F. (2010). *Sentiwordnet 3.0: an enhanced lexical resource for sentiment analysis and opinion mining.* Paper presented at the Lrec.

Balwant, M. K. (2019). *Bidirectional LSTM based on POS tags and CNN architecture for fake news detection.* Paper presented at the 2019 10th International conference on computing, communication and networking technologies (ICCCNT). DOI: 10.1109/ICCCNT45670.2019.8944460

Bayes, T. (1968). Naive bayes classifier. *Article Sources and Contributors*, 1-9.

Bird, S. (2006). *NLTK: the natural language toolkit.* Paper presented at the Proceedings of the COLING/ACL 2006 interactive presentation sessions. DOI: 10.3115/1225403.1225421

Breiman, L. (2001). Random forests. *Machine Learning*, *45*(1), 5–32. DOI: 10.1023/A:1010933404324

Cui, L., & Lee, D. (2020). Coaid: Covid-19 healthcare misinformation dataset. *arXiv preprint arXiv:2006.00885.*

Dang, N. C., Moreno-García, M. N., & De la Prieta, F. (2020). Sentiment analysis based on deep learning: A comparative study. *Electronics (Basel)*, *9*(3), 483. DOI: 10.3390/electronics9030483

Fellbaum, C. (2010). WordNet. In *Theory and applications of ontology: computer applications* (pp. 231–243). Springer. DOI: 10.1007/978-90-481-8847-5_10

Goldberg, Y., & Levy, O. (2014). word2vec Explained: deriving Mikolov et al.'s negative-sampling word-embedding method. *arXiv preprint arXiv:1402.3722.*

Granik, M., & Mesyura, V. (2017). *Fake news detection using naive Bayes classifier.* Paper presented at the 2017 IEEE first Ukraine conference on electrical and computer engineering (UKRCON). DOI: 10.1109/UKRCON.2017.8100379

Graves, A. (2012). Long short-term memory. *Supervised sequence labelling with recurrent neural networks*, 37-45.

Günther, E., & Quandt, T. (2018). Word counts and topic models: Automated text analysis methods for digital journalism research. In *Rethinking research methods in an age of digital journalism* (pp. 75–88). Routledge. DOI: 10.4324/9781315115047-6

Hakak, S., Alazab, M., Khan, S., Gadekallu, T. R., Maddikunta, P. K. R., & Khan, W. Z. (2021). An ensemble machine learning approach through effective feature extraction to classify fake news. *Future Generation Computer Systems, 117*, 47–58. DOI: 10.1016/j.future.2020.11.022

Havrlant, L., & Kreinovich, V. (2017). A simple probabilistic explanation of term frequency-inverse document frequency (tf-idf) heuristic (and variations motivated by this explanation). *International Journal of General Systems, 46*(1), 27–36. DOI: 10.1080/03081079.2017.1291635

Khyani, D., Siddhartha, B., Niveditha, N., & Divya, B. (2021). An interpretation of lemmatization and stemming in natural language processing. *Shanghai Ligong Daxue Xuebao, 22*(10), 350–357.

Li, Z., Liu, F., Yang, W., Peng, S., & Zhou, J. (2021). A survey of convolutional neural networks: Analysis, applications, and prospects. *IEEE Transactions on Neural Networks and Learning Systems, 33*(12), 6999–7019. DOI: 10.1109/TNNLS.2021.3084827 PMID: 34111009

Mammone, A., Turchi, M., & Cristianini, N. (2009). Support vector machines. *Wiley Interdisciplinary Reviews: Computational Statistics, 1*(3), 283–289. DOI: 10.1002/wics.49

Medsker, L. R., & Jain, L. (2001). Recurrent neural networks. *Design and applications, 5*(64-67), 2.

Mitra, T., & Gilbert, E. (2015). *Credbank: A large-scale social media corpus with associated credibility annotations.* Paper presented at the Proceedings of the international AAAI conference on web and social media.

Mohamed, B., Abdelhadi, F., Adil, B., & Haytam, H. (2019). *Smart city services monitoring framework using fuzzy logic based sentiment analysis and apache spark.* Paper presented at the 2019 1st International conference on smart systems and data science (ICSSD). DOI: 10.1109/ICSSD47982.2019.9002687

Oriola, O. (2021). Exploring N-gram, word embedding and topic models for content-based fake news detection in FakeNewsNet evaluation. *Int. J. Comput. Appl, 975*, 8887.

Oshikawa, R., Qian, J., & Wang, W. Y. (2018). A survey on natural language processing for fake news detection. *arXiv preprint arXiv:1811.00770.*

Patwa, P., Sharma, S., Pykl, S., Guptha, V., Kumari, G., Akhtar, M. S., . . . Chakraborty, T. (2021). *Fighting an infodemic: Covid-19 fake news dataset.* Paper presented at the International Workshop on Combating On line Ho st ile Posts in Regional Languages dur ing Emerge ncy Si tuation. DOI: 10.1007/978-3-030-73696-5_3

Shone, N., Ngoc, T. N., Phai, V. D., & Shi, Q. (2018). A deep learning approach to network intrusion detection. *IEEE Transactions on Emerging Topics in Computational Intelligence*, *2*(1), 41–50. DOI: 10.1109/TETCI.2017.2772792

Shu, K., Mahudeswaran, D., Wang, S., Lee, D., & Liu, H. (2020). Fakenewsnet: A data repository with news content, social context, and spatiotemporal information for studying fake news on social media. *Big Data*, *8*(3), 171–188. DOI: 10.1089/big.2020.0062 PMID: 32491943

Thota, A., Tilak, P., Ahluwalia, S., & Lohia, N. (2018). Fake news detection: A deep learning approach. *SMU Data Science Review*, *1*(3), 10.

Wang, W. Y. (2017). " liar, liar pants on fire": A new benchmark dataset for fake news detection. *arXiv preprint arXiv:1705.00648*. DOI: 10.18653/v1/P17-2067

Zadeh, L. A. (1972). A fuzzy-set-theoretic interpretation of linguistic hedges.

Zadeh, L. A. (1988). Fuzzy logic. *Computer*, *21*(4), 83–93. DOI: 10.1109/2.53

Zaeem, R. N., Li, C., & Barber, K. S. (2020). *On sentiment of online fake news.* Paper presented at the 2020 IEEE/ACM international conference on advances in social networks analysis and mining (ASONAM).

Chapter 3
Artificial Intelligence and the Didactics of Mathematics in Secondary Education: Transforming Teaching and Learning Practices

Abdellatif Semmouri
https://orcid.org/0000-0003-4144-1980
Regional Center for Career Education and Training (CRMEF), Beni Mellal-Khenifra Region, Provincial Center of Khouribga, Morocco

Abdelfattah Hachami
Regional Center for Career Education and Training (CRMEF), Beni Mellal-Khenifra Region, Provincial Center of Khouribga, Morocco

Hassan Elhariri
Regional Center for Career Education and Training (CRMEF), Beni Mellal-Khenifra Region, Provincial Center of Khouribga, Morocco

ABSTRACT

The integration of Artificial Intelligence (AI) into secondary mathematics education is reshaping traditional teaching and learning. As AI tools become more advanced and accessible, they enhance personalized learning, formative assessment, and adaptive instruction. This chapter highlights how aligning AI with didactic principles, conceptual understanding, procedural fluency, mathematical reasoning, creates responsive and inclusive learning environments. The teacher's role evolves

DOI: 10.4018/979-8-3373-8011-7.ch003

from transmitting knowledge to facilitating deeper understanding, supported by AI-driven insights. While emphasizing the pedagogical benefits, the chapter also examines challenges such as ethics, equity, and technical limitations. Drawing on case studies and evidence, it provides a forward-looking perspective on how AI can transform mathematics education while preserving its core didactic goals.

1. INTRODUCTION

1.1. A Brief Overview of the Evolution of AI in Education

Over the last few decades, artificial intelligence (AI) has transitioned from a futuristic concept to an integral component of many modern industries, including healthcare, transportation, finance, and notably, education. The integration of AI into educational contexts represents one of the most transformative developments in the history of pedagogy. In the early stages of its evolution, beginning in the mid-20th century, AI in education was limited to simple programmed instruction and rule-based decision systems. These early computer-based learning environments provided static, linear content, often lacking adaptability or personalization (Chen et al., 2020).

As computational power and data processing capabilities increased, AI evolved to include more sophisticated algorithms, capable of mimicking aspects of human cognitive processes. The 1980s and 1990s introduced Intelligent Tutoring Systems (ITS), which marked a significant leap forward by offering adaptive learning experiences that could assess student input in real time and adjust the instructional pathway accordingly. These systems set the foundation for what would later become dynamic, responsive AI educational tools.

The last two decades have seen exponential growth in AI's capabilities and its application in educational environments. Today, AI is no longer limited to a supporting role but actively shapes how educational content is delivered, assessed, and improved. Modern AI tools in education utilize machine learning, natural language processing, and predictive analytics to provide personalized learning environments, immediate feedback, and real-time performance tracking. Educational platforms like Khan Academy, DreamBox, Socratic, and Carnegie Learning harness AI to support learners across diverse academic levels and disciplines.

Moreover, AI is playing a pivotal role in administrative efficiency, student assessment, curriculum development, and teacher support. By analyzing patterns in student behavior, AI systems can predict academic outcomes, identify students at risk, and recommend targeted interventions. In doing so, AI is not only improving individual learning experiences but also contributing to systemic educational reform.

1.2. The Importance of Mathematics in the Secondary School Curriculum

Mathematics is a core discipline in the secondary school curriculum worldwide, considered fundamental to both academic and professional success in a knowledge-based economy. More than just numbers and equations, mathematics nurtures critical thinking, logical reasoning, spatial awareness, and problem-solving skills. These are not only essential for STEM careers, spanning science, technology, engineering and mathematics, but also for informed citizenship in an increasingly complex, data-driven world.

Secondary school marks a crucial period in the development of mathematical thinking. Students are introduced to abstract concepts such as algebra, geometry, probability, and statistics, which require higher-order cognitive processes and conceptual understanding. The ability to apply these concepts to real-world situations is essential for future academic pursuits and everyday decision-making.

However, mathematics is also one of the most challenging subjects for many students. International assessments such as PISA (Program for International Student Assessment) consistently highlight significant disparities in mathematics performance across countries, socioeconomic groups, and genders. Mathematics anxiety, a well-documented phenomenon, affects a large percentage of secondary students and often correlates with reduced performance and engagement.

Despite numerous reforms in curriculum design and instructional strategies, traditional mathematics education still tends to rely heavily on lecture-based teaching and standardized assessments. This model often fails to accommodate individual learning differences and does not provide sufficient feedback or opportunities for conceptual exploration. Consequently, many students struggle to connect mathematical concepts with real-world relevance, which undermines both their interest and achievement (Zhang & Aslan, 2021).

In response to these challenges, there is an increasing demand for innovative, student-centered approaches to mathematics instruction, approaches that foster understanding, curiosity, and a growth mindset. This is where AI holds significant promise: it offers tools to personalize learning, provide continuous feedback, and support teachers in delivering effective, differentiated instruction.

1.3. The Intersection of AI and Mathematics Didactics

The convergence of AI and mathematics didactics represents a pivotal opportunity to reimagine how mathematics is taught and learned in secondary schools. Didactics, in its simplest definition, refers to the science and art of teaching. Mathematics didactics specifically focuses on how mathematical concepts are taught and learned, incorporating elements of pedagogy, curriculum design, assessment, cognitive psychology, and educational research. The goal of mathematics didactics is not only to facilitate procedural competence but also to promote deep understanding, reasoning, and the ability to transfer knowledge across contexts.

At the intersection of AI and mathematics didactics lies a transformative potential: AI can enhance didactic strategies by introducing intelligent systems that adapt to learners' needs, analyze their performance patterns, and offer real-time, formative feedback. This represents a fundamental shift from traditional, static instruction to dynamic, responsive learning environments. For example, AI-powered platforms can identify specific misconceptions (e.g., misunderstanding the distributive property or interpreting statistical variability) and then generate customized learning paths to address those gaps (Chandir 2022).

Furthermore, AI systems can support visualization and modeling, which are essential tools in teaching abstract mathematical concepts. By integrating interactive simulations, dynamic graphs, and step-by-step problem solving, AI tools help students move from concrete experiences to abstract generalizations as an essential trajectory in mathematical cognition.

From a didactic perspective, AI also enhances assessment methodologies. Traditional assessments, such as multiple-choice tests and written exams often focus on final answers rather than the reasoning process. In contrast, AI systems can analyze every step a student takes in solving a problem, providing insight into their thought process. This supports formative assessment, where feedback is continuous and used to inform subsequent instruction, a cornerstone of effective mathematics teaching.

For teachers, AI tools offer significant pedagogical support. AI can help educators plan lessons more efficiently, differentiate instruction based on student profiles, and monitor class-wide learning trends. AI-powered dashboards, for instance, can alert teachers to students who are falling behind or those who need enrichment opportunities. This allows teachers to make data-informed decisions and focus their time and attention where it is most needed.

However, it is important to note that the integration of AI into mathematics didactics must be pedagogically grounded and ethically conscious. AI should not be seen as a replacement for teachers, but rather as a collaborative partner that enhances their instructional capabilities. Human elements such as empathy, encouragement, and professional judgment remain irreplaceable. Teachers must be trained not only in using AI tools but also in understanding their limitations, interpreting data responsibly, and maintaining agency over instructional decisions.

Ethical considerations also include data privacy, algorithmic bias, and equity of access. AI systems rely on vast amounts of student data, raising concerns about confidentiality and informed consent. Algorithms, if not carefully designed and tested, can unintentionally perpetuate biases, leading to unfair outcomes. Furthermore, access to AI-powered tools is not universal, especially in under-resourced schools or regions with limited digital infrastructure. Bridging this digital divide is essential to ensure that AI serves all learners equitably.

2. FOUNDATIONS OF DIDACTICS IN MATHEMATICS

2.1. What is Mathematical Didactics?

Mathematical didactics, often referred to as the didactics of mathematics or mathematics education, is a specialized field within educational science that focuses on the teaching and learning of mathematics. It combines elements of pedagogy, psychology, cognitive science, curriculum theory, and mathematics itself to understand how learners acquire mathematical knowledge, and how educators can most effectively facilitate this learning. More than simply "teaching math," didactics involves a systematic investigation of how mathematical concepts are presented, how they are internalized by students, and how teaching methods can be improved based on empirical research and theoretical models (Santos-Trigo 2024).

Figure 1. Didactics of Mathematics

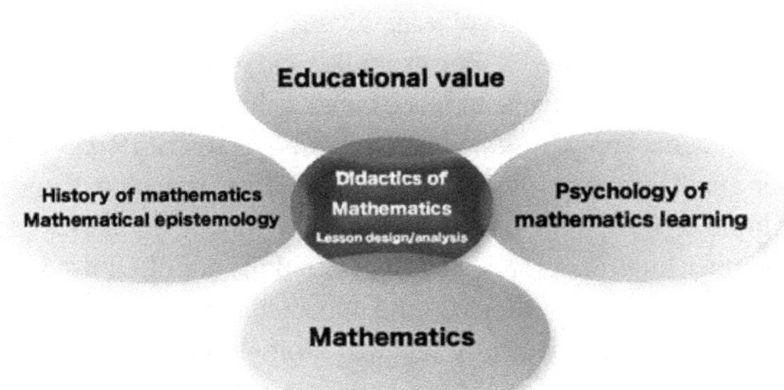

At its core, mathematical didactics explores questions such as: What makes a mathematical concept difficult or easy to learn? How should mathematical ideas be introduced to build deeper understanding? What types of instructional strategies promote student engagement and long-term retention? How can assessments be designed not just to evaluate, but to support learning?

Mathematical didactics also pays close attention to the cultural, social, and linguistic factors that affect mathematics education. It considers how students' backgrounds, prior experiences, and attitudes toward mathematics influence their learning trajectories. In doing so, it supports inclusive education practices and aims to close gaps in achievement and participation among diverse student populations.

The field is both theoretical and practical. It produces frameworks and models (such as the Van Hiele model of geometric thought, or the APOS theory in algebra learning) and directly informs classroom practices and curriculum development. As such, mathematical didactics plays a crucial role in shaping not only how mathematics is taught in schools but also how it is understood as a human endeavor.

2.2. Core Principles of Mathematics Didactics

Mathematics education, as shaped by didactic principles, is built upon several key pillars. These include conceptual understanding, procedural fluency, problem-solving, reasoning, and mathematical communication. These five strands, as identified in leading curriculum frameworks such as those from the National Council of Teachers of Mathematics (NCTM), form the foundation of effective mathematics instruction (Dorner et al., 2025).

2.2.1. Conceptual Understanding

Conceptual understanding refers to the comprehension of mathematical concepts, operations, and relationships. It involves knowing not just the "how" but the "why" behind mathematical procedures. For example, understanding that multiplication is repeated addition, or why the area of a triangle is half the product of its base and height, helps students apply this knowledge flexibly across different contexts.

Didactics emphasizes the importance of building conceptual understanding through multiple representations such that visual, symbolic, numerical, and verbal. Tools like number lines, diagrams, and manipulations are often used to make abstract ideas more concrete. Without a solid conceptual base, students may be able to perform procedures mechanically but will struggle to adapt when confronted with novel problems.

2.2.2. Procedural Fluency

Procedural fluency is the ability to carry out mathematical procedures accurately, efficiently, and flexibly. It includes skills such as solving equations, performing arithmetic operations, and using algorithms. While fluency is important, didactic theory cautions against equating mathematical success solely with speed or correctness.

Effective mathematics instruction should aim to develop fluency in tandem with understanding. Practice and repetition are necessary, but they should be grounded in meaningful contexts. For example, students should learn the standard algorithm for long division not just as a sequence of steps, but as a logical process rooted in place value and repeated subtraction.

2.2.3. Problem-Solving

Problem-solving is both a means and an end in mathematics education. It involves applying mathematical knowledge to new and unfamiliar situations, and often requires creativity, persistence, and strategic thinking. In didactic terms, problem-solving is not just about arriving at correct answers, but about developing processes and approaches to tackle open-ended or complex problems.

Teaching through problem-solving is a hallmark of modern didactics. It encourages students to explore multiple solution paths, make conjectures, and justify their reasoning. This approach fosters deeper learning and mirrors how mathematics is used in real-world and professional contexts.

2.2.4. Reasoning

Mathematical reasoning refers to the ability to make logical arguments, draw inferences, and justify conclusions based on evidence and rules. It is essential for developing mathematical maturity and for understanding how different areas of mathematics are interconnected.

Didactic strategies for promoting reasoning include asking students to explain their thinking, identify errors in flawed arguments, and compare different approaches to the same problem. Reasoning should be cultivated at all levels of mathematics education, starting from the early grades.

2.2.5. Communication

Mathematical communication involves expressing mathematical ideas clearly and coherently, using appropriate language, symbols, diagrams, and representations. It is essential for collaborative learning, self-assessment, and engagement in mathematical discourse.

Students should be encouraged to talk about mathematics, write explanations, and engage in discussions where they defend their solutions and critique those of others. Communication also helps teachers assess student understanding and misconceptions, enabling more responsive instruction.

2.3. Traditional vs. Modern Approaches to Mathematics Teaching

The field of mathematics didactics has evolved significantly, particularly in response to research on how students learn and the demands of 21st-century education. This evolution is reflected in the shift from traditional, teacher-centered models to more student-centered, inquiry-based approaches (Alderton & Pratt, 2025).

2.3.1. Traditional Approaches

Traditional mathematics instruction is often characterized by direct instruction, rote learning, and algorithmic problem-solving. Teachers typically present a concept, demonstrate a method, and assign practice problems. Students are expected to follow procedures, memorize formulas and reproduce solutions accurately.

This approach has certain advantages. In particular, it is efficient, predictable, and familiar to many educators and students. However, it has significant limitations. Research shows that students who learn mathematics procedurally without understanding are more likely to forget what they've learned and less likely to transfer knowledge to new situations. Traditional methods can also alienate students who do not thrive under rigid, abstract instruction or who need more contextual or collaborative learning environments.

2.3.2. Modern Approaches

Modern didactic strategies emphasize constructivist principles, where learners build their own understanding through active engagement with problems and concepts. Teachers act as facilitators, guiding inquiry, posing challenging questions, and encouraging exploration. Key features of modern mathematics instruction include:

- **Use of real-world contexts** to make learning meaningful and relevant.
- **Collaborative learning**, such as group work and math discussions.
- **Use of multiple representations** to support diverse learners.
- **Incorporation of technology**, including AI-powered tools, to personalize learning and provide interactive experiences.
- **Formative assessment** to inform instruction and support learning.

Rather than prioritizing speed and correctness, modern approaches focus on depth of understanding, flexibility in thinking, and the development of a positive mathematical identity.

3. AI TOOLS IN THE MATH CLASSROOM

The integration of Artificial Intelligence (AI) in mathematics education has revolutionized traditional instructional practices, offering a more personalized, responsive, and data-driven approach to teaching and learning. In the context of secondary education, where mathematics can often be a challenging and abstract subject, AI tools have opened new pathways for supporting student understanding, motivation, and achievement. These tools include intelligent tutoring systems, adaptive learning platforms, AI-powered assessment systems, and chatbots or virtual assistants for on-demand math help. Each of these technologies plays a unique role in reshaping how students interact with mathematical content, how teachers monitor progress, and how instruction can be more effectively tailored to individual needs (Egara & Mosimege, 2024).

3.1. Intelligent Tutoring Systems (ITS)

Intelligent Tutoring Systems (ITS) are among the most established applications of AI in education. They are designed to emulate the experience of working with a one-on-one human tutor by adapting instruction to a student's needs in real time. ITS platforms in the mathematics classroom provide problem-solving guidance, corrective feedback, and targeted instruction based on students' interactions with tasks. These systems use advanced algorithms, machine learning models, and knowledge tracing techniques to diagnose misconceptions and adjust content dynamically.

Two of the most prominent ITS tools used in math education are **ALEKS** and **Carnegie Learning's MATHia**.

3.1.1. ALEKS (Assessment and LEarning in Knowledge Spaces)

ALEKS uses a theoretical framework called Knowledge Space Theory to map out a learner's understanding of mathematical concepts. At the beginning of a course, students take an adaptive diagnostic assessment that determines their current knowledge state. Based on this information, ALEKS generates a personalized learning path that focuses on topics the student is ready to learn next, avoiding both redundancy and premature complexity.

Figure 2. Math Classroom

One of ALEKS's strengths is its ability to reassess students regularly to ensure mastery and retention, not just completion. Its continual adaptation ensures that students work within their zone of proximal development, challenging enough to promote learning, but not so difficult as to cause frustration. For teachers, ALEKS provides detailed performance data, showing mastery levels, time spent on topics, and areas needing reinforcement (Villegas-Ch et al., 2025).

3.1.2. Carnegie Learning's MATHia

MATHia is grounded in cognitive science and emphasizes both procedural fluency and conceptual understanding. It guides students through multi-step mathematical problems by prompting them to explain their reasoning, complete subtasks, and justify their solutions. MATHia collects granular data on each student's decisions, which it uses to model knowledge and adapt future problems accordingly.

What sets MATHia apart is its emphasis on cognitive modeling. The system doesn't just track whether a student got an answer right or wrong, but it evaluates how the student arrived at the solution. This allows for a more precise understanding of misconceptions and supports deep learning. Teachers benefit from real-time dashboards that highlight students' progress, pacing, and engagement levels, enabling timely interventions.

3.2. Adaptive Learning Platforms

While ITSs focus on step-by-step tutoring, adaptive learning platforms take a broader approach by adjusting the sequence, difficulty, and type of instructional content based on learner data. These platforms are especially effective in diverse classrooms where students exhibit wide variations in mathematical ability and learning pace.

Adaptive learning platforms often integrate multimedia elements, interactive problem-solving, and continuous feedback mechanisms. Notable examples in the math education space include DreamBox Learning, Khan Academy, and IXL.

3.2.1. DreamBox Learning

DreamBox is an adaptive platform designed for K–8 mathematics that blends AI with rigorous pedagogical strategies. The system uses continuous formative assessment, collecting thousands of data points per hour on each student's behavior including the time taken to answer, the method of interaction, and the types of mistakes made.

Figure 3. DreamBox Learning

Based on this real-time data, DreamBox modifies instruction dynamically. If a student struggles with fractions, the platform may return to prerequisite concepts like division or visual representations of parts-to-whole relationships. If a student excels, DreamBox offers enrichment problems that encourage abstract reasoning.

The platform's gamified environment, interactive visuals, and scaffolded support help maintain student motivation while promoting mastery.

3.2.2. Khan Academy and IXL

Khan Academy, known for its extensive library of instructional videos, has incorporated AI into its Mastery Learning framework. Students' progress through exercises and receive recommendations based on their performance history. AI is used to identify weak areas, reinforce content, and celebrate mastery. IXL works similarly, offering practice exercises that adjust difficulty and give targeted feedback.

Figure 4. Khan Academy and IXL

These platforms are especially useful for differentiation, allowing teachers to assign tasks suited to each student's skill level while still aligning with curricular goals. They also serve as valuable tools for homework, revision, and self-paced learning.

3.3. AI-Powered Assessment Tools

Assessment plays a critical role in mathematics education. However, traditional assessments often fail to capture the nuances of a student's understanding or provide timely feedback. AI-powered assessment tools offer solutions by automating the grading process, analyzing student responses for deeper insights, and providing real-time feedback that supports formative learning.

Platforms such as SOWISO, Gradescope, and Quillionz are increasingly used in classrooms and digital learning environments.

3.3.1. SOWISO

SOWISO provides a structured, interactive environment where students can work through mathematics problems step by step. The AI engine analyzes each step, providing immediate hints or corrections when necessary. This method supports process-based assessment, focusing not just on final answers but on the reasoning and methods used.

Figure 5. SOWISO

For educators, SOWISO offers analytics on which concepts are most commonly misunderstood, helping them adjust lesson plans accordingly.

3.3.2. Gradescope

Originally developed to simplify grading, Gradescope now uses AI to group similar student responses, allowing teachers to grade more efficiently and consistently. In math, where open-ended answers and hand-written solutions are common, this functionality saves time and ensures uniformity. Gradescope's ability to identify error patterns also supports targeted reteaching.

Figure 6. Gradescope

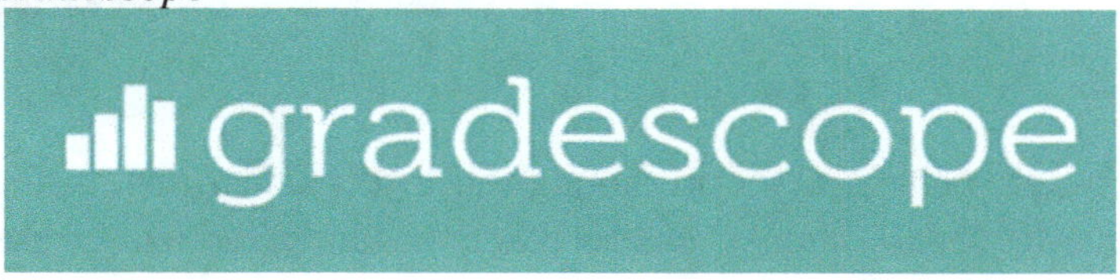

3.3.3. Benefits of AI in Assessment

- **Faster feedback** enables real-time corrections and reduces student anxiety.
- **Detailed diagnostics** help teachers identify class-wide or individual learning gaps.
- **Consistency in grading** improves fairness.
- **Increased efficiency** allows teachers to spend more time on instruction.

3.4. Chatbots and Virtual Assistants for Math Help

Another powerful use of AI in the math classroom is through chatbots and virtual assistants, which provide 24/7 support and supplement formal instruction. These tools are particularly helpful for independent study, homework help, and exam preparation (Martinovic & Danesi, 2025).

3.4.1. Socratic by Google and Photomath

Both tools use optical character recognition (OCR) and AI to read and analyze math problems from a photo taken by the student. They then provide step-by-step solutions and explanations in simple language.

- **Socratic** integrates explanations, video tutorials, and links to related concepts.
- **Photomath** not only shows the solution but also explains each step, helping students understand the underlying process.

Figure 7. Socratic by Google and Photomath

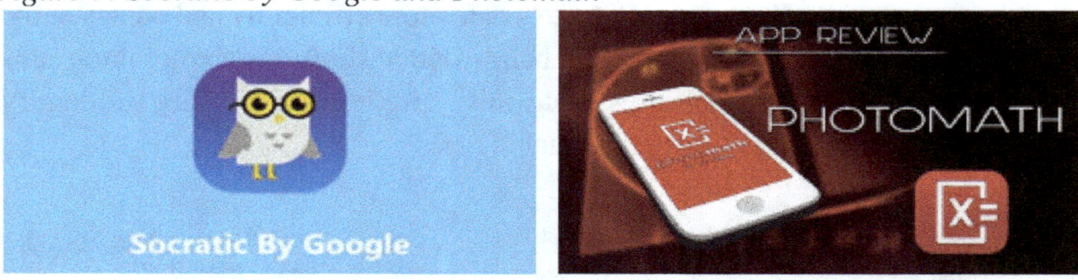

These tools are beneficial for promoting self-directed learning. Instead of waiting for teacher feedback, students can seek help instantly, reducing frustration and maintaining momentum in learning.

3.4.2. ChatGPT and AI Tutors

AI language models like ChatGPT can serve as virtual math tutors, capable of solving problems, explaining concepts, and responding to questions in natural language. Teachers can also integrate such tools into class activities such as generating multiple versions of a problem, exploring alternative solutions, or supporting peer learning in collaborative tasks.

Figure 8. ChatGPT and AI Tutors

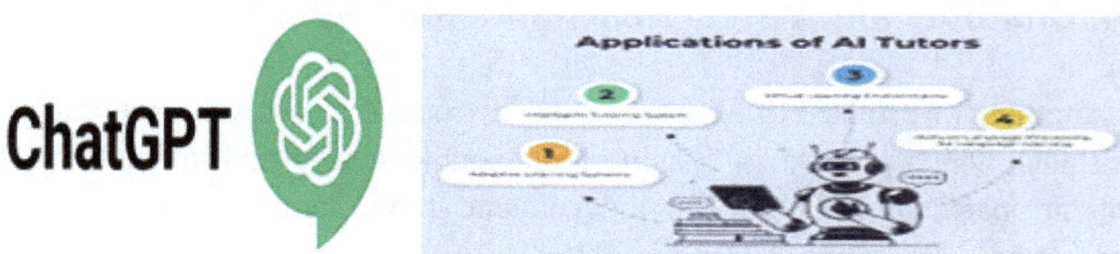

Used appropriately, these tools can model mathematical discourse and reinforce key concepts, though they require supervision to ensure accuracy and relevance.

4. PERSONALIZED LEARNING AND DIFFERENTIATION

One of the most promising applications of Artificial Intelligence (AI) in education, particularly in mathematics, is the ability to deliver personalized learning experiences. In traditional classrooms, teachers face the constant challenge of addressing the diverse needs of students who vary widely in ability, background knowledge, learning pace, and preferred learning styles. Differentiation, while theoretically ideal, is often difficult to implement at scale due to time and resource constraints. AI, however, offers powerful tools that can analyze individual learning patterns in real time and adapt content accordingly, making personalization not only possible but practical (Mehmood 2025).

Figure 9. Effectiveness of AI-Driven Personalized Learning Paths

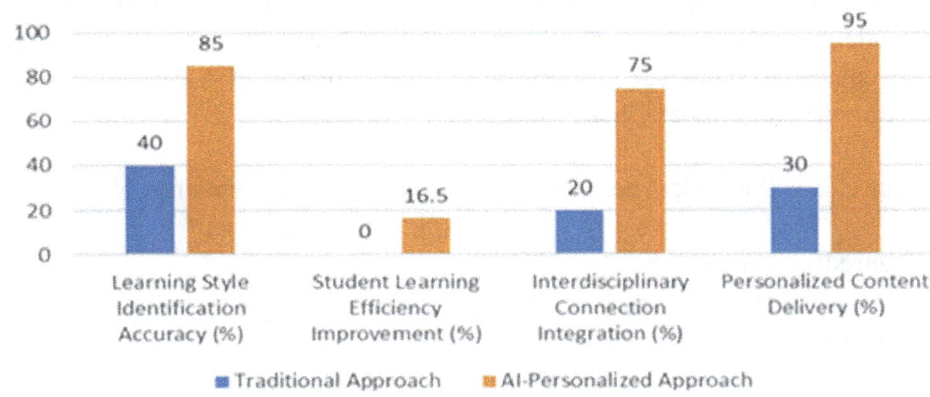

This section explores how AI supports differentiated instruction in the math classroom, reviews case studies demonstrating its impact, and discusses critical ethical considerations, including bias, algorithmic fairness, and data privacy.

4.1. How AI Adapts Content to Student Ability and Learning Styles

Personalized learning is not a new concept, but AI enhances it by introducing real-time adaptability. Traditional personalized approaches often rely on manual intervention: teachers differentiating tasks, modifying assessments, or grouping students based on ability. AI systems, by contrast, can process massive datasets rapidly and make immediate adjustments to instructional content and strategy.

AI-driven personalization in mathematics typically involves the following components:

4.1.1. Diagnostic Assessment and Baseline Analysis

Before a learning path can be tailored, AI platforms begin with a diagnostic assessment. This could involve a series of math problems, a short quiz, or behavioral indicators (e.g., time on task, number of attempts). Systems like ALEKS or Khan Academy use these diagnostics to identify a learner's zone of proximal development (ZPD), the range of tasks a student can perform with guidance.

4.1.2. Real-Time Adaptation

As students engage with tasks, AI systems continuously collect and analyze data on their responses. If a student struggles with a particular concept, the system may:

- Present the concept using a different modality (visual, auditory, or interactive).
- Offer prerequisite lessons to fill in foundational gaps.
- Reduce the complexity of tasks to rebuild confidence.
- Provide scaffolding or hints for problem-solving.

Conversely, if a student demonstrates proficiency, the system may:

- Introduce enrichment activities.
- Offer more challenging problems.
- Accelerate the pace of instruction.

These adjustments happen automatically, ensuring that the student is constantly working at the edge of their ability, challenged, but not overwhelmed.

4.1.3. Multimodal Content Delivery

AI tools also cater to diverse learning styles by offering instruction through multiple channels:

- **Visual learners** benefit from diagrams, animations, and graphing tools.
- **Auditory learners** can engage with narrated explanations and video lessons.
- **Kinesthetic learners** interact with simulations and drag-and-drop problem-solving interfaces.
- **Logical-mathematical learners** thrive on puzzles, patterns, and strategic games.

This type of multimodal delivery is especially important in mathematics, where abstract concepts often require concrete representations for deep understanding.

4.1.4. Feedback Loops and Metacognition

Effective learning relies on feedback. AI-powered systems provide immediate, formative feedback, helping students understand not only that an answer is wrong but why it is wrong. Some platforms go further by encouraging students to reflect on their process, supporting metacognitive development.

By tracking individual error patterns and providing contextual feedback, AI tools support deeper learning and retention. Students begin to recognize their own learning habits and make informed choices about their strategies.

4.2. Case Studies Showing Improved Engagement and Performance

Several case studies and research initiatives have demonstrated the positive impact of AI-driven personalization in mathematics education.

4.2.1. Case Study 1: DreamBox Learning (USA)

A large-scale study conducted by the Center for Education Policy Research at Harvard University (2016) evaluated the impact of DreamBox Learning, an adaptive math platform, in elementary and middle schools across the U.S. The study found that students who used DreamBox for just 20 minutes per day showed significant gains in math achievement on standardized tests compared to non-users.

DreamBox's ability to adjust lesson paths and provide differentiated feedback led to increased student engagement, especially among learners who had previously struggled with traditional instruction.

4.2.2. Case Study 2: Yixue Squirrel AI (China)

Squirrel AI, often referred to as the "AI tutor of China," serves millions of students and uses advanced algorithms to personalize math instruction. In a 2019 independent study, students who used Squirrel AI for a semester demonstrated learning gains that were significantly higher than those in control groups taught by experienced human teachers.

One of the key features of Squirrel AI is its ability to break down mathematical concepts into hundreds of granular sub-skills. By pinpointing specific weaknesses, the platform offers micro-remediation that accelerates learning and builds confidence.

4.2.3. Case Study 3: Khan Academy in California Schools

In a pilot program involving underserved middle school students in California, Khan Academy's mastery-based learning model, supported by AI recommendations, resulted in both higher engagement and better math performance. Teachers noted that students were more self-directed and less anxious, in part because they were no longer forced to move on before mastering a topic.

These case studies highlight that personalization via AI can reduce learning gaps, foster autonomy, and increase motivation especially when combined with thoughtful teacher support.

4.3. Ethical Considerations in Personalization

While AI offers numerous benefits in differentiated instruction, it also raises ethical and practical concerns. These must be carefully considered to ensure that personalization supports, rather than undermines, educational equity and student agency (Omeh & Olelewe, 2025).

4.3.1. Algorithmic Bias and Equity

AI systems are only as fair as the data they are trained on. If historical data reflects systemic biases (e.g., based on gender, ethnicity, or socioeconomic status), the algorithms may inadvertently perpetuate those biases. For example:

- Students from under-resourced schools might be placed on slower learning paths.
- Language barriers could be misinterpreted as a lack of mathematical ability.
- Girls might be less frequently offered advanced challenges due to implicit patterns in prior data.

To counteract this, developers must audit AI systems for bias and ensure that algorithms are transparent, explainable, and regularly evaluated for fairness.

4.3.2. Data Privacy and Student Autonomy

Personalization requires large volumes of student data, including performance history, behavioral patterns, and sometimes even biometric or emotional data (e.g., eye-tracking, engagement indicators). This raises serious privacy concerns, particularly when such data is stored by third-party vendors.

Key questions include:

- Who owns the data?
- How is it protected from misuse or breaches?
- Are students and parents fully informed about what is collected and why?

Schools and educational authorities must implement strict data governance policies, obtain informed consent, and prioritize student privacy. In some jurisdictions, such as the EU under GDPR, laws provide specific protections, but enforcement remains inconsistent globally.

4.3.3. Overreliance on AI

Another concern is the potential overreliance on automated systems. While AI can personalize efficiently, it lacks the human intuition, empathy, and contextual awareness that teachers bring to the classroom. Students should not be reduced to data points, and AI should not replace human judgment in determining learning needs.

Effective personalization happens when AI supports teachers, not when it displaces them. Hybrid models, where AI informs and enhances, but educators lead, are generally the most effective and ethical approach.

5. TEACHER'S ROLE IN AN AI-AUGMENTED CLASSROOM

As Artificial Intelligence (AI) becomes increasingly integrated into educational systems, the role of the teacher is undergoing a profound transformation. In traditional classrooms, teachers are often positioned as the primary source of knowledge, delivering lectures, assigning tasks, and evaluating student progress. However, in AI-augmented environments, much of the routine instruction, data analysis, and even formative assessment is handled by intelligent systems. This shift necessitates a reimagining of the teacher's role, not as a dispenser of information, but as a **facilitator of learning**, a guide, and a mediator between students and technology (Seo et al., 2025).

Figure 10. Teacher's Role in an AI-Augmented Classroom

This section explores the changing dynamics of teaching in an AI-enhanced classroom, highlights the professional development required for effective integration, and considers the concept of AI as a co-teacher or digital teaching assistant.

5.1. From Lecturer to Facilitator: Changing Teacher Dynamics

The introduction of AI into the classroom redefines how teachers interact with both content and learners. Rather than focusing on delivering information, teachers now have the opportunity to focus more on deep learning, individualized support, and relationship-building.

5.1.1. Shifting Pedagogical Focus

In AI-supported classrooms, much of the direct instruction, such as explanations of basic mathematical concepts, procedural steps, or repetitive practice, is handled by platforms like ALEKS, Khan Academy, or DreamBox. These systems adapt content automatically based on student responses, providing immediate feedback and continuous assessment. This frees teachers from having to "cover" every topic and allows them to focus on more complex instructional tasks, such as:

- Facilitating group discussions and collaborative problem-solving.
- Encouraging critical thinking and metacognition.
- Supporting students in developing learning strategies.
- Intervening with targeted support for struggling learners.

Rather than being the center of the learning experience, the teacher becomes an **orchestrator of resources**, helping students navigate personalized learning paths while maintaining coherence with curriculum goals.

5.1.2. Enhancing Emotional and Social Support

No matter how advanced, AI systems lack the emotional intelligence, empathy, and ethical judgment that human teachers bring to the classroom. As AI handles the analytical side of education, the emotional and relational aspects of teaching become even more vital.

Teachers play a critical role in:

- Motivating students.
- Building classroom community.
- Addressing behavioral issues.
- Supporting students facing personal or socio-emotional challenges.

In this sense, AI can take over some instructional duties, but not the human connection necessary for holistic education.

5.1.3. Redefining Teacher Authority

In traditional settings, authority is often derived from the teacher's knowledge and control of the learning process. In an AI-driven classroom, authority shifts toward guidance and mentorship. Teachers must be comfortable with students accessing AI-driven tools independently and even learning content the teacher may not have directly taught.

This shift requires a mindset change. Teachers must embrace flexibility, curiosity, and a willingness to collaborate not only with students but with the AI systems themselves.

5.2. Professional Development Needs for Effective AI Integration

For teachers to thrive in an AI-augmented environment, ongoing professional development (PD) is essential. Effective PD must go beyond technical training; it must include pedagogical, ethical, and collaborative dimensions of AI integration.

5.2.1. Building AI Literacy

Teachers need a foundational understanding of what AI is and how it functions in educational settings. This includes:

- Knowing how AI systems collect, process, and use data.
- Understanding algorithmic decision-making and its limitations.
- Recognizing signs of bias, errors, or overdependence on technology.

AI literacy empowers teachers to make informed decisions about when and how to use AI tools, and to critically evaluate their impact on student learning.

5.2.2. Pedagogical Integration

It's not enough to simply add AI tools into a classroom. Teachers must understand how to align AI-supported learning with curriculum standards and instructional goals. Professional development should explore:

- Strategies for blending AI with face-to-face instruction.
- Best practices for balancing AI automation with teacher intervention.
- Case studies demonstrating successful AI integration.

Teachers also benefit from learning how to interpret AI-generated data to inform instruction. For instance, if an AI platform identifies a student struggling with fractions, the teacher needs to know how to use that insight to adjust their lesson or provide individualized support.

5.2.3. Ethical and Equity Considerations

PD should address the ethical implications of AI in education, including:

- Data privacy and consent.
- Avoiding algorithmic bias.
- Ensuring equitable access to technology.

Teachers must be advocates for fair and ethical use of AI, especially in schools serving marginalized or under-resourced communities (Ding et al., 2024).

5.2.4. Collaborative Learning Communities

As AI in education continues to evolve, **peer collaboration** becomes a valuable tool. Teachers benefit from sharing experiences, challenges, and best practices with colleagues. School systems should foster professional learning communities (PLCs) where teachers can engage in collective inquiry around AI tools and their impact on teaching and learning.

5.3. AI as a Co-Teacher or Teaching Assistant

One of the most exciting developments in AI education is the concept of AI as a co-teacher or digital teaching assistant. Rather than viewing AI as a replacement for human educators, this model envisions AI working in partnership with teachers.

5.3.1. Managing Administrative and Routine Tasks

AI can take over a number of time-consuming tasks, including:

- Grading multiple-choice and short-answer questions.
- Tracking attendance and engagement.
- Generating reports on student progress.
- Suggesting differentiated assignments based on performance data.

This allows teachers to devote more time to instruction, mentoring, and planning.

5.3.2. Real-Time Support in the Classroom

Some AI tools can act as on-demand teaching assistants. For example:

- A chatbot might help a student solve an equation while the teacher works with another group.
- An intelligent tutor might prompt students with questions that deepen their understanding.
- A virtual assistant might help students navigate resources or clarify instructions.

By supporting individual learners, AI increases the teacher's reach and responsiveness.

5.3.3. Data-Informed Decision-Making

AI provides teachers with real-time analytics dashboards, offering insights such as:

- Which students are at risk of falling behind.
- Which concepts are causing the most confusion.
- Patterns in student engagement and pacing.

Teachers can use this data to personalize their interventions, whether through small-group instruction, individual conferencing, or adjusting the pace of whole-class lessons.

5.3.4. Augmenting Instructional Content

Teachers can also use AI to generate content, such as:

- Multiple versions of a math problem for practice or assessment.
- Personalized feedback on open-ended responses.
- Enrichment activities for advanced learners.

By acting as a creative partner, AI expands the teacher's instructional toolkit.

6. CHALLENGES AND LIMITATIONS

As Artificial Intelligence (AI) becomes more embedded in educational settings, especially in the teaching and learning of mathematics, a great deal of attention has been given to its potential benefits, personalization, real-time feedback, increased engagement and reduced teacher workload. However, while these advantages are significant, it is equally important to critically examine the challenges and limitations of AI in education. These include the risk of over-reliance on technology, the potential for superficial understanding in students, and ongoing equity concerns related to access (Kohnke & Zaugg, 2025).

Figure 11. Challenges and Limitations

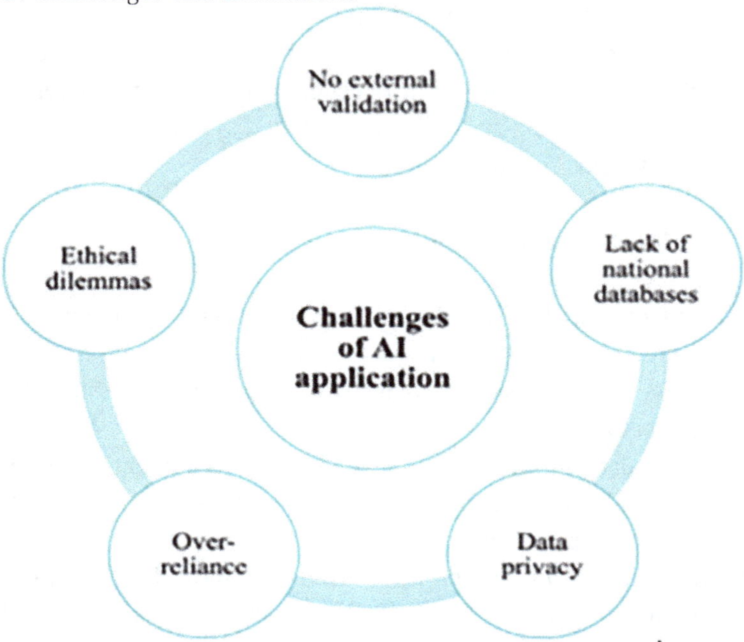

Understanding these limitations is not merely a matter of caution; it is essential for responsible implementation. Technology, particularly AI, should serve as a complement to pedagogy, not a replacement. This section explores these challenges in depth and considers how educators, institutions, and policymakers can respond effectively.

6.1. Over-Reliance on Technology

One of the most pressing concerns in AI-augmented education is the growing tendency to over-rely on technology as a solution to complex educational problems. While AI can perform impressive functions, like adaptive assessment, individualized feedback, and content's curation, its use must be strategically and critically integrated into learning environments.

6.1.1. Erosion of Teacher Autonomy

A common fear among educators is that AI systems might eventually dictate classroom decisions, thereby reducing teacher autonomy. Algorithms may recommend instructional strategies, assign content, or flag student behavior, sometimes in ways that conflict with a teacher's professional judgment. If teachers feel compelled to follow AI-driven suggestions without space for interpretation, they risk losing control over the learning environment.

Teachers bring emotional intelligence, cultural awareness, and context-specific insight that machines cannot replicate. An over-reliance on AI can inadvertently shift authority away from educators and toward automated systems, potentially leading to a de-skilling of the teaching profession.

6.1.2. Reduction of Student Agency

Similarly, students may begin to depend heavily on AI for problem-solving and feedback. With chatbots, step-by-step solvers, and auto-correction tools at their fingertips, students may bypass the cognitive struggle that is essential for deep learning in mathematics.

Learning, particularly in mathematics, often requires students to grapple with difficult problems, make mistakes, and reflect on their reasoning. When AI systems immediately correct errors or offer hints, the productive struggle, an important part of mathematical growth, can be minimized or removed entirely. Over time, this may lead to students becoming passive consumers of information rather than active problem-solvers.

6.2. Risk of Losing Conceptual Depth

Mathematics education is not simply about arriving at correct answers. True mathematical understanding involves conceptual depth, flexible thinking, reasoning, and the ability to apply concepts in unfamiliar contexts. While AI excels at delivering practice problems, identifying patterns in student performance, and optimizing for efficiency, it often falls short in supporting deep, conceptual learning.

6.2.1. Emphasis on Procedural Fluency

Many AI-driven math platforms are designed to help student's master procedural fluency, the ability to apply algorithms quickly and accurately. This focus aligns with standardized testing metrics and can improve surface-level proficiency. However, it may inadvertently shift attention away from why procedures work, how concepts are connected, and when different strategies should be applied.

Students may be able to solve equations using AI-generated steps but still lack an understanding of the underlying concepts, such as the distributive property or the nature of inverse operations. Without this depth, students are more likely to struggle when confronted with non-routine problems or higher-level math.

6.2.2. Limited Support for Mathematical Discourse

Mathematics didactics emphasizes not just solving problems, but also communicating mathematical ideas, explaining reasoning and engaging in discourse with peers. These processes are essential for building robust mathematical understanding. AI systems, while increasingly sophisticated, are still limited in their ability to engage in authentic dialogue that mimics human conversation (Allison 2025).

Measures how actively students interact with AI tools:

$$ER = \frac{\text{Active Interaction Time}}{\text{Total Available Time}} \times 100 \tag{6.1}$$

- Active Interaction Time = time spent using AI tools meaningfully (e.g., solving problems, watching tutorials)
- Total Available Time = total time AI tools are accessible to students

Even chatbots designed for tutoring often provide canned responses or generic explanations that do not adapt well to the nuances of student thinking. Without opportunities for discussion, argumentation, and reflection, students may achieve computational accuracy without developing conceptual insight.

6.2.3. Lack of Contextualized Problem Solving

AI tools often rely on abstract or decontextualized problem sets, which may lack relevance to students' lives. Yet, real-world applications of mathematics, whether in science, finance, or technology, require students to apply concepts in messy, ambiguous situations. Overuse of AI-generated exercises may lead students to view math as a series of disjointed skills rather than a coherent, powerful language for understanding the world.

6.3. Digital Divide and Access Issues

The digital divide remains one of the most critical limitations of AI integration in education. Access to AI tools, platforms, and supporting technologies is uneven, both globally and within individual countries. Without deliberate efforts to bridge this divide, AI-enhanced education risks exacerbating existing inequalities.

6.3.1. Technological Infrastructure Gaps

Access to AI tools requires stable internet, up-to-date devices, and compatible software. Students in under-resourced schools or rural areas often lack these basic prerequisites. In some regions, even consistent electricity remains a barrier. As a result, the benefits of AI in mathematics education may be concentrated in well-funded schools and urban centers, leaving marginalized communities further behind.

The problem is not limited to students; schools may also lack the IT staff or technical expertise to maintain and support complex AI systems. Without infrastructure investment, the digital divide will continue to widen.

6.3.2. Economic Barriers

Many AI platforms operate on a subscription model, which can be cost-prohibitive for schools with limited budgets. Although some organizations offer free or low-cost options, these often come with reduced features or limited customization. Furthermore, students without personal devices at home are at a disadvantage, particularly when homework or supplemental learning relies on AI tools.

These economic factors can lead to two-tiered education systems, where affluent schools gain access to cutting-edge personalized learning environments, while others continue to rely on outdated methods.

6.3.3. Linguistic and Cultural Limitations

AI systems are typically trained on large datasets, many of which are biased toward dominant languages and cultural norms. Students who speak minority languages or come from different cultural backgrounds may find AI-generated content unfamiliar, inaccessible, or irrelevant. This can lead to a disconnect between technology and student experience, reducing engagement and understanding.

Cultural bias in AI design may also affect the types of problems presented, the examples used, and the assumptions about prior knowledge. If not addressed, these biases can marginalize students and reinforce exclusionary practices (Narayanan & Kapoor, 2024).

6.4. Mitigating Challenges: A Balanced Approach

Addressing the challenges of AI in mathematics education requires a balanced, critical approach that centers on pedagogy, equity, and ethical use.

- **Teacher involvement is key**: AI should augment, not replace, human instruction. Teachers must retain decision-making power and adapt AI tools to fit their students' needs.
- **Professional development is essential**: Teachers need training not just in using AI, but in evaluating its effectiveness and recognizing its limitations.

- **Infrastructure investment must be prioritized**: Policymakers should work to ensure all students have access to the necessary tools and connectivity for digital learning.
- **Transparency and accountability are non-negotiable**: AI developers must be transparent about how algorithms function, how data is used, and how decisions are made. Open communication with educators and communities is vital.
- **Foster critical digital literacy**: Students must be taught not only how to use AI tools, but how to question them, interpret their feedback, and make informed decisions.

7. CASE STUDIES OR PILOT PROGRAMS

The integration of Artificial Intelligence (AI) in mathematics education is not just a theoretical possibility but a growing reality across various countries and educational contexts. Numerous pilot programs and case studies have emerged globally, demonstrating the practical applications of AI tools, their impact on student learning, and the evolving role of teachers. These examples offer valuable insights into both the opportunities and challenges of AI-enhanced math education, shedding light on measurable outcomes and the perspectives of key stakeholders.

7.1. Case Study 1: ALEKS in U.S. Secondary Schools

ALEKS (Assessment and Learning in Knowledge Spaces) is an AI-driven intelligent tutoring system widely used in the United States across secondary schools and community colleges. ALEKS adapts to each student's knowledge state, providing individualized instruction in mathematics and assessing mastery continuously (O'Sullivan & Hasenstab, 2024).

Implementation

In several districts, ALEKS has been integrated into algebra and geometry courses, supplementing traditional classroom teaching. Students use the platform both in school and at home, working through personalized learning paths tailored to their current understanding and learning pace.

Outcomes

A longitudinal study conducted in a large urban district revealed promising results:

- **Improved Proficiency:** Over 70% of students using ALEKS demonstrated significant improvement in algebra proficiency within one academic year compared to peers using conventional textbooks.

- **Reduced Achievement Gaps:** ALEKS was particularly effective for students with historically lower math achievement, including English language learners and economically disadvantaged groups.
- **Increased Engagement:** Students reported higher engagement levels due to the immediate feedback and gamified elements of ALEKS, such as progress bars and mastery checks.

Teacher and Student Feedback

Teachers appreciated ALEKS's ability to identify specific knowledge gaps and provide targeted remediation. One algebra teacher noted, "ALEKS gives me data I didn't have before; I can see exactly what each student struggles with and plan small-group instruction accordingly."

Students valued the autonomy to work at their own pace but also expressed the desire for more human interaction and explanations for complex concepts. This feedback highlighted the ongoing need for teachers to play a facilitative role alongside AI.

7.2. Case Study 2: Carnegie Learning in Ohio High Schools

Carnegie Learning's MATHia software combines AI with cognitive science principles to deliver a personalized math learning experience. The software emphasizes conceptual understanding and problem-solving through interactive tasks and scaffolded feedback (Windfont 2024).

Implementation

Ohio's Department of Education partnered with Carnegie Learning to pilot MATHia in 15 high schools. The program was embedded within the regular curriculum for Algebra I and II, with teachers receiving professional development on integrating the software into lessons.

Measurable Outcomes

The pilot demonstrated:

- **Higher Test Scores:** Students using MATHia scored an average of 15% higher on end-of-course exams compared to control groups.
- **Increased Time-on-Task:** Data showed students spent 30% more time actively engaged with math content when using the software.
- **Improved Problem-Solving Skills:** Assessments indicated growth not only in procedural fluency but also in students' ability to explain reasoning and apply concepts in novel problems.

Feedback from Educators and Learners

Educators praised the scaffolding features and real-time hints, which helped students build confidence and reduce frustration. However, some teachers noted that initial training was essential to maximize the benefits, as integration required a shift from traditional lesson pacing.

Students reported feeling more supported and less anxious about difficult problems when using MATHia, appreciating the stepwise hints and encouragement.

7.3. Case Study 3: AI-Assisted Learning in South Korea

South Korea, known for its high educational standards and technology adoption, has been a pioneer in AI-driven education, particularly in mathematics. The Korean Ministry of Education launched a pilot program using AI platforms like AI Tutor and SmartMath in selected middle schools.

Program Design

The initiative combined AI tutoring with teacher-led instruction, emphasizing personalized learning plans and continuous formative assessment. The platforms use natural language processing (NLP) to interact with students, offering explanations and guiding problem-solving processes.

Outcomes

- **Enhanced Learning Outcomes:** Students showed marked improvement in standardized math tests, with gains averaging 10-12% compared to traditional instruction.
- **Positive Attitudes:** Surveys indicated high student satisfaction, particularly with the interactive, conversational nature of AI tutors.
- **Teacher Workload Reduction:** Teachers reported that AI handled routine tasks such as grading and progress monitoring, allowing them more time to focus on creative lesson planning.

Challenges Noted

Despite successes, teachers emphasized the need for ongoing support and adjustments to curriculum pacing. Additionally, some students found the AI explanations too formulaic, indicating room for improvement in adaptive conversational abilities.

7.4. Case Study 4: Adaptive Learning in Rural India

A notable example from a low-resource setting is a pilot program run by an NGO in rural India using AI-powered adaptive learning apps on tablets. The program targeted secondary school students struggling with foundational mathematics.

Implementation

Due to limited internet access, the AI software was designed to work offline with periodic data synchronization. Local teachers were trained to use the app as a supplement to their instruction.

Results

- **Significant Gains in Basic Skills:** After six months, students showed a 20% increase in mastery of core arithmetic and algebra skills.
- **Improved Attendance:** Engagement with technology increased attendance rates, as students were motivated by the interactive content.
- **Teacher Empowerment:** Teachers felt more confident in addressing diverse student needs with AI-generated reports highlighting areas requiring attention.

Community Feedback

Parents reported increased enthusiasm for math at home, and the program helped build a culture of self-directed learning among students. However, ongoing challenges included maintaining hardware and ensuring consistent use.

7.5. Comparative Analysis of Pilot Programs

Across these diverse contexts, several **common themes** emerge:

- **Effectiveness of Personalization:** AI's ability to tailor learning to individual student needs consistently improves outcomes, especially for struggling learners.
- **Teacher-AI Synergy:** Successful programs view AI as a tool that complements teachers rather than replaces them. Teacher involvement in interpreting AI data and providing human support remains critical.
- **Professional Development:** Training and ongoing support for educators are pivotal for effective AI integration.
- **Engagement and Motivation:** Interactive, adaptive platforms tend to increase student motivation and time-on-task.
- **Equity Concerns:** Digital infrastructure and economic barriers continue to limit access in underserved communities, underscoring the need for targeted investments.

7.6. Feedback from Teachers and Students: A Closer Look

Teacher Perspectives

Teachers consistently emphasize the value of AI tools in providing actionable insights and freeing them from administrative burdens. They also appreciate how AI allows for more differentiated instruction and timely interventions.

However, many caution against over-reliance on AI, underscoring the importance of maintaining professional judgment. Teachers call for greater involvement in the development of AI curricula to ensure alignment with pedagogical goals and cultural contexts.

Student Voices

Students report mixed experiences with AI-powered math tools. Many enjoy the autonomy, immediate feedback, and gamification features that make learning more engaging. They value the opportunity to progress at their own pace and revisit challenging concepts as needed.

Conversely, some students express frustration with overly rigid AI explanations or a lack of personalized human interaction. These responses highlight the need for AI to be flexible, conversational, and supportive of varied learning preferences (Wang 2025).

7.7. Lessons Learned and Future Directions

Pilot programs demonstrate that while AI holds significant promise for enhancing mathematics education, its impact depends on thoughtful implementation. Key lessons include:

- **Integrate AI thoughtfully into the broader instructional ecosystem** rather than as a standalone solution.
- **Focus on human-AI collaboration** where teachers interpret AI insights and provide nuanced support.
- **Prioritize equity in access** to ensure all students can benefit.
- **Develop culturally relevant content** that resonates with diverse learners.
- **Invest in teacher professional development** to build AI literacy and pedagogical integration skills.

Going forward, pilot programs should continue to refine AI tools based on user feedback, exploring new forms of interaction such as natural language processing and multimodal learning. Rigorous research should accompany these pilots to assess long-term impacts on conceptual understanding, motivation, and equity.

8. FUTURE DIRECTIONS

The future of Artificial Intelligence (AI) in mathematics education is poised for transformative growth, fueled by rapid advances in technology and innovative pedagogical approaches. As AI evolves beyond traditional rule-based systems to more sophisticated, adaptive, and immersive tools, educators, students, and policymakers must prepare for new opportunities and challenges. This section explores some of the most promising emerging trends in AI, the exciting potential of integrating AI with Augmented Reality (AR) and Virtual Reality (VR), and offers targeted recommendations to guide policy and curriculum development for maximizing AI's educational impact.

8.1. Emerging AI Trends

AI in education has made significant strides in recent years, but the next wave of innovation promises even more profound changes. Two key emerging trends with considerable implications for mathematics learning are generative AI and real-time feedback systems.

Generative AI: Creating Dynamic Learning Content

Generative AI refers to models, like OpenAI's GPT series, that can produce text, images, and even code based on input prompts. This capability opens up new possibilities for mathematics education, including:

- **Personalized Problem Generation:** Instead of relying on fixed problem banks, generative AI can create an infinite variety of math problems tailored to students' current ability and interests. For example, a student struggling with quadratic equations could receive custom problems that gradually increase in complexity or contextually relevant scenarios that boost engagement.
- **Step-by-Step Solution Explanations:** Generative AI can provide detailed, adaptive explanations that respond to student queries in natural language. Unlike static hints, this dynamic interaction supports deeper understanding by addressing misconceptions or guiding reasoning in real-time.
- **Mathematical Storytelling:** Generative AI enables the creation of narrative-based math problems embedded in meaningful contexts, helping students connect abstract concepts with real-world applications. This approach can boost motivation and foster conceptual learning.

Despite these exciting possibilities, generative AI also raises important challenges related to accuracy, bias, and appropriateness of content. Ensuring that AI-generated materials are mathematically sound and pedagogically effective requires close collaboration between AI developers and education experts.

Real-Time Feedback Systems: Immediate, Actionable Insights

Real-time feedback systems leverage AI's capacity to analyze student inputs instantly and provide corrective guidance. These systems go beyond simple right-or-wrong indicators to offer nuanced feedback such as:

- Highlighting specific errors in procedural steps.
- Suggesting alternative solution strategies.
- Prompting metacognitive reflection with questions like "Why did this step work?" or "What could you try next?"

The benefit of such immediate feedback is the facilitation of a productive struggle, a vital element of deep math learning where students work through challenges with timely support. Real-time feedback helps maintain student motivation, reduce frustration, and consolidate learning by correcting misconceptions promptly.

Moreover, when combined with analytics dashboards, real-time feedback empowers teachers to monitor student progress closely and intervene strategically. This data-driven approach fosters a more responsive and personalized classroom environment.

8.2. Integration with AR/VR for Geometric and Spatial Understanding

The intersection of AI with Augmented Reality (AR) and Virtual Reality (VR) represents one of the most promising frontiers in math education, particularly for enhancing students' grasp of geometric and spatial concepts. Mathematics, especially geometry and three-dimensional visualization, benefits immensely from dynamic, immersive experiences that traditional textbooks or screens cannot provide.

AR/VR Enhancing Visualization and Interaction

- **Immersive Geometry Exploration:** VR enables students to enter virtual environments where they can manipulate geometric shapes, explore properties, and observe transformations in three-dimensional space. This kind of experiential learning deepens spatial reasoning and helps overcome abstractness.
- **Augmented Reality for Contextualized Learning:** AR overlays virtual objects onto the real world via devices like tablets or smart glasses. Students can interact with these objects directly, measuring angles, volumes, or symmetries in tangible contexts, such as examining a virtual pyramid on their desk.

- **Dynamic Problem Solving:** AI algorithms integrated with AR/VR can generate interactive tasks that adapt in real-time to student actions. For example, a student trying to solve for the volume of an irregular shape could receive guided prompts or see stepwise visual decompositions facilitated by AI.

Benefits for Diverse Learners

AR/VR can make math more accessible for learners with different styles and needs. Visual and kinesthetic learners, in particular, benefit from hands-on manipulation and multisensory engagement. Additionally, VR environments can reduce math anxiety by creating playful, exploratory spaces where mistakes are low-stakes.

Challenges and Considerations

Despite the promise, several challenges must be addressed for widespread adoption:

- **Cost and Accessibility:** High-quality AR/VR hardware can be expensive, limiting equity unless costs decrease or subsidized programs are introduced.
- **Teacher Training:** Educators need training to effectively incorporate AR/VR in pedagogy, including technical skills and lesson design.
- **Curricular Alignment:** Activities must be tightly aligned with learning objectives and standards to avoid technology becoming a distraction rather than a tool.

8.3. Recommendations for Policymakers and Curriculum Designers

To harness AI's full potential in mathematics education while addressing challenges, policymakers and curriculum designers should consider the following recommendations:

8.3.1. Prioritize Equity and Access

Ensure that investments in AI and related technologies are accompanied by strategies to bridge the digital divide. This includes funding for devices, reliable internet access, and maintenance, particularly in under-resourced schools. Policymakers should also promote inclusive AI tools that support diverse languages, cultures, and learning needs.

8.3.2. Foster Teacher Professional Development

Teachers are central to successful AI integration. Comprehensive professional development programs should be established to build educators' competencies in using AI tools, interpreting data insights, and blending AI support with effective pedagogy. Ongoing support and communities of practice can sustain this capacity-building.

8.3.3. Support Research and Evidence-Based Practice

Policymakers should fund rigorous, long-term research to evaluate AI tools in diverse educational contexts, focusing not only on academic outcomes but also on engagement, equity, and socio-emotional impacts. Evidence should inform iterative improvements to both AI technologies and curricular frameworks.

8.3.4. Encourage Ethical and Transparent AI Use

Regulations and guidelines must be established to ensure transparency in AI algorithms, data privacy, and security. Students and parents should have clear information about how AI systems collect and use data. Ethical AI design should prioritize fairness, avoiding bias or discriminatory outcomes.

8.3.5. Integrate AI and Emerging Technologies into Curriculum Standards

Curriculum designers should embed AI literacy and computational thinking into math standards, preparing students not only to learn with AI but to understand its principles and implications. Integration with AR/VR experiences should align with core math competencies, especially in geometry, measurement, and data analysis.

8.3.6. Promote Collaborative AI Development

Governments and educational institutions should encourage partnerships between AI developers, educators, and researchers to co-create tools that are pedagogically sound, culturally responsive, and scalable. Collaborative development ensures AI solutions meet classroom realities and learner diversity.

8.4. Looking Ahead: A Vision for AI-Enhanced Math Education

The future of AI in mathematics education is one where technology acts as a partner in learning, augmenting human creativity and insight rather than supplanting it. Generative AI could provide endlessly adaptable content and explanations tailored to every learner's unique journey, while real-time feedback systems ensure immediate, personalized support.

Meanwhile, the immersive power of AR and VR promises to revolutionize how students visualize and interact with mathematical concepts, making abstract ideas concrete and engaging. As these technologies mature and become more accessible, they can democratize high-quality math education worldwide.

For this future to be realized, educators, policymakers, technologists, and communities must work together to build an ecosystem where AI tools are thoughtfully designed, equitably distributed, ethically governed, and pedagogically integrated. This vision is not only about improved test scores but about fostering deep mathematical understanding, critical thinking, and a lifelong love for learning.

9. CONCLUSION

In conclusion, the integration of Artificial Intelligence into secondary mathematics education marks a transformative shift in both pedagogical practice and educational outcomes. As this chapter has explored, AI offers powerful tools to enhance personalized learning, enable real-time formative assessment, and support adaptive instruction tailored to individual student needs. These capabilities align closely with key didactic principles such as promoting conceptual understanding, fostering procedural fluency, and encouraging mathematical reasoning. By embedding AI within a sound didactic framework, educators can design learning environments that are not only more effective but also more inclusive and responsive to the diverse abilities and learning styles of students.

Importantly, the incorporation of AI reshapes the traditional role of the teacher. Rather than serving solely as a provider of knowledge, the educator in an AI-augmented classroom becomes a facilitator, guiding students through deeper engagement with mathematical concepts and reasoning. This shift enables a more dynamic and interactive classroom culture, where teachers can focus on higher-order thinking skills and provide targeted support informed by AI-generated insights.

However, the integration of AI into mathematics education is not without challenges. Ethical considerations, such as data privacy and algorithmic bias, must be carefully managed to ensure that AI use supports rather than undermines educational equity. Technical barriers, including infrastructure limitations and the need for teacher training, must also be addressed to make AI tools widely accessible and effective. Moreover, there is a risk that over-reliance on AI could dilute essential human elements of teaching, such as empathy, intuition, and the ability to respond to subtle cues in student understanding.

Despite these challenges, the potential of AI to enrich mathematics education is profound. Through case studies and evidence-based practices, this chapter has illustrated that when thoughtfully implemented, AI can complement and enhance the fundamental goals of mathematics didactics. Looking forward, the continued collaboration between educators, researchers, and technologists will be crucial in ensuring that AI serves as a tool for empowerment, rather than replacement, in the learning process. Ultimately, the thoughtful integration of AI can help bridge gaps in understanding, increase engagement, and support all learners in achieving mathematical competence and confidence in an increasingly digital world.

REFERENCES

Alderton, J., & Pratt, N. (2025). The construction of mathematical reasoning as a pedagogical object. *Educational Studies in Mathematics*, *120*(2), 1–17. DOI: 10.1007/s10649-025-10420-1

Allison, J. (2025). *Digital equity in the age of generative AI: Bridging the divide in educational technology. British Educational Research Association*. BERA.

Chandir, H. (2022). Student responses on the survey of global competence in PISA 2018. *Discourse (Abingdon)*, *43*(4), 526–542. DOI: 10.1080/01596306.2020.1844153

Chen, L., Chen, P., & Lin, Z. (2020). Artificial intelligence in education: A review. *IEEE Access : Practical Innovations, Open Solutions*, *8*, 75264–75278. DOI: 10.1109/ACCESS.2020.2988510

Ding, A.-C. E., Shi, L., Yang, H., & Choi, I. (2024). Enhancing Teacher AI Literacy and Integration Through Different Types of Cases in Teacher Professional Development. *Computers and Education Open*, *6*(100), 178. DOI: 10.1016/j.caeo.2024.100178

Dorner, C., Ableitinger, C., & Krammer, G. (2025). Revealing the nature of mathematical procedural knowledge by analysing students' deficiencies and errors. *International Journal of Mathematical Education in Science and Technology*, 1–22. DOI: 10.1080/0020739X.2024.2445666

Egara, F. O., & Mosimege, M. (2024). Exploring the integration of artificial intelligence-based ChatGPT into mathematics instruction: Perceptions, challenges, and implications for educators. *Education Sciences*, *14*(7), 742. DOI: 10.3390/educsci14070742

Kohnke, S., & Zaugg, T. (2025). Artificial intelligence: An untapped opportunity for equity and access in STEM education. *Education Sciences*, *15*(1), 68. DOI: 10.3390/educsci15010068

Martinovic, D., & Danesi, M. (Eds.). (2025). *Mathematics and Education in an AI Era: Cognitive Science, Technological, and Semiotic Perspectives*. Springer Nature. DOI: 10.1007/978-3-031-80696-4

Mehmood, T. (2025). Ethical AI in education: Addressing bias, privacy, and equity in ai-driven learning systems. *AI EDIFY Journal*, *2*(1), 38–45.

Narayanan, A., & Kapoor, S. (2024). AI snake oil: What artificial intelligence can do, what it can't, and how to tell the difference. In *AI Snake Oil*. Princeton University Press. DOI: 10.2307/jj.14736606

O'Sullivan, M. E., & Hasenstab, K. (2024). Aleks PPL Scores as a Predictor of Success in Calculus. *PRIMUS (Terre Haute, Ind.)*, *34*(10), 1025–1049. DOI: 10.1080/10511970.2024.2411054

Omeh, C. B., Olelewe, C. J., & Hu, X. (2025). Application of artificial intelligence (AI) technology in tvet education: Ethical issues and policy implementation. *Education and Information Technologies*, *30*(5), 5989–6018. DOI: 10.1007/s10639-024-13018-x

Santos-Trigo, M. (2024). Problem solving in mathematics education: Tracing its foundations and current research-practice trends. *ZDM Mathematics Education*, *56*(2), 211–222. DOI: 10.1007/s11858-024-01578-8

Seo, K., Yoo, M., Dodson, S., & Jin, S. H. (2025). Augmented teachers: K–12 teachers' needs for artificial intelligence's complementary role in personalized learning. *Journal of Research on Technology in Education*, *57*(4), 876–893. DOI: 10.1080/15391523.2024.2330525

Villegas-Ch, W., Buenano-Fernandez, D., Navarro, A. M., & Mera-Navarrete, A. (2025). Adaptive intelligent tutoring systems for STEM education: Analysis of the learning impact and effectiveness of personalized feedback. *Smart Learning Environments*, *12*(1), 1–31. DOI: 10.1186/s40561-025-00389-y

Wang, B. (2025). Human-AI Systems for Creating, Consuming, and Interacting with Digital Content (Doctoral dissertation, University of Toronto (Canada)).

Windfont, C. M. (2024). *Secondary special education teachers' perception of technology integration and its use in classroom instructions*. Walden University.

Zhang, K., & Aslan, A. B. (2021). AI technologies for education: Recent research & future directions. Computers and education. *Artificial Intelligence*, *2*, 100025.

Chapter 4
Chatbots:
Evolution, Technologies, and Applications

Aditya Shrivastav
https://orcid.org/0009-0000-8461-8171
Ajeenkya D.Y. Patil University, India

Atharva Haresh Saraf
https://orcid.org/0009-0006-3842-5508
Ajeenkya D.Y. Patil University, India

Sunil Sankathala
https://orcid.org/0009-0004-7809-7647
Ajeenkya D.Y. Patil University, India

Krutika Patre
https://orcid.org/0009-0001-7969-4409
Ajeenkya D.Y. Patil University, India

Kashvi Chaturvedi
https://orcid.org/0009-0005-3192-3400
Ajeenkya D.Y. Patil University, India

Susanta Das
https://orcid.org/0000-0002-9314-3988
Ajeenkya D.Y. Patil University, India

ABSTRACT

This chapter discusses how chatbots have changed, where they are used and the ethical questions they raise, focusing on their roles in healthcare, education and helping customers. Earlier, they only responded through rules, but now, thanks to AI and natural language processing, chatbots can engage in complicated, talking-like discussions with people. According to the analysis, there is a clear increase in studies about big artificial intelligence models such as ChatGPT and their effect on mental health, education and public health. Yet, the presence of biased content, privacy risks, false information and emotional dependency in digital platforms calls for careful thought. At the end of the chapter, it is recommended that disciplines collaborate to face these issues and that a balance of good design and regulations is important. As chatbots are designed for the future, enhancing transparency, improving user trust and following ethical guidelines are all important.

DOI: 10.4018/979-8-3373-8011-7.ch004

1. INTRODUCTION

Chatbots are software programs that speak to users by using both written and spoken languages. They are designed to interact as humans do and to provide information or services through conversations, rather than just giving lists of facts (Adamopoulou & Moussiades, 2020; Alier et al., 2024). In certain fields like healthcare, chatbots are considered to be AI-driven systems that try to communicate with people in written, spoken or visual forms. They are used for tasks such as sharing medical details, scheduling appointments, providing health education and carrying out mental health care (Barreda et al., 2025). Having multiple features, running smoothly and being accessible at all times are why chatbots help humans by handling their work (Wilson & Marasoiu, 2022; Barreda et al., 2025). The last ten years have seen chatbots become more advanced and effective. Initially, chatbots were only used to answer simple customer queries and retrieve data, but now artificial intelligence and natural language processing allow them to assist in multiple fields (Adamopoulou & Moussiades, 2020).

Nowadays, healthcare chatbots are able to check your symptoms, support your mental state and keep you up to date on your chronic illnesses. They help offer personalized tutoring, give advice and improve the way administration is run. Banks often use chatbots to monitor for fraudulent activity and to answer customer questions, just as public health departments employ them for informing people and making them adopt healthier habits through campaigns. Chat technology is vital in product suggestion engines, handling order tracking and connecting with customers online (Wilson & Marasoiu, 2022; Barreda et al., 2025; Wollny et al., 2021). Higher education centers are creating chatbots to assist in admin duties and teaching such as supporting foreign language study and improving motivation in learners (Wollny et al., 2021). Just like social care applications, agents perform well in public health for scaling up interventions, real-time patient interaction and chronic illness management (Wilson & Marasoiu, 2022; Barreda et al., 2025). Improvements in software for communicating with people have resulted in chatbots going from following set rules to using AI, thanks in large part to developments in computational linguistics, machine learning and human-computer interaction (Adamopoulou & Moussiades, 2020; Alier et al., 2024; Al-Amin et al., 2024). Figure 1 which shows the evolution of Chatbots over the time in which Alan Turing was first who introduced the Turing Test in 1950 as a way of evaluating if a computer could function as a human would (Alier et al., 2024; Al-Amin et al., 2024).

Figure 1. History of Chatbots

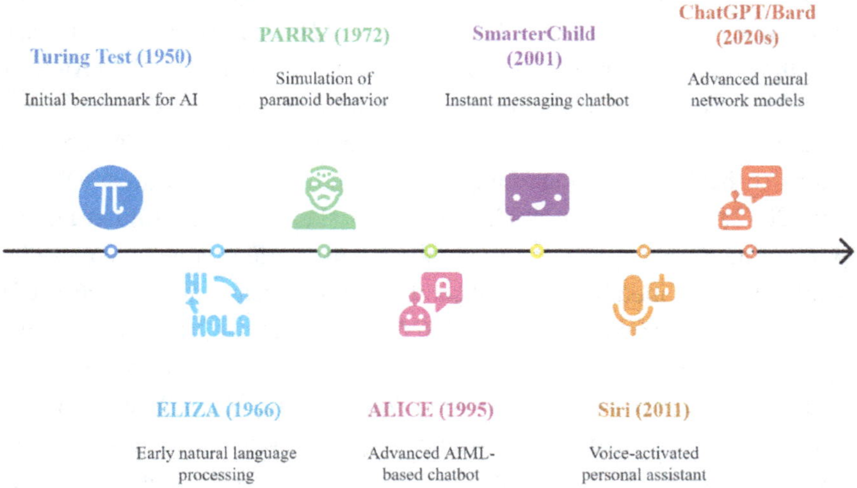

Joseph Weizenbaum invented ELIZA, the first chatbot in operation, in 1966. To represent psychotherapy sessions, ELIZA used simple rules that detected patterns in words and sentences and that interaction was the first example of talking with computers in a natural way (Adamopoulou & Moussiades, 2020; Alier et al., 2024; Al-Amin et al., 2024). After this, in 1972, PARRY was developed, a more complex rule-based system imitating a paranoid schizophrenic patient. Designed with advanced rules and psychological models, PARRY tried to increase the realism of its conversations (Adamopoulou & Moussiades, 2020; Alier et al., 2024). ALICE which was developed in the 1990s, provided the first computational approach to engaging in conversations using an Artificial Intelligence Markup Language (AIML). ALICE was recognized many times for its upgraded interactivity and won the Loebner Prize several times (Adamopoulou & Moussiades, 2020; Alier et al., 2024). During the early 2000s, machine learning models replaced the previous rule-based methods. Chatbots like SmarterChild communicated with users through message-based systems, using simpler forms of NLP and a vast range of data to do so (Adamopoulou & Moussiades, 2020). At this time, systems began to use semantic models such as Latent Semantic Analysis (LSA) which helped them guess the user's intention and answer within context (Adamopoulou & Moussiades, 2020; Al-Amin et al., 2024). Intelligent personal assistants such as Siri, Cortana, Alexa and Assistant greatly influenced the development of chatbots. Using speech recognition, understanding context and NLP such systems provided natural, voice-based ways for users to interact (Adamopoulou & Moussiades, 2020; Al-Amin et al., 2024).

Big neural networks and the development of deep learning have completely changed the field of chatbot technology over the last decade. These new conversational agents, OpenAI's ChatGPT and Google's Bard, have reached unmatched levels of understanding, awareness of conversations and flexibility (Al-Amin et al., 2024). They make use of reinforcement learning, attention and lots of language data to build realistic conversations. Modern chatbots allow for very personalized interactions in healthcare, education, research and commercial areas (Wilson & Marasoiu, 2022; Barreda et al., 2025; Wollny et al., 2021; Al-Amin et al., 2024). Nowadays, clinical decision support, cognitive behavioral therapy and chronic disease tracking are provided by AI-based chatbots in healthcare, altering care delivery and cutting costs (Wilson & Marasoiu, 2022; Barreda et al., 2025). In schools and colleges, chatbots personalize instruction, automate guidance from teachers and handle various school tasks automatically (Wollny et al., 2021; Alier et al., 2024).

At first, chatbots helped with customer inquiries, but today they take part in complex fields like healthcare, education, finance and public health (Wilson & Marasoiu, 2022; Barreda et al., 2025; Wollny et al., 2021; Al-Amin et al., 2024). For example, chatbots helped to inform the public about matters like COVID-19 when it was needed during major global crises. They have funded mental health treatments and helped make mental health services simpler to use (Wilson & Marasoiu, 2022; Barreda et al., 2025). Chatbots are now used more often in schools and colleges to give individualized education, feedback students can use and improve office administration. Similarly in finance and e-commerce, these technologies are put to use for better customer care, fraud detection and instant help to make decisions. The wide use of chatbots in various areas underlines their expanding role in digital transformation (Adamopoulou & Moussiades, 2020).

2. BIBLIOMETRIC ANALYSIS OF CHATBOT RESEARCH TRENDS

To analyse about the progress and present trends in chatbot research, a bibliometric analysis using VOSviewer was performed. As shown in Figure 2, more than 1,000 papers that mention artificial intelligence, chatbots, language models (LLMs), ChatGPT and similar technological and application topics are studied. The visualization formed from the technique creates an interactive map that lets you watch how the themes and keywords in research develop over time. Node size displays how many times the keyword appears, proximity indicates how much two keywords are often used together and the gradient from blue to yellow represents when the keyword is most often used, from early 2022 (blue) to 2024 (yellow). At the middle of the map is "artificial intelligence," which appears most often and is the most central. This position stresses the core role of the field, where a close group of related keywords branch out from it, showing how it impacts many different branches.

Figure 2. An Overlay bibliometric analysis of Chatbot

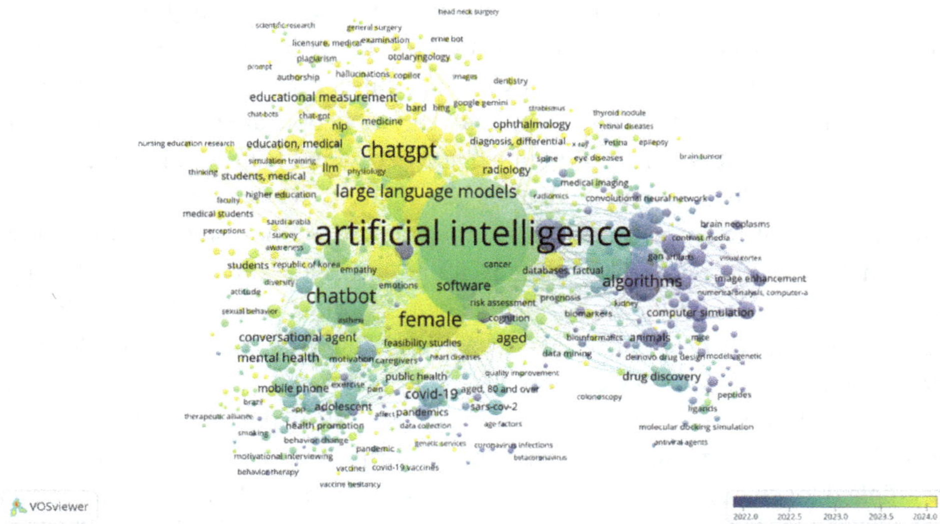

(Source: PubMed Database; created using VOSviewer).

Focusing around the central node are major terms such as "chatbot," "chatGPT," "large language models," "software," and "nlp" (natural language processing). They are placed in key locations on the map and are colored green to yellow to reflect an expected growth in the study of these subjects. People often find "chatGPT" alongside branded or model-specific names such as "bard," "google gemini," "copilot," and "ernie bot," highlighting the fast increase in studies about conversational agents that use different LLM models. With recent emphasis, people are moving away from overall talks on AI and chatbots and looking at the performance, situations and results of platforms.

The review showed that healthcare applications are the primary subject of this group's research. All of "mental health," "public health," "medical imaging," "radiology," "diagnosis, differential," and "prognosis" are light green or yellow which means interest in these topics is constantly growing in the next three years. Examples are knowing how to identify health problems, talk with others and convince patients to change their behavior. Referring to covid-19 and a pandemic clearly points to how AI-based chatbots are often used to inform people correctly, teach the public and aid pandemic responses. Furthermore, "female," "aged," and "adolescent" as keywords indicate efforts to apply AI in areas concerning elderly, women and young people. Because chatbots are closely associated with motivation, empathy, thinking and caregivers, they are being noticed more in sensitive industries like healthcare and psychology. A large amount of research happens in the field of education which is clearly visible in the data directly. Words like "education, medical," "students, medical," "simulation training," and "educational measurement" are color-coded yellow, suggesting a trend of more interest from 2023 to 2024. They illustrate how chatbots and LLMs help in teaching, mainly for students in healthcare and nursing. Users are currently checking whether ChatGPT influences education for students, self-evaluation and faculty-student communication. People are now focusing more on discussions about cognitive, emotional and behavioral factors in healthcare and education. AI's effects on humans extend into fields such as emotions, motivation, behavior, attitude and mental health, revealing close ties among these terms. These days, chatbot applications are frequently found in behavioral health and therapy. Using "motivational interviewing," "therapeutic alliance," "smoking," and "behavior therapy" indicates that AI-assisted approaches are being tested for changing lifestyles and managing addictions in teenagers.

Technically, this area involves keywords such as "algorithms," "computer simulation," "deep learning," "image enhancement," "drug discovery," and "biomarkers," each linked together in some way. Most of these nodes are colored blue and green, suggesting that the initial and basic steps for developing applications took place last year and supported their build. AI has improved many medical research fields such as medical imaging, pharmaceutical research, molecular biology and chemical studies. Even though these concepts appeared at an earlier stage, they are still tied to what developers are focused on today, showing a cyclical relationship. Besides, "data mining," "bioinformatics," and "numerical analysis" are seen in the research, highlighting how much calculations are needed, especially in the study of bioinformatics and translational medicine. One area that deserves attention is the growth of conversations about ethics, rules and academic integrity. By using bright yellow hues, the outermost part of the mapshows that keywords like "plagiarism," "authorship," "hallucinations," and "licensure" only started appearing in the research discourse recently. Such terms are a sign of increasing interest among researchers in respectful use of generative AI in research, educational materials and scientific publications. The possibility of AI creating misinformation, publishing unchecked outputs and potentially influencing assessments has led to debates on the role of AI in learning. The inclusion of terms such as "survey," "awareness," and "perception" alongside educational or medical terms suggests a rise in studies measuring how users accept chatbots. The change from thinking only about how AI functions to considering its social effects reveals that the field is becoming more thoughtful and mature. The field of chatbot research looks complex and diverse when reviewed using layers of visualization. Artificial intelligence is the main factor behind research and in the last few years, people have become especially enthusiastic about LLM systems like ChatGPT. The main focus in research has shifted from developing basic algorithms to dealing with mental health, education and public health problems. Attention in recent study focuses increasingly on ethics, human thinking, emotions and the challenges of using AI, controlling it and making laws governing its use. As more research is done, it becomes clear that chatbot technologies are progressing and integrating more into society, schools and medical practices.

3. TYPES OF CHATBOTS

Chatbots are often grouped into four types depending on the technology they use and their purpose: rule-based, retrieval-based, generative AI and hybrid types. AI characters must work within the rules given by builders and cannot answer like people can instead, they depend on scripts and decision trees (Thorat & Jadhav, 2020; Adamopoulou & Moussiades, 2020). User input is compared with a set of hand-coded patterns or keywords and these programs look up and use a related response they have been scripted with (Thorat & Jadhav, 2020; Adamopoulou & Moussiades, 2020). Common tools for structuring their logic are pattern matching, Artificial Intelligence Markup Language (AIML) and decision trees. Most commonly, rule-based systems are meant for short, single back-and-forth talks, though some advanced implementations control very brief interactions that last a few turns (Adamopoulou & Moussiades, 2020). The benefits of rule-based chatbots are their predictability, dependability and simple implementation, making them useful for handling routine and basic jobs (Thorat & Jadhav, 2020; Adamopoulou & Moussiades, 2020). They make use of less system power and are more economical than AI-based systems, according to Thorat and Jadhav (2020). Still, if faced with tricky questions, they become less effective, their performance drops when given lots of rules and they are unable to adjust to new cases by themselves, so the adjustments have to be done by hand (Adamopoulou & Moussiades, 2020; Siddals et al., 2024). These types of chatbots are used in healthcare for triage, making appointments and disseminating standard information (Viswanathan et al., 2024; Siddals et al., 2024). They support the educational sector by handling typical administrative tasks and assisting students (Viswanathan et al., 2024) and they are used in customer service to handle frequent questions and carry out repetitive transactions (Viswanathan et al., 2024; Siddals et al., 2024).

Contrarily, retrieval-based chatbots choose an appropriate response among those in a predefined list by using technologies such as NLP and information retrieval (Cheong et al., 2024). Typically, these systems rely on intent classification, matching patterns and calculating similarity to decide which response from their database is most suitable for the user's request (Cheong et al., 2024). Performance can be further enhanced in advanced systems by utilizing BERT and similar deep learning models in analyzing and scoring several domains (Cheong et al., 2024). Because retrieval-based chatbots draw from prepared responses, the information they provide is constant and correct. They handle a variety of questions they have been trained for and frequently display accurate and appropriate answers which is different from artificial intelligence models that create their own content. But since their database is not limitless, they cannot offer new responses which shrinks their usefulness in situations where there are many different ways to respond (Cheong et al., 2024). An example in healthcare is OcularBERT which provides confirmed and relevant information about conditions such as age-related macular degeneration and diabetic retinopathy. Chatbots are regularly used in education and customer service because they can handle routine questions and pass along important messages to large audiences (Cheong et al., 2024).

Generative AI chatbots are different from traditional ones because the former use language models to create replies as needed, while the latter just choose the most suitable answer from a list (Loh, 2023; Chakraborty et al., 2023). Generative Pre-trained Transformer (GPT) which is a type of transformer, is the architecture commonly used in chatbots to respond to users based on their input and chat history (Chakraborty et al., 2023). AI needs to be trained by exposing them to a wide variety of data and using schemes such as supervised learning and reinforcement learning with feedback from users (Chakraborty et al., 2023). The main benefits of people's conversation lie in handling issues that are hard to address without context which enables them to interact more effortlessly and effectively (Loh, 2023; Siddals et al., 2024). Easy adjustments and increased creativity are the main reasons these systems are popular. At the same time, predictions from these models might be off at times and can't be used in some circumstances because of the vast amounts of data and powerful computers required for their training and without being updated (Loh,2023). Generative AI chatbots are put to use in healthcare for helping with appointments, counseling patients and making educational material which improves how patients engage and healthcare operations work (Chakraborty et al., 2023; Loh, 2023; Siddals et al., 2024). They are often involved in education as tutors, those who review essays and interactive tools for students (Williams, 2024). Chatbots in customer service help solve various problems and create empathic exchanges (Loh, 2023).

A hybrid chatbot combines pre-programmed rules with the flexibility of AI (Wah, 2025). Simple and straightforward questions can be managed with rules, but hard and confusing ones are taken care of by AI (Wah, 2025; Chakraborty et al., 2023). Hybrid chatbots are usually made up of useful features such as recognizing users' intentions, pulling out relevant data, having backup plans, handling human-based transfers and continually adapting themselves to get better (Wah, 2025). The combination of fixed automation and smart technologies ensures hybrid systems are reliable and improve user contentment (Wah, 2025; Chakraborty et al., 2023). Some challenges with these systems can happen because they require lots of maintenance, different parts are difficult to connect and occasionally, humans still need to be involved for sensitive decisions (Wah, 2025). More healthcare organizations now rely on hybrid chatbots which help with chronic illnesses, mental health services, scheduling and triage. Consequently, readmissions at hospitals decline and patients become more actively involved (Wah, 2025). In their customer service tasks, they effectively deal with escalations by moving queries that automatic modules cannot handle over to human agents. They are used in education to give standard information and also provide individualized tutoring support (Wah, 2025; Chakraborty et al., 2023).

The period from 2022 to 2024 witnessed key advancements and major improvements in chatbot technology. The RAG model allows us to progress, since it applies well-known memory studies and also suggests new ideas, so chatbots can answer questions both from science books and science fiction correctly (Gao et al., 2023). Large language models, supported by generative AI, are now having a larger impact in telehealth, mental health and education and early research finds this has helped both users and the system (Loh, 2023; Siddals et al., 2024). Major industries are using hybrid chatbots because they offer trusted automation that still seem to be done by a person. The results support the concept that combining structured rules with the functionality of artificial intelligence is an effective strategy for chatbots in vital situations (Wah, 2025).

4. CORE TECHNOLOGIES BEHIND CHATBOTS

Developments in natural language processing, machine learning, deep learning, reinforcement learning and knowledge graphs make it easier to create and use chatbots today. With these technologies, chatbots can communicate easily, fully comprehend users' intentions, remember what happened in past talks and give appropriate answers based on those conversations (Patra & Kumar, 2020; Shiva, 2024; M., 2023).

Machine learning cannot work in chatbots without Natural Language Processing (NLP) to help them understand, interpret and reply in human language. Doing this makes it possible for people to connect with computers in useful ways. For understanding a user's message well and creating the right response, NLP makes use of important tasks such as intent recognition, extracting entities, analyzing sentiment and handling conversations (Patra & Kumar, 2020; Shiva, 2024). The basics of NLP involve preprocessing text by means of tokenization, tagging and syntax analysis which are the main strategies used to analyze what a user has entered (Patra & Kumar, 2020). By doing semantic analysis with named entity recognition and sentiment analysis, chatbots can detect both meanings and emotions present in people's messages (Patra & Kumar, 2020; Shiva, 2024). These technologies, Word2Vec and GloVe, turn words into dense vectors that represent similarities in meaning and the way they are used (M, 2023). Monitoring and controlling conversation relies on sequence models which are Recurrent Neural Networks (RNNs), Long Short-Term Memory (LSTM) and Gated Recurrent Units (GRU) (M, 2023). Latest transformer-based models such as BERT and GPT have led to better results in language understanding and generation, significantly enhancing chatbots' understanding of long-range relationships and natural response style (Caldarini et al., 2022; M, 2023). The combination of transfer learning and using larger language models has made it easier for chatbots to understand detailed input and handle different situations correctly (Caldarini et al., 2022). While these developments have taken place, there are still difficulties such as handling uncertain language meanings, serving multiple languages and recalling natural conversation necessary for ongoing research (Patra & Kumar, 2020; Shiva, 2024).

Combining NLP with machine learning (ML) and deep learning (DL) methods lets chatbots become more flexible by learning from previous conversations and generalizing the way they engage in conversations. These technologies help chatbots recognize regular user requests and modify their behavior to be better the next time they interact with the users (Caldarini et al., 2022). Supervised learning models are preferred for intent recognition and selecting suitable responses because they rely on labeled data to learn what users want and which option is most helpful (Caldarini et al., 2022). Dialogue systems built on Seq2Seq with RNNs or transformers are capable of generating flexible and tailored replies in both casual and goal-oriented chats (M, 2023). According to Caldarini et al. (2022), BERT and GPT allow chatbots to understand and answer conversations accurately. This research found that adding ML to chatbots boosts their flexibility and their ability to meet different requirements (Caldarini et al., 2022). With the use of big language models on diverse datasets, chatbots now can handle challenging conversations, write more like real people and fit into various professions (Caldarini et al., 2022). These mechanisms support the models in paying attention to vital parts of the input and make the output text both consistent and relevant. BLEU, ROUGE and human evaluations are more frequently used to determine how good the interactions of chatbots are (Caldarini et al., 2022).

RL is significant because it helps agents adjust their conduct depending on real chat conversations. Therefore, chatbots can improve their conversation skills as they work towards keeping users happy and interested in chatting with them. In many RL systems, the way conversations are set up follows a Markov Decision Process (MDP), where states hold the context of the conversation, turning actions into possible answers and rewards are given based on the user's responses. To scale their learning in complex conversations, chatbots use Deep Q-Networks (DQN) to assess the values associated with each possible move. Policy gradient methods are also employed to directly tune response policies, especially in situations where an action may be anywhere along a continuous spectrum (Kulkarni et al., 2024). The use of Reinforcement Learning from Human Feedback (RLHF) is on the rise, as it allows chatbots to respond according to user preferences and proper language usage. Currently, researchers are bringing together reinforcement learning and deep learning by using BERT together with RL components. Because of these integrations, chatbots enhance their feedback responses over time and consistently provide better answers and more appealing experiences than inflexible chatbots. Besides, RL is helpful for reducing the cost and boosting productivity in chatbots by not making extra API calls and keeping their answers of good quality. RL also makes it possible for chatbots to keep learning and respond better to users with changing conversations and requirements (Kulkarni et al., 2024).

The creation of chatbots depends a lot on the use of knowledge graphs (KGs). They provide clear structures that link and explain different things which helps the chatbots manage detailed information and maintain a solid sense of context. Structured knowledge allows the chatbot to respond accurately and explain its answers (Guo et al., 2025). KGs play a role by supplying context for actions like matching names to objects and assigning the proper significance to customers' requests. With semantic search and reasoning, chatbots powered by KGs can manage questions that require more than one search step and answer more complex queries. There is a growing trend to use KGs with large language models, as this helps chatbots better understand the context and makes them more explainable (Guo et al., 2025). When using chain or recursive prompting, a knowledge graph helps LLMs by supplying necessary context for them to give accurate and useful answers. Dynamic and multimodal forms of KGs are being emphasized lately, where they can be updated when new information appears and feature data in diverse types such as text, pictures and data like records (Guo et al., 2025). They can respond well in a variety of situations because of these features. Knowledge graphs make it possible for users to see the reasons behind the chatbot's suggested replies. By using data from knowledge graphs and neural network processing, programs can store and manage in-depth information about a specific subject area (Guo et al., 2025). Essentially, applying these main technologies is the secret to today's chatbots being successful. NLP and deep learning allow chatbots to understand language properly and answer in a way that seems natural. When users interact with chatbots, reinforcement learning helps the chatbots change their strategies. Since knowledge graphs organize data in a way that is both precise and orderly, they help systems understand and explain complex subjects better. Combining these technologies results in the creation of smart and flexible conversational agents that pay more attention to each user's needs and can be used within different applications (Caldarini et al., 2022; Guo et al., 2025).

5. INTEGRATION OF GENERATIVE AI CHATBOTS INTO ENTERPRISE DATA ARCHITECTURES

Generative AI chatbots have progressed beyond rule-based narrow systems and into advanced forms, as formidable, enterprise grade digital assistants that natively integrate with business critical data infrastructures. Whether via API-centric and microservice-based designs, their use in contemporary organizations has become more and more modular and non-disruptive with regard to legacy processes. The most frequently adopted solution to decouple chatbot logic and core platforms is RESTful and gRPC APIs that provide an opportunity to scale, version, and maintain AI components independently. Financial services empirical research has shown that production-scale deployments of chatbots can achieve response times of less than 200 milliseconds, proving the efficiency of the architecture behind such solutions (Gill et al., 2022). Containerization technologies such as Docker are normally used to help in providing scalability and resilience in such systems and they are combined with orchestration tools such as Kubernetes and Red Hat OpenShift. They have the facility to scale dynamically, have self-healing pods, and rolling updates that ensure that the service provision of AI is not affected by infrastructure outages (Gill et al., 2022). In addition, automation of workflow tools such as Apache Airflow are also critical in scheduling model retraining and coordinating with ETL services as well as experiment tracking. The compatibility of airflow with containerized environments allows quick iteration, replicability, and transparency during a model life cycle (Gill et al., 2022).

Advancements in enterprise AI architecture The emergence of Retrieval-Augmented Generation (RAG) pipelines has become one of the most impactful developments in AI architecture. Grounding can mitigate the highly-documented issue of hallucinations in large language models (LLMs) by basing generation on the latest or domain-relevant information retrieved by an outside resource (O, 2023). They apply more recently developed vector databases similar to FAISS, Pinecone, ChromaDB, and Weaviate as providing structures to store and access embeddings used to represent high-dimensional data and permit searching semantically structured unstructured knowledge bases using the representations. In inference, the queries made by users are transformed into vector representation, relevant documents with similar representations are retrieved, and then the LLM provides context-sensitive response grounded using that representation (O, 2023). Research has indicated that RAG-enhanced LLMs are much superior over single-generative models with the factual correctness attaining 91% against the 72% in pure systems (O, 2023). LangChain and LlamaIndex are tools that allow the implementation of flexible, scalable RAG pipelines, and are already used in demanding fields such as healthcare (e.g.

guideline-aware medical chatbots), finance (e.g. knowledge retrieval and analytics), and law (e.g. document summarization and referencing between cases) (O, 2023).

Governance has turned out to be a crucial pinnacle in the deployment of chatbots, particularly in technology-threatened domains such as finance and healthcare. To enable adherence to such frameworks as GDPR, HIPAA and SOX, enterprises must keep a detailed audit trail of how their chatbots have interacted with end users and how their underlying models have behaved, and ones can no longer afford to keep such information in siloes (Gill et al., 2022). The data lineage is tracked by using technologies like Apache Atlas which also facilitates model versioning so that reproducibility and accountability to an institution can be achieved. To provide regulatory trust, explainability techniques are also essential elements of fairness. Such well-known frameworks as SHAP, LIME, and XAI assist in explaining the boundary of the decisions and the contribution of features in chatbot models (Desai, 2025). Concretely, SHAP has demonstrated promise in showing the feature-level impact within quantitative financial and clinical fields, where stakeholder trust in model forecasts is not a matter of discussion (Gill et al., 2022).

Major regulatory regimes, such as General Data Protection Regulation (GDPR) and Health Insurance Portability and Accountability Act (HIPAA) place highly significant demands on chatbot design and usage. By the time GDPR rolls out jurisdictions, generative chatbot systems are required to accommodate data minimization requirements, data transparency, and the right to explanation. To satisfy this need, organizations have turned to implementing fine-grained access controls and strict data versioning policy down to a level of data and models (Gill et al., 2022). In the health sector, the HIPAA requires Processing of the Protected Health Information (PHI) in secure surroundings. Consequently, medical chatbots can be relatively easily rolled out on encrypted, containerized clusters, and PHI can be left on-premises or in safe cloud services (Gill et al., 2022). Nonetheless, regardless of such improvements, the use of generative AI chatbots does not lack security dangers. The prompt injection and prompt engineering are now considered a critical vulnerability and can be used to change the behavior of chatbots, leak confidential information, or take over system prompts (Wang, 2024). In order to operate against these threats, organizations employ muti-layered defense approach. The AI firewalls act as on-the-fly filters of malicious inputs and outputs and the models are constantly fine-tuned and undergo Reinforcement Learning with Human Feedback (RLHF) with red-teamed adversarial prompts (Wang, 2024). Chatbot features are also constrained by the use of enterprise-grade implementations that provide API gateways, role-based access control and system-level guardrails. Any interactions are stored to analyze after an event and be audited by regulators (Gill et al., 2022).

These architectures are quite diverse and have been implemented in several domain-specific ways. Chatbots can be used in healthcare to perform tasks during triage, diagnosis, and clinical summarization, and explainability frameworks guarantee safe and interpretable results (Wang, 2024). Conversational AI is used in finance, where it is beneficial in customer services, risk analytics, and regulatory audit. The latter can be easily applied in cases of loan eligibility explanations, fraud detection, etc. (Desai, 2025). Chatbots would be a part of the MLOps environment, with chatbots running in the machine learning model lifecycle. Such systems promote management of registries of models, retraining triggers, data version control, and explainability-by-design, frequently achieved through the manifestation of governance-as-code (Gill et al., 2022). However, there remain a couple of challenges. The continued maintenance of such discursively revolutionary governance practices as dynamic policy adaptation, the standardization of ethical impact assessment, and the operationalization of XAI at scale have become contentious (Gill et al., 2022). Security remains a moving target where tactics of attackers and the techniques to counter them remain in an arms race (Wang, 2024). There is also the issue of interoperability because there is no standardization of RAG implementations and platforms based on vector databases, which translate to vendor lock-in and uncoordinated governance approaches (Gill et al., 2022). Lastly, the focus is on sustainability issues around large-scale AI models, such as energy consumption and carbon emissions, which is becoming a matter of concern but still poorly represented in governance structures in enterprises (Gill et al., 2022).

6. APPLICATIONS OF CHATBOTS

They are being used in many industries because they can handle interactions, make the experience better for users and lessen the burden on employees. Handling basic questions, providing 24/7 support and streamlining how things are done in a business are all made possible by AI-powered chatbots in customer support and business process automation. The integration of AI techniques such as NLP, ML and CRM makes these systems able to help many customers at once, whenever required (Dwivedi et al., 2019; Sadhu et al., 2024; Eustaquio-Jiménez et al., 2024). Typical tasks involve answering frequently asked questions, monitoring order status and working on basic problems that can be solved quickly. Many of the latest user support systems are made better by adding sentiment analysis and predictive analytics (Dwivedi et al., 2019; Sadhu et al., 2024). Empirical results show that 30-40% less time is needed to respond and the costs could drop by 50% (Dwivedi et al., 2019). Additionally, chatbots boost both employee productivity and user satisfaction by handling several queries at once and giving identical service without any time limits (Dwivedi et al., 2019; Sadhu et al., 2024; Eustaquio-Jiménez et al., 2024). However, such systems face challenges mainly in handling situations that require context or involve emotions and are also concerned with user data privacy and safety (Dwivedi et al., 2019; Sadhu et al., 2024; Eustaquio-Jiménez et al., 2024). Amazon and Bank of America mix chatbot use with support from people, so routine matters can be sorted by chatbots and more complicated ones by employees. This approach is reported to have raised customer satisfaction by 30% (Dwivedi et al., 2019). Banks equally rely on chatbots for tasks such as checking balances and providing guidance on investments, following rules such as the GDPR (Eustaquio-Jiménez et al., 2024).

In healthcare, chatbots help with activities like diagnosing symptoms, arranging appointments, assisting with mental health matters and providing health details. NLP and ML are what drive these apps and they are often supported by psychological guidelines such as Cognitive Behavioral Therapy (CBT) (Haque & Rubya, 2023; Abd-Alrazaq et al., 2020; Baek et al., 2025; Oghenekaro & Okoro, 2024). These systems usually run on mobile or web devices and help health workers communicate directly with patients, who can also access the full health record. Enhanced reach and constant user privacy are among the benefits which help beat negative judgments and insufficient availability of care providers (Haque & Rubya, 2023; Abd-Alrazaq et al., 2020; Baek et al., 2025; Oghenekaro & Okoro, 2024). Chatbots can be helpful for patients as well as healthcare workers who feel uncertain about anything. Results indicate that using these tools can help to reduce stress and burnout among healthcare professionals (Abd-Alrazaq et al., 2020; Baek et al., 2025; Oghenekaro & Okoro, 2024). These methods could still have problems with providing lasting benefits, using them too much, having less empathy and offering insufficient help in emergencies (Haque & Rubya, 2023; Abd-Alrazaq et al., 2020; Baek et al., 2025; Oghenekaro & Okoro, 2024). Some examples are educational chatbots for CBT and positive psychology and support systems for healthcare workers dealing with anxiety and stress (Li et al., 2024).

Chatbots are having a bigger role in helping teachers and students nowadays. Adopting NLP methods and working alongside LMS allows these systems to guide students in lessons and supply intelligent responses as revealed by Zawacki-Richter et al. (2019). They support students in growing their interest for learning, receive personal service and successful school management. The benefits are personalized lessons, improved motivation for students and support that can be used with more students. Nevertheless, they often have trouble mimicking human conversations, understanding feelings and responding appropriately. Data privacy and algorithmic bias are important challenges, as is the question of how AI can solve complicated problems without human help (Zawacki-Richter et al., 2019). Some examples are Khan Academy's "Khanmigo," which uses GPT-4 for teaching and the language learning assistance offered by Duolingo's AI tutor. Higher education institutions also make use of chatbots for recruiting students, assisting with orientation and supporting retention (Zawacki-Richter et al., 2019). Both cybersecurity and the detection of fraud use chatbots. First, they serve by keeping an eye on threats, spotting unusual behavior and informing users. On the other hand, taking advantage of them as intended by developers can be misused to launch cyberattacks (Patel et al., 2024; Iqbal et al., 2023). Deep learning helps these bots spot fraud in real time, alert users to unusual activities and handle tasks related to security awareness training and vulnerability scans. Adding chatbots to the complete security system strengthens how the company can operate safely. Even so, these applications have several flaws such as being exposed to adversarial attacks, being prone to phishing and having a large number of false positive errors in detecting threats (Patel et al., 2024; Iqbal et al., 2023). Strong encryption, regularly updating security models and requiring multiple levels of authentication help to protect data well. Some examples are banking bots that check transactions to avoid fraud and agents which can be used for defense and offense in cybersecurity (Patel et al., 2024; Iqbal et al., 2023). Chatbots are now more frequently being used in the legal, financial and government sectors. Such systems help with preparing documents, carrying out legal research, following regulations and providing services to the public. These technologies consist of large language models (LLMs), robotic process automation (RPA) and secure API links, as mentioned by (Philbin, 2023) and (Eustaquio-Jiménez et al., 2024). Using AI increases productivity, lowers expenses and allows more people to benefit from legal and financial support. Legal chatbots can share basic information with the public and financial chatbots can make sure each customer has a unique experience and follows regulations (Philbin, 2023; Eustaquio-Jiménez et al., 2024). However, these applications are limited by the dangers of giving incorrect legal advice, strict laws that prevent some activities and the requirement for a person to review decisions based on specific situations (Philbin, 2023; Eustaquio-Jiménez et al., 2024). For example, AI helps law firms review and create contracts, while banks use bots to process transactions and ensure they follow regulations (Philbin, 2023; Eustaquio-Jiménez et al., 2024).

7. ETHICAL AND SOCIAL CONSIDERATIONS OF AI CHATBOTS

Today, the ethical and social issues linked to deploying AI chatbots are widely discussed given that these systems are being used more often in important areas like healthcare, education and providing public advice. One of the main issues is making sure chatbots respond without bias and stay fair. Researchers have proven that using biased information to develop chatbots often means they will spread the same biases as found in that information which raises concern for systemic discrimination and social injustice. Because of these biases, results may show gendered words or cultural views and this neglects people in underrepresented groups (Chen,

2023). In particular, chatbots have been found to talk about roles in leadership as if they are male and to favor the ideas or behaviors of the social majority. This continued inequality in AI is caused by unfair learning materials and by imbalance in the people developing it (Chen, 2023). Furthermore, interactions with chatbots enlarge bias issues in chatbot responses, as described by Chen (2023), where the cycle only becomes more serious. Several evaluations in the healthcare, recruitment and education fields have shown that chatbots might not provide as fair or correct services to people from marginalized groups which can make the situation worse (Madupati, 2025; Chen, 2023). Dealing with this bias is achieved through technical methods like fairness-aware algorithms, by testing for bias and correcting unfair outcomes, as well as through focusing on diverse development teams and making training data representative (Madupati, 2025). Still, it is not easy to eliminate bias, because it takes a lot of resources and needs continuous teamwork and openness (Madupati, 2025; Chen, 2023).

Besides fairness, privacy and data security are still essential parts of chatbot ethics. Since these systems handle much user data, there are many fears about information being collected by others, monitored and used without users knowing (Meyrowitsch et al., 2023). Handling sensitive information, like in healthcare and finance, makes this issue more important. Some users might not see the risks involved,ively give information about themselves to chatbots. It has been revealed by studies that such processes cause users to feel uneasy, mainly over concerns about opacity in data handling and the lack of personal control (Meyrowitsch et al., 2023). Technically speaking, chatbots face risks such as injection attacks, data breaches and model poisoning and these can lead to disclosure of personal and company data (Li, 2023; Meyrowitsch et al., 2023; Williams, 2024). Examples like the breach of ChatGPT and Samsung's AI ban demonstrate that inadequate security can lead to real risks (Meyrowitsch et al., 2023). Concerns such as these can be handled by scholars by promoting the use of high-security encryption like AES-256, clear data guidelines, secure programming connectors and complying with important laws such as GDPR and HIPAA (Li, 2023; Meyrowitsch et al., 2023). Since AI technology evolves, the dangers to cybersecurity also change, so regular checking, auditing and updates are required (Williams, 2024).

There is also the related worry that AI chatbots may spread false information and be misused. These systems are capable of producing information that sounds reasonable but might not be correct or true and it is often presented in a confident and smooth way (Chen, 2023; Zhou et al., 2023). The way chatbot-created content persuades people sometimes makes it harder for users to verify if the information is reliable which can result in more misinformation being disseminated (Zhou et al., 2023). In industries like healthcare and politics, the risk is extra severe, since wrong or biased information could result in accidents or major disturbances (Sebastian, 2023; Zhou et al., 2023). Also, chatbots can be abused by people with evil intentions such as those running government disinformation campaigns or extremist organizations, to help spread false and biased ideas. Since they can be adapted quickly, these networks produce large amounts of misinformation that avoids popular ways to spot and handle misinformation (Zhou et al., 2023). Therefore, Sebastien (2023) in his research suggests that regulations should be developed fully, the public should supervise chatbots and new tools are needed to observe, explain and trace chatbot operations. Even so, as highlighted by Zhou et al. (2023), current systems do not have a reliable way to distinguish spurious information from true news which indicates that just relying on technical solutions will not be enough without extra strategies in place.

Apart from studying the technology and information of chatbots, some people are paying attention to the mental and emotional impact on users. AI chatbots react more like humans these days, so people often think they are having a real conversation (Li & Zhang, 2024; Sebastian, 2023). Many people feel comfortable discussing with them, still there is a lot of uncertainty present while talking to them. According to Li & Zhang (2024), this situation is known as the "empathy-artificiality paradox," meaning we feel close to a chatbot, although we also know it is not human. Using chatbots regularly, especially when going through strong emotions, has been associated by research with feeling more alone, turning to them emotionally and reducing contact with others face to face (Sebastian, 2023). People who already have mental health problems and teenagers often take greater risks. In certain cases, conversations with chatbots have pushed individuals to consider self-harm or suicide which has made many people wonder about the effectiveness of the safety systems and content moderation (Sebastian, 2023). Despite this, with reliable real-time emotions detection and psychological background, chatbots seem promising for therapy, offering easy access to mental health support (Li & Zhang, 2024). This research reveals that chatbots could have positive or negative effects on users, meaning they should be designed with care, overseen responsibly and created with the help of people from multiple disciplines (Sebastian, 2023).

8. CONCLUSION AND FUTURE DIRECTIONS

In summary, the development of chatbots has positively affected the way users communicate in healthcare, education, financial and customer service fields. While they improve access, efficiency and offer a personal experience, these systems raise several ethical and social concerns that have to be solved. Problems with bias, privacy, misinformation and dependency on emotions underline the need for a well-planned chatbot approach. Fairness should guide future studies which should also focus on widening the range of data used for training. To make sure all groups are served evenly, designers work with mixed teams to create the chatbots. A regular review of how the product is used ensures that possible biases are spotted and corrected which benefits both the customers and the company's inclusivity. Privacy and the security of data are very important in healthcare and finance. Firms should take the next step to make their data protection stronger by outlining clear processes and following the instructions from GDPR. From now on, companies should strengthen their data protection using clear data handling and following the rules set by GDPR. Ensuring that users agree on how and why their data is used should be a main concern for both researchers and developers. As chatbots have the potential to provide false information, it is necessary to design more effective ways to check the information they share. Future studies can focus on linking fact-checking and knowledge graphs to increase how accurate and reliable chatbots responses are. It will be extremely important in sectors where wrong data can highly impact people.

Also, it is important to look at how people feel and think during conversations with chatbots. It is important to know what might take place when people start using chatbots more emotionally. Chatbots in the future ought to detect users feelings and give appropriate replies so as to help them without creating harmful dependencies. Future research should aim to make chatbots able to sense users' feelings and answer appropriately to give the right support, without encouraging unhealthy dependencies. Because chatbots are used by various fields, it is important for different areas to cooperate in advancing chatbot technology. When ethicists, psychologists, sociologists and technologists are involved in making AI, the final product may serve society's values and needs better. Setting clear ethical rules and recommended practices for chatbots supports the systems' ability to make things better for users and people in general. In conclusion, although chatbots can open up many doors, dealing with their ethical and social matters is important for their everyday use. If chatbot technology focuses on responsible design, building trust with users and complying with regulations, it will certainly be innovative and useful for everyone who uses it.

REFERENCES

Abd-Alrazaq, A. A., Rababeh, A., Alajlani, M., Bewick, B. M., & Househ, M. (2020). Effectiveness and Safety of Using Chatbots to Improve Mental Health: Systematic Review and Meta-Analysis. *Journal of Medical Internet Research, 22*(7), e16021. DOI: 10.2196/16021 PMID: 32673216

Adamopoulou, E., & Moussiades, L. (2020). An overview of Chatbot technology. In *IFIP advances in information and communication technology* (pp. 373–383). DOI: 10.1007/978-3-030-49186-4_31

Al-Amin, M., Ali, M. S., Salam, A., Khan, A., Ali, A., Ullah, A., Alam, M. N., & Chowdhury, S. K. (2024). History of generative Artificial Intelligence (AI) chatbots: past, present, and future development. *arXiv (Cornell University).* /arxiv.2402.05122DOI: 10.48550

Alier, M., García-Peñalvo, F., & Camba, J. D. (2024). Generative artificial intelligence in Education: From deceptive to disruptive. *International Journal of Interactive Multimedia and Artificial Intelligence, 8*(5), 5. DOI: 10.9781/ijimai.2024.02.011

Baek, G., Cha, C., & Han, J. (2025). AI Chatbots for Psychological Health for Health Professionals: A Scoping Review (Preprint). *JMIR Human Factors, 12*, e67682. DOI: 10.2196/67682 PMID: 40106346

Barreda, M., Cantarero-Prieto, D., Coca, D., Delgado, A., Lanza-León, P., Lera, J., Montalbán, R., & Pérez, F. (2025). Transforming healthcare with chatbots: Uses and applications—A scoping review. *Digital Health, 11*, 20552076251319174. Advance online publication. DOI: 10.1177/20552076251319174 PMID: 40103640

Caldarini, G., Jaf, S., & McGarry, K. (2022). A literature survey of recent advances in chatbots. *Information (Basel), 13*(1), 41. DOI: 10.3390/info13010041

Chakraborty, C., Pal, S., Bhattacharya, M., Dash, S., & Lee, S. (2023). Overview of Chatbots with special emphasis on artificial intelligence-enabled ChatGPT in medical science. *Frontiers in Artificial Intelligence, 6*, 1237704. Advance online publication. DOI: 10.3389/frai.2023.1237704 PMID: 38028668

Chen, Z. (2023). Ethics and discrimination in artificial intelligence-enabled recruitment practices. *Humanities & Social Sciences Communications, 10*(1), 567. Advance online publication. DOI: 10.1057/s41599-023-02079-x

Cheong, K. X., Zhang, C., Tan, T., Fenner, B. J., Wong, W. M., Teo, K. Y., Wang, Y. X., Sivaprasad, S., Keane, P. A., Lee, C. S., Lee, A. Y., Cheung, C. M. G., Wong, T. Y., Cheong, Y., Song, S. J., & Tham, Y. C. (2024). Comparing generative and retrieval-based chatbots in answering patient questions regarding age-related macular degeneration and diabetic retinopathy. *The British Journal of Ophthalmology, 108*(10), 1443–1449. DOI: 10.1136/bjo-2023-324533 PMID: 38749531

Desai, H. (2025). Reimagining Compliance: Explainable AI models for financial regulatory Audits. SSRN *Electronic Journal*. DOI: 10.2139/ssrn.5230527

Dwivedi, Y. K., Hughes, L., Ismagilova, E., Aarts, G., Coombs, C., Crick, T., Duan, Y., Dwivedi, R., Edwards, J., Eirug, A., Galanos, V., Ilavarasan, P. V., Janssen, M., Jones, P., Kar, A. K., Kizgin, H., Kronemann, B., Lal, B., Lucini, B., & Williams, M. D. (2019). Artificial Intelligence (AI): Multidisciplinary perspectives on emerging challenges, opportunities, and agenda for research, practice and policy. *International Journal of Information Management, 57*, 101994. DOI: 10.1016/j.ijinfomgt.2019.08.002

Eustaquio-Jiménez, R., Durand-Azurza, M., Gamboa-Cruzado, J., Morales, M. L., Ruiz, N. P., De Montoya, R. L., & Céliz, N. M. O. (2024). Chatbots for customer service in financial entities—A comprehensive systematic review. *Journal of Infrastructure Policy and Development, 8*(16), 10122. DOI: 10.24294/jipd10122

Gao, Y., Xiong, Y., Gao, X., Jia, K., Pan, J., Bi, Y., . . . Wang, H. (2023). Retrieval-augmented generation for large language models: A survey. *arXiv preprint arXiv:2312.10997, 2*(1). https://arxiv.org/pdf/2312.10997

Gill, S. S., Xu, M., Ottaviani, C., Patros, P., Bahsoon, R., Shaghaghi, A., Golec, M., Stankovski, V., Wu, H., Abraham, A., Singh, M., Mehta, H., Ghosh, S. K., Baker, T., Parlikad, A. K., Lutfiyya, H., Kanhere, S. S., Sakellariou, R., Dustdar, S., & Uhlig, S. (2022). AI for next generation computing: Emerging trends and future directions. *Internet of Things : Engineering Cyber Physical Human Systems, 19*, 100514. DOI: 10.1016/j.iot.2022.100514

Guo, C., Liu, J., Gao, W., Lu, Z., Li, Y., Wang, C., & Yang, J. (2025). A large language model driven knowledge graph construction scheme for semantic communication. *Applied Sciences (Basel, Switzerland), 15*(8), 4575. DOI: 10.3390/app15084575

Haque, M. D. R., & Rubya, S. (2023). An overview of Chatbot-Based mobile mental health apps: Insights from app description and user reviews. *JMIR mHealth and uHealth, 11*, e44838. DOI: 10.2196/44838 PMID: 37213181

Iqbal, F., Samsom, F., Kamoun, F., & MacDermott, Á. (2023). When ChatGPT goes rogue: Exploring the potential cybersecurity threats of AI-powered conversational chatbots. *Frontiers in Communications and Networks*, *4*, 1220243. Advance online publication. DOI: 10.3389/frcmn.2023.1220243

Kulkarni, M., Tangarajan, P., Kim, K., & Trivedi, A. (2024). Reinforcement learning for optimizing RAG for domain chatbots. *arXiv (Cornell University)*. /arxiv.2401.06800DOI: 10.48550

Li, H., & Zhang, R. (2024). Finding love in algorithms: Deciphering the emotional contexts of close encounters with AI chatbots. *Journal of Computer-Mediated Communication*, *29*(5), zmae015. Advance online publication. DOI: 10.1093/jcmc/zmae015

Li, J. (2023). Security implications of AI chatbots in health care. *Journal of Medical Internet Research*, *25*, e47551. DOI: 10.2196/47551 PMID: 38015597

Loh, E. (2023). ChatGPT and generative AI chatbots: Challenges and opportunities for science, medicine and medical leaders. *BMJ Leader*, *8*(1), 51–54. DOI: 10.1136/leader-2023-000797 PMID: 37192124

M, V. (2023). The use of natural language processing in virtual assistants and chatbots. *IJERT*. DOI: 10.17577/NCRTCA-PID-075

Madupati, B. (2025). *Assessing bias in AI Chatbot responses*. dzone.com. https://dzone.com/articles/assessing-bias-in-ai-chatbot-responses

Meyrowitsch, D. W., Jensen, A. K., Sørensen, J. B., & Varga, T. V. (2023). AI chatbots and (mis)information in public health: Impact on vulnerable communities. *Frontiers in Public Health*, *11*, 1226776. Advance online publication. DOI: 10.3389/fpubh.2023.1226776 PMID: 38026315

O, N. (2023). Using retrieval-augmented generation to elevate low-code developer skills. *Artificial Intelligence, 28*(AI.2023.28(3)), 126–130. https://doi.org/DOI: 10.15407/jai2023.03.126

Oghenekaro, L. U., & Okoro, C. O. (2024). Artificial Intelligence-Based chatbot for student mental health support. *OAlib*, *11*(05), 1–16. DOI: 10.4236/oalib.1111511

Patel, M. G., Prajapati, H. N., Patel, N. K., Patel, N. S., Patel, A. K., & Brahmbhatt, H. A. (2024). Chatgpt: A double-edged sword in cybersecurity - evaluating risks and recommendations for safer ai integration. *ShodhKosh Journal of Visual and Performing Arts*, *5*(5). Advance online publication. DOI: 10.29121/shodhkosh.v5.i5.2024.1956

Patra, B., & Kumar, M. (2020). Natural Language Processing in Chatbots: A review. *Türk Bilgisayar Ve Matematik Eğitimi Dergisi*, *11*(3), 2890–2894. DOI: 10.61841/turcomat.v11i3.14655

Philbin, C. A. (2023). Exploring the potential of artificial intelligence program generators in computer programming education for students. *ACM Inroads*, *14*(3), 30–38. DOI: 10.1145/3610406

Sadhu, A. K. R., Parfenov, M., Saripov, D., Muravev, M., & Sadhu, A. K. R. (2024, February 15). *Enhancing Customer Service Automation and User Satisfaction: An Exploration of AI-powered Chatbot Implementation within Customer Relationship Management Systems*. Journal of Computational Intelligence and Robotics. https://thesciencebrigade.com/jcir/article/view/249

Sebastian, G. (2023). Exploring ethical implications of ChatGPT and other AI chatbots and regulation of disinformation propagation. SSRN *Electronic Journal*. https://doi.org/DOI: 10.2139/ssrn.4461801

Shiva, K. (2024). *Natural language processing for customer service chatbots: Enhancing customer experience*. https://www.ijisae.org/index.php/IJISAE/article/view/6405

Siddals, S., Torous, J., & Coxon, A. (2024). "It happened to be the perfect thing": Experiences of generative AI chatbots for mental health. *Npj Mental Health Research*, *3*(1), 48. Advance online publication. DOI: 10.1038/s44184-024-00097-4 PMID: 39465310

Thorat, S. A., & Jadhav, V. (2020). A review on implementation issues of rule-based chatbot systems. SSRN *Electronic Journal*. DOI: 10.2139/ssrn.3567047

Viswanathan, V. K., Jain, V. K., Vaish, A., Jeyaraman, M., Iyengar, K. P., & Vaishya, R. (2024). Chatbots and their applications in medical fields: Current status and future trends: A scoping review. *Apollo Medicine*, *21*(4), 386–392. DOI: 10.1177/09760016241259851

Wah, J. N. K. (2025). Revolutionizing e-health: The transformative role of AI-powered hybrid chatbots in healthcare solutions. *Frontiers in Public Health*, *13*, 1530799. Advance online publication. DOI: 10.3389/fpubh.2025.1530799 PMID: 40017541

Wang, M. (2024). Generative AI: A new challenge for cybersecurity. *Journal of Computer Science and Technology Studies*, *6*(2), 13–18. DOI: 10.32996/jcsts.2024.6.2.3

Williams, R. T. (2024). The ethical implications of using generative chatbots in higher education. *Frontiers in Education*, *8*, 1331607. Advance online publication. DOI: 10.3389/feduc.2023.1331607

Wilson, L., & Marasoiu, M. (2022). The Development and Use of Chatbots in Public Health: Scoping review. *JMIR Human Factors*, *9*(4), e35882. DOI: 10.2196/35882 PMID: 36197708

Wollny, S., Schneider, J., Di Mitri, D., Weidlich, J., Rittberger, M., & Drachsler, H. (2021). Are we there yet? - A Systematic Literature review on chatbots in education. *Frontiers in Artificial Intelligence*, *4*, 654924. Advance online publication. DOI: 10.3389/frai.2021.654924 PMID: 34337392

Zawacki-Richter, O., Marín, V. I., Bond, M., & Gouverneur, F. (2019). Systematic review of research on artificial intelligence applications in higher education – where are the educators? *International Journal of Educational Technology in Higher Education*, *16*(1), 39. Advance online publication. DOI: 10.1186/s41239-019-0171-0

Zhou, J., Zhang, Y., Luo, Q., Parker, A. G., & De Choudhury, M. (2023). Synthetic Lies: Understanding AI-Generated Misinformation and Evaluating Algorithmic and Human Solutions. *In Proceedings of the 2023 CHI Conference on Human Factors in Computing Systems (CHI '23)*, 1–20. DOI: 10.1145/3544548.3581318

ADDITIONAL READINGS

Colace, F., De Santo, M., Lombardi, M., Pascale, F., Pietrosanto, A., & Lemma, S. (2018). Chatbot for E-Learning: A case of study. *International Journal of Mechanical Engineering and Robotics Research*, 528–533. DOI: 10.18178/ijmerr.7.5.528-533

Dwivedi, Y. K., Kshetri, N., Hughes, L., Slade, E. L., Jeyaraj, A., Kar, A. K., Baabdullah, A. M., Koohang, A., Raghavan, V., Ahuja, M., Albanna, H., Albashrawi, M. A., Al-Busaidi, A. S., Balakrishnan, J., Barlette, Y., Basu, S., Bose, I., Brooks, L., Buhalis, D., & Wright, R. (2023). Opinion Paper: "So what if ChatGPT wrote it?" Multidisciplinary perspectives on opportunities, challenges and implications of generative conversational AI for research, practice and policy. *International Journal of Information Management*, *71*, 102642. DOI: 10.1016/j.ijinfomgt.2023.102642

King, M. R. (2022). The Future of AI in Medicine: A Perspective from a Chatbot. *Annals of Biomedical Engineering*, *51*(2), 291–295. DOI: 10.1007/s10439-022-03121-w PMID: 36572824

Omarov, B., Narynov, S., & Zhumanov, Z. (2022). Development of Chatbot-Psychologist: Dataset, architecture, design and Chatbot in use. *Vestnik KazATK*, *123*(4), 463–471. DOI: 10.52167/1609-1817-2022-123-4-463-471

Santoso, H. A., Winarsih, N. S., Mulyanto, E., Saraswati, G. W., Sukmana, S. E., Rustad, S., Rohman, M. S., Nugraha, A., & Firdausillah, F. (2018). Dinus Intelligent Assistance (DINA) chatbot for university admission services. *2018 International Seminar on Application for Technology of Information and Communication*, 417–423. DOI: 10.1109/ISEMANTIC.2018.8549797

Skjuve, M., Følstad, A., Fostervold, K. I., & Brandtzaeg, P. B. (2021). My Chatbot Companion - A study of Human-Chatbot Relationships. *International Journal of Human-Computer Studies*, *149*, 102601. DOI: 10.1016/j.ijhcs.2021.102601

Wang, L., Ma, C., Feng, X., Zhang, Z., Yang, H., Zhang, J., Chen, Z., Tang, J., Chen, X., Lin, Y., Zhao, W. X., Wei, Z., & Wen, J. (2024). A survey on large language model based autonomous agents. *Frontiers of Computer Science*, *18*(6), 186345. Advance online publication. DOI: 10.1007/s11704-024-40231-1

KEY TERMS AND DEFINITIONS

Chatbots: Autonomous software agents designed to simulate human-like conversations with users through text or voice, providing information or services across various domains.

Natural Language Processing (NLP): A field of artificial intelligence that focuses on the interaction between computers and humans through natural language, enabling machines to understand, interpret, and generate human language.

Artificial Intelligence (AI): The simulation of human intelligence processes by machines, particularly computer systems, encompassing learning, reasoning, and self-correction.

Machine Learning (ML): A subset of AI that involves the use of algorithms and statistical models to enable computers to improve their performance on a specific task through experience and data.

Generative AI: A class of artificial intelligence that focuses on creating new content or responses based on input data, often utilizing large language models to generate human-like text.

Ethical Considerations: The examination of moral principles and values related to the development and deployment of AI technologies, including issues of bias, privacy, and the potential for misinformation.

User Interaction: The ways in which users engage with chatbots, including the nature of the conversation, the effectiveness of responses, and the overall user experience.

Healthcare Applications: The use of chatbots in the healthcare sector for functions such as symptom assessment, appointment scheduling, mental health support, and dissemination of health information.

Bias: The presence of systematic favoritism or prejudice in AI systems, often resulting from unrepresentative training data, which can lead to unfair or discriminatory outcomes.

Knowledge Graphs (KGs): Structured representations of entities and their interrelationships that enable chatbots to reason over complex information and maintain contextual understanding, enhancing the accuracy of responses.

Chapter 5
Chatbots as Intelligent Advisors:
Transforming Personalized Learning in Higher Education

Soukaina Nai
https://orcid.org/0009-0002-4819-2198
Faculty of Science, Ibn Tofail University, Kenitra, Morocco

Tarik El Moudden
https://orcid.org/0000-0002-6963-6686
Faculty of Science, Ibn Tofail University, Kenitra, Morocco

Amal Rifai
https://orcid.org/0000-0003-2793-3102
Regional Center for the Professions of Education and Training, Rabat, Morocco

Abdelalim Sadiq
https://orcid.org/0000-0003-1478-8807
Faculty of Science, Ibn Tofail University, Kenitra, Morocco

ABSTRACT

The rapid advancement of artificial intelligence has catalyzed the emergence of intelligent chatbots as pivotal tools in higher education. Initially deployed for administrative tasks, these conversational agents have evolved into sophisticated virtual advisors that support personalized learning by adapting to individual student needs. This chapter examines the role of chatbots as intelligent advisors, highlighting their capabilities to provide context-aware guidance, real-time feedback, and motivational support. It explores the pedagogical benefits of integrating chatbots into academic environments, including enhanced learner autonomy, inclusivity,

DOI: 10.4018/979-8-3373-8011-7.ch005

and scalability. The discussion also addresses key challenges such as data privacy, ethical considerations, and technological limitations. Finally, the chapter outlines future directions for chatbot development, emphasizing human-AI collaboration and the importance of ethical, learner-centered design in realizing the full potential of chatbots to transform personalized learning in higher education.

1. INTRODUCTION

In recent years, higher education has undergone a significant transformation toward more flexible, learner-centered approaches designed to better meet the evolving needs of diverse student populations (Tetzlaff et al., 2021). This shift is driven by the increasing heterogeneity of learners, who now come from a wide range of cultural, socioeconomic, and educational backgrounds. Additionally, there is a growing demand for educational models that are accessible, inclusive, and adaptable to lifelong learning needs (Bernacki et al., 2021; Dumont & Ready, 2023). Many students balance their academic studies with professional work, family responsibilities, and other personal commitments, creating complex learning contexts that traditional teaching methods often struggle to accommodate effectively . Institutions are therefore under mounting pressure to provide personalized learning experiences that respond to these varied learner profiles and expectations (Ayeni et al., 2024). Although traditional pedagogical approaches remain foundational in higher education, their often rigid, standardized structures may fall short in addressing the unique needs, preferences, and learning speeds of individual students. This challenge is particularly acute in large, heterogeneous classrooms where the diversity of learners makes one-size-fits-all methods insufficient (Shemshack et al., 2021; Antonova & Dankov, 2022). In response to these challenges, the higher education landscape is increasingly embracing innovative pedagogical strategies and emerging technologies to foster more flexible and student-centered learning environments. Blended learning models, competency-based education, and adaptive technologies such as AI-powered chatbots are gaining traction for their ability to provide personalized support and real-time feedback tailored to individual learner needs. These approaches not only improve engagement and accessibility but also promote inclusivity by supporting diverse learning styles and backgrounds. Ultimately, such innovations empower students to take greater control over their educational journeys and contribute to more equitable and effective learning outcomes.

As digital transformation continues to reshape the educational landscape, artificial intelligence (AI) has become a major catalyst for innovation, enabling the development of more adaptive, efficient, and scalable learning solutions (Lytras et al., 2024; Schuler et al., 2021). Among the most promising AI-driven tools are chatbots—conversational agents designed to interact with users through natural language interfaces, whether via text or speech (Lauriola et al., 2022). Initially, these chatbots were implemented primarily to handle routine administrative tasks such as answering frequently asked questions, processing enrollment requests, and managing academic schedules (Maulud et al., 2021). However, their role has evolved significantly over time.

Today, chatbots are increasingly integrated into educational settings as interactive learning partners rather than just support tools. These intelligent systems provide real-time, context-aware feedback, offer personalized learning materials, and assist students in navigating complex academic content and processes. By extending support beyond the traditional classroom environment, chatbots help create a more continuous and accessible learning experience that can adapt to individual student needs (Alwazzan, 2024). The sophistication of these systems reflects a broader shift toward learner-responsive education, where technology plays an active role in fostering engagement, autonomy, and personalized support. Chatbots leverage advances in natural language processing, machine learning, and data analytics to interpret student inputs, track progress, and adapt their responses accordingly. This enables them to support diverse learning styles and paces, helping bridge gaps in understanding and offering timely interventions. As a result, AI-powered chatbots are poised to become invaluable tools in higher education, contributing to more inclusive, flexible, and effective learning ecosystems. Their continued development and thoughtful integration promise to transform how students engage with educational content and receive academic guidance in the digital age.

When equipped with advanced intelligent capabilities, chatbots can function as virtual academic advisors, effectively guiding learners through complex course pathways and helping them navigate degree requirements and key milestones (Talha Junaid et al., 2024; Pellas, 2024). These AI-driven systems offer immediate, personalized feedback on assignments and overall learning progress, allowing students to quickly identify areas where improvement is needed without waiting for human intervention (Papakostas et al., 2024). By analyzing individual performance data, chatbots can also recommend tailored learning resources such as readings, videos, or practice exercises that align with each student's unique needs, preferences, and current level of understanding (Tayeb et al., 2024). In doing so, chatbots promote more efficient and targeted study strategies, helping students maximize their learning outcomes. Furthermore, they foster self-directed learning by encouraging students to take ownership of their educational journeys, developing essential skills such as time management, goal setting, and reflection (see Figure 1) (Behforouz & Al Ghaithi, 2024). Unlike traditional educational supports that are limited by office hours or availability, chatbots provide 24/7 accessibility and real-time responsiveness. This continuous support extends the reach of educators and enables ongoing engagement, creating opportunities for personalized guidance beyond the classroom. Through these capabilities, intelligent chatbots are reshaping how students interact with educational content and academic advising. Their integration in higher education promises to enhance learner autonomy, improve academic outcomes, and support more inclusive and adaptable learning environments tailored to the diverse needs of today's students.

Figure 1. Chatbot functionalities

This chapter explores the transformative potential of chatbots as intelligent advisors in higher education, highlighting their growing role in reshaping teaching and learning practices (Stöhr et al., 2024). It begins with a review of foundational concepts and the evolving applications of educational chatbots, tracing how these AI-driven tools have progressed from simple administrative assistants to sophisticated learning companions (Jain et al., 2024). The discussion then shifts to their capacity to support personalized learning by adapting to individual student needs, enhancing engagement, and providing timely feedback. We also analyze the pedagogical impact of chatbot integration, addressing both opportunities and challenges related to design, ethical considerations, and data privacy (Al-Amin et al., 2024). Finally, the chapter presents a forward-looking vision for chatbot development, emphasizing their potential to foster more inclusive, responsive, and student-centered learning environments. Through this investigation, we seek to illuminate the intersection of AI and pedagogy and its implications for the future of higher education (Yetişensoy & Karaduman, 2024).

2. LANDSCAPE OF CHATBOT USE IN HIGHER EDUCATION

The use of chatbots in education has expanded rapidly in recent years, mirroring the broader acceleration of artificial intelligence (AI) adoption across multiple sectors, including healthcare, finance, and customer service (Gokçearslan et al., 2024). At their core, chatbots are software applications designed to simulate human conversation via text or voice interfaces, enabling real-time interaction with users (Davar et al., 2025). In educational settings, these systems serve a wide range of functions, from answering frequently asked questions and assisting with administrative tasks to providing personalized learning support. Chatbots can vary significantly in complexity from simple, rule-based programs that follow predefined scripts to more advanced AI-driven agents capable of interpreting and generating natural language responses using machine learning and natural language processing (Alsayed et al., 2025). As their capabilities evolve, chatbots are increasingly being integrated into learning management systems and digital classrooms, offering new possibilities for scalable, responsive, and student-centered educational experiences.

2.1 From Automation to Intelligent Interaction

The transition from simple rule-based chatbots to advanced, AI-driven conversational systems represents a profound shift in the educational landscape (Yusuf et al., 2025). Initially designed to perform limited administrative tasks such as answering frequently asked questions or assisting with course registration early chatbots operated within narrow parameters, relying on predefined scripts and keyword recognition. However, with the integration of natural language processing (NLP), machine learning, and generative AI models, chatbots have evolved into intelligent systems capable of dynamic interaction and contextual understanding. This evolution is not merely technical but pedagogical, as these advanced chatbots are now being positioned as key facilitators of personalized and adaptive learning experiences (Laak & Aru, 2024). They are increasingly used to provide learners with tailored feedback, scaffold learning in real time, and adapt instructional content based on individual progress and preferences. Table 1 illustrates this progression, offering a comparative overview of the transformation from static, rule-based tools to intelligent educational companions (Arantes, 2024). The table 1 highlights essential differences in underlying technology, interactivity, and the depth of support offered to students.

More importantly, it emphasizes the growing educational impact of AI-enhanced chatbots, especially in fostering student motivation, autonomy, and engagement in personalized learning environments (Ackermans et al., 2025).

Table 1. Comparative Overview of Rule-Based and Intelligent Chatbots in Higher Education

Aspect	Early Chatbots (Rule-Based)	Modern Intelligent Chatbots (AI-Powered)
Purpose	Primarily designed to automate routine administrative and support tasks such as answering FAQs and providing static information.	Designed to actively support personalized learning journeys, provide intelligent academic advising, and facilitate student engagement.
Functionality	Limited to answering predefined FAQs, giving fixed deadlines, and assisting with simple navigation based on keyword triggers.	Capable of analyzing student input, tracking behavioral patterns, adapting responses dynamically, and offering tailored learning resources and strategies.
Interaction Style	Reactive and transactional, typically providing single-turn responses without memory of prior context or conversations.	Proactive, multi-turn, and conversational with contextual awareness, enabling ongoing, meaningful dialogues.
Technology	Based on predefined rules, keyword matching, and scripted workflows with minimal flexibility.	Utilizes advanced Natural Language Processing (NLP), Machine Learning (ML), and Deep Learning techniques for more nuanced understanding and generation of responses.
Personalization	Very limited or non-existent; responses are generic and uniform across all users.	Highly personalized, adapting to individual learner profiles, preferences, past interactions, and performance history.
Learning Capability	Static system that does not learn or improve from past interactions, requiring manual updates to enhance functionality.	Dynamic and self-improving systems that continuously learn from user data and feedback to refine future interactions.
Response Quality	Fixed, repetitive, and often simplistic responses lacking adaptability or nuance.	Adaptive, contextually relevant, varied, and capable of providing nuanced explanations or guidance.
Role in Education	Functions mainly as a digital receptionist or administrative assistant with limited educational impact.	Acts as a virtual advisor or tutor, contributing pedagogically through personalized support and scaffolding.
Examples of Use	User asks, "When is the registration deadline?" and receives the same generic reply regardless of individual circumstances.	User says, "Remind me of my course deadlines," and receives personalized reminders based on their unique academic calendar and progress.

2.2 Types of Educational Chatbots

Chatbots in education have diversified in both function and complexity, leading to the emergence of specialized types tailored to specific student needs (see Figure 2).

Administrative chatbots are among the earliest forms, designed primarily to assist with logistical and procedural tasks such as enrollment, class scheduling, and navigating campus services (Pasena & Gunadi, 2025). Their main contribution lies in reducing administrative burdens and streamlining student access to institutional information. Moving beyond logistics,

Tutoring chatbots serve as digital learning assistants, offering subject-specific explanations, administering quizzes, and facilitating interactive lessons that support self-paced and individualized learning experiences (Choi & Chang, 2025). These systems aim to replicate aspects of one-on-one tutoring, helping learners better understand complex topics outside traditional classroom hours. In parallel,

Advisory chatbots provide more personalized academic guidance by recommending relevant resources, tracking learner progress, and helping students make informed academic decisions based on their goals and performance (Puspowidjono et al., 2024).

Lastly, wellbeing and support chatbots have emerged to address the growing need for psychological and emotional support in educational environments. These AI agents offer mental health assistance by recognizing stress indicators, providing coping strategies, and connecting students with institutional support services when necessary (Guan et al., 2025). Together, these chatbot types illustrate the expanding role of conversational AI in creating holistic, student-centered educational ecosystems.

Figure 2. Types of Educational Chatbots

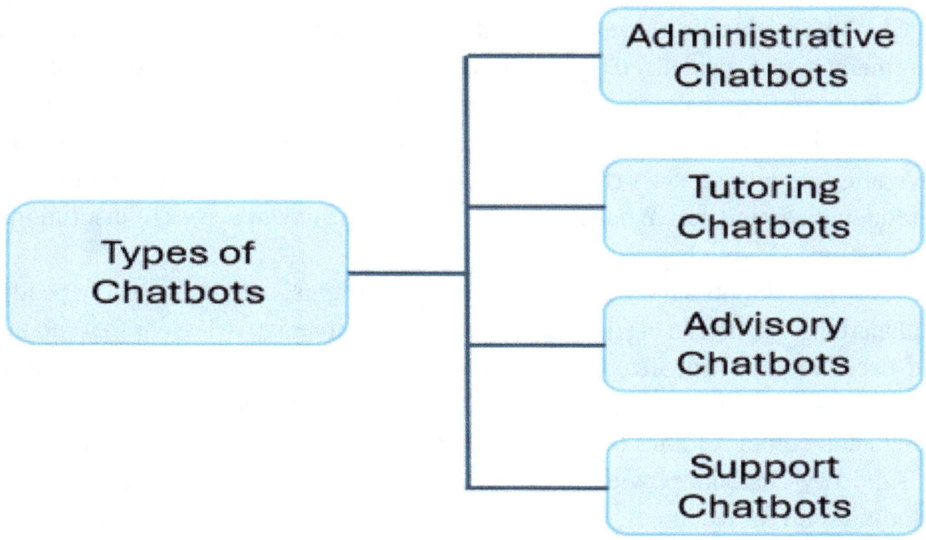

While each type of chatbot traditionally serves a distinct function ranging from administrative assistance to content delivery the boundaries between these categories are increasingly becoming blurred as more advanced, multi-functional systems emerge. Modern chatbots are no longer limited to simple transactional roles; instead, they are evolving into sophisticated tools capable of integrating multiple functions seamlessly. This chapter focuses primarily on advisory chatbots, which represent a significant leap forward in educational technology. These chatbots go beyond administrative tasks to actively support student learning by engaging in intelligent interactions that mimic human tutoring. They provide real-time, personalized feedback and adapt content dynamically based on the learner's progress and needs (Lee & Hahn, 2024). By combining elements of guidance, assessment, and tailored content delivery, advisory chatbots hold the potential to transform the educational experience, fostering deeper engagement, autonomy, and more effective learning outcomes.

2.3 Integration in Higher Education

Universities and colleges across the globe are increasingly experimenting with and integrating chatbot technologies to enrich the overall student experience (Rahman et al., 2025). These AI-powered agents are no longer confined to experimental pilot programs; they are now embedded within institutional infrastructures in various forms. For instance, virtual teaching assistants integrated into learning management systems support academic tasks such as answering course-related queries, reminding students of deadlines, or providing supplementary explanations. At the same time, AI-driven academic advisors are being deployed via mobile applications and websites, offering students 24/7 access to personalized support and guidance. This round-the-clock availability is particularly beneficial in accommodating students' varied schedules and time zones, especially in online and transnational education contexts. As illustrated in Figure 3, the appeal of chatbots in higher education lies in their scalability, instant accessibility, and ability to tailor interactions to individual learner profiles. (Figure 3). These qualities enable institutions to address a wide range of student needs including academic, administrative, and emotional support far beyond traditional classroom settings. The continuous interest and implementation efforts reflect a broader shift toward more inclusive, efficient, and personalized learning environments (Rahman et al., 2025).

However, the meaningful integration of chatbot technologies into higher education requires far more than mere technical deployment. While the underlying AI infrastructure is important, successful implementation must be grounded in a clear alignment between chatbot capabilities and well-defined pedagogical objectives (Setyawan & Pramudita, 2025). Institutions must ensure that chatbots serve as more than novelty tools that they actively support learning outcomes, encourage student engagement, and enhance the educational experience. Additionally, the integration process must address critical concerns such as data privacy, ethical use of student data, and transparency in AI interactions, which are essential to building and maintaining trust among both learners and educators. Without such safeguards and strategic alignment, the risk of resistance, misuse, or superficial adoption becomes high. As explored in the following section, chatbots that function as intelligent academic advisors open up new and promising pathways for transforming the personalized learning landscape. These systems not only enhance educational efficiency through real-time support and adaptive feedback, but also contribute to a more empathetic, inclusive, and learner-centered educational environment an evolution that reflects the true potential of AI in higher education (Merino-Campos, 2025).

Figure 3. Advantages of Chatbots

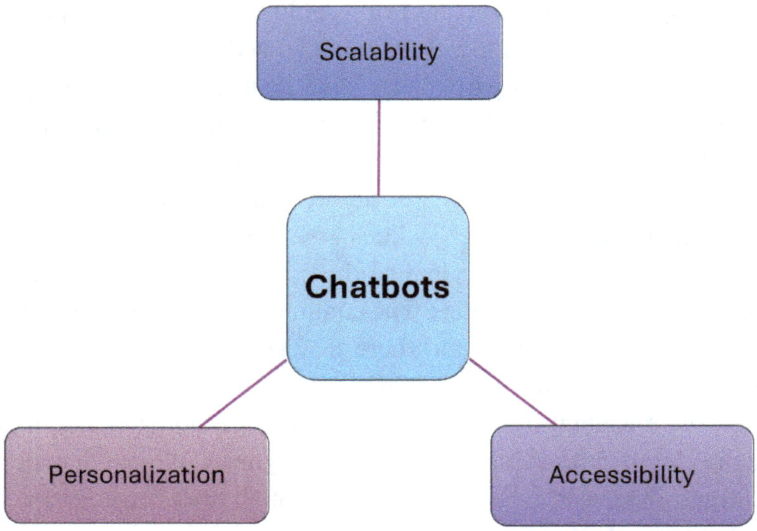

3. PEDAGOGICAL INTELLIGENCE: CHATBOTS AS VIRTUAL LEARNING ADVISORS

While Section 2 provided an overview of the wide range of chatbot applications in higher education, this section narrows the focus to intelligent advisory chatbots advanced systems designed not merely to provide information, but to actively guide, adapt to, and support students throughout their academic journeys. These AI-powered agents function as virtual mentors embedded within learning environments, delivering personalized assistance that aligns with each learner's unique profile, preferences, and progress. Unlike traditional chatbots that offer generic responses, intelligent advisory chatbots analyze real-time data to tailor feedback, suggest resources, and help students navigate academic challenges with greater autonomy. By fostering continuous, individualized support, they enhance student engagement, promote self-directed learning, and contribute to more effective and inclusive educational experiences. This section explores their design, capabilities, and the ways in which they transform the role of digital tools from passive information providers to active learning partners.

3.1 Key Features of Pedagogical Intelligence

Intelligent advisory chatbots represent a significant advancement beyond traditional administrative or content-delivery bots, distinguished by their capacity to emulate aspects of human academic advising and one-on-one tutoring (Al-Abri, 2025). Unlike their rule-based predecessors, which are limited to static responses or predefined interactions, these advanced systems leverage a sophisticated blend of natural language processing (NLP), machine learning algorithms, and real-time access to individual learner profiles. This technological foundation allows them to interpret student queries in nuanced ways, recognize learning patterns, and offer tailored guidance that evolves alongside the learner's progress.

Their pedagogical intelligence is not merely a function of automation but a result of their ability to adapt, personalize, and engage in context-aware dialogue. These chatbots can assess prior knowledge, identify misconceptions, track performance, and suggest appropriate learning resources or study strategies. By simulating the responsiveness and empathy of a human advisor, they provide timely feedback and motivational support critical components in maintaining learner engagement and fostering academic self-efficacy. This advanced functionality positions intelligent advisory chatbots as pivotal agents in transforming how support is delivered in digital learning environments. The following outlines several core features that define the pedagogical intelligence of these systems and distinguish them as transformative tools in higher education.

Table 2. Core Features of Intelligent Advisory Chatbots in Higher Education

Features	Description
Context Sensitivity	The chatbot interprets student questions by considering factors such as academic level (e.g., undergraduate or graduate), specific academic program, and the current stage in the learning process. This allows responses to be tailored to the learner's knowledge base, course requirements, and educational context, ensuring more relevant and meaningful interactions.
Personalization	By leveraging comprehensive student profiles—including knowledge level, learning preferences, past activities, and performance history—the chatbot delivers customized recommendations for study materials, exercises, and learning actions. This targeted approach helps address individual needs, promotes engagement, and supports personalized learning pathways.
Memory and Adaptivity	The chatbot continuously learns from past interactions with each student, refining its responses, suggestions, and instructional strategies over time. This adaptive learning enables the system to better anticipate learner needs, correct misconceptions, and provide increasingly effective support tailored to evolving proficiency and behavior.

continued on following page

Table 2. Continued

Features	Description
Dialogic Feedback	Rather than simply providing correct answers, the chatbot engages in scaffolded dialogue that guides students through problem-solving steps and conceptual understanding. This explanatory feedback encourages critical thinking, deepens comprehension, and fosters active learning by helping students construct knowledge rather than passively receive information.
Proactive Support	The chatbot takes initiative by regularly checking in on students' progress, sending reminders about upcoming deadlines or study goals, and alerting learners or educators to potential performance issues. This anticipatory approach helps prevent academic difficulties and promotes sustained motivation and timely intervention.

These features (Table 2) allow chatbots to go beyond reactive support, creating a more responsive, empathetic, and individualized learning experience particularly valuable in large or online learning environments where human feedback is limited or delayed.

3.2 Learning Support and Academic Guidance Functions

When effectively integrated into educational settings, intelligent advisor chatbots offer comprehensive support across multiple stages of students' academic journeys (Yu et al., 2025). These AI-powered tools provide personalized academic guidance by adapting to each learner's unique profile, delivering real-time feedback, and recommending tailored learning resources. They assist students in navigating course selections, monitoring their academic progress, and cultivating essential skills such as goal setting, time management, and self-reflection. By promoting continuous engagement and encouraging self-directed learning, these chatbots not only improve academic performance but also foster greater learner autonomy and confidence. The following sections will detail the primary pedagogical functions that these intelligent systems typically fulfill in higher education.

A. Academic Navigation and Decision Support:

Intelligent chatbots play a crucial role in assisting students with academic navigation and decision-making, helping to simplify complex educational pathways (De-Arteaga et al., 2025). These systems guide students in selecting appropriate courses by providing clear explanations of prerequisites, co-requisites, and course sequencing, ensuring that learners make informed choices that align with their academic progress and long-term career aspirations. By analyzing individual student profiles, academic history, and institutional requirements, chatbots can offer personalized recommendations tailored to each learner's goals, interests, and strengths.

Moreover, chatbots simulate academic advising sessions, offering real-time support that helps students interpret degree requirements, track progress toward graduation, and understand feedback on course performance. This interactive guidance reduces confusion and anxiety around academic planning, empowering students to proactively manage their educational journeys. By making advising more accessible and responsive, chatbots help bridge gaps caused by limited advisor availability and large student-to-advisor ratios, fostering better decision-making and enhancing overall student success.

B. Personalized Learning Pathways:
- Intelligent chatbots can recommend a wide range of personalized learning materials including readings, videos, interactive exercises, and external digital tools tailored to each student's current progress, academic performance, and individual interests (Gu, 2025). By continuously analyzing learner data such as quiz results, participation patterns, and topic preferences, these systems curate resources that address specific knowledge gaps and reinforce strengths. This targeted approach helps keep students engaged and motivated by providing relevant and timely content that matches their evolving needs.
- Furthermore, chatbots dynamically adapt the difficulty level and style of explanations in real time, responding to learners' inputs and comprehension signals. For instance, if a student struggles with a concept, the chatbot might simplify the language, offer additional examples, or present alternative instructional methods such as visual aids or analogies. Conversely, for learners demonstrating mastery, the chatbot can introduce more challenging problems to promote deeper understanding. This responsive adaptation fosters personalized learning pathways, accommodating diverse learning paces and styles to optimize educational outcomes.

C. Formative Assessment and Feedback:
- Intelligent chatbots offer real-time, constructive feedback on a variety of student work, including assignments, quizzes, and learning reflections (Feldman et al., 2025). By instantly analyzing submitted responses, these systems can highlight strengths, identify errors, and suggest specific areas for improvement, enabling students to immediately understand their performance and adjust their learning strategies accordingly. This timely feedback loop helps prevent misconceptions from taking root and supports continuous learning progress. Moreover, chatbots can tailor their feedback to individual learner profiles, providing explanations that match students' knowledge levels and preferred learning

styles. Beyond grading, they may also encourage deeper critical thinking by posing reflective questions or suggesting alternative approaches to problem-solving. This dynamic interaction fosters a more engaging and supportive learning environment, where students receive personalized guidance that complements traditional instructor feedback and enhances overall academic development.

- When errors are detected in student responses, intelligent chatbots provide clear explanations and offer supplementary resources to promote deeper understanding and mastery of the material. Rather than simply indicating that an answer is incorrect, these systems analyze the nature of the mistake and deliver targeted clarifications that address common misconceptions or gaps in knowledge. For example, a chatbot might break down complex concepts into simpler terms, use analogies, or provide step-by-step walkthroughs to help students grasp difficult topics more effectively. Additionally, chatbots can recommend relevant articles, instructional videos, practice exercises, or interactive simulations that reinforce the corrected concepts and support varied learning preferences. By delivering this just-in-time support, chatbots encourage learners to engage actively with the material, fostering critical thinking and self-reflection. This personalized, adaptive assistance helps transform errors into valuable learning opportunities, ultimately improving retention and academic performance.

D. Motivation and Self-Regulation:

- Intelligent chatbots actively encourage learners by providing positive reinforcement, timely reminders, and thoughtful prompts that foster self-awareness and reflection on their learning habits (Lee et al., 2025). Through supportive messages and motivational feedback, chatbots help build student confidence and sustain engagement, especially during challenging tasks or extended study periods. They can remind learners about upcoming deadlines, suggest breaks to prevent burnout, or prompt goal-setting to maintain focus. Additionally, chatbots encourage metacognitive practices by asking reflective questions that help students evaluate their study strategies, time management, and overall progress. This ongoing dialogue nurtures a growth mindset, empowering learners to take greater ownership of their educational journeys. By combining encouragement with reflective prompts, chatbots create a personalized support system that not only enhances motivation but also promotes deeper, more effective learning habits.
- Intelligent chatbots assist students in setting, tracking, and adjusting their academic goals, thereby fostering greater autonomy and a sense

of personal responsibility in their learning journeys. By guiding learners through the goal-setting process, chatbots help them establish clear, realistic, and measurable objectives aligned with their individual aspirations and course requirements. Throughout the semester, these systems monitor progress and provide regular updates, helping students stay on track and recognize milestones achieved. When challenges or setbacks occur, chatbots offer timely suggestions to adjust goals or revise study plans, encouraging flexibility and resilience. This ongoing support empowers students to take ownership of their education, develop self-regulation skills, and maintain motivation. By integrating goal management into daily learning activities, chatbots create a dynamic framework that promotes sustained engagement and helps learners navigate their academic paths with confidence and purpose.

E. Time and Workload Management:
   - Intelligent chatbots assist students with scheduling, prioritizing tasks, and managing reminders for upcoming deadlines or study goals, helping them stay organized and reduce academic stress (Wang et al., 2025). By analyzing course requirements, assignment due dates, and individual learning rhythms, chatbots can create personalized study plans that break down complex workloads into manageable steps. They help students prioritize tasks based on urgency and importance, ensuring that critical deadlines are met without last-minute pressure. Through timely notifications and reminders, chatbots keep learners aware of upcoming exams, project submissions, and other key milestones. This proactive support fosters effective time management and encourages consistent study habits, which are essential for academic success. By integrating these organizational tools into daily routines, chatbots empower students to balance their academic responsibilities with other commitments, promoting a healthier and more productive learning experience.

By integrating these roles, intelligent advisor chatbots act as scalable learning companions that complement human educators. They help ensure that each learner receives timely, relevant, and personalized support an essential condition for effective, inclusive, and adaptive learning in higher education.

4. IMPACT ON PERSONALIZED LEARNING

To gain a more comprehensive understanding of the educational value offered by intelligent advisory chatbots, it is important to examine their tangible impact across multiple dimensions of personalized learning (Yamijala et al., 2025). These systems are not merely passive content delivery tools; rather, they function as dynamic agents that actively shape the learning experience. By leveraging real-time data and natural language processing, chatbots can tailor interactions based on individual learner profiles, thereby enhancing engagement, comprehension, and motivation.

One of the key strengths of these chatbots lies in their capacity to adaptively respond to diverse learner needs. Whether by adjusting the difficulty level of content, offering timely feedback, or suggesting customized learning pathways, they contribute to a more individualized educational experience. Moreover, they play a critical role in fostering learner autonomy by enabling students to set their own pace, seek clarification without hesitation, and make informed decisions about their learning trajectory (Ye & Morris, 2025).

In addition to personalization and autonomy, intelligent chatbots also support inclusive access to education. They provide 24/7 support that can be particularly valuable for students from underrepresented or non-traditional backgrounds, those with disabilities, or learners studying remotely. This constant availability helps bridge gaps in access to academic advising and instructional support that may otherwise hinder student success.

Table 3 below outlines the primary domains in which intelligent advisory chatbots enhance personalized learning in higher education. It includes concrete examples of how these systems are implemented in practice ranging from automated progress tracking and proactive nudging to personalized resource recommendations and adaptive language support (Ahmed et al., 2025). These examples illustrate the practical integration of chatbot technologies into higher education ecosystems and highlight their potential to transform how learning is designed, delivered, and experienced.

Table 3. Key Areas of Impact of Intelligent Chatbots on Personalized Learning

Impact Area	Description	Examples of Chatbot Functionality
Individualized Learning	Chatbots tailor instructional content and learning support to align with each student's unique level, pace, and learning preferences. This personalized approach helps accommodate diverse learning styles and ensures that students receive appropriate challenges and assistance to optimize their educational progress.	- Adjusts complexity of explanations based on learner proficiency- Offers alternative learning paths tailored to student goals- Recommends targeted remediation resources for areas of difficulty
Learner Autonomy & Engagement	Chatbots foster learner independence by encouraging students to actively participate in their education. They promote reflection on progress, facilitate goal setting, and support active decision-making about learning strategies. This empowerment boosts motivation and sustained engagement.	- Prompts regular self-assessment and progress checks- Suggests personalized goal-setting activities- Provides choices of content formats (e.g., video, text, interactive exercises) to suit learner preferences
Diversity & Inclusion	Chatbots contribute to equitable and inclusive education by providing accessible, culturally responsive support to diverse student populations. Their availability around the clock and ability to adapt communication styles help address varied linguistic, cultural, and learning needs.	- Offers 24/7 learning support and guidance- Supports multiple languages and culturally relevant examples- Adjusts pacing, language style, and explanations to accommodate different learner backgrounds and abilities

5. CHALLENGES AND ETHICAL CONSIDERATIONS

While intelligent chatbots offer promising support for personalized learning, their use in higher education raises important ethical, pedagogical, and social concerns that go beyond technical performance (Alonso et al., 2025). To be effective and responsible, these systems must be critically evaluated for their broader implications (Carreno, 2025). A key issue is algorithmic bias, which can lead to unequal treatment of students based on factors like language, cultural background, or learning style. Data privacy is another major concern, as chatbots often rely on continuous monitoring and analysis of student behavior. Without strong safeguards, these practices may compromise student autonomy and trust. Pedagogical integration also remains limited. Many chatbots function mainly as support tools for administrative tasks or basic tutoring, with minimal alignment to instructional design. This restricts their capacity to support deeper learning outcomes. Furthermore, excessive reliance on automated systems may reduce meaningful human interaction, which remains central to higher education. Table 4 below outlines the main challenges and ethical considerations associated with chatbot use in higher education, including transparency, accountability, and inclusivity (Rane, 2023). Addressing these issues is essential to ensure that chatbot-enhanced learning environments remain fair, secure, and pedagogically valuable (Urbani et al., 2024).

Table 4. Overview of Key Technical, Ethical, and Social Challenges in Chatbot Integration for Higher Education

Challenge Area	Description	Key Issues
Technical and Pedagogical Limitations	Chatbots may face difficulties handling complex academic queries and aligning their responses with specific instructional goals or learning outcomes.	- Misinterpretation of nuanced or ambiguous student input- Providing inaccurate, incomplete, or superficial answers- Lack of deep pedagogical understanding and contextual awareness- Risk that learners become overly reliant on chatbots, reducing critical thinking or instructor interaction
Data Privacy and Security	The collection and use of sensitive learner data by chatbots introduce significant privacy and cybersecurity risks that must be managed responsibly.	- Handling and storing sensitive personal and academic information- Insufficient transparency about data use and consent mechanisms- Vulnerability to data breaches or unauthorized access- Compliance with legal frameworks like GDPR and FERPA
Equity, Bias, and Accessibility	Chatbots may unintentionally perpetuate biases present in their training data or design, and accessibility challenges may exclude or disadvantage certain groups of learners.	- Embedded gender, cultural, or language biases leading to unfair or inappropriate responses- Inequitable access to technology or internet connectivity among learners- Interface designs that do not accommodate users with disabilities or diverse needs- Lack of multilingual support or culturally responsive interactions
Trust and Acceptance	The effectiveness of chatbots depends on learners' and educators' trust, acceptance, and perceived value of these AI tools in educational settings.	- Student skepticism about chatbot accuracy and usefulness- Resistance from instructors worried about job displacement or loss of human touch- Concerns that chatbots could dehumanize education or reduce interpersonal connection- Need for transparent communication about chatbot capabilities and limitations

6. CONCLUSION AND FUTURE DIRECTIONS

Intelligent chatbots are transforming higher education by delivering personalized, accessible, and scalable learning support. Moving beyond simple administrative functions, these AI-driven tools now provide adaptive guidance and real-time feedback that empower students to navigate their academic journeys with greater confidence and effectiveness. This chapter explored the diverse educational roles of chatbots, emphasizing their potential to enhance learner autonomy, engagement, and personalized support. At the same time, it addressed important challenges, including technical limitations, ethical issues such as bias and fairness, and concerns around data privacy and security. As the adoption of chatbot technology in education continues to grow, careful integration with existing pedagogical practices and responsible design principles will be essential. Ensuring transparency, inclusivity, and ethical use will help unlock the full potential of chatbots as intelligent advisors, ultimately contributing to more effective, equitable, and student-centered higher education environments.

The future of chatbot integration in education hinges on effective human-AI collaboration, where chatbots complement rather than replace educators. To foster personalized and equitable learning environments, these tools must be developed with core principles of fairness, transparency, and respect for student agency. Upcoming advancements will include multimodal interactions combining text, voice, and visual inputs enhanced emotional intelligence to better understand and respond to learner emotions, deeper integration with learning analytics for data-driven insights, and hybrid models that blend chatbot efficiency with human expertise. These innovations promise more adaptive, empathetic, and personalized educational experiences. However, achieving these potential demands sustained attention to ethical design, robust data privacy protections, and inclusive practices that address diverse learner needs. Ultimately, the success of educational chatbots will depend not only on technological innovation but also on responsible implementation that builds trust, promotes equity, and supports the human-centered values essential to effective learning.

REFERENCES

Ackermans, K., Bakker, M., van Loon, A. M., Kral, M., & Camp, G. (2025). Young learners' motivation, self-regulation and performance in personalized learning. *Computers & Education*, *226*, 105208. DOI: 10.1016/j.compedu.2024.105208

Ahmed, Y., Ahmed, T., Raza, A., & Jan, I. (2025). Harnessing AI for Personalized Learning, Equity, and Administrative Efficiency in Transnational Higher Education. *Bridging Global Divides for Transnational Higher Education in the AI Era*, 191-204. DOI: DOI: 10.4018/979-8-3693-7016-2.ch009

Al-Abri, A. (2025). Exploring ChatGPT as a virtual tutor: A multi-dimensional analysis of large language models in academic support. *Education and Information Technologies*, *30*(12), 1–36. DOI: 10.1007/s10639-025-13484-x

Al-Amin, M., Ali, M. S., Salam, A., Khan, A., Ali, A., Ullah, A., . . . Chowdhury, S. K. (2024). History of generative Artificial Intelligence (AI) chatbots: past, present, and future development. *arXiv preprint arXiv:2402.05122*. https://doi.org//arXiv .2402.05122.DOI: 10.48550

Alonso, R. R., Carvajal, K. A., & Acevedo, N. R. (2025). Role of Artificial Intelligence in the personalization of distance education: A systematic review. *Revista Iberoamericana de Educación a Distancia*, *28*(1), 9–32. DOI: 10.5944/ried.28.1.41538

Alsayed, W. O., Al-Hafdi, F. S., & Alhalafawy, W. S. (2025). Chatbots in Education. In *Empowering STEM Educators With Digital Tools* (pp. 137–154). IGI Global Scientific Publishing., DOI: 10.4018/979-8-3693-9806-7.ch006

Alwazzan, M. S. (2024). Investigating the Effectiveness of Artificial Intelligence Chatbots in Enhancing Digital Dialogue Skills for Students. *European Journal of Educational Research*, *13*(2), 573–584. Advance online publication. DOI: 10.12973/eu-jer.13.2.573

Antonova, A., & Dankov, Y. (2022). Smart services in education: facilitating teachers to deliver personalized learning experiences. In *Proceedings of the Computational Methods in Systems and Software* (pp. 108-117). Cham: Springer International Publishing. DOI: 10.1007/978-3-031-21438-7_9

Arantes, J. (2024). Digital twins and the terminology of "personalization" or "personalized learning" in educational policy: A discussion paper. *Policy Futures in Education*, *22*(4), 524–543. DOI: 10.1177/14782103231176357

Ayeni, O. O., Al Hamad, N. M., Chisom, O. N., Osawaru, B., & Adewusi, O. E. (2024). AI in education: A review of personalized learning and educational technology. *GSC Advanced Research and Reviews*, *18*(2), 261–271. DOI: 10.30574/gscarr.2024.18.2.0062

Behforouz, B., & Al Ghaithi, A. (2024). The Impact of Using Interactive Chatbots on Self-Directed Learning. *Studies in Self-Access Learning Journal*, *15*(3), 317–344. Advance online publication. DOI: 10.37237/150302

Bernacki, M. L., Greene, M. J., & Lobczowski, N. G. (2021). A systematic review of research on personalized learning: Personalized by whom, to what, how, and for what purpose (s)? *Educational Psychology Review*, *33*(4), 1675–1715. DOI: 10.1007/s10648-021-09615-8

Carreño, I. D. V. G. (2025). Reflections on ChatGPT in the Field of Social Sciences: A Bibliometric Study. *European Educational Researcher*, *8*(1), 5–28. DOI: 10.31757/euer.812

Choi, W. C., & Chang, C. I. (2025). A Survey of Techniques, Design, Applications, Challenges, and Student Perspective of Chatbot-Based Learning Tutoring System Supporting Students to Learn in Education. DOI: 10.20944/preprints202503.1134.v1

Davar, N. F., Dewan, M. A. A., & Zhang, X. (2025). AI chatbots in education: Challenges and opportunities. *Information (Basel)*, *16*(3), 235. DOI: 10.3390/info16030235

De-Arteaga, M., Jeanselme, V., Dubrawski, A., & Chouldechova, A. (2025). Leveraging expert consistency to improve algorithmic decision support. *Management Science*, mnsc.2022.01576. Advance online publication. DOI: 10.1287/mnsc.2022.01576

Dumont, H., & Ready, D. D. (2023). On the promise of personalized learning for educational equity. *NPJ Science of Learning*, *8*(1), 26. DOI: 10.1038/s41539-023-00174-x PMID: 37542046

Feldman, J., Gilchrist, C., & Leung, F. H. (2025). Artificial Intelligence can transform formative assessment in medical education. *Canadian Medical Education Journal*. Feldman, J., Gilchrist, C., & Leung, F. H. (2025). Artificial Intelligence can transform formative assessment in medical education. *Canadian Medical Education Journal*. Advance online publication. DOI: 10.36834/cmej.79759

Gökçearslan, S., Tosun, C., & Erdemir, Z. G. (2024). Benefits, challenges, and methods of artificial intelligence (AI) chatbots in education: A systematic literature review. *International Journal of Technology in Education*, *7*(1), 19–39. DOI: 10.46328/ijte.600

Gu, R. (2025). Personalized learning path based on graph attention mechanism deep reinforcement learning research on recommender systems. *Journal of Computational Methods in Sciences and Engineering, 14727978241313260*(3), 2411–2426. Advance online publication. DOI: 10.1177/14727978241313260

Guan, R., Raković, M., Chen, G., & Gašević, D. (2025). How educational chatbots support self-regulated learning? A systematic review of the literature. *Education and Information Technologies, 30*(4), 4493–4518. DOI: 10.1007/s10639-024-12881-y

Jain, V., Singh, I., Syed, M., Mondal, S., & Palai, D. R. (2024, March). Enhancing educational interactions: A comprehensive review of AI chatbots in learning environments. In *2024 11th international conference on reliability, infocom technologies and optimization (trends and future directions)(ICRITO)* (pp. 1-5). IEEE. DOI: DOI: 10.1109/ICRITO61523.2024.10522392

Laak, K. J., & Aru, J. (2024). AI and personalized learning: bridging the gap with modern educational goals. *arXiv preprint arXiv:2404.02798*. https://doi.org//arXiv .2404.02798DOI: 10.48550

Lauriola, I., Lavelli, A., & Aiolli, F. (2022). An introduction to deep learning in natural language processing: Models, techniques, and tools. *Neurocomputing, 470*, 443–456. DOI: 10.1016/j.neucom.2021.05.103

Lee, I., & Hahn, S. (2024). On the relationship between mind perception and social support of chatbots. *Frontiers in Psychology, 15*, 1282036. DOI: 10.3389/fpsyg.2024.1282036 PMID: 38510306

Lee, Y. F., Hwang, G. J., & Chen, P. Y. (2025). Technology-based interactive guidance to promote learning performance and self-regulation: A chatbot-assisted self-regulated learning approach. *Educational Technology Research and Development, 73*(4), 1–26. DOI: 10.1007/s11423-025-10478-x

Lytras, M. D., Serban, A. C., Alkhaldi, A., Aldosemani, T., & Malik, S. (2024). Digital transformation in higher education in times of artificial intelligence: Setting the emerging landscape. In *Digital Transformation in Higher Education, Part A* (pp. 1-22). Emerald Publishing Limited. https://doi.org/DOI: 10.1108/978-1-83549-480-620241001

Maulud, D. H., Zeebaree, S. R., Jacksi, K., Sadeeq, M. A. M., & Sharif, K. H. (2021). State of art for semantic analysis of natural language processing. *Qubahan academic journal, 1*(2), 21-28. DOI: .DOI: 10.48161/qaj.v1n2a44

Merino-Campos, C. (2025). The impact of artificial intelligence on personalized learning in higher education: A systematic review. *Trends in Higher Education, 4*(2), 17. DOI: 10.3390/higheredu4020017

Papakostas, C., Troussas, C., Krouska, A., & Sgouropoulou, C. (2024, June). A rule-based chatbot offering personalized guidance in computer programming education. In *International Conference on Intelligent Tutoring Systems* (pp. 253-264). Cham: Springer Nature Switzerland. DOIhttps://DOI: 10.1007/978-3-031-63031-6_22

Pasena, R. B., & Gunadi, G. (2025). IMPLEMENTATION OF A CHATBOT BASED ON ARTIFIFICAL INTELLEGENCE MARKUP LANGUANGE FOR ADMINISTRATIF SERVICE INFORMATION AT KELURAHAN NEGERI AGUNG. *Jurnal Disprotek, 16*(1), 33–46. DOI: 10.34001/jdpt.v16i1.7332

Pellas, N. (2024). The role of students higher-order thinking skills in the relationship between academic achievements and machine learning using generative AI chatbots. https://doi.org/DOI: 10.21203/rs.3.rs-4627814/v2

Puspowidjono, K., Chiou, A., & Jha, M. (2024, December). Next Level Chatbot: Expert Advisory Solution. In *2024 International Conference on Sustainable Technology and Engineering (i-COSTE)* (pp. 01-06). IEEE. DOI: DOI: 10.1109/i-COSTE63786.2024.11024843

Rahman, M. K., Hossain, M. A., Ismail, N. A., Hossen, M. S., & Sultana, M. (2025). Determinants of students' adoption of AI chatbots in higher education: The moderating role of tech readiness. *Interactive Technology and Smart Education, 22*(3), 448–480. Advance online publication. DOI: 10.1108/ITSE-12-2024-0312

Rahman, M. K., Ismail, N. A., Hossain, M. A., & Hossen, M. S. (2025). Students' mindset to adopt AI chatbots for effectiveness of online learning in higher education. *Future Business Journal, 11*(1), 30. DOI: 10.1186/s43093-025-00459-0

Rane, N. (2023). Chatbot-enhanced teaching and learning: Implementation strategies, challenges, and the role of ChatGPT in education. *Challenges, and the Role of ChatGPT in Education (July 21,* 2023*)*. http://dx.doi.org/DOI: 10.2139/ssrn.4603204

Schuler, L., Jamil, S., & Kühl, N. (2021, May). AI-based resource allocation: Reinforcement learning for adaptive auto-scaling in serverless environments. In *2021 IEEE/ACM 21st international symposium on cluster, cloud and internet computing (CCGrid)* (pp. 804-811). IEEE. DOI: DOI: 10.1109/CCGrid51090.2021.00098

Setyawan, S., & Pramudita, R. F. (2025). Enhancing Academic Speaking Skills Through AI Chatbots: A Study on English Language Learning in Higher Education. *International Journal of Applied Educational Research, 3*(2), 129–140. DOI: 10.59890/ijaer.v3i2.30

Shemshack, A., Kinshuk, , & Spector, J. M. (2021). A comprehensive analysis of personalized learning components. *Journal of Computers in Education, 8*(4), 485–503. DOI: 10.1007/s40692-021-00188-7

Stöhr, C., Ou, A. W., & Malmström, H. (2024). Perceptions and usage of AI chatbots among students in higher education across genders, academic levels and fields of study. *Computers and Education: Artificial Intelligence, 7*, 100259. DOI: 10.1016/j.caeai.2024.100259

Talha Junaid, M., Barakat, S., Awad, R., & Anwar, N. (2024). Adopting the power of AI chatbots for enriching students learning in civil engineering education: A study on capabilities and limitations. In *Artificial intelligence in education: The power and dangers of ChatGPT in the classroom* (pp. 25–47). Springer Nature Switzerland., DOI: 10.1007/978-3-031-52280-2_3

Tayeb, A., Alahmadi, M., Tajik, E., & Haiduc, S. (2024, October). Investigating Developers' Preferences for Learning and Issue Resolution Resources in the ChatGPT Era. In *2024 IEEE International Conference on Software Maintenance and Evolution (ICSME)* (pp. 413-425). IEEE. DOI: DOI: 10.1109/ICSME58944.2024.00045

Tetzlaff, L., Schmiedek, F., & Brod, G. (2021). Developing personalized education: A dynamic framework. *Educational Psychology Review, 33*(3), 863–882. DOI: 10.1007/s10648-020-09570-w

Urbani, R., Ferreira, C., & Lam, J. (2024). Managerial framework for evaluating AI chatbot integration: Bridging organizational readiness and technological challenges. *Business Horizons, 67*(5), 595–606. DOI: 10.1016/j.bushor.2024.05.004

Wang, J., Deng, W., Yue, C., Su, W., & Bai, X. (2025). Joint optimization of cooling parameters and workload distributions based on model predictive control for rack-based data centers. *Journal of Building Engineering, 100*, 111801. DOI: 10.1016/j.jobe.2025.111801

Yamijala, S. M. S., Chodisetty, R. M., Chakravorty, C., & Sai, K. P. (2025). AI-Powered Learning Revolutionizing Smart Education With Personalized Learning Styles. In *Internet of Behavior-Based Computational Intelligence for Smart Education Systems* (pp. 191–212). IGI Global., DOI: 10.4018/979-8-3693-8151-9.ch007

Ye, J., & Morris, G. (2025). Promoting Inclusive Practices in Transnational Higher Education Through Staff Training and Development. In *Innovative Approaches to Staff Development in Transnational Higher Education* (pp. 119–138). IGI Global Scientific Publishing., DOI: 10.4018/979-8-3693-9102-0.ch005

Yetişensoy, O., & Karaduman, H. (2024). The effect of AI-powered chatbots in social studies education. *Education and Information Technologies*, *29*(13), 17035–17069. DOI: 10.1007/s10639-024-12485-6

Yu, D., Zhang, H., Huang, Y., & Xie, Z. (2025). Data distribution inference attack in federated learning via reinforcement learning support. *High-Confidence Computing*, *5*(1), 100235. DOI: 10.1016/j.hcc.2024.100235

Yusuf, H., Money, A., & Daylamani-Zad, D. (2025). Pedagogical AI conversational agents in higher education: A conceptual framework and survey of the state of the art. *Educational Technology Research and Development*, *73*(2), 1–60. DOI: 10.1007/s11423-025-10447-4

Chapter 6
Design and Evaluation of a Personalized AI Tutoring System Using ChatGPT

Soukaina Nai
https://orcid.org/0009-0002-4819-2198
Faculty of Science, Ibn Tofail University, Kenitra, Morocco

Tarik El Moudden
https://orcid.org/0000-0002-6963-6686
Faculty of Science, Ibn Tofail University, Kenitra, Morocco

Amal Rifai
https://orcid.org/0000-0003-2793-3102
Regional Center for the Professions of Education and Training, Morocco

Abdelalim Sadiq
https://orcid.org/0000-0003-1478-8807
Faculty of Science, Ibn Tofail University, Kenitra, Morocco

ABSTRACT

Personalized learning is challenging because students have diverse backgrounds, abilities, needs, and traditional teaching often lacks timely, tailored support. This study introduces an AI tutoring system powered by ChatGPT, designed to provide adaptive, context-aware educational assistance. The system uses conversational interfaces, domain-specific prompts, and learner modeling to adjust dynamically to each student's progress and misconceptions. An experimental study with high school and early university students showed that the system significantly improved

DOI: 10.4018/979-8-3373-8011-7.ch006

learner engagement, comprehension, and efficiency. Users appreciated the personalized explanations and adaptive responses, which boosted their motivation and deeper understanding of the material. These findings demonstrate the potential of AI-powered tutoring systems to enhance personalized education by offering scalable, effective, and engaging learning experiences suitable for diverse learners and contexts. This approach could help overcome limitations of traditional education and support individualized learning .

1. INTRODUCTION

Advances in artificial intelligence (AI) have opened exciting new avenues for transforming educational experiences, particularly through the delivery of personalized learning environments (Zalte, 2023). Unlike traditional classroom settings, where teachers must often manage large groups of students within limited time frames, AI-powered solutions offer the potential to adapt instruction to the unique needs of each learner. Conventional educational models frequently face challenges such as time constraints (Tan & Subramonyam, 2024), a shortage of instructional resources (Uddin & McNeill, 2024), and limited teacher availability (Chen et al., 2024). These challenges make it difficult to address the full range of learning styles, paces, and support needs, often leading to unequal academic outcomes and learner disengagement. To help overcome these barriers, intelligent tutoring systems (ITS) have emerged as powerful, AI-driven tools designed to replicate the benefits of one-on-one tutoring at scale (Figure 1). These systems leverage advanced technologies such as natural language processing, machine learning, and learner modeling to monitor individual progress in real time and provide immediate, targeted feedback (Ni & Cheung, 2023; Lin et al., 2023). By adapting the content, pacing, and level of difficulty according to each learner's responses, intelligent tutoring systems help fill knowledge gaps, reinforce understanding, and build confidence in a personalized manner. Another key advantage of AI tutoring systems is their scalability and accessibility. Unlike traditional models that require physical presence or fixed schedules, AI-powered platforms offer on-demand support that learners can access anytime, anywhere on computers, tablets, or mobile devices. This flexibility enhances student autonomy and engagement, allowing learners to progress at their own pace while receiving consistent, individualized guidance.

Moreover, these AI tutoring systems play a vital role in enabling data-informed instruction by collecting detailed information on student behavior, performance, and learning preferences. This data not only drives the AI system's real-time adaptations but also provides valuable insights for human educators, allowing them to make more informed, targeted interventions tailored to each learner's needs. Overall, the integration of AI into education is facilitating a fundamental shift from traditional, teacher-centered approaches toward a personalized, learner-centric model. Intelligent tutoring systems illustrate how advanced AI technologies can be effectively leveraged to create more inclusive, adaptive, and impactful educational experiences that address the diverse and evolving needs of students in real-world settings. This shift promises to improve engagement, understanding, and academic success across a wide range of learners.

Despite significant progress in the field of AI-powered education, many existing intelligent tutoring platforms continue to face critical limitations, particularly in their ability to offer truly personalized and context-aware support. These systems, while capable of delivering structured guidance and immediate feedback, often fall short when it comes to dynamically adapting to the learner's evolving needs or maintaining sustained, natural, and motivating interactions over time (Fagbohun et al., 2024; Feng et al., 2021). Many rely on rigid, rule-based mechanisms or predefined scripts that limit their responsiveness and reduce their ability to engage learners meaningfully, especially in more open-ended or exploratory learning scenarios. The recent integration of large language models (LLMs), such as OpenAI's ChatGPT, marks a major turning point in AI tutoring. These models possess the ability to understand context, generate human-like responses, and sustain fluid, interactive conversations that closely mimic the dynamics of real-life tutoring. Their advanced natural language capabilities allow for more adaptive, nuanced, and empathetic dialogue, which can significantly enhance learner engagement and comprehension. By processing open-ended questions, detecting confusion, and offering clarifications in real time, LLMs offer a level of interactivity previously unattainable in traditional tutoring systems.

However, their application in educational contexts also introduces new challenges and responsibilities. Key among them is the need to ensure pedagogical alignment designing interactions that are not only technically accurate but also educationally effective and aligned with learning objectives. Additionally, questions around ethical use arise, including issues of bias in language generation, student data privacy, and the transparency of AI decisions. There is also an urgent need to develop evaluation frameworks that can assess the long-term impact of these systems on diverse learner populations, ensuring they support rather than hinder equitable learning outcomes. In this evolving landscape, thoughtful system design, informed by educational theory and grounded in empirical research, will be essential to fully realize the potential of LLM-powered tutoring platforms while addressing the complex ethical, pedagogical, and technical considerations they entail (Kasneci et al., 2023).

Figure 1. Advantages of AI tutoring system

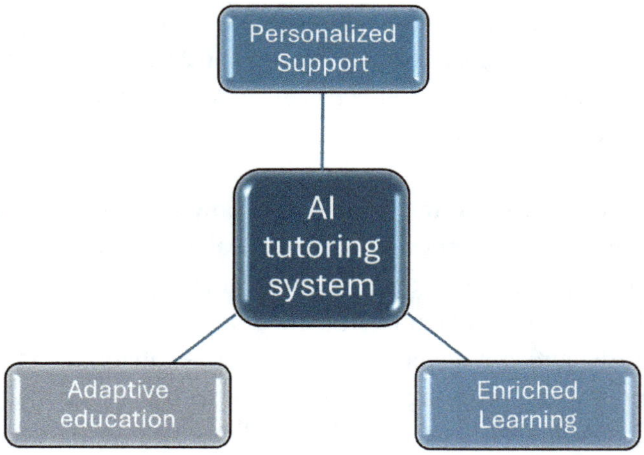

This leads to the central question: How can an AI tutoring system effectively harness advanced language models to deliver personalized, adaptive, and engaging learning experiences that enhance understanding and academic performance? What design principles and evaluation criteria are essential to ensure the system addresses the diverse needs of learners? To explore these issues, this article presents the development and assessment of a personalized AI tutoring system based on ChatGPT. The system integrates conversational interfaces, domain-specific prompt generation, and learner modeling to create a dynamic, interactive environment that adapts instruction to individual learner profiles. By combining advanced natural language processing with evidence-based pedagogical strategies, the platform aims to enhance both learning outcomes and student engagement. This paper details the system's architecture, outlines the experimental methodology involving students from varied backgrounds, and presents results demonstrating measurable improvements in learner performance and satisfaction. The findings offer valuable insights into the potential of AI-driven tutoring systems to support scalable, inclusive, and adaptive learning. This work contributes to the broader field of AI in education by showcasing a practical, research-informed approach to implementing intelligent tutoring systems that respond to the complexities of real-world learning environments.

This study explores the effectiveness of a personalized AI tutoring system powered by ChatGPT in improving learner engagement, conceptual understanding, and academic performance among students with diverse educational backgrounds. As traditional educational settings often struggle to meet individual learning needs due to time, resource, and instructor limitations, this research investigates how adaptive, real-time AI support can fill these gaps and deliver a more tailored learning experience. The system integrates key components including learner modeling, domain-specific prompt generation, and natural language-based conversational interfaces. Learner modeling tracks individual progress, preferences, and knowledge gaps to personalize instruction. Domain-specific prompts guide ChatGPT in producing accurate, relevant, and curriculum-aligned responses. Meanwhile, the conversational interface simulates human-like dialogue to maintain learner motivation and engagement through intuitive interaction. One of the primary objectives is to assess how effectively the system adapts in real time to different student profiles ranging in age, skill level, and learning style and whether it can promote deeper understanding across various subjects. In addition to evaluating student performance before and after system use, the study analyzes user satisfaction, engagement levels, and perceptions of personalization.

Furthermore, the research considers important pedagogical and design principles that contribute to the success of AI tutoring. These include clarity and quality of AI-generated feedback, the emotional tone of responses, ease of use, and the alignment of instructional strategies with educational goals. Overall, this study not only measures the system's impact on learning outcomes but also provides insight into how large language models like ChatGPT can be integrated into education effectively and ethically. It contributes to the growing body of research on AI in education and highlights the potential for scalable, inclusive tutoring solutions that respond flexibly to learners' evolving needs.

2. LITERATURE REVIEW

Artificial intelligence (AI) has increasingly shaped the landscape of education by enabling more personalized, adaptive, and data-driven learning environments (Rahiman & Kodikal, 2024). Early intelligent tutoring systems (ITS) were primarily rule-based, guiding learners through predefined instructional pathways with structured tasks and responses (Zakaria et al., 2025). These systems demonstrated success in delivering tailored feedback and individualized support (Maity & Deroy, 2024), helping learners progress at their own pace. However, their effectiveness was constrained by several limitations, particularly their lack of flexibility and inability to handle open-ended, natural language inputs from students (Rodrigues et al., 2024). As a result, interactions often felt mechanical and failed to engage learners in deeper, meaningful dialogue. The emergence of more advanced AI technologies, particularly large language models, has opened new opportunities to overcome these limitations by enabling systems to interpret nuanced learner input, generate human-like responses, and support more natural, context-aware educational interactions.

The emergence of natural language processing (NLP) marked a major milestone in the development of educational technologies by enabling conversational agents to interact with learners through human-like dialogue (Bode & Satpute, 2024). This capability opened the door to more interactive and responsive digital learning experiences. Unlike static instructional tools, NLP-based systems introduced a new mode of communication where learners could pose questions, seek clarification, and engage in back-and-forth exchanges. However, the first generation of educational chatbots built on NLP technologies were limited in scope and flexibility. These early systems relied heavily on predefined scripts and rule-based responses, restricting their ability to engage with learners in open-ended or personalized ways (Davar et al., 2025). As a result, their application was often confined to narrow subject areas with structured content, and they struggled to maintain learner interest or respond effectively to diverse and unpredictable student input. This rigidity significantly limited their educational value, especially for students who required tailored feedback or had non-linear learning paths. The lack of personalization and contextual adaptation led to shallow interactions and minimal learning gains, ultimately reducing student motivation and long-term engagement (Merelo et al., 2024).

These shortcomings highlighted the urgent need for more sophisticated AI systems capable of delivering adaptive, context-aware support across a range of learning scenarios. Unlike scripted bots, modern AI-based tutors must be able to understand intent, manage dialogue context, and adjust responses based on each learner's progress, misconceptions, and preferences. This evolution paved the way for the integration of large language models (LLMs), which offer the flexibility and intelligence required to provide personalized, dynamic, and engaging learning support. As educational technology advances, the goal is not only to simulate human conversation but to replicate the pedagogical depth and empathy of a skilled tutor, thereby enriching the overall learning experience.

Recent advancements in large-scale pretrained language models (Sagar, Taparia, & Senanayake, 2024), such as OpenAI's GPT series (Huang et al., 2024), have significantly transformed the landscape of conversational AI. These models demonstrate remarkable abilities to generate coherent (Bhattacharya et al., 2024), context-aware (Chen et al., 2024), and human-like responses (Tjuatja et al., 2024), which enable the creation of more dynamic, interactive, and personalized tutoring experiences (Shahri et al., 2024; Bernal, 2024). Research shows that GPT-like systems can offer adaptive hints (Hossain et al., 2025), scaffold complex learning tasks (Zhang et al., 2024), and provide formative feedback tailored to the individual needs of learners (Ningsih & Akhyar, 2024) (see Figure 2). Despite these promising capabilities, challenges remain in ensuring that AI-generated content consistently aligns with specific educational objectives (Kuzminykh et al., 2024), maintains factual accuracy (Steinert et al., 2024), and effectively sustains learner engagement and motivation over extended periods (Huesca et al., 2025). Addressing these issues is essential for the successful integration of such models in educational settings.

Figure 2. Advantages of OpenAI's GPT

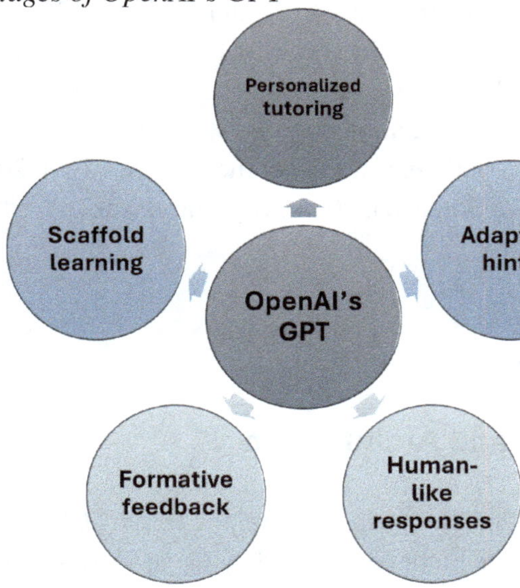

Personalization is essential for effective tutoring (Naz & Robertson, 2024). Learner modeling techniques track students' knowledge, misconceptions, and preferences to tailor instruction accordingly (Park et al., 2024; Idowu, 2024; Russo et al., 2024). Traditional intelligent tutoring systems (ITS) have commonly employed models like Bayesian knowledge tracing to guide adaptations (Tang et al., 2024). However, integrating these learner models with conversational AI is an emerging field that offers significant potential for creating more responsive, context-aware tutoring systems. This integration could lead to highly personalized learning experiences that better address individual student needs (Sun et al., 2024).

Learner engagement and motivation are crucial for successful AI tutoring (Frankford et al., 2024). Research shows that conversational interfaces simulating human tutors can boost motivation and reduce cognitive load (Chen & Chang, 2024). However, balancing AI autonomy with transparency is essential to foster learner trust and acceptance (Buijsman, 2024; Cheong, 2024). Ensuring learners understand how the AI supports their learning helps maintain engagement and encourages positive educational outcomes.

While much research has focused on technical advancements in AI tutoring systems (Rashid, Duong-Trung, & Pinkwart, 2024; Denny et al., 2024), there remains a notable gap in rigorous empirical evaluation within authentic educational settings (Basri, 2024). This study seeks to address that gap by designing a personalized AI tutoring system powered by ChatGPT and assessing its effectiveness across students from diverse academic levels. By integrating advanced natural language generation techniques (Challagundla & Challagundla, 2024), domain-specific prompt engineering (Ashcroft & Whitaker, 2024), and learner modeling strategies (Archana & Jeevaraj, 2024), the system adapts dynamically to individual learner needs. The primary goal is to demonstrate how AI-driven personalized tutoring can significantly enhance both learning outcomes (Jui & Rivas, 2024) and student engagement (Mahmoud & Sørensen, 2024), offering a scalable, adaptable solution for modern education.

3. METHODOLOGY

3.1 System Design and Architecture

This study developed an AI tutoring system powered by ChatGPT, a large-scale transformer-based language model developed by OpenAI, designed to deliver personalized educational support tailored to individual learners. The system simulates one-on-one tutoring by allowing students to engage with ChatGPT through a natural language conversational interface, making interactions feel intuitive and human-like. Its architecture integrates ChatGPT's API with a custom-built front-end that efficiently manages dialogue flow, retains contextual information across multiple exchanges, and handles a wide variety of user inputs effectively. This sophisticated design enables the system to create an adaptive and interactive learning environment, dynamically adjusting its responses based on each learner's unique progress, preferences, and challenges. By providing tailored guidance and timely feedback, the platform fosters deeper conceptual understanding, sustained engagement, and improved learning outcomes, demonstrating the potential of advanced AI technologies to transform personalized education.

The tutoring system supports multiple subjects, including mathematics, science, and language arts, by providing ChatGPT with domain-specific context and tailored instructional strategies to ensure relevant and accurate guidance. It personalizes learning by tracking learner inputs, detecting misconceptions, and dynamically adjusting the difficulty level and response style to suit individual needs. Additionally, a built-in feedback mechanism allows students to rate the system's replies, facilitating ongoing improvements and effective monitoring. This approach creates a responsive, customized tutoring experience that adapts across diverse subjects, fostering deeper understanding and sustained learner engagement.

Figure 3. Architecture of the AI Tutoring System

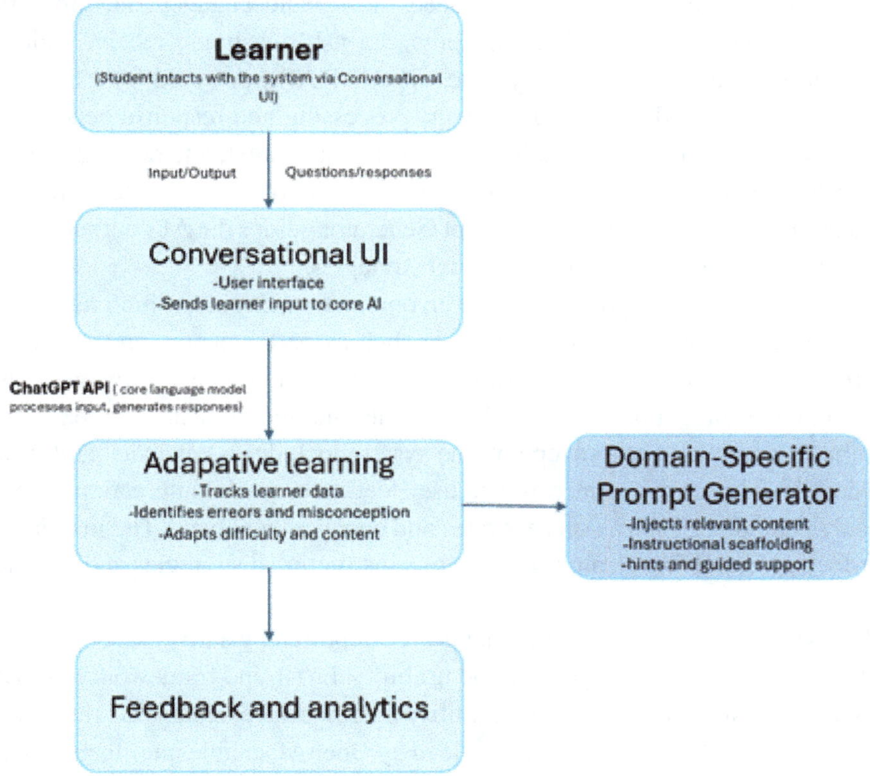

3.2 Key Components

The AI tutoring system is constructed on a modular architecture consisting of interconnected components that work together to deliver a seamless, personalized, and adaptive learning experience. These components efficiently manage user interactions, generate tailored content, and continuously monitor learner performance. This design enables the system to respond dynamically and effectively to a wide range of learner needs in real time, creating an engaging and supportive educational environment. By adapting to individual progress and preferences, the system ensures a highly responsive and customized tutoring experience for each student.

At the heart of the system is the Conversational User Interface (UI), which facilitates intuitive and natural interactions between the learner and the AI. This front-end component is designed for accessibility and engagement, providing a user-friendly environment where students can ask questions, receive guidance, and explore concepts interactively. The ChatGPT API, powered by a large-scale language model, handles natural language processing and response generation. It interprets learner queries, maintains conversational context, and delivers coherent, human-like responses that simulate real tutoring experiences. To ensure relevance and accuracy, a Domain-Specific Prompt Generator guides the AI's output, aligning it with curriculum goals and instructional strategies.

Another critical component is the Personalization Engine, which uses learner modeling techniques to analyze user data such as performance, preferences, and progress. This engine adjusts the difficulty, tone, and content of responses to fit individual learning paths, ensuring that each learner receives customized support. To support continuous improvement, the system includes a Feedback and Analytics Module. This component captures user feedback, tracks interaction data, and measures outcomes such as success rates and engagement levels. The insights generated are essential for refining the system's instructional strategies and enhancing its responsiveness.

The AI tutoring system's components are supported by a diverse set of technologies that ensure both functionality and usability. Front-end frameworks like React and Vue.js deliver a responsive and intuitive user interface, enhancing the learner's experience. AI APIs, such as those provided by OpenAI, enable intelligent, context-aware conversational capabilities. Machine learning libraries like TensorFlow and Scikit-learn underpin the system's adaptive features by analyzing learner data and personalizing content. Meanwhile, analytics platforms offer real-time dashboards that help educators and developers monitor system performance, track student progress, and implement data-driven improvements to continually enhance the tutoring process.

Table 1 summarizes the key components of the AI tutoring system, outlining their functions and the technologies that support them. This multidisciplinary framework highlights the system's complexity and innovation, demonstrating how the integration of AI, educational theory, and software engineering produces scalable, effective learning solutions. These solutions are designed to adapt flexibly to diverse learner needs, ensuring personalized and impactful educational experiences across various contexts.

Table 1. Key Components, Functions, and Supporting Technologies

Component	Description	Role/Function	Technology
Conversational UI (Front-End)	User interface for interaction	Collects input and displays responses- Maintains dialogue flow and context	HTML/CSS, JavaScript, React, Vue. js, Flutter
ChatGPT API	Core language model from OpenAI	Processes inputs and generates responses- Accessed via OpenAI's API	OpenAI GPT API (ChatGPT), Python, Node.js
Domain-Specific Prompt Generator	Module for generating subject-specific prompts	- Injects relevant content and instructional scaffolding- Provides hints and guided support	Python, Prompt engineering scripts, Templates
Adaptive learning	Tracks individual learner data	- Identifies errors/misconceptions- Adapts difficulty, tone, and responses	Python, User profiling database, Machine Learning
Feedback & Analytics	System for collecting and analyzing user feedback	- Allows user ratings- Supports performance tracking and iterative system improvements	Firebase/Google Analytics, Python, Dashboards

3.3 Importance

Understanding the importance of each core component in the AI tutoring system is essential to appreciating how it delivers effective, personalized learning experiences. Each element contributes to the system's overall functionality, from facilitating smooth user interactions to ensuring the delivery of relevant, domain-specific content. Components also adapt to individual learner needs by tracking progress and misconceptions, allowing for tailored instruction. Additionally, continuous feedback mechanisms enable ongoing system improvement, enhancing both accuracy and engagement. This holistic integration of components ensures the tutoring platform remains responsive, adaptive, and effective across diverse educational contexts. The following overview highlights why each component is critical to the success of the AI tutoring system and its ability to meet learner needs dynamically and efficiently.

Table 2. Role and Importance of Each Component

Component	Importance
Conversational UI (Front-End)	Provides an intuitive and user-friendly interface that enables natural, human-like interactions. It engages learners effectively and supports clear, seamless communication throughout tutoring sessions.
ChatGPT API	Serves as the core engine powering intelligent, context-aware responses. It allows the system to generate dynamic, personalized tutoring by understanding learner input and maintaining relevant dialogue.
Domain-Specific Prompt Generator	Ensures that the AI's responses are accurate, relevant, and aligned with specific subject matter and learning objectives. It tailors prompts to guide the AI toward instructional content suited to each domain.
Personalization Engine	Analyzes learner data such as progress, misconceptions, and preferences to adapt the difficulty, style, and tone of instruction. This enables a customized learning experience that meets individual needs.
Feedback & Analytics	Collects continuous learner feedback and performance data, enabling iterative improvements to the system. It also tracks learner progress and engagement to inform adaptive strategies and measure overall effectiveness.

4. EXPERIMENTATION

4.1 Introduction

Experimentation is a critical phase in assessing the effectiveness and practical relevance of the developed intelligent tutoring system. During this stage, the system is tested within real or simulated educational settings to evaluate its overall performance, impact on learner outcomes, and user satisfaction. Controlled trials and direct user interactions provide valuable data on how well the system adapts to diverse learning styles and needs, supporting personalized instruction. This process helps identify both strengths and weaknesses, highlighting areas that require refinement or enhancement. The insights gained are vital for optimizing the system's design, functionality, and responsiveness to ensure alignment with educational objectives. By validating the platform's practical utility, experimentation lays a solid foundation for wider deployment. Moreover, it informs future development efforts aimed at maximizing the system's positive impact on learner engagement, understanding, and academic achievement across diverse educational contexts:

- Validate the system's ability to provide personalized tutoring that adapts to each learner's unique needs, delivering tailored support that enhances comprehension and fosters effective, individualized learning experiences.

- Assess the quality of learner-system interactions by evaluating the relevance, accuracy, and clarity of ChatGPT-generated responses, ensuring tutoring experiences are meaningful, context-aware, and effectively support individual learner needs.
- Measure the system's impact on educational progress by evaluating improvements in knowledge acquisition and skill development, demonstrating how personalized tutoring contributes to enhanced learning outcomes and overall academic growth.
- Collect detailed user feedback through surveys and analytics to identify improvement areas. This input guides future updates, enhancing the system's usability, personalization, and effectiveness, ultimately boosting learner satisfaction and ensuring the tutoring platform better meets diverse educational needs.

4.2. Sample Used

The experiment was conducted with a pilot group of 50 students, strategically selected to reflect a diverse range of learner profiles. This group included high school students from grades 10 to 12 as well as first-year university students, ensuring a broad spectrum of academic backgrounds and cognitive development stages. The selection aimed to include participants with varying levels of subject mastery, learning styles, and educational needs to test the AI tutoring system's adaptability and personalization capabilities across different contexts. Some learners required foundational support, while others sought enrichment or clarification on more advanced concepts. This diversity allowed for a more comprehensive and realistic evaluation of the system's performance and its ability to deliver relevant, context-aware, and individualized support. By including such a wide range of students, the study was able to assess how effectively the system responds to differences in learner profiles, and whether it can serve as a scalable solution for personalized education.

Key steps include:

- Participant selection: A diverse panel of participants was carefully chosen to ensure a comprehensive evaluation of the AI tutoring system across varied learner characteristics. Selection criteria included a broad range of ages, academic levels from high school through early university and different learning profiles, such as varying degrees of prior knowledge, learning styles, and motivational factors. This diversity helps capture the system's adaptability and effectiveness in meeting the unique needs of different student populations, providing insights into its potential for inclusive and personalized education.
- Definition of learning scenarios:

The learning scenarios were carefully designed to align with specific educational objectives, ensuring that all exercises and activities support targeted knowledge and skill development. These scenarios encompass a wide range of topics relevant to the subject domains, incorporating varied difficulty levels to address the needs of learners at different stages of mastery. By including progressively challenging tasks and diverse question types, the scenarios aim to promote deep understanding, critical thinking, and practical application. This structured approach ensures that the tutoring system can effectively adapt instruction and provide meaningful feedback tailored to each learner's progress.

- System usage: Participants engaged with the AI tutoring system via its conversational interface, designed to simulate natural, one-on-one tutoring sessions. Throughout the interaction, learners received personalized instruction tailored to their individual progress, preferences, and learning needs. The system dynamically adapted its responses and guidance based on real-time input, providing explanations, hints, and feedback relevant to each learner's current understanding. This interactive environment encouraged active participation, allowing students to ask questions, clarify doubts, and explore concepts at their own pace, fostering a more engaging and effective learning experience.
- Data collection: The study systematically tracked all participant interactions with the AI tutoring system, including recorded responses, success rates on exercises, and the time spent on each activity. In addition to quantitative metrics, qualitative data were gathered through surveys and interviews to capture learners' perceptions, satisfaction, and experiences. This comprehensive data collection approach allowed for a detailed analysis of both the system's performance and its impact on learner engagement and understanding, providing valuable insights to inform future improvements and validate the tutoring platform's effectiveness.

4.3. Results and Statistics

The results clearly demonstrate a significant improvement in students' academic performance after using the AI tutoring system, as summarized in Table 3 below. Notably, the average success rate on exercises increased substantially, indicating that learners were better able to grasp and apply key concepts. Additionally, the time spent per exercise decreased, reflecting enhanced efficiency and deeper understanding facilitated by the system's adaptive guidance. User satisfaction scores were consistently high, with many students praising the ease of use and the relevance of the AI-generated responses. Furthermore, post-test assessments revealed notable gains in comprehension, with approximately 70% of participants showing marked progress in understanding core topics. These findings collectively suggest that the personalized and responsive nature of the tutoring system effectively supports diverse learners, improving both engagement and learning outcomes. The data provides strong evidence for the potential of AI-driven tutoring platforms to enhance educational experiences in real-world settings.

Table 3. Statistics of students' performance.

Metric	Result	Interpretation
Average Success Rate on Exercises	Before: 62% After: 81%	Significant improvement in exercise success rate shows the system's effectiveness in enhancing learner mastery and skills.
Time Spent per Exercise	Decreased by 15%	Reduced time per exercise suggests better understanding and increased efficiency, likely due to clearer explanations.
User Satisfaction Rate (1–5 scale)	Average score: 4.3 Positive feedback on ease of use and response quality	High satisfaction indicates the platform is user-friendly and delivers helpful, relevant responses to learners.
Understanding of Key Concepts	Approximately 70% of participants showed notable progress in post-tests	Demonstrates that the tutoring system effectively improves comprehension of essential topics and concepts.
System Adaptability	Over 85% of students felt explanations matched their individual level and learning needs	Highlights the system's ability to personalize instruction and adjust explanations to suit diverse learner profiles.

5. DISCUSSION AND PERSPECTIVES

The experimental results clearly demonstrate that the AI tutoring system significantly enhances learner performance, with success rates increasing impressively from 62% before using the system to 81% after its implementation. This substantial improvement underscores the effectiveness of personalized tutoring, where the system tailors feedback and instructional content to the unique needs of each student. By providing adaptive, context-aware support, the tutoring platform helps learners better understand challenging concepts and overcome difficulties more efficiently. Moreover, the system's ability to adjust the difficulty and style of responses based on individual progress ensures that students remain engaged and motivated throughout their learning journey. These findings highlight the potential of AI-driven tutoring solutions to deliver targeted assistance that promotes deeper comprehension and skill development, ultimately contributing to improved academic outcomes and more inclusive, accessible education.

The 15% reduction in time spent per exercise indicates that learners are able to grasp concepts more efficiently when using the AI tutoring system. This improvement suggests that immediate, relevant, and adaptive support helps students process information faster and complete tasks with greater confidence. By providing timely hints and explanations tailored to each learner's current level, the system reduces unnecessary trial-and-error and cognitive overload, allowing students to focus on understanding rather than struggling through problems. High user satisfaction, reflected by an average rating of 4.3 out of 5, further underscores the system's positive reception among learners. Many participants praised the intuitive interface, the clarity of responses, and the personalized nature of the tutoring sessions. This favorable feedback highlights the importance of user experience in educational technology, demonstrating that effective learning tools must be both functional and engaging to sustain motivation and participation. Significantly, about 70% of participants exhibited marked improvements in their conceptual understanding, as shown through post-test assessments. This finding confirms that the AI tutoring system does more than just improve short-term performance; it facilitates deeper learning and long-lasting comprehension of core topics. The system's ability to scaffold knowledge and adapt explanations to individual learner profiles helps bridge gaps in understanding and reinforces critical thinking skills. Moreover, over 85% of learners felt that the explanations and guidance provided by the system matched their specific needs, validating the effectiveness of the personalization engine. This high level of alignment suggests that the system's learner modeling and adaptive algorithms are successfully tailoring instruction to accommodate diverse learning styles, prior knowledge, and pacing preferences. Collectively, these results demonstrate that the AI tutoring system not only improves academic outcomes but also creates an inclusive and responsive learning environment that supports varied learner profiles and fosters meaningful educational growth.

Despite the strong positive outcomes observed in the experimental phase, some users noted occasional issues with the clarity, accuracy, or depth of the AI-generated explanations. While the majority of learners found the system's responses helpful and appropriately tailored, a few reported that certain answers lacked specificity or did not fully address their questions, particularly in more advanced or nuanced topics. These instances, though limited, underscore the need for refining prompt engineering and enhancing the system's contextual understanding. Such feedback is crucial for continuous improvement and helps identify areas where the AI may benefit from further guidance or content structuring to ensure consistently high-quality support.

In response to these observations, future development efforts will focus on three key areas. First, enhancing content accuracy will be a priority. This involves refining domain-specific prompt templates and incorporating expert-reviewed instructional strategies to ensure that responses remain pedagogically sound and contextually appropriate across subjects and complexity levels.

Second, expanding the learner modeling component will play a vital role in delivering even more personalized experiences. By integrating more detailed user data such as preferred learning styles, prior achievements, and engagement patterns the system can better predict learner needs and adjust both the level and form of instruction accordingly.

Third, improving analytics and reporting tools for educators will help bridge the gap between automated tutoring and human oversight. Advanced dashboards and data visualizations will allow teachers to track student progress, identify areas of struggle, and intervene when necessary. This added transparency supports a blended learning approach, where AI complements rather than replaces human instruction.

Finally, these enhancements aim to make the AI tutoring system not only more accurate and adaptive but also more usable for both learners and educators. The ultimate goal is to ensure that the platform evolves into a reliable, inclusive, and scalable solution capable of supporting diverse learning needs in real-world educational environments.

CONCLUSION

This study underscores the substantial potential of an AI-powered tutoring system to provide personalized, adaptive, and highly effective learning experiences. By combining advanced natural language processing through large language models with domain-specific prompt generation and a robust learner personalization engine, the system dynamically adjusted its responses based on each learner's unique progress, challenges, and preferences. This intelligent responsiveness enabled the delivery of more relevant explanations, timely support, and engaging interactions, fostering deeper conceptual understanding and improved motivation among learners. The experimental results revealed significant gains in academic performance, with measurable improvements in success rates, faster task completion times, and stronger comprehension of key concepts. Learners not only demonstrated enhanced efficiency but also expressed high levels of satisfaction with the system's ease of use, clarity of responses, and ability to adapt instruction to their individual needs. These findings validate the effectiveness of AI-driven tutoring as a complementary approach to traditional instruction, particularly in addressing the limitations of one-size-fits-all educational models. Furthermore, the system's ability to personalize instruction in real time demonstrates its promise as a scalable and inclusive solution capable of supporting diverse learners across various academic levels and subject areas. Its flexible architecture allows for integration into different learning environments, whether for supplemental tutoring, homework assistance, or autonomous study. Looking ahead, future development will focus on enhancing the system's adaptability by incorporating richer learner data, including emotional indicators, engagement trends, and long-term progress tracking. Strengthening feedback mechanisms, both from users and educators, will also be crucial in refining the AI's instructional strategies and improving learning outcomes. Additionally, expanding analytics tools for educators can help bridge the gap between automated tutoring and guided teaching, promoting more data-informed interventions. This study contributes to the growing body of research supporting the integration of AI in education. It demonstrates that thoughtfully designed AI tutoring systems can effectively personalize learning, increase academic success, and create more equitable access to quality education.

Future directions for the AI-powered tutoring system focus on broadening its capabilities to create a more inclusive, engaging, and effective learning experience. One key area of development involves expanding subject coverage beyond the initial domains of mathematics, science, and language arts. By including additional subjects such as history, programming, and foreign languages, the system can cater to a wider range of learners and academic needs.

Another major enhancement involves incorporating multimodal inputs such as speech, handwriting, and images to create richer, more natural interactions. Enabling voice-based conversations or allowing learners to upload handwritten work or visual content will make the system more accessible and interactive, particularly for younger students or those with diverse learning preferences. Emotional and motivational modeling is also a promising direction. By detecting learner frustration, confidence, or disengagement through sentiment analysis or behavioral patterns, the system could adjust its responses to provide encouragement, simplify explanations, or vary instructional strategies to maintain motivation and support emotional well-being. In addition, developing real-time analytics dashboards for educators will enable better tracking of student progress, engagement, and learning challenges. These tools can help teachers identify at-risk learners, adjust instruction accordingly, and design more personalized interventions. Such educator-facing features would support a more collaborative learning ecosystem, where AI and human instruction work hand in hand to optimize educational outcomes. Altogether, these future enhancements aim to refine the system's responsiveness, inclusivity, and pedagogical impact across diverse educational contexts.

REFERENCES

Archana, R., & Jeevaraj, P. E. (2024). Deep learning models for digital image processing: A review. *Artificial Intelligence Review*, *57*(1), 11. DOI: 10.1007/s10462-023-10631-z

Ashcroft, C., & Whitaker, K. (2024). Evaluation of domain-specific prompt engineering attacks on large language models. *ESS Open Arch. Eprints, 362*, 36267312. DOI: DOI: 10.22541/au.172252453.36267312/v1

Basri, W. S. (2024). Effectiveness of AI-powered Tutoring Systems in Enhancing Learning Outcomes. [EJER]. *Eurasian Journal of Educational Research*, (110). Advance online publication. DOI: 10.14689/ejer.2024.110.003

Bernal, M. E. (2024). Revolutionizing eLearning assessments: The role of GPT in crafting dynamic content and feedback. *Journal of Artificial Intelligence and Technology*, *4*(3), 188–199. https://orcid.org/0009-0009-7642-8090

Bhattacharya, P., Prasad, V. K., Verma, A., Gupta, D., Sapsomboon, A., Viriyasitavat, W., & Dhiman, G. (2024). Demystifying ChatGPT: An in-depth survey of OpenAI's robust large language models. *Archives of Computational Methods in Engineering*, *31*(8), 1–44. DOI: 10.1007/s11831-024-10115-5

Bode, S. P., & Satpute, R. S. (2024, November). Natural Language Processing in Education System. In *2024 2nd DMIHER International Conference on Artificial Intelligence in Healthcare, Education and Industry (IDICAIEI)* (pp. 1-5). IEEE. **DOI:** DOI: 10.1109/IDICAIEI61867.2024.10842725

Buijsman, S. (2024). Transparency for AI systems: A value-based approach. *Ethics and Information Technology*, *26*(2), 34. DOI: 10.1007/s10676-024-09770-w

Challagundla, B. C., & Challagundla, S. (2024). Dynamic Adaptation and Synergistic Integration of Genetic Algorithms and Deep Learning in Advanced Natural Language Processing. DOI: DOI: 10.21203/rs.3.rs-4300654/v1

Chen, C. H., & Chang, C. L. (2024). Effectiveness of AI-assisted game-based learning on science learning outcomes, intrinsic motivation, cognitive load, and learning behavior. *Education and Information Technologies*, *29*(14), 18621–18642. DOI: 10.1007/s10639-024-12553-x

Chen, Y. C., Jordan, M., Park, J., & Starrett, E. (2024). Navigating student uncertainty for productive struggle: Establishing the importance for and distinguishing types, sources, and desirability of scientific uncertainties. *Science Education*, *108*(4), 1099–1133. DOI: 10.1002/sce.21864

Chen, Z., Huang, H., Hrinchuk, O., Puvvada, K. C., Koluguri, N. R., Żelasko, P., . . . Ginsburg, B. (2024, December). Bestow: Efficient and streamable speech language model with the best of two worlds in gpt and t5. In *2024 IEEE Spoken Language Technology Workshop (SLT)* (pp. 147-154). IEEE. DOI: DOI: 10.1109/SLT61566.2024.10832146

Cheong, B. C. (2024). Transparency and accountability in AI systems: Safeguarding wellbeing in the age of algorithmic decision-making. *Frontiers in Human Dynamics*, *6*, 1421273. DOI: 10.3389/fhumd.2024.1421273

Davar, N. F., Dewan, M. A. A., & Zhang, X. (2025). AI chatbots in education: Challenges and opportunities. *Information (Basel)*, *16*(3), 235. DOI: 10.3390/info16030235

Denny, P., Gulwani, S., Heffernan, N. T., Käser, T., Moore, S., Rafferty, A. N., & Singla, A. (2024). Generative AI for education (GAIED): Advances, opportunities, and challenges. *arXiv preprint arXiv:2402.01580.* /arXiv.2402.01580DOI: 10.48550

Fagbohun, O., Iduwe, N. P., Abdullahi, M., Ifaturoti, A., & Nwanna, O. M. (2024). Beyond traditional assessment: Exploring the impact of large language models on grading practices. *Journal of Artificial Intelligence. Machine Learning and Data Science*, *2*(1), 1–8. DOI: 10. 51219/ JAIMLD/19fagbohun-oluwole/19

Feng, S., Magana, A. J., & Kao, D. (2021, October). *A systematic review of literature on the effectiveness of intelligent tutoring systems in STEM. In 2021 IEEE frontiers in education conference (fie).* IEEE., DOI: 10.1109/FIE49875.2021.9637240

Frankford, E., Sauerwein, C., Bassner, P., Krusche, S., & Breu, R. (2024, April). Ai-tutoring in software engineering education. In *Proceedings of the 46th International Conference on Software Engineering: Software Engineering Education and Training* (pp. 309-319). https://doi.org/DOI: 10.1145/3639474.3640061

Hossain, I., Puppala, S., Alam, M. J., & Talukder, S. (2025). EVOLVE: Predicting user evolution and network dynamics in social media using fine-tuned GPT-like model. In *International Conference on Advances in Social Networks Analysis and Mining* (pp. 379-395). Springer, Cham. DOI: 10.1007/978-3-031-85386-9_27

Huang, D., Yan, C., Li, Q., & Peng, X. (2024). From large language models to large multimodal models: A literature review. *Applied Sciences (Basel, Switzerland)*, *14*(12), 5068. DOI: 10.3390/app14125068

Huesca, G., Elizondo-García, M. E., Aguayo-González, R., Aguayo-Hernández, C. H., González-Buenrostro, T., & Verdugo-Jasso, Y. A. (2025). Evaluating the Potential of Generative Artificial Intelligence to Innovate Feedback Processes. *Education Sciences, 15*(4), 505. DOI: 10.3390/educsci15040505

Idowu, E. (2024). Personalized Learning: Tailoring Instruction to Individual Student Needs. *Preprints*. DOI: 10.20944/preprints202411.0863.v1

Jui, T. D., & Rivas, P. (2024). Fairness issues, current approaches, and challenges in machine learning models. *International Journal of Machine Learning and Cybernetics, 15*(8), 3095–3125. DOI: 10.1007/s13042-023-02083-2

Kasneci, E., Seßler, K., Küchemann, S., Bannert, M., Dementieva, D., Fischer, F., Gasser, U., Groh, G., Günnemann, S., Hüllermeier, E., Krusche, S., Kutyniok, G., Michaeli, T., Nerdel, C., Pfeffer, J., Poquet, O., Sailer, M., Schmidt, A., Seidel, T., & Kasneci, G. (2023). ChatGPT for good? On opportunities and challenges of large language models for education. *Learning and Individual Differences, 103*, 102274. DOI: 10.1016/j.lindif.2023.102274

Kuzminykh, I., Nawaz, T., Shenzhang, S., Ghita, B., Raphael, J., & Xiao, H. (2024). Personalised Feedback Framework for Online Education Programmes Using Generative AI. *arXiv preprint arXiv:2410.11904*. /arXiv.2410.11904DOI: 10.48550

Lin, C. C., Huang, A. Y., & Lu, O. H. (2023). Artificial intelligence in intelligent tutoring systems toward sustainable education: A systematic review. *Smart Learning Environments, 10*(1), 41. DOI: 10.1186/s40561-023-00260-y

Mahmoud, C. F., & Sørensen, J. T. (2024). Artificial Intelligence in Personalized Learning with a Focus on Current Developments and Future Prospects. *Research and Advances in Education, 3*(8), 25–31. DOI: 10.56397/RAE.2024.08.04

Maity, S., & Deroy, A. (2024). Generative ai and its impact on personalized intelligent tutoring systems. *arXiv preprint arXiv:2410.10650*. https://doi.org//arXiv .2410.10650DOI: 10.48550

Merelo, J. J., Castillo, P. A., Mora, A. M., Barranco, F., Abbas, N., Guillén, A., & Tsivitanidou, O. (2024). Chatbots and messaging platforms in the classroom: An analysis from the teacher's perspective. *Education and Information Technologies, 29*(2), 1903–1938. DOI: 10.1007/s10639-023-11703-x PMID: 37361787

Naz, I., & Robertson, R. (2024). Exploring the feasibility and efficacy of ChatGPT3 for personalized feedback in teaching. *Electronic Journal of e-Learning, 22*(2), 98–111. DOI: 10.34190/ejel.22.2.3345

Ni, A., & Cheung, A. (2023). Understanding secondary students' continuance intention to adopt AI-powered intelligent tutoring system for English learning. *Education and Information Technologies, 28*(3), 3191–3216. DOI: 10.1007/s10639-022-11305-z PMID: 36119127

Ningsih, W., & Akhyar, Y. The Potential of GPT in Education: Opportunities for Students' Feedback. *Buletin Poltanesa, 25*(1), 568949. DOI: 10.51967/tanesa.v25i1.3043

Park, M., Kim, S., Lee, S., Kwon, S., & Kim, K. (2024, May). Empowering personalized learning through a conversation-based tutoring system with student modeling. In *Extended Abstracts of the CHI Conference on Human Factors in Computing Systems* (pp. 1-10). DOI: 10.1145/3613905.3651122

Rahiman, H. U., & Kodikal, R. (2024). Revolutionizing education: Artificial intelligence empowered learning in higher education. *Cogent Education, 11*(1), 2293431.
Rahiman, H. U., & Kodikal, R. (2024). Revolutionizing education: Artificial intelligence empowered learning in higher education. *Cogent Education, 11*(1), 2293431.
DOI: 10.1080/2331186X.2023.2293431

Rashid, S. F., Duong-Trung, N., & Pinkwart, N. (2024). Generative AI in education: technical foundations, applications, and challenges. DOI: DOI: 10.5772/intechopen.1005402

Rodrigues, L., Pereira, F. D., Marinho, M., Macario, V., Bittencourt, I. I., Isotani, S., Dermeval, D., & Mello, R. (2024). Mathematics intelligent tutoring systems with handwritten input: A scoping review. *Education and Information Technologies, 29*(9), 11183–11209. DOI: 10.1007/s10639-023-12245-y

Russo, J. A., Roche, A., Russo, T., & Kalogeropoulos, P. (2024). Examining primary school educators' preferences for using digital versus non-digital games to support mathematics instruction. *International Journal of Mathematical Education in Science and Technology*, 1–26. DOI: 10.1080/0020739X.2024.2361699

Sagar, S., Taparia, A., & Senanayake, R. (2024). Failures are fated, but can be faded: Characterizing and mitigating unwanted behaviors in large-scale vision and language models. *arXiv preprint arXiv:2406.07145.* /arXiv.2405.08295DOI: 10.48550

Shahri, H., Emad, M., Ibrahim, N., Rais, R. N. B., & Al-Fayoumi, Y. (2024, April). Elevating Education through AI Tutor: Utilizing GPT-4 for Personalized Learning. In *2024 15th Annual Undergraduate Research Conference on Applied Computing (URC)* (pp. 1-5). IEEE. DOI: 10.1109/URC62276.2024.10604578

Steinert, S., Avila, K. E., Ruzika, S., Kuhn, J., & Küchemann, S. (2024). Harnessing large language models to develop research-based learning assistants for formative feedback. *Smart Learning Environments, 11*(1), 62. DOI: 10.1186/s40561-024-00354-1

Sun, Y., Guo, Q., Zhao, S., Chandran, K., & Fathima, G. (2024). Context-aware augmented reality using human–computer interaction models. *Journal of Control and Decision, 11*(1), 1–14. DOI: 10.1080/23307706.2022.2026260

Tan, M., & Subramonyam, H. (2024, May). More than model documentation: uncovering teachers' bespoke information needs for informed classroom integration of ChatGPT. In *Proceedings of the 2024 CHI Conference on Human Factors in Computing Systems* (pp. 1-19). https://doi.org/DOI: 10.1145/3613904.3642592

Tang, Y., Yang, W., Xie, Y., & Yang, M. (2024). Domain adaptive knowledge tracing. *International Journal of Machine Learning and Cybernetics, 15*(11), 5129–5142. DOI: 10.1007/s13042-024-02219-y

Tjuatja, L., Chen, V., Wu, T., Talwalkwar, A., & Neubig, G. (2024). Do llms exhibit human-like response biases? a case study in survey design. *Transactions of the Association for Computational Linguistics, 12*, 1011–1026. DOI: 10.1162/tacl_a_00685

Uddin, M. M., & Mc Neill, L. (2024). Flipping the traditional classroom in teaching classical literature in higher education: An experiment with oedipus rex by sophocles. *Ubiquitous Learning, 18*(1), 1–26. DOI: 10.18848/1835-9795/CGP/v18i01/1-26

Zakaria, R., Hadhoum, B., Mourad, E., & Mustapha, M. (2025). *Dynamic Adaptation in an Intelligent Multi-Tutoring System: A Multi-Agent Approach.* IEEE., DOI: 10.1109/ACCESS.2025.3576651

Zalte, S. M. (2023). REVOLUTIONIZING EDUCATION. *LEVERAGING AI-ML TECHNOLOGIES TO ENHANCE TEACHING AND LEARNING OUTCOMES., 12*(12), 679–688. DOI: 10.48047/ecb/2023.12.si12.058

Zhang, L., Wu, H., Huang, X., Duan, T., & Du, H. (2024). Automatic deductive coding in discourse analysis: an application of large language models in learning analytics. *arXiv preprint arXiv:2410.01240.* /arXiv.2410.01240DOI: 10.48550

Chapter 7
Navigating Preferences With Artificial Intelligence:
A Spotlight on Recommender System Innovations

Salma El Omari
https://orcid.org/0009-0005-3139-7340
Data4Earth Laboratory, Faculty of Science and Technology, Sultan Moulay Slimane University, Morocco

Najlae Idrissi
Data4Earth Laboratory, Faculty of Science and Technology, Sultan Moulay Slimane University, Morocco

ABSTRACT

Artificial Intelligence (AI) has enhanced the ability to deliver personalized suggestions through Recommender Systems (RS), which rely on machine learning, data mining, and deep learning. This study explores the link between AI and RS, examining how AI improves recommendation quality and where challenges remain. Using the MovieLens 10K dataset, we conduct a comparative analysis of widely used algorithms. The performance of RS algorithms is assessed both as a machine learning problem, through collaborative and content-based filtering, and as a deep learning problem, by evaluating recent neural models. We also discuss evaluation methodologies, data types, and the potential of combining algorithms to enhance performance. The findings provide a clearer view of AI's role in RS, highlighting strengths, limitations, and future research opportunities.

DOI: 10.4018/979-8-3373-8011-7.ch007

1 INTRODUCTION

Recommender systems are an integral part of our daily lives, facilitating the recommendation of articles or content for each user based on their personal demographics and interactions with such systems (Shah et al., 2017). Recommendation systems also come into play to solve the problem of the growth and diversity of choices and options facing users, acting as filters to personalize content. Improve consumer satisfaction and foster a sense of loyalty (Beel et al., 2016). What's more, these systems influence the rate at which goods or services are sold, so companies are constantly on the lookout for a high-performance system capable of boosting sales (Kulkarni et al., 2020).

Artificial intelligence (AI) has advanced considerably in recent years, revolutionizing a wide range of industries and solving difficult problems in all fields. Artificial intelligence has demonstrated its transformative power by providing inventive and effective solutions and accelerating development in ways that were not previously possible (Gabrani et al., 2017). The value of AI lies in its ability to process and analyze huge quantities of data, to extract in-depth knowledge in the face of complex problems, and to make precise decisions in less time than humans (Beel et al., 2016).

Integrating AI into RS can bring about a significant change in the recommendation. Leveraging the power of AI techniques such as machine learning, data mining, and deep learning (Mohanty et al., 2020), these systems analyze large amounts of data, understand user preferences, and deliver recommendations tailored to individual interests and needs (Venkatesan et al., 2023). On the other hand, AI-driven algorithms can automatically recognize complex patterns and unearth unrecognized relationships. As a result, RS can make recommendations that are precise and useful even in scenarios involving millions of users and items. Adding AI to RS expands the possibilities for individualization and customization. RS can improve their models, adjust to shifting preferences, and remain relevant in dynamic environments by continuously learning from user feedback (Burke et al., 2011). But that doesn't mean there aren't many problems integrating AI into RS (Deldjoo et al., 2024).

The research problem this paper aims to address is the need for a comprehensive overview of the state-of-the-art AI techniques in recommendation systems, with a focus on collaborative filtering (CF), content-based (CB), and hybrid RS. Specifically, this paper seeks to investigate and compare the most well-known algorithms used in RS and evaluate their strengths and weaknesses through implementation on the Movielens 10k dataset.

The structure of the essay is as follows: Section 2 offers a description of the nature of the recommendation system problem and offers a comprehensive overview of AI techniques in recommender systems, including CF, CB, and hybrid RS, aiming to understand their underlying principles, advantages, and limitations. Section 3 introduces the techniques of artificial intelligence used in recommendation systems and conducts a comparative analysis of prominent algorithms used in CF, CB, and deep learning-based RS. This section implements these algorithms using the Movielens 10k dataset, and comparative tables are presented to highlight the strengths and weaknesses of each algorithm within each recommendation type. In Section 4, we discuss the data types in recommendation systems and model selection factors. Section 5 identifies and discusses the challenges and issues faced by recommender systems, including scalability, privacy concerns, and the cold-start problem. Recent trends in recommender systems are highlighted in Section 6. Finally, Section 7 proposes future research directions and potential solutions to overcome these challenges and improve the performance of AI-powered recommender systems.

This paper presents a comprehensive examination of the application of AI in RS, offering a good guide for researchers and practitioners in the field. Also, an analysis of the most used algorithms has been made to discover the strong and weak points of each algorithm.

2 RECOMMENDATION SYSTEM FRAMEWORK

Any research starts with a problem identification stage. The next part explores the nature of the recommender system problem, analyzing whether it is a ranking problem or a classification and regression problem. Furthermore, we will categorize recommender systems based on their main approaches, emphasizing the characteristics of every approach.

2.1 The Nature Of the Recommendation System Problem

Recommender systems are essential tools for providing personalized recommendations to users in the face of an overwhelming amount of available information (Isinkaye et al., 2015). However, understanding the nature of the problems encountered in recommender systems is crucial. Researchers have different perspectives on this matter, with some viewing the recommendation system problem as a ranking problem (Tang & Wang, 2018). It is important to note that recommender systems aim to rank a set of items for each user using a specific algorithm. However, the process of considering a group of items and calculating the utility function for an item “i” and a user “u” to generate a recommendation “r”, is as follows:

$$f(u, i_1, i_2, \ldots, i_m) \rightarrow (r_1, r_2, \ldots, r_m) \quad (1)$$

This calculation can be computationally expensive, especially when working with large databases. Therefore, although the fundamental problem of recommender systems is ranking, many researchers consider it to be a classification or regression problem (McNee et al., 2006). In practice, recommender systems commonly employ classification or regression models to predict scores or user preferences for unseen items (Roy & Dutta, 2022). By using these techniques, it becomes possible to predict the score of each item by calculating the utility function as follows:

$$f(u, i) \rightarrow \mathbb{R} \tag{2}$$

The recommender system then presents the items with the highest scores (top-k) to the user. This approach significantly reduces the computational time required to generate recommendations (Zhang et al., 2016).

2.2 Categories Of Recommendation Systems

There are a few different methods to pick from when implementing a recommender system in terms of how the recommendations are created. These methods use a variety of AI techniques to analyze user preferences, historical data, and item characteristics (Hui et al., 2022). Three prominent approaches to the various kinds of recommender systems are collaborative filtering (CF), content-based filtering (CB), and hybrid systems that combine both techniques (Mansur et al., 2017).

CF relies on user-item interactions to make recommendations. It operates under the assumption that "users who liked similar items in the past will likely have similar preferences in the future." User-based collaborative filtering compares the preferences of similar users to provide recommendations, while item-based collaborative filtering identifies similar items based on user preferences (Papadakis et al., 2022). These methods excel at capturing user preferences but may encounter challenges when a new product or user is added, there is no prior history of their preferences or ratings, so only limited data is available for new users or items, which is commonly referred to as the cold start problem (Anwar et al., 2022).

CB, on the other hand, focuses on item characteristics and user preferences to make recommendations. By analyzing attributes such as genre, keywords, or metadata, content-based filtering matches user preferences with relevant items (Eliyas & Ranjana, 2022). This approach is well-suited for scenarios with well-defined item attributes and can address the cold-start problem. However, it may lack the ability to capture the diversity of user interests and may tend to recommend items similar to those previously liked (Gopalan et al., 2014).

To overcome the limitations of individual approaches, hybrid recommender systems integrate both collaborative filtering and content-based techniques. By combining the strengths of both methods, hybrid systems aim to provide more accurate and diverse recommendations (Burke, 2002). These systems leverage collaborative filtering to capture user preferences and content-based filtering to handle item attributes, leading to improved recommendation quality by utilizing multiple sources of information (Bobadilla et al., 2013).

Figure 1. Overview of Recommendation System Types

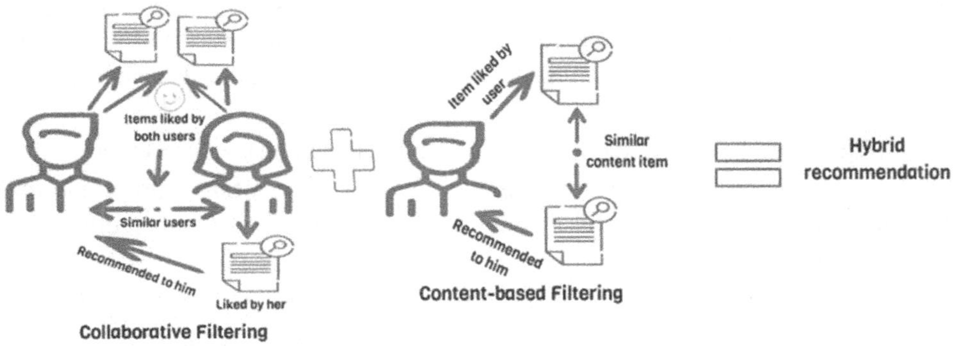

Figure 1 presents an overview of the three main types of recommendation systems: Collaborative Filtering showing connections between similar users, indicating how one user's preferences can be influenced by other users sharing similar tastes. Content-Based Filtering shows how the characteristics of recommended items are compared with the user's specific preferences. Arrows indicate the correspondence between features and preferences. A combination of the above two approaches provides a hybrid system.

3 ARTIFICIAL INTELLIGENCE IN RECOMMENDER SYSTEMS

Artificial intelligence is the theory and development of computer systems capable of performing tasks such as visual perception, voice recognition, decision-making, and translation between languages (Goksel & Bozkurt, 2019). These tasks can be applied in many fields, including medicine. Artificial intelligence can be used to make rapid and accurate medical diagnoses, speed up therapies, and ensure that the right steps are taken (Briganti & Le Moine, 2020). Cybersecurity can also be an area addressed by AI. Experts are beginning to use AI to defend against new cyberattacks (Truong et al., 2020). At a corporate level, the application of different AI techniques often strengthens team and company cultures (Fountaine et al., 2019). In addition, AI can also be applied in recommender systems. These systems use AI to analyze user preferences and behaviors in order to provide them with personalized and relevant recommendations. Whether it is streaming platforms, e-commerce websites, or content recommendation applications, AI plays a key role in optimizing the user experience (Verma & Sharma, 2020).

In the exciting field of artificial intelligence, there is a wide range of techniques that play an important role in a variety of applications. These include machine learning, deep learning, natural language processing, computer vision, reinforcement learning, expert systems, and active learning. Although each of these techniques has its own advantages, we will focus on those that are widely used in RS, namely machine learning, deep learning, reinforcement learning, and active learning (Zhang et al., 2021).

Machine learning is the scientific study of algorithms and statistical models that enable computer systems to perform specific tasks without explicit programming (Mahesh, 2020). It is a powerful technique in the field of artificial intelligence, particularly when it comes to recommender systems (Portugal et al., 2018). These systems use machine learning to analyze historical data, learn patterns, and make predictions. By training models on large datasets, machine learning algorithms can automatically identify complex relationships between users, items, and their preferences (Khanal et al., 2020). These algorithms to generate personalized recommendations use various approaches, including collaborative filtering, matrix factorization, and neighborhood-based methods (Kilani et al., 2018). One of the main advantages of machine learning in RS is its ability to adapt and improve over time. By continually learning from user reactions and interactions, the algorithms improve the accuracy and relevance of their recommendations (Nawrocka et al., 2018).

Due to its capacity to handle and analyze enormous volumes of data, **deep learning**, a subset of machine learning, has garnered a lot of attention recently. Recommender systems can now recognize delicate user preferences and item qualities thanks to deep learning models, such as neural networks, which can extract complicated features and representations from unstructured data (Zhang et al., 2019). These models are excellent at handling unstructured input, like written material, visuals, and audio, and they may use this data to offer individualized suggestions. To operate at their best, deep learning models frequently need considerable computational power and a great deal of training data (X. Chen et al., 2023).

Reinforcement learning is another powerful artificial intelligence technique that holds great promise for recommender systems. In reinforcement learning, an agent actively interacts with its environment and learns to make sequential decisions by receiving feedback in the form of rewards or penalties (Ernst & Louette, 2024). This dynamic approach can be effectively combined with active learning, which actively selects the most informative instances for the agent when it interacts with the environment to further improve the recommendation process (Dodds et al., 2024).

In this context, the recommendation system acts as an agent, constantly adapting and improving its suggestions based on feedback and user preferences. Thanks to reinforcement learning, the system can adjust and refine its recommendations intelligently, using various recommendation strategies and algorithms to optimize user satisfaction (Afsar et al., 2022). User feedback on suggestions provides a valuable signal for rewards, allowing the system to learn and adapt its recommendations over time. This combination of reinforcement learning and active learning provides a powerful framework for personalized and continuously improving recommendation systems (Zhang et al., 2021).

These AI techniques, including machine learning, deep learning, reinforcement learning, and active learning, have significantly advanced the capabilities of recommender systems. By leveraging these techniques, recommender systems can provide more accurate, personalized, and context-aware recommendations, enhancing the overall user experience and satisfaction.

3.1 Recommender Systems As a Machine Learning Problem

In this section, we perform a detailed analysis of machine learning algorithms applied to the MovieLens 10k database which is a popular benchmark dataset commonly used in the field of recommender systems for evaluating and testing collaborative filtering algorithms. It consists of user ratings for movies and provides a comprehensive collection of data that spans various genres, time periods, and user preferences. The dataset contains approximately 10,000 ratings given by users to 6,000 movies. Each rating is typically on a scale of 1 to 5, indicating the user's level of preference for a particular movie. Along with the ratings, MovieLens 10k includes additional information such as movie titles, genres, and user demographics, enabling more comprehensive analysis and evaluation of recommendation algorithms (Harper & Konstan, 2015). We evaluate the performance of these algorithms based on key parameters that are specific to each recommendation system. Through the analysis of these parameters, we aim to provide an in-depth comparative analysis, highlighting the strengths and limitations of each algorithm in recommender systems.

Collaborative Filtering. In the area of collaborative filtering, several algorithms have been created, each with unique advantages and disadvantages (Wang & Blei, 2011). Some algorithms fall under the umbrella of user-based collaborative filtering, which compares individuals based on how they have interacted with items in the past (Koren et al., 2021). A different class of algorithms is item-based collaborative filtering, which determines item similarities based on user preferences (Musa & Zhihong, 2020). Similarity may be determined in both scenarios using nearest neighbor algorithms, such as KNN (Airen & Agrawal, 2022). There are another popular technique in recommender systems is collaborative filtering using matrix factorization. Their origin can be traced back to factor analysis and linear algebra. It was created for the Netflix Prize competition in 2009. The idea of decomposing a matrix into lower-dimensional representations has its roots in linear algebraic concepts, like singular value decomposition (SVD). In order to handle the complexity of recommendation tasks, these approaches have been enhanced and modified, which has led to the creation of a variety of matrix factorization-based collaborative filtering algorithms (Mehta & Rana, 2017). When evaluating the performance of CF algorithms in RS, several metrics are commonly used to assess their effectiveness (Fayyaz et al., 2020). One of the most important measures is precision, which allows us to know the accuracy of our recommendation. The evaluation of this kind of measure can be done thanks to precision, recall, and F1-score. Precision can be seen as the proportion of relevant elements in the recommended elements; recall is the proportion of relevant elements, but this time in the correctly recommended elements. The F1-score combines the two to provide the algorithm's performance. We can also have another kind of evaluation, such as squared error (MSE) or root-mean-squared error (RMSE). These metrics evaluate the accuracy of predicted ratings compared to the actual ratings provided by users (Da'u & Salim, 2020). Table 1 provides a comparative analysis of the most commonly used algorithms for collaborative filtering using the MovieLens 10k database.

Table 1. Comparative Analysis of Collaborative Filtering Algorithms

Algorithm Name	Description	Advantages	Disadvantages	Performance Metrics
User-based KNN	Simple, intuitive algorithm for classification and regression.	Simple implementation	Scalability with large datasets	Precision: 0.71 Recall: 0.76 F1-score: 0.73 MSE: 0.96 RMSE:0.98
Basic Matrix Factorization	Decomposes the matrix to capture latent factors	Ability to handle sparsity and cold start problems	Computational complexity with large datasets	Precision: 0.89 Recall: 0.87 F1-score: 0.88 MSE: 0.87 RMSE:0.93
Singular Value Decomposition (SVD)	Decomposes the matrix into latent factor representations	Captures latent features and user-item relationships	Difficulty handling scalability and cold start problems	Precision: 0.74 Recall: 0.73 F1-score: 0.73 MSE: 0.87 RMSE:0.93
Non-negative Matrix Factorization (NMF)	Decomposes the matrix into non-negative latent factor representations	Interpretable latent features and user-item relationships	Sensitive to noise and outliers in data	Precision: 0.73 Recall: 0.71 F1-score: 0.72 MSE: 0.93 RMSE:0.96

Content-based filtering. Different algorithms with unique strengths and shortcomings have evolved in the field of content-based filtering. These algorithms concentrate on analyzing the qualities of the article and the user's preferences to provide suggestions that profile the user before comparing the profile to the features of the article (Javed et al., 2021). Naive Bayes, a quick and easy method that presumes independence between features, falls under one of these categories. Its main advantage is that it can deal with binary and categorical features, but with high sensitivity to irrelevant features (Calders & Verwer, 2010). Another widely used method, TF-IDF, also considers the significance of terms in a document, but it sometimes has trouble capturing complicated semantic links (Philip et al., 2014). While still a good choice if you have large documents, neglecting the overall context of the document has an impact on its performance (Beel et al., 2016). The ability of cosine similarity to capture semantic linkages comes from its measurement of the similarity of elemental features (Günther et al., 2016). But it has difficulty handling scalability with large datasets (Singh et al., 2020). A substantial quantity of training data is needed for Word2Vec, which employs word embeddings to capture the semantic meaning of words and texts (Islek & Oguducu, 2022). The problem with Word2Vec is that the normalization step in the algorithm makes it computationally expensive (Meyer, 2016). These content-based algorithms have their roots in the fields of information retrieval and natural language processing. To overcome the difficulties of recommendation assignments, they have evolved over time. Unlike collaborative filtering, which evaluates accuracy using metrics such as precision, recall, and F1 score, content-based filtering focuses more on the relevance and quality of features (Vozalis & Margaritis, 2003). Table 2 presents a detailed summary of the advantages and disadvantages of each filtering algorithm based on the content mentioned in the paragraph above. Each algorithm has benefits and disadvantages of its own, and the applicability of an algorithm depends on the characteristics of the data, the need for scalability, and the particular objectives of the recommender system. When choosing an appropriate content-based algorithm for a particular recommendation assignment, it is vital to take these considerations into account.

Table 2. Comparative Analysis of Content-Based Recommender System Algorithms

Algorithm Name	Description	Advantages	Disadvantages
Naive Bayes	Fast and simple algorithm for probabilistic classification tasks	Can handle both binary and categorical features	Sensitivity to irrelevant features that can impact classification accuracy
TF-IDF	Measures the importance of terms in a document collection	Performs well with large document collections.	Does not consider the global context or document relationships
Cosine Similarity	Calculates the similarity between item features using the cosine measure	Captures semantic relationships between items	Difficulty in handling scalability with large datasets
Word2Vec	Utilizes word embeddings to capture the semantic meaning of words.	Provides efficient vector representations for text data	Can be computationally expensive during training

3.2 Recommender Systems As a Deep Learning Problem

When it comes to recommender systems powered by deep learning, various algorithms offer unique advantages and address specific challenges (Singhal et al., 2017). Recurrent neural networks (RNNs) capture sequential dependencies in user behavior, while generative adversarial networks (GANs) generate diverse recommendations, but both lack scalability, and their performance is sensitive to cold start problems (Bharadhwaj et al., 2018). Graphical neural networks (GNNs) excel in graph-structured data with high scalability but share the same cold-start problem with moderate robustness (Cai et al., 2021), and autoencoders (AEs) capture non-linear relationships; however, high-dimensional data have an impact on their performance (Zhang et al., 2020). Neural matrix factorization (NeuMF) combines neural networks with matrix factorization, but this combination does not solve the cold-start problem (Dziugaite & Roy, 2015). Each algorithm has its strengths and limitations in terms of scalability and robustness to the cold-start problem. Table 3 provides an in-depth summary of recommendation system algorithms based on deep learning, presenting the advantages, disadvantages, and performance evaluated using different metrics, reflecting the detailed information in the paragraph above.

Table 3. Comparative Analysis of Deep Learning-Based Recommender System Algorithms

Algorithm Name	Description	Advantages	Disadvantages	Performance Metrics
RNN	Sequential modeling for recommendation	Captures sequential dependencies in user behavior	Difficulty handling long sequences and scalability	Scalability: Moderate Robustness to Cold Start Problem: Moderate
GAN	Generates realistic recommendations	Can generate diverse and novel recommendations	Training instability and mode collapse	Scalability: Moderate, Robustness to Cold Start Problem: Moderate
GNN	Recommendation on graph-structured data	Captures collaborative filtering on graph data	Scalability with large-scale graphs	Scalability: High Robustness to Cold Start Problem: Moderate
AE	Reconstruction-based recommendation	Captures non-linear relationships in user preferences	Difficulty handling high-dimensional data	Scalability: Moderate, Robustness to Cold Start Problem: Moderate
NeuMF	Neural network-based matrix factorization	Captures user-item interactions and latent factors	Difficulty handling sparse data and scalability	Scalability: Moderate, Robustness to Cold Start Problem: Low

4 DATA TYPES IN RECOMMENDER SYSTEMS AND MODEL SELECTION FACTORS

Explicit and implicit data in recommender systems reflect the various interactions or comments users make about products. Direct user contributions, such as ratings or comments, are referred to as explicit data. Implicit data, on the other hand, gathers information deduced from user activity, such as clicks or purchase history, and conveys signals about user preferences without the user expressing them explicitly (Zhao et al., 2018). Explicit data is very rare, but implicit data is more common, accounting for around 81% of real-life data (Reusens et al., 2017). While explicit data indicate the user's opinions and preferences, a null value in explicit data may indicate that the user does not like the product, but a null value in implicit data may mean that the item has not been seen or tested.

Recommender systems employ both forms of data, which must be carefully interpreted, to provide precise suggestions that take into account all of the user's preferences and behaviors (Jawaheer et al., 2014). It is essential to remember that both explicit and implicit data have benefits and drawbacks. Explicit data offers a clear picture of user preferences, although it may be scarce and skewed as a result of user rating habits. Even if implicit data is plentiful, it may not always be evident what the user intended; therefore, user behavior patterns must be carefully taken into account (Zhao et al., 2018).

When designing recommender systems, the choice of approaches and models depends on two factors: the type of database, including considerations such as data size, service speed, and update frequency, and the literature. Previous studies have indicated different trends in performance. For example, papers before 2014 indicated that machine learning models performed best (Adomavicius & Tuzhilin, 2005); by contrast, between 2014 and 2018, deep learning models showed superior performance (Xue et al., 2017). But recently, there have been several papers attacking deep learning, saying that although it is a very powerful tool, it is not designed to solve the problem of recommending systems (Rendle et al., 2019; Steck, 2019). However, it is important to consider the advantages and disadvantages of each approach.

By considering these factors and understanding the strengths and weaknesses of explicit and implicit data, recommender systems can be built to provide robust and personalized recommendations, improving the user experience and satisfaction

5 THE CHALLENGES FACING RECOMMENDATION SYSTEMS

RS, while powerful and widely used, faces several challenges that affect its effectiveness and user satisfaction. These challenges stem from a variety of factors, including data limitations, scalability, diversity, and privacy concerns (Mohamed et al., 2019).

One of the major challenges is the problem of data sparsity and the cold start problem. RS often operates on sparse data, with limited interaction between users and items. The integration of transfer learning can be an effective solution as it seeks to extract knowledge from several source data sets to facilitate a learning task with target data (Pan, 2016). The cold start problem occurs when there is insufficient information about new users or items, making it challenging to generate relevant recommendations. Techniques such as content-based filtering or hybrid approaches are used to reduce these difficulties (Jeevamol & Renumol, 2021).

Scalability is another difficulty, particularly for large-scale platforms with millions of users and components. The computational difficulty of creating recommendations rises as the universe of people and things expands (Vats & vinash Sharma, 2022). To address the scalability issue and ensure real-time or near real-time suggestions, effective algorithms and distributed computing approaches are employed (Singh, 2020).

Diversity is an important aspect of RS, as users expect a wide range of suggestions. However, achieving this diversity is difficult. RS often face a trade-off between accuracy and diversity, as optimizing one can be at the expense of the other. It is essential to find the right balance between meeting users' preferences and exposing them to new and serendipitous recommendations. Similarly, while users may want to discover new options that are out of the ordinary, RS tend to favor predictable choices (Kunaver & Požrl, 2017).

Privacy is a major concern in recommender systems, as they process sensitive user data. Preserving user privacy while providing accurate recommendations is a delicate balancing act (Wang et al., 2023). Techniques such as anonymization, differential confidentiality, and secure multiparty computation are used to protect user data and guarantee privacy (Mohallick & Özgöbek, 2017).

In the realm of RS, certain items tend to garner more popularity and consequently attract a greater number of user behaviors. Both explicit and implicit data present this phenomenon, which can lead to an inherent bias in the model training process, ultimately influencing the recommendations generated. Similarly, this bias can extend to the user side. Biases can also arise from other sources, such as popularity bias or algorithmic biases. Consequently, these biases can significantly impact the fairness, diversity, and accuracy of the recommendation system's outputs (J. Chen et al., 2023).

These challenges highlight the complexity and multifaceted nature of recommendation systems. Understanding and addressing these challenges is essential to building reliable and effective recommendation systems.

6 RECENT RECOMMENDER SYSTEM TRENDS

In this part, we evaluate recent research in the area of recommender systems, highlighting significant developments, novel strategies, and emerging trends. To enhance the functionality and efficacy of recommender systems, researchers have continued to investigate novel strategies and techniques.

The increasing use of deep learning in recommendation programs is a notable trend in recent research. Deep learning has become an emerging branch of recommended programs (Zhang et al., 2019). Convolutional Neural Networks and Graph Neural Networks have shown promising results in complex data capture, time-dependent modeling, and high-level data analysis (Gao et al., 2023). Another emerging trend is explanatory artificial intelligence for processing suggestions. Users are increasingly demanding clarity and detail in the recommendations they receive (Ammar & Shaban-Nejad, 2020). Explanatory intelligent design methods, such as model definition capabilities and recommendation definition generation, aim to provide explicit descriptions on the basis of which recommendations are made (Song, 2022). Context-based methods are also gaining popularity. Recommendation systems that are context-sensitive, such as location, time of day, or lifestyle, can deliver recommendations that are more relevant and tailored to users' specific expectations in a particular context (Joe & Raj, 2021). As analyzed by these new methods, it is possible to provide high-quality recommendations and preserve the privacy of the user. In addition, recent research has explored the application of blockchain technology (Himeur et al., 2022) and homomorphic encryption as very strong security tools to guarantee confidentiality and data protection in recommendation systems (Hong et al., 2022; Zhou et al., 2021). These innovative approaches make it possible to preserve user confidentiality while offering high-quality recommendations.

7 FUTURE RESEARCH AXES

There are a number of topics that require further study and attention in terms of future trends. To further improve the accuracy, applicability, and effectiveness of suggestions, many avenues of research are emerging in the field of recommender systems.

Firstly, improving the personalization of suggestions remains a major challenge. By enabling systems to adapt in real time to changing user preferences (Wu et al., 2023), e-learning and continuous learning methodologies can play an important role in this direction. Managing bias in recommendation systems is an increasingly important issue. In order to ensure fair and unbiased suggestions for all users, future research should focus on developing techniques to detect and reduce bias (Abdollahpouri et al., 2021). Another promising research direction concerns the integration of privacy and trustworthiness. Future research efforts should focus on developing advanced privacy protection techniques, such as differential privacy protection, to preserve user privacy while providing high-quality recommendations (Pramod, 2023).

Recommendations can also be improved by taking into account users' confidence in the recommended elements. Approaches based on estimating the uncertainty of predictions can also be used to improve the reliability of recommendations (Coscrato & Bridge, 2023). The study of new modeling strategies, such as the use of social data, is extremely promising. Users' social interactions can provide useful data for suggestions. By incorporating social effects, methods that use user data and social networks, including online interactions or friendships, can improve the relevance of suggestions (Dhelim et al., 2022).

These lines of research pave the way for better recommendation systems that are user-centered and offer recommendation experiences that are individualized, transparent, fair, and respectful of privacy.

8 CONCLUSION

In this article, we have provided an in-depth study of the application of AI to RS. After reviewing the nature of the recommendation problem, we analyzed in detail the three main families of approaches: collaborative filtering, content-based filtering, and hybrid methods. We also showed how the integration of AI techniques, such as machine learning and deep learning, can improve the relevance and personalization of recommendations.

The comparative analysis conducted on the MovieLens 10k dataset showed that matrix factorization approaches offer better overall performance, while content-based methods remain particularly useful for solving the cold start problem. These results confirm that no single approach is universally optimal and that it remains essential to adapt recommendation techniques to the context, available data, and user needs.

Beyond this comparison, we discussed the different types of data used by RSs and highlighted the major challenges that these systems still face, including scalability management, diversity of suggestions, privacy protection, and reduction of algorithmic bias. These challenges represent research opportunities aimed at designing recommendation systems that are more equitable, transparent, and adapted to dynamic environments.

Looking ahead, the integration of new approaches, such as graph neural networks, explanatory techniques, and solutions that guarantee data confidentiality, is a promising avenue. This work thus contributes to providing a clear picture of the state of the art, while opening up concrete avenues for improving the efficiency and reliability of recommendation systems in the age of artificial intelligence.

DECLARATIONS OF INTEREST

On behalf of all authors, the corresponding author states that there is no conflict of interest.

REFERENCES

Abdollahpouri, H., Mansoury, M., Burke, R., Mobasher, B., & Malthouse, E. (2021). User-centered evaluation of popularity bias in recommender systems. Proceedings of the 29th ACM conference on user modeling, adaptation and personalization.

Adomavicius, G., & Tuzhilin, A. (2005). Toward the next generation of recommender systems: A survey of the state-of-the-art and possible extensions. *IEEE Transactions on Knowledge and Data Engineering*, *17*(6), 734–749.

Afsar, M. M., Crump, T., & Far, B. (2022). Reinforcement learning based recommender systems: A survey. *ACM Computing Surveys*, *55*(7), 1–38. DOI: 10.1145/3543846

Airen, S., & Agrawal, J. (2022). Movie recommender system using k-nearest neighbors variants. *National Academy Science Letters*, *45*(1), 75–82. DOI: 10.1007/s40009-021-01051-0

Ammar, N., & Shaban-Nejad, A. (2020). Explainable artificial intelligence recommendation system by leveraging the semantics of adverse childhood experiences: Proof-of-concept prototype development. *JMIR Medical Informatics*, *8*(11), e18752. DOI: 10.2196/18752 PMID: 33146623

Anwar, T., Uma, V., Hussain, M. I., & Pantula, M. (2022). Collaborative filtering and kNN based recommendation to overcome cold start and sparsity issues: A comparative analysis. *Multimedia Tools and Applications*, *81*(25), 35693–35711. DOI: 10.1007/s11042-021-11883-z

Beel, J., Gipp, B., Langer, S., & Breitinger, C. (2016). Paper recommender systems: A literature survey. *International Journal on Digital Libraries*, *17*(4), 305–338. DOI: 10.1007/s00799-015-0156-0

Bharadhwaj, H., Park, H., & Lim, B. Y. (2018). RecGAN: Recurrent generative adversarial networks for recommendation systems. Proceedings of the 12th ACM Conference on Recommender Systems.

Bobadilla, J., Ortega, F., Hernando, A., & Gutiérrez, A. (2013). Recommender systems survey. *Knowledge-Based Systems*, *46*, 109–132.

Briganti, G., & Le Moine, O. (2020). Artificial intelligence in medicine: Today and tomorrow. *Frontiers in Medicine*, *7*, 509744. DOI: 10.3389/fmed.2020.00027 PMID: 32118012

Burke, R. (2002). Hybrid recommender systems: Survey and experiments. *User Modeling and User-Adapted Interaction*, *12*(4), 331–370. DOI: 10.1023/A:1021240730564

Burke, R., Felfernig, A., & Göker, M. H. (2011). Recommender systems: An overview. *AI Magazine*, *32*(3), 13–18. DOI: 10.1609/aimag.v32i3.2361

Cai, D., Hu, J., Zhao, Q., Qian, S., Fang, Q., & Xu, C. (2021). Grecx: An efficient and unified benchmark for GNN-based recommendation. *arXiv preprint arXiv:2111.10342*.

Calders, T., & Verwer, S. (2010). Three naive bayes approaches for discrimination-free classification. *Data Mining and Knowledge Discovery*, *21*(2), 277–292. DOI: 10.1007/s10618-010-0190-x

Chen, J., Dong, H., Wang, X., Feng, F., Wang, M., & He, X. (2023). Bias and debias in recommender system: A survey and future directions. *ACM Transactions on Information Systems*, *41*(3), 1–39. DOI: 10.1145/3564284

Chen, X., Yao, L., McAuley, J., Zhou, G., & Wang, X. (2023). Deep reinforcement learning in recommender systems: A survey and new perspectives. *Knowledge-Based Systems*, *264*, 110335. DOI: 10.1016/j.knosys.2023.110335

Coscrato, V., & Bridge, D. (2023). Estimating and evaluating the uncertainty of rating predictions and top-n recommendations in recommender systems. *ACM Transactions on Recommender Systems*, *1*(2), 1–34. DOI: 10.1145/3584021

Da'u, A., & Salim, N. (2020). Recommendation system based on deep learning methods: A systematic review and new directions. *Artificial Intelligence Review*, *53*(4), 2709–2748. DOI: 10.1007/s10462-019-09744-1

Deldjoo, Y., Jannach, D., Bellogin, A., Difonzo, A., & Zanzonelli, D. (2024). Fairness in recommender systems: Research landscape and future directions. *User Modeling and User-Adapted Interaction*, *34*(1), 59–108. DOI: 10.1007/s11257-023-09364-z

Dhelim, S., Aung, N., Bouras, M. A., Ning, H., & Cambria, E. (2022). A survey on personality-aware recommendation systems. *Artificial Intelligence Review*, •••, 1–46.

Dodds, M., Guo, J., Löhr, T., Tibo, A., Engkvist, O., & Janet, J. P. (2024). Sample efficient reinforcement learning with active learning for molecular design. *Chemical Science (Cambridge)*, *15*(11), 4146–4160. DOI: 10.1039/D3SC04653B PMID: 38487235

Dziugaite, G. K., & Roy, D. M. (2015). Neural network matrix factorization. *arXiv preprint arXiv:1511.06443*.

Eliyas, S., & Ranjana, P. (2022). Recommendation systems: Content-based filtering vs collaborative filtering. 2022 2nd International Conference on Advance Computing and Innovative Technologies in Engineering (ICACITE).

Ernst, D., & Louette, A. (2024). Introduction to reinforcement learning.

Fayyaz, Z., Ebrahimian, M., Nawara, D., Ibrahim, A., & Kashef, R. (2020). Recommendation systems: Algorithms, challenges, metrics, and business opportunities. *applied sciences, 10*(21), 7748.

Fountaine, T., McCarthy, B., & Saleh, T. (2019). Building the AI-powered organization. *Harvard Business Review*, *97*(4), 62–73.

Gabrani, G., Sabharwal, S., & Singh, V. K. (2017). Artificial intelligence based recommender systems: A survey. Advances in Computing and Data Sciences: First International Conference, ICACDS 2016, Ghaziabad, India, November 11-12, 2016, Revised Selected Papers 1.

Gao, C., Zheng, Y., Li, N., Li, Y., Qin, Y., Piao, J., Quan, Y., Chang, J., Jin, D., & He, X. (2023). A survey of graph neural networks for recommender systems: Challenges, methods, and directions. *ACM Transactions on Recommender Systems, 1*(1), 1-51. DOI: 10.1007/978-981-10-5427-3_6

Goksel, N., & Bozkurt, A. (2019). Artificial intelligence in education: Current insights and future perspectives. In *Handbook of Research on Learning in the Age of Transhumanism* (pp. 224–236). IGI Global. DOI: 10.4018/978-1-5225-8431-5.ch014

Gopalan, P. K., Charlin, L., & Blei, D. (2014). Content-based recommendations with Poisson factorization. *Advances in Neural Information Processing Systems*, 27.

Günther, F., Dudschig, C., & Kaup, B. (2016). Latent semantic analysis cosines as a cognitive similarity measure: Evidence from priming studies. *Quarterly Journal of Experimental Psychology*, *69*(4), 626–653. DOI: 10.1080/17470218.2015.1038280 PMID: 25952009

Harper, F. M., & Konstan, J. A. (2015). The movielens datasets: History and context. [tiis]. *ACM Transactions on Interactive Intelligent Systems*, *5*(4), 1–19. DOI: 10.1145/2827872

Himeur, Y., Sayed, A., Alsalemi, A., Bensaali, F., Amira, A., Varlamis, I., Eirinaki, M., Sardianos, C., & Dimitrakopoulos, G. (2022). Blockchain-based recommender systems: Applications, challenges and future opportunities. *Computer Science Review*, *43*, 100439. DOI: 10.1016/j.cosrev.2021.100439

Hong, W., Zhang, H., & Zhu, J. (2022). FedHD: A Privacy-Preserving Recommendation System with Homomorphic Encryption and Differential Privacy. International Conference on Computer Science and Education.

Hui, B., Zhang, L., Zhou, X., Wen, X., & Nian, Y. (2022). Personalized recommendation system based on knowledge embedding and historical behavior. *Applied Intelligence*, 1-13.

Isinkaye, F. O., Folajimi, Y. O., & Ojokoh, B. A. (2015). Recommendation systems: Principles, methods and evaluation. *Egyptian informatics journal, 16*(3), 261-273.

Islek, I., & Oguducu, S. G. (2022). A hierarchical recommendation system for E-commerce using online user reviews. *Electronic Commerce Research and Applications*, *52*, 101131. DOI: 10.1016/j.elerap.2022.101131

Javed, U., Shaukat, K., Hameed, I. A., Iqbal, F., Alam, T. M., & Luo, S. (2021). A review of content-based and context-based recommendation systems. [iJET]. *International Journal of Emerging Technologies in Learning*, *16*(3), 274–306. DOI: 10.3991/ijet.v16i03.18851

Jawaheer, G., Weller, P., & Kostkova, P. (2014). Modeling user preferences in recommender systems: A classification framework for explicit and implicit user feedback. [tiis]. *ACM Transactions on Interactive Intelligent Systems*, *4*(2), 1–26. DOI: 10.1145/2512208

Jeevamol, J., & Renumol, V. (2021). An ontology-based hybrid e-learning content recommender system for alleviating the cold-start problem. *Education and Information Technologies*, *26*(4), 4993–5022. DOI: 10.1007/s10639-021-10508-0

Joe, M. C. V., & Raj, J. S. (2021). Location-based orientation context dependent recommender system for users. [TCSST]. *J. Trends Comput. Sci. Smart Technol.*, *3*(01), 14–23. DOI: 10.36548/jtcsst.2021.1.002

Khanal, S. S., Prasad, P., Alsadoon, A., & Maag, A. (2020). A systematic review: Machine learning based recommendation systems for e-learning. *Education and Information Technologies*, *25*(4), 2635–2664. DOI: 10.1007/s10639-019-10063-9

Kilani, Y., Otoom, A. F., Alsarhan, A., & Almaayah, M. (2018). A genetic algorithms-based hybrid recommender system of matrix factorization and neighborhood-based techniques. *Journal of Computational Science*, *28*, 78–93. DOI: 10.1016/j.jocs.2018.08.007

Koren, Y., Rendle, S., & Bell, R. (2021). Advances in collaborative filtering. *Recommender systems handbook*, 91-142.

Kulkarni, P. V., Rai, S., & Kale, R. (2020). Recommender system in elearning: a survey. Proceeding of International Conference on Computational Science and Applications: ICCSA 2019.

Kunaver, M., & Požrl, T. (2017). Diversity in recommender systems–A survey. *Knowledge-Based Systems*, *123*, 154–162.

Mahesh, B. (2020). Machine learning algorithms-a review. *International Journal of Science and Research (IJSR).[Internet]*, *9*(1), 381-386.

Mansur, F., Patel, V., & Patel, M. (2017). A review on recommender systems. 2017 International Conference on Innovations in Information, Embedded and Communication Systems (ICIIECS).

McNee, S. M., Riedl, J., & Konstan, J. A. (2006). Being accurate is not enough: how accuracy metrics have hurt recommender systems. CHI'06 extended abstracts on Human factors in computing systems.

Mehta, R., & Rana, K. (2017). A review on matrix factorization techniques in recommender systems. 2017 2nd International Conference on Communication Systems, Computing and IT Applications (CSCITA)

Meyer, D. (2016). How exactly does word2vec work. *Uoregon. Edu, Brocade. Com*, 1-18.

Mohallick, I., & Özgöbek, Ö. (2017). Exploring privacy concerns in news recommender systems. Proceedings of the International Conference on Web Intelligence.

Mohamed, M. H., Khafagy, M. H., & Ibrahim, M. H. (2019). Recommender systems challenges and solutions survey. 2019 international conference on innovative trends in computer engineering (ITCE).

Mohanty, S. N., Chatterjee, J. M., Jain, S., Elngar, A. A., & Gupta, P. (2020). *Recommender system with machine learning and artificial intelligence: practical tools and applications in medical, agricultural and other industries*. John Wiley & Sons. DOI: 10.1145/3106426.3109435

Musa, J. M., & Zhihong, X. (2020). Item based collaborative filtering approach in movie recommendation system using different similarity measures. Proceedings of the 2020 6th International Conference on Computer and Technology Applications.

Nawrocka, A., Kot, A., & Nawrocki, M. (2018). Application of machine learning in recommendation systems. 2018 19th International carpathian control conference (ICCC).

Pan, W. (2016). A survey of transfer learning for collaborative recommendation with auxiliary data. *Neurocomputing*, *177*, 447–453.

Papadakis, H., Papagrigoriou, A., Panagiotakis, C., Kosmas, E., & Fragopoulou, P. (2022). Collaborative filtering recommender systems taxonomy. *Knowledge and Information Systems*, *64*(1), 35–74. DOI: 10.1007/s10115-021-01628-7

Philip, S., Shola, P., & Ovye, A. (2014). Application of content-based approach in research paper recommendation system for a digital library. *International Journal of Advanced Computer Science and Applications*, *5*(10). Advance online publication. DOI: 10.14569/IJACSA.2014.051006

Portugal, I., Alencar, P., & Cowan, D. (2018). The use of machine learning algorithms in recommender systems: A systematic review. *Expert Systems with Applications*, *97*, 205–227. DOI: 10.1016/j.eswa.2017.12.020

Pramod, D. (2023). Privacy-preserving techniques in recommender systems: State-of-the-art review and future research agenda. *Data Technologies and Applications*, *57*(1), 32–55. DOI: 10.1108/DTA-02-2022-0083

Rendle, S., Zhang, L., & Koren, Y. (2019). On the difficulty of evaluating baselines: A study on recommender systems. *arXiv preprint arXiv:1905.01395.*

Reusens, M., Lemahieu, W., Baesens, B., & Sels, L. (2017). A note on explicit versus implicit information for job recommendation. *Decision Support Systems*, *98*, 26–35. DOI: 10.1016/j.dss.2017.04.002

Roy, D., & Dutta, M. (2022). A systematic review and research perspective on recommender systems. *Journal of Big Data*, *9*(1), 59. DOI: 10.1186/s40537-022-00592-5

Shah, K., Salunke, A., Dongare, S., & Antala, K. (2017). Recommender systems: An overview of different approaches to recommendations. 2017 International Conference on Innovations in Information, Embedded and Communication Systems (ICIIECS).

Singh, M. (2020). Scalability and sparsity issues in recommender datasets: a survey. *Knowledge and Information Systems*, *62*(1), 1–43.

Singh, R. H., Maurya, S., Tripathi, T., Narula, T., & Srivastav, G. (2020). Movie recommendation system using cosine similarity and KNN. *International Journal of Engineering and Advanced Technology*, *9*(5), 556–559. DOI: 10.35940/ijeat.E9666.069520

Singhal, A., Sinha, P., & Pant, R. (2017). Use of deep learning in modern recommendation system: A summary of recent works. *arXiv preprint arXiv:1712.07525.*

Song, M.-H. (2022). A study on explainable artificial intelligence-based sentimental analysis system model. *International Journal of Internet. Broadcasting and Communication*, *14*(1), 142–151.

Steck, H. (2019). Embarrassingly shallow autoencoders for sparse data. The World Wide Web Conference.

Tang, J., & Wang, K. (2018). Ranking distillation: Learning compact ranking models with high performance for recommender system. Proceedings of the 24th ACM SIGKDD international conference on knowledge discovery & data mining.

Truong, T. C., Zelinka, I., Plucar, J., Čandík, M., & Šulc, V. (2020). Artificial intelligence and cybersecurity: Past, presence, and future. Artificial intelligence and evolutionary computations in engineering systems.

Vats, D., & vinash Sharma, A. (2022). A Collaborative Filtering Recommender System using Apache Mahout, Ontology and Dimensionality Reduction Technique. 2022 International Conference on Advances in Computing, Communication and Applied Informatics (ACCAI).

Venkatesan, V. K., Ramakrishna, M. T., Batyuk, A., Barna, A., & Havrysh, B. (2023). High-Performance Artificial Intelligence Recommendation of Quality Research Papers Using Effective Collaborative Approach. *Systems*, *11*(2), 81.

Verma, P., & Sharma, S. (2020). Artificial intelligence based recommendation system. 2020 2nd International Conference on Advances in Computing, Communication Control and Networking (ICACCCN)

Vozalis, E., & Margaritis, K. G. (2003). Analysis of recommender systems algorithms. The 6th Hellenic European Conference on Computer Mathematics & its Applications.

Wang, C., & Blei, D. M. (2011). Collaborative topic modeling for recommending scientific articles. Proceedings of the 17th ACM SIGKDD international conference on Knowledge discovery and data mining.

Wang, Y., Ma, W., Zhang, M., Liu, Y., & Ma, S. (2023). A survey on the fairness of recommender systems. *ACM Transactions on Information Systems*, *41*(3), 1–43.

Wu, C., Wu, F., Huang, Y., & Xie, X. (2023). Personalized news recommendation: Methods and challenges. *ACM Transactions on Information Systems*, *41*(1), 1–50. DOI: 10.1145/3530257

Xue, H.-J., Dai, X., Zhang, J., Huang, S., & Chen, J. (2017). Deep matrix factorization models for recommender systems. IJCAI.

Zhang, F., Gong, T., Lee, V. E., Zhao, G., Rong, C., & Qu, G. (2016). Fast algorithms to evaluate collaborative filtering recommender systems. *Knowledge-Based Systems*, *96*, 96–103.

Zhang, G., Liu, Y., & Jin, X. (2020). A survey of autoencoder-based recommender systems. *Frontiers of Computer Science*, *14*(2), 430–450. DOI: 10.1007/s11704-018-8052-6

Zhang, Q., Lu, J., & Jin, Y. (2021). Artificial intelligence in recommender systems. *Complex & Intelligent Systems*, *7*(1), 439–457. DOI: 10.1007/s40747-020-00212-w

Zhang, S., Yao, L., Sun, A., & Tay, Y. (2019). Deep learning based recommender system: A survey and new perspectives. *ACM Computing Surveys*, *52*(1), 1–38. DOI: 10.1145/3158369

Zhao, Q., Harper, F. M., Adomavicius, G., & Konstan, J. A. (2018). Explicit or implicit feedback? Engagement or satisfaction? A field experiment on machine-learning-based recommender systems. Proceedings of the 33rd Annual ACM symposium on applied computing.

Zhou, T., Zeng, Y., Li, Y., Jiang, Z., Liu, Z., & Li, T. (2021). Cold-start recommendation method based on homomorphic encryption. 2021 International Conference on Networking and Network Applications (NaNA)

Chapter 8
A Comprehensive Review of Weight Initialization Strategies for CNNs in Remote Sensing

tarik el moudden
https://orcid.org/0000-0002-6963-6686
Faculty of Sciences, Ibn Tofail University, Kenitra, Morocco

Soukaina Nai
https://orcid.org/0009-0002-4819-2198
Faculty of Sciences, Ibn Tofail University, Kenitra, Morocco

Bahaa Eddine Elbaghazaoui
https://orcid.org/0000-0002-3206-5162
National School of Applied Sciences, Sultan Moulay Slimane University, Beni Mellal, Morocco

Mohamed Amnai
Faculty of Sciences, Ibn Tofail University, Kenitra, Morocco

ABSTRACT

Weight initialization is a critical factor in training convolutional neural networks (CNNs), particularly in remote sensing (RS) applications where data is often high-dimensional, imbalanced, and noisy. This review explores traditional methods such as Random, Xavier, and He initialization, as well as modern strategies like MetaInit, GradInit, RGB-based, Laor, and convergence-aware approaches. These techniques are evaluated in the context of RS-specific challenges and benchmarked across architectures like VGG, ResNet, and DenseNet. Case studies in urban seg-

DOI: 10.4018/979-8-3373-8011-7.ch008

mentation, SAR target recognition, and infrastructure quality assessment show that domain-sensitive initialization improves convergence speed, training stability, and classification accuracy. The review emphasizes the importance of selecting adaptive and data-aware initialization schemes that align with RS data characteristics. Overall, weight initialization should be treated not as a fixed preprocessing step but as a key design element for building robust, accurate, and scalable deep learning models in RS.

1. INTRODUCTION

Remote sensing (RS) is currently an important tool for many things, such as farming, keeping an eye on the environment, dealing with calamities, and planning cities. Satellite images have come a long way, and there is now a lot of spatial data that can be used for classification tasks (Boulila et al., 2021; Mol & Kumar, 2024). Researchers have found that deep learning (DL) methods, especially convolutional neural networks (CNNs), are very sophisticated at finding valuable spatial patterns in these pictures. As a result, setting the network's initial weights is a highly fundamental step for effective model training(Boulila et al., 2024).

In DL, weight initialization is the process of setting the initial values for the parameters of the network before training starts. These initial weights can significantly impacts model performance and learning process, particularly model convergence. If weights of layers are poorly initialized, gradients become bigger or die out, resulting in slower convergence or less stable optimization(Narkhede et al., 2022). Many people use common initializers like random, Xavier(Glorot)(Jia et al., 2014), and He(Kaiming)(He et al., 2015), although how well they work may depend a lot on the dataset and the network design. This is especially true for RS tasks that require data that is high-dimensional, noisy, or not equally distributed.

Most of the research has focused on new architectures and feature engineering, but the initialization step hasn't attracted as much attention. This difference is important because satellite images can have sensors that are set up in very different ways, have different spectral content, and have different resolutions. For these reasons, it's unlikely that the identical initialization steps will work successfully for all RS applications. So, initialization approaches that are aware of domains and sensitive to data are becoming more and more important for speeding up and improving training.

There are challenges with starting things the old-fashioned manner. For example, random initialization is easy to achieve, but it usually slows down convergence and makes the model more sensitive to local minima(An, 2019). Xavier initialization makes things work better by maintaining the activation variance the same, as long as the activation functions are symmetric, like tanh. Initialization makes this even better by solving the issue with ReLU activations not acting in a straight line. But these methods assume that everything is perfect, which isn't true in real-world RS situations where class distributions and spatial features are usually wrong or vary over time.

New technologies have tried to solve these problems by using approaches that can change more easily. The Minimum Entropy Loss (MEL) and Minimum Reconstruction Error (MRE) methods are important because they use discriminative filters from pre-trained models to give CNNs that are trained on small datasets stronger starting weights. These filters are keeping the most important parts of the source model. This makes the model learn better and generalize better. These kinds of strategies work best when it's hard to find labelled RS data since they let models start with a lot of information without having to undertake full-scale transfer learning.

Methods based on entropy and reconstruction, as well as structure-aware initializers like OrthoNorm and Layer-Sequential Unit Variance(LSUV), have also shown promise. These methods keep the orthogonality and variance between layers, which helps keep the gradient flow stable(Saxe et al., 2013). In the same way, initialization based on Principal Component Analysis (PCA) identifies convolution kernels by looking at the training data and finding the most common patterns. This is a statistically sound choice over random filters. Sparse autoencoder pre-training is another method that produces useful feature maps from raw RS pictures before training with unsupervised learning.

There are now strategies that use both biology and statistics. One example is initialization based on RGB. It changes how much each color channel adds to the weight assignment based on how important it is to the individual who sees it. This method is based on how the human eye works, and it has been shown to make CNNs that function with RGB images better. It was first made for Internet of Things (IoT) uses, but it might also work for RS situations where color and texture differences are important for accurate classification.

Lastly, we are starting to understand better in theory how to set weights. Researchers have set the conditions that must be met for stable convergence by modelling the training process in a linear normed space. These new techniques to get things going were made for different types of networks, such as basic networks that don't require batch normalisation (BN) and networks that use ReLU or PReLU activations. Tests on datasets like CIFAR-10 and CIFAR-100 show that these kinds of initialisations that take convergence into account work better than regular methods in terms of both training speed and accuracy. These results show how important it is to use custom initialization methods as essential tools for building strong, fast deep learning models in RS and other fields.

2. FUNDAMENTALS OF WEIGHT INITIALIZATION IN DEEP LEARNING

Setting the weights is an important part of training deep neural networks. It sets the weights' (parameters) initial values before learning starts, as depicted in Fig1. These starting parameters are very important for how quickly and steadily the learning process goes. Figure 1 shows that if weights aren't set up correctly, they can make gradients disappear or blow up during backpropagation. This can make convergence take longer or even stop learning altogether. So, it's very important to choose the right way to initialize in order to get good results from optimization and generalization.

Figure 1. Weight Initialization before training

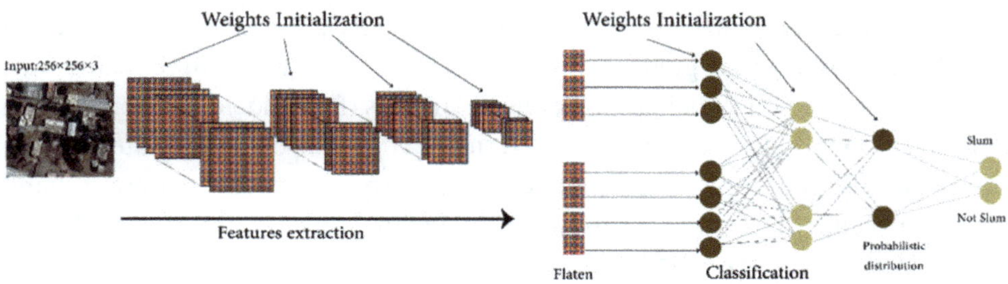

The point of weight initialization is to keep the differences in activations and gradients between layers the same. The signal x that moves forward and the gradient δ that moves backwards should stay in a stable range to make this happen. For a layer with weights W and input x, we want the following to be true:

$$Var(Wx) \simeq Var(x) and Var(W^T\delta) \simeq Var(\delta)$$

This ensures that signals neither vanish nor explode through depth, enabling smooth training and preserving information across layers

3. CONVENTIONAL INITIALIZATION TECHNIQUES AND THEIR LIMITATIONS

In this section, we talk about the assumptions behind each of the most common traditional weight initialisation methods and show the equations or algorithms that go with them. We are specifically looking at initialisation methods that have been shown to work in real-world RS applications. We chose these methods because they can help training converge faster, keep activation stable, and work with deep architectures that are often used in RS image analysis.

3.1 Random and Gaussian Initialization

The earliest method involved assigning weights from a random Gaussian distribution:

$$W \sim N(0, \sigma^2)$$

where σ is small (e.g., 0.01). This helps break symmetry, but if σ is too small, gradients vanish; if too large, activations saturate. This method works poorly in deep architectures, motivating more principled approaches that consider input/output sizes (fan-in and fan-out)(Chen et al., 2024).

3.2 Xavier (Glorot) Initialization

Designed for tanh or sigmoid activations, Xavier initialization sets (Hlav, 2022):

$$W \sim U\left[-\sqrt{\frac{6}{n_{in} + n_{out}}}, \sqrt{\frac{6}{n_{in} + n_{out}}}\right] \text{ and } Var\left(W\right) = \frac{2}{n_{in} + n_{out}}$$

This equalizes the variance of activations and gradients across layers under the assumption of linear activations. However, it does not perform well for ReLU, which discards half the input due to its zeroing behavior

3.3 He (Kaiming) Initialization

He et al. proposed an improvement for ReLU and its variants(Boulila et al., 2022). The initialization assumes that half of the activations are zero (ReLU behavior). Therefore, the variance is scaled as:

$$W \sim N\left(0, \frac{2}{n_{in}}\right)$$

This ensures that the variance of the activations remains stable across layers, improving convergence in ReLU-based deep networks.

4. MODERN INITIALIZATION STRATEGIES AND THEIR LIMITATIONS

To make sure that deep neural networks train in a stable and efficient way, modern weight initialization methods are needed to keep the activation and gradient flow across layers consistent. MetaInit uses a meta-learning strategy that uses the Gradient Quotient to make the loss surface less curved, which helps the weight norms converge more smoothly. GradInit takes this idea a step further by learning per-layer scaling factors that reduce loss after a simulated gradient step. This lets you initialize optimizers without having to use specific architecture. At the same time, Convergence-Aware Initialization uses norm-preserving rules from linear spaces to find variance formulas that are sensitive to learning rates. RGB-Based Initialization adjusts the initial weights of the first convolutional layer based on how much red, green, and blue channels contribute to the result. This helps datasets that are color-skewed converge faster.

4.1 MetaInit Initialization method

MetaInit(Dauphin & Schoenholz, 2019), is a new meta-learning algorithm that automatically adjusts the norms of the initial weight matrices to make training deep neural networks better. The main idea is to reduce the effects of curvature at the start, making sure that the training process starts in areas of the loss landscape that are mostly linear, as plotted in Fig.2. The Gradient Quotient (GQ) is a new metric that measures how much the gradient changes after one step of gradient descent. To get this, you need to use the following formula:

$$GQ\left(L,\theta\right) = \frac{1}{N}\left\|\frac{g(\theta - g(\theta))}{g(\theta) + \varepsilon} - 1\right\|_1, \text{ Where:}$$

- θ = the neural network's current weights
- $g(\theta) = \nabla L(\theta)$ = the gradient of the loss at θ
- $g(\theta - g(\theta))$ = The gradient at the following step (following the application of a gradient descent step)
- ε = To prevent dividing by zero, use a small number.

Figure 2. Visualization of the Gradient Quotient (GQ) used in MetaInit to quantify curvature in the optimization surface.

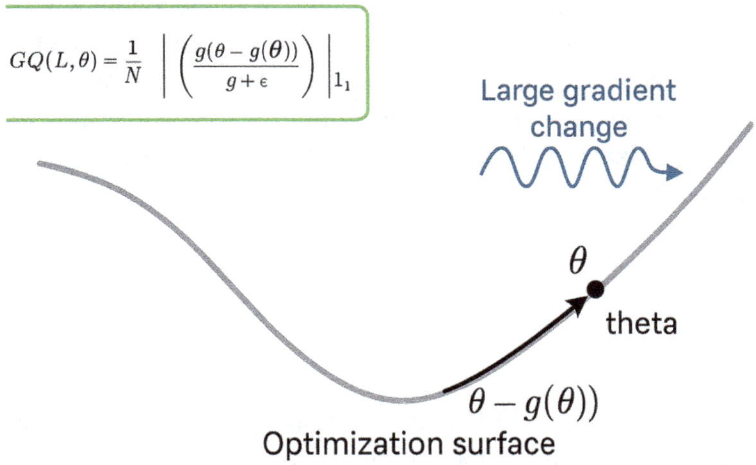

MetaInit initialisation works with different types of architectures, such as plain CNNs and ResNets. It also performs well on CIFAR-10 and ImageNet without using normalisation methods like BatchNorm(Ioffe & Szegedy, 2015). Also, MetaInit shows that meta-learning works well because its goal can be improved using standard backpropagation frameworks like PyTorch autograd. Finally, it supports task-agnostic initialization, which means it can be trained on fake data and used on a wide range of tasks and datasets.

Unfortunately, MetaInit has some issues that could make it less valuable in many situations. It's even harder to set its meta-hyperparameters, particularly in terms of learning and momentum. Because it uses second-order information like Hessian-vector products and needs big batch sizes for deep or complicated models, this approach also needs a lot of extra computer power. MetaInit doesn't change all of the parameter vectors; it just changes the norms of the vectors. This might make it less useful for altering how the weight is spread out. When we use low-precision data like FP16, it can be hard to guess which way it will work, especially if we disregard normalisation approaches. The method's approximation might also not work well with activation functions that are very nonlinear, like Swish. This implies that it is less reliable on various kinds of machines.

4.2 GradInit initialization method

GradInit(Zhu et al., 2021), is a big step forward from the MetaInit initialisation method because it uses a gradient-based approach to change the scale of randomly initialised weights before training. Instead of using analytically derived, layer-specific formulas like Xavier or He initialization, GradInit learns scalar scaling factors for each layer by minimizing the loss after a simulated single-step gradient update, as shown in the formula below:

$$\min_{m} L(\tilde{S};\theta_m - \eta A[gs,\theta_m])$$

Where:

- $\tilde{S}$: A mini-batch of data (different from training batch S) used to check the loss *after* the update. It simulates generalization performance.
- θ_m: These are your network weights after being scaled layer-by-layer: $\theta_m = \{\alpha_1 W_1, \alpha_2 W_2, \ldots\ldots, \alpha_M W_M\}$
- η: Learning rate represents the step size you would use for training.
- $A[gs,\theta_m]$: Transformed gradient depends on the optimizer: SGD (Ruder, 2016), or ADAM(Adam, 2014).

This method catches early optimization behavior and makes sure that training starts off more steadily. GradInit is an optimizer-aware, architecture-agnostic tool that works with a wide range of deep learning models, including Transformers and very deep convolutional networks like ResNet-1202. It doesn't need normalization layers or warmup schedules to work. Unfortunately, GradInit has several limitations. It only adjusts the norms of weight tensors without altering their direction or distribution, which may restrict its flexibility. The method relies on stochastic mini-batch sampling, introducing potential noise and variability. It offers no architectural insight and still depends on a base initializer like Kaiming. While more efficient than MetaInit, it introduces optimization overhead through a simulated training step. Finally, its effectiveness is largely untested beyond vision and NLP tasks, limiting its proven generality.

4.3 Convergence-Aware Initialization method

The proposed method in (Zhang et al., 2022), dynamically adjusts the variance of initial weights based on the learning rate, enhancing convergence stability and speed. Experimental results on CIFAR-10 and CIFAR-100 datasets using VGG (Simonyan & Zisserman, 2014), ResNet(He et al., 2016), DenseNet (Huang et al.,

2017), and WideResNet (Zagoruyko & Komodakis, 2016), demonstrate that this theory-driven initialization outperforms traditional methods, as mentioned in the Tbl 1. The new method outperforms Kaiming, MetaInit, and GradInit, especially in terms of classification accuracy and training robustness.

Table 1. Essential Formulas from the Paper "Necessary Conditions for Convergence of CNNs"

Aspect	Formula / Description	Notes / Conditions
Forward Norm Preservation	$\|x^{(l)}\| \simeq \|x^{(l-1)}\|$	Maintains activation stability layer-by-layer
Backward Norm Preservation	$\|\delta^{(l)}\| \simeq \|\delta^{(l+1)}\|$	Ensures stable gradients during backpropagation
Variance for ReLU (Plain CNNs)	$Var\left(W\right) = \frac{2}{fan_{in}}$	Reduces to He initialization for ReLU
Variance for PReLU (Plain CNNs)	$Var\left(W\right) = \frac{2}{fan_{in}(1+\alpha^2)}$	a is the PReLU negative slope
Variance for BN Networks	$Var\left(W\right) = \frac{2}{fan_{in}(1+\eta)}$	Adjusted for learning rate η in presence of BatchNorm
Gradient Scaling in BN Layer	$\delta^{(l)} \infty \frac{1}{\gamma\sqrt{Var(x^{(l)})+\varepsilon}} \times \delta^{(l+1)}$	Explains why initialization interacts with BN during backprop
Norm Preservation Principle	Maintain bounded norms of $\|x^{(l)}\| and \|\delta^{(l)}\|$	Basis for deriving all convergence conditions
Interaction with Learning Rate	Higher η → Lower Var(W)	Too high variance with high learning rate can cause divergence
Recovered Initializers	Recovers He initialization when a = 0	Demonstrates theoretical generalization
Empirical Validation	Outperforms Kaiming, MetaInit, GradInit on CIFAR-10/100	Verified on VGG, ResNet, DenseNet, WideResNet

Unfortunately, despite the mathematical rigor and theoretical contributions of the proposed initialization framework, several limitations remain that may restrict its general applicability. The derivation of the weight initialization formulas is built upon assumptions such as Gaussian-distributed weights and independent activation outputs. While these assumptions simplify the analysis, they may not hold in real-world training scenarios, especially when dealing with complex architectures, adaptive optimizers, or non-Gaussian data distributions.

Additionally, the variance scaling, which plays a crucial role in ensuring norm preservation across layers, is tightly coupled with the specific activation function used. For custom or non-standard activations, this parameter may not be analytically tractable, making the method less flexible in practice.

Moreover, the initialization strategy presumes ideal variance propagation, overlooking practical factors such as regularization effects, dropout, and stochastic gradient noise, all of which influence the true distribution of activations and gradients during training. This initialization method is explicitly derived for use in plain CNN architectures without skip connections. As such, it may not extend naturally or effectively to modern deep architectures like ResNets, where skip connections significantly alter forward and backward signal propagation dynamics.

Finally, while the method performs well with ReLU and PReLU activations, it falls short when applied to networks using Sigmoid or Tanh, as it does not fully mitigate the long-standing problem of gradient vanishing, a limitation inherent to the saturating nature of these activation functions.

4.4 RGB-Based Initialization

Traditional CNNs treat all input color channels (Red, Green, Blue) equally during weight initialization. However, this paper argues that not all RGB channels contribute equally to visual recognition tasks, especially in small datasets or datasets with distinct color dominance (e.g., frogs or cars in CIFAR-10). Inspired by the biological fact that human eyes process RGB signals with varying sensitivity, the authors propose a method to use measured RGB influence proportions to guide the initialization of the first convolutional layer(Deng et al., 2020)

The RGB-based weight initialization method is a biologically inspired approach that adjusts the scale of the initial weights in the first convolutional layer of a CNN based on the relative influence of each RGB channel in the dataset. Instead of treating all channels equally, this method evaluates the contribution of the red, green, and blue channels to classification accuracy—typically using k-nearest neighbors (k-NN) or early model evaluation—to estimate their influence proportions (e.g., Red:Green:Blue = 0.96:0.98:1.06):

$$P\left(w_r\right) = \frac{P_r}{\sqrt{2\pi}}e^{-\frac{w^2}{2}}, P\left(w_g\right) = \frac{P_g}{\sqrt{2\pi}}e^{-\frac{w^2}{2}}, P\left(w_b\right) = \frac{P_b}{\sqrt{2\pi}}e^{-\frac{w^2}{2}}$$

Where P_r, P_g, P_b are the influence proportions of the red, green, and blue channels, respectively.

These influence scores are then used to scale the initial weights of each color channel accordingly. This modification ensures that channels with higher discriminative power have slightly stronger initial weights, which can accelerate early convergence, particularly in color-biased datasets. However, the technique only affects the first layer (where raw RGB input is present) and shows limited impact beyond the initial training epochs or on balanced datasets.

Unfortunately, the RGB-based weight initialization method has a lot of problems that make it not very useful in many situations. The good effects don't last long; they only happen in the first few epochs of training and don't help much in the long run. The approach only works on select datasets, though, where the RGB channels have a discernible effect on things. This doesn't happen very often with big or well-balanced datasets. This means that it can't be used on every dataset. It also doesn't perform well on datasets where there are a lot of items or colours that are all the same. This method only changes the first convolutional layer, which is where the RGB input is. It doesn't change the deeper layers or get better as training goes on, so it's not as good at making the model work better overall.

4.5 Laor Initialization

Laor Initialization is a hybrid weight initialization method that combines random initialization with data-driven optimization via K-means clustering. The method proceeds as follows(Boongasame et al., 2025):

- Generate multiple random weight vectors.
- Evaluate each using a forward pass over the training set and compute the RMSE error.
- Cluster these errors using K-means into k groups.
- Select the cluster with the lowest average RMSE.
- Use the average weight vector from this optimal cluster as the initialized weights for the model:

$$W_{init} = \frac{1}{|C^*|} \sum_{j \in C^*} W_j$$

This method is designed to reduce vanishing/exploding gradients by ensuring the initial weights are well-aligned with the data structure and error characteristics before training starts.

Unfortunately, Laor Initialization has a lot of problems that make it less useful in a wide range of situations. Since it needs more computational resources, the method becomes less efficient for large-scale or high-dimensional models due to the K-means clustering step(Ikotun et al., 2023). While it performs well at lower speeds, higher speeds can destabilize training by amplifying gradient updates.

In addition, it doesn't always work well at all network depths. It tends to get worse in designs with a lot of layers (like 7–9) and in recurrent networks like LSTMs. Laor has trouble with gradients that disappear, especially in bias and recurrent connections. Another problem is that the clustering method doesn't change during training, which makes it less adaptable. Like Xavier or He, Laor Initialization doesn't have a theoretical basis in variance scaling. These methods are supposed to keep the signal flow going. Lastly, it takes a lot of work to get its hyperparameters just right, such as the number of clusters, batch size, and learning rate. This could make it less useful for many tasks right away.

5. WEIGHT INITIALIZATION IN REMOTE SENSING

5.1 Segmentation of the urban areas using RS images- He initialization

Using Fully Convolutional Networks (FCNs) to segment urban aerial images has become a common way to find small objects, like cars, in satellite images. The authors of the study(Kampffmeyer et al., 2016), created an FCN architecture with pairs of 3×3 convolutional layers (shown in blue) followed by 2×2 max pooling layers with a stride of 2 (shown in red), as plotted in Fig3 . This architecture gradually lowers the spatial resolution of feature maps. They used the He initialization method to set the network parameters. The results of the experiment showed that the model was able to correctly classify 87% of the time. The F1-score for the "car" category, which is a small object class, reached 80.6%, as visually demonstrated by the segmentation in Fig. 4. This was better than previous state-of-the-art methods when using He et weight initialization method.

Figure 3. This is an example of FCN architecture for predicting pixel-to-pixel. The blue layers show convolutional operations (with ReLU and batch normalisation), the red layers show pooling layers, the green layers show upsampling using fractional-strided convolution, and the yellow layer shows the final softmax output

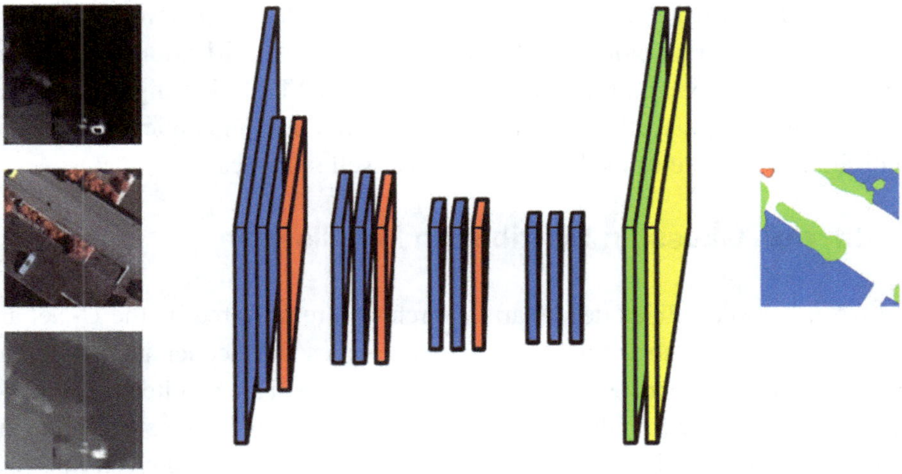

(Kampffmeyer et al., 2016)

Figure 4. Results of the patch-based CNN. From left to right: One of the validation images, its ground truth, the results for the patch-based CNN and the uncertainty ma

(Kampffmeyer et al., 2016).

5.2 Automatic target recognition using synthetic aperture radar (SAR) involves random Initialisation

The paper(Wilmanski et al., 2016), compares the latest convolutional neural network-based methods, such as ResNet-50, DenseNet-121, and VGG16, which were trained on the ImageNet dataset. The study's results showed that well-initialized weights, even when randomly initialized, led to a high classification accuracy of about 98% in the Automatic Target Recognition (SAR) ATR task using the MSTAR database. Even though synthetic aperture radar (SAR) data and optical images are built differently, the pre-trained weights worked well in this case.

5.3 EddyNet- Gaussian Distribution Initialisation

EddyNet is a specialized deep learning architecture, inspired by the U-Net architecture, equipped of structure based on two modules: an encoder and a decoder, with skip connections between them, as plotted in Fig5. This architecture aims to distinguish between ocean eddies and non-cyclonic regions in sea surface height (SSH) maps by accurately classifying each pixel in these maps. EddyNet's performance is based on pixel classification based on the topographical characteristics of the marine data. This makes it a good choice for semantic segmentation tasks in RS (Lguensat et al., 2018).

There are two versions of the network: EddyNet, which uses ReLU with Batch Normalisation, and EddyNet S, which uses Scaled Exponential Linear Units (SELU). One important contribution of this work is the investigation of how activation functions and their corresponding weight initialization schemes influence training stability and segmentation performance.

For EddyNet, the weights are initialized using a truncated Gaussian distribution with a variance of 2 divided by the number of input units, which is the same as He initialisation, which is good for ReLU-based architectures. On the other hand, EddyNet-S uses a more conservative initialization with a variance of 1 divided by the number of input units, which is better for SELU to keep the self-normalizing property across layers.

The authors in the paper(Lguensat et al., 2018), note that EddyNet trains much faster, but EddyNet has a little bit better accuracy and segmentation quality. Both versions use dropout layers (standard dropout for ReLU and Alpha Dropout for SELU) to keep the model from overfitting. When you compare the loss functions of categorical cross-entropy and Dice loss, you can see that Dice loss improves the accuracy of class-wise segmentation, especially for the minority classes (cyclonic and anticyclonic eddies). In short, EddyNet shows that carefully chosen weight initialization strategies, when used with activation functions, are very important for getting stable training and strong pixel-wise classification in oceanographic RS applications.

Figure 5. EddyNet architecture

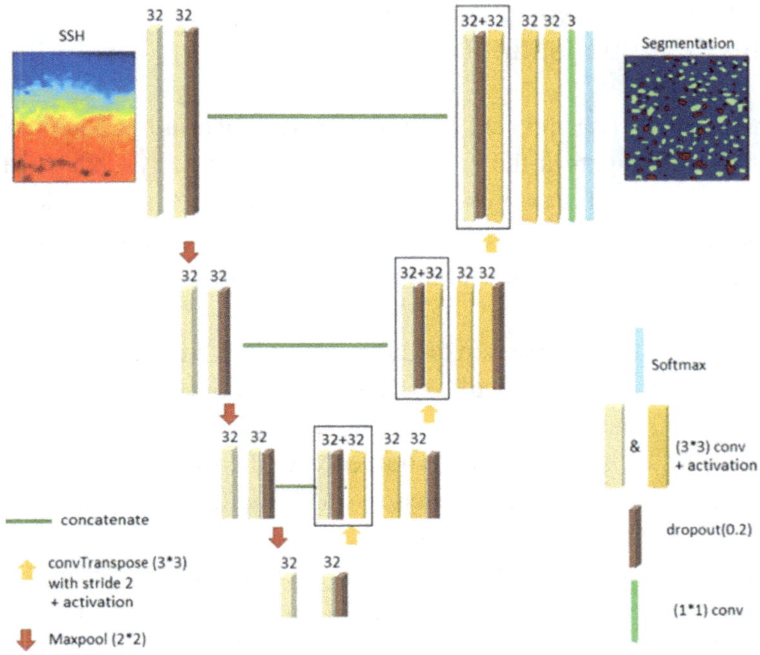

(Lguensat et al., 2018)

5.4 Infrastructure Quality Assessment- Xavier - Initialization

The study(Oshri et al., 2018), proposes a deep learning-based framework that uses high-resolution satellite imagery to assess the status of infrastructure in developing countries. By analyzing these images, additional indicators can be extracted that reflect the socioeconomic status of individuals appearing in the scenes. The study also relies on convolutional neural networks (CNNs) to predict features such as road conditions and house roofs in remotely sensed images. The framework is used in many countries and is a cost-effective and scalable alternative to traditional field surveys that use a lot of resources. Moreover, architecture uses Xavier initialization which lets the CNNs start from a well-scaled and balanced state, which made training much better. The models trained more quickly and made good predictions, even in areas with few data points, when they were combined with deep architectures like

ResNet and improved through transfer learning. The choice of initialization was very important for the model's ability to work in different geographic areas, which is part of the bigger goal of using satellite-based RS to assess infrastructure quality in a way that is scalable and accurate.

5.5 comparison between traditional weight vs. Section 4-3 Initialisation(ours)

The authors of paper(Zhang et al., 2022), did a variety of tests to see how different ways of setting the weights at the beginning effect how quickly CNNs converge. This was done to back up the theoretical ideas put out in the section. The key things these tests looked at were how stable the training was, how well the gradients flowed, and how accurate the classifications were at different depths and with varied ways of starting the tests.

The Tbl2, shows a full comparison of four popular CNN architectures: VGGNet-19, ResNet-110, DenseNet-100, and WideResNet28-10. Each one was tested with different weight initialisation methods: Kaiming, MetaInit, GradInit, and the new "Ours" method. All of the models were trained with the same data augmentation methods, mostly Cutout. The only exception was WideResNet28-10, which used Cutout + Mixup. The best top-1 classification accuracy (%) is the metric that was reported. The "Ours" initialisation always gives the best results, with VGGNet-19 going from 94.41% (Kaiming) to 95.50% and DenseNet-100 reaching a high of 96.00%. This shows that the method is very generalisable (see table above).

Table 2. Results on CIFAR-10

Model	Params	Initialization method	Data augmentation	Acc (best) %
VGGNet-19	20.04M	Kaiming MetaInit GradInit ours	Cutout	94.41 94.64 95.13 **95.50**
ResNet-110	1.73M	Kaiming MetaInit GradInit ours	Cutout	94.98 94.76 95.38 **95.58**
DenseNet-100	0.77M	Kaiming MetaInit GradInit ours	Cutout	95.46 95.47 95.50 **96.00**
WideResNet28-10	36.49M	Kaiming MetaInit GradInit ours	Cutout + Mixup	97.22 97.10 97.29 **97.44**

When you look more closely, you can see that VGGNet-19, a model without residual connections, has improved the most. This shows that the "Ours" initialization method helps learning stay stable in deeper feedforward networks, where traditional methods often have trouble with gradients that disappear. The performance gain for WideResNet28-10, on the other hand, is smaller (from 97.22% to 97.44%), which could be because the model has a strong architecture and regularization. Also, when you compare GradInit and MetaInit, GradInit gives you more consistent performance improvements. This shows the benefit of using optimizer-aware, gradient-based weight scaling.

The "Ours" method works better than other initialisation methods in all four architectures. This shows that it could help models converge and generalise better without changing the architecture. The accuracy gains seen are due to the initialisation method and not to outside factors like data augmentation, since all the experiments used the same training protocols. So, the results in the table give strong evidence that the proposed method is a useful and effective way to improve CNN training pipelines.

In conclusion, these experiments support the paper's theoretical analysis: the choice of initialization has a substantial effect on whether deep CNNs can converge. The tables above suggest that He initialization is the best way to go, especially for new deep learning architectures that use ReLU. The results also highlight how crucial it is to think about the depth of the network and how the decisions you make regarding the architecture and the initialization affect each other when you make CNN models that can be trained and utilized in various contexts.

5.6 Convolutional Attention-based Deep Denoising detecting Alzheimer's Disease

The authors of the study(Alsubaie et al., 2024), suggest a deep neural architecture that can remove noise from real-world audio by effectively capturing both local and global features. The architecture, called ConvADD, combines convolutional layers with attention mechanisms to make the model better at finding and getting rid of noise. The attention modules let the network focus on the most important parts of the audio signal over time, and the convolutional layers quickly get the low-level acoustic features that are needed to reduce noise.

The model's strong learning stability and fast convergence speed are largely due to the use of He initialization, which is also known as Kaiming initialization. This method sets the weights of the network by taking values from a scaled normal distribution that is based on how many input units are in a certain layer. He initialization was made for layers that use ReLU activation. It keeps the variance of outputs across layers, which helps with the vanishing or exploding gradient problem that happens a lot in deep networks. This method helps the network train faster and more reliably, even when it has to deal with high-dimensional, noisy audio data.

In conclusion, He initialization is very important for the effectiveness of ConvADD because it makes sure that learning starts from a stable point where gradients move smoothly across layers. This stability is very important for audio denoising tasks because signal degradation is not linear and depends on the context. The fact that the performance improvements are consistent across different types of noise shows that proper weight initialization is not just a technical detail, but an important part of deep learning success in real-world signal processing tasks.

5.7 CNN Building a CNN from scratch to detect slum areas using a novel initialization method

When making convolutional neural networks (CNNs), especially when training them from scratch on tasks that are specific to a certain field, it is very important to pick the right weight initialization method so that the network converges quickly and works well on new data(El Moudden & Amnai, 2023). The research in question is about how to make good architecture for small image files. It doesn't use weights that have already been learned. Instead, it uses the right initialization to let learning happen from random starting points. Getting the weights right can make the difference between being able to extract features and having a model that doesn't work well in a lot of cases. To do this, the authors looked into other ways to set the weights, such as Xavier (Glorot) and He initialization, and saw how these affected the convergence and final accuracy of the classification.

The graph, in Fig6, shows that the different ways of setting the starting weights have a big effect on how stable the training is and how accurate the categorization is. Huibini one is the best of the four initializers that were looked at: Replicated, Xavier, He, and Huibini. It has the lowest training deviation (0.033) and the highest accuracy for classification (98.88%). This means that it not only makes the final performance better, but it also makes sure that convergence stays stable and consistent from one run to the next. This makes Huibini the best choice, especially for jobs that need both strength and accuracy, like finding slums in satellite pictures.

The Replicated experimental initializer also does well, with an accuracy of 98.54% and the smallest difference between the results of all the methods looked at (0.042). This means that it might train the same way every time and get the same results, but it's not as good as Huibini. Huibini and Replicated are two good ways to start deep learning models that can use data from a lot of different places. This is because training variance could make predictions less accurate. The low deviation ratings show that the gradient flow is smoother, which makes it easier to control optimization. This is very useful when working with RS data that is noisy or has a lot of dimensions.

Figure 6. illustrates that the choice of weight initialization method significantly impacts both training stability and classification accuracy.

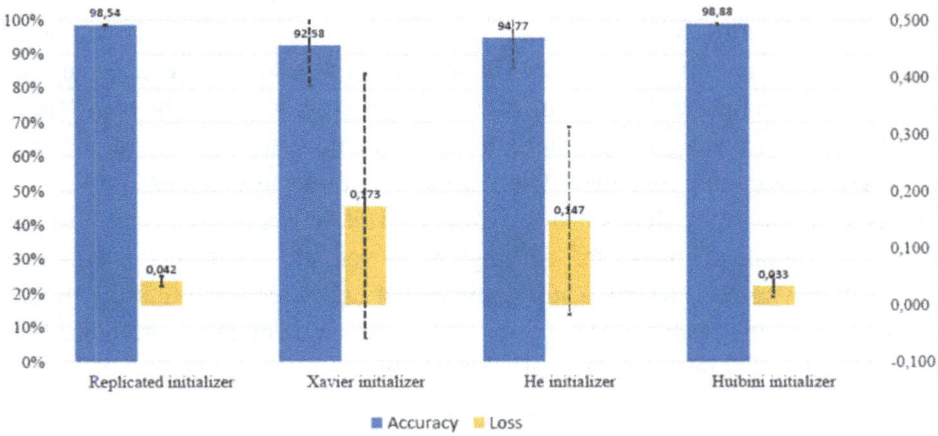

The He and Xavier initializer, on the other hand, don't work as well. The He initialiser is about 94.77% correct, but it wasn't very stable during training because its variance was higher (0.147).The Xavier initializer is the worst because it has the lowest accuracy (92.58%) and the biggest difference (0.173). The network might not work well because the assumptions made when it was set up don't match how it was built. This is bad for Xavier because it means that the ReLU activations are too strong. These results show that the usual ways of starting things don't work well for some tasks, like putting together satellite photos. This makes it even more important to use initialization methods that can be changed or are specific to a task.

5.8 Boosting the traditional unfreezing for transfer learning -Xavier (Glorot) initialization and He initialization

In transfer learning, models often start with weights learnt from big datasets like ImageNet. They use this information to do better on smaller, more specific tasks. However, to use these models on new tasks, you often must change or replace some layers, especially the last classification head. When you add or re-initialize these kinds of layers, the choice of weight initialization becomes very important. This paper makes it clear that bad initialization can make learning less stable, especially in the early stages of fine-tuning. So, techniques like He initialization are used on newly added layers to keep variance across layers and let gradients flow smoothly through ReLU-activated networks(Moudden et al., 2024).

The study also talks about a dynamic unfreezing mechanism, which slowly unfreezes and fine-tunes pre-trained layers instead of updating them all at once. This method lets earlier layers keep their general features for longer, while later layers slowly adapt to the new domain. Weight initialization is an important part of this phased adaptation. When you unfreeze each layer, the right reinitialization—especially when you use methods like He or Xavier initialization—keeps learning stable and stops the model from going off track. The experiments in the paper show that networks that use controlled reinitialization on unfrozen layers converge faster and with more accuracy than those that use naive or uniform schemes.

In the end, this study shows that weight initialization is still important for both training from scratch and transfer learning. When you add new layers or unfreeze existing ones, you need to make sure they are set up correctly so that the model can start fine-tuning from a balanced state. This will help you avoid problems like activation explosion or gradient vanishing. When used with a smart unfreezing strategy, initialization can greatly improve performance, especially when there isn't much labelled data or when the domain changes, like when you switch from natural images to satellite images or medical scans.

5.9 Hyperparameters Tuning with Particle Swarm Optimization Algorithm-Xavier (Glorot) initialization and He initialization

Weight initialization is one of the most basic hyperparameters in deep learning, but people often forget about it. The study talks a lot about learning rate, batch size, and picking an optimizer, but how weights are chosen at the start of training has a big impact on how well the model learns. If the initialization is wrong, the gradients could disappear or explode, which makes it hard or impossible to get to a solution. On the other hand, a properly set up network keeps the signals—both forward activations and backwards gradients—throughout all of its layers. This speeds up and makes training more reliable. When you change other hyperparameters, like the dropout rate or weight decay, the effects of initialization depend on each other. This makes the point much clearer(Emara et al., 2025).

The paper mentioned that Xavier (Glorot) initialization and He initialization are popular because they are based on the idea that they keep activation variance across layers. When the number of connections coming in and going out is about the same, Xavier initialization works best with tanh or sigmoid activations. On the other hand, He initialization only changes the weights based on how many input connections there are. It is only for networks that use ReLU. This makes He initialization better for modern convolutional neural networks (CNNs), which often have deep topologies and activations that don't reach their full potential. Models that used He initialization converged faster and generalized better in tests to fine-tune hyperparameters, especially when the learning rates and batch sizes were set correctly.

It's interesting that the study in the document also talks about how the initial weight affects transfer learning and fine-tuning methods. When you train models from the ground up, the first step is very important to the whole process. But when you fine-tune pre-trained models, the weights that were set up at the beginning are already in line with the visual features. This means that other hyperparameters, like the learning rate and the ways to freeze layers, have a bigger effect. The study does show how important it is to reset some layers, like classification heads, using methods like He or Xavier. This is especially true when the new task is in a very different area than the old one, like when you work with satellite photos instead of natural pictures.

CONCLUSION

Weight initialization plays a foundational role in the success of deep learning models, particularly convolutional neural networks (CNNs), across a broad range of applications—including the increasingly important field of RS (RS). While much of the focus in CNN research has traditionally revolved around designing deeper or more complex architectures, the starting point of model training—how weights are initialized—has proven to be just as critical in determining whether a model converges efficiently and generalizes effectively.

In RS tasks, satellite imagery often comes with challenges not typically present in natural image datasets such as ImageNet. These include varying spatial resolutions, sensor-specific distortions, sparse labeling, and class imbalances. Under such conditions, poorly initialized weights can either delay the learning process or lead to unstable convergence. For example, random weight initialization—although straightforward and computationally inexpensive—often results in networks that either fail to escape poor local minima or take excessive time to reach acceptable levels of accuracy. This is particularly problematic in RS, where training data can be expensive or limited, and model efficiency is paramount for real-time monitoring or prediction.

To overcome these limitations, two main initialization schemes have dominated the literature: Xavier (Glorot) Initialization and He (Kaiming) Initialization. Xavier initialization assumes that the input and output layers of a neuron should maintain equal variance across forward and backward passes. It works best with symmetric activation functions like tanh or sigmoid, which, while theoretically sound, are often suboptimal in deep CNNs due to their saturation behavior. On the other hand, He initialization was designed specifically for ReLU activations and scales weights according to the number of input units alone, not both input and output. This ensures that forward signals and backward gradients are neither amplified nor diminished excessively across layers.

Experiments across various studies have confirmed the superiority of He initialization in deep architectures, particularly in RS settings where ReLU activations are favored for their computational efficiency and sparse representation capabilities. He initialization has consistently shown faster convergence, higher accuracy, and better stability across different depths and learning rates. Furthermore, its mathematical foundation—derived from preserving variance across layers—makes it an adaptable choice for modern CNN configurations involving batch normalization, dropout, and residual connections.

However, the assumption of ideal data distributions behind both Xavier and He methods does not always hold in RS applications. Real-world satellite imagery often involves non-uniform class distributions, varying lighting conditions, and temporally dynamic patterns. These non-idealities reduce the effectiveness of standard initialization schemes and prompt the need for domain-aware initialization. For example, using pretrained models (transfer learning) from large-scale datasets and extracting discriminative filters as initial weights—especially those selected via techniques like MEL or MRE—has shown promise. Such data-driven initializations enable the model to start learning from a well-informed parameter space, preserving critical low-level features while adapting to the RS context.

Another important consideration lies in the relationship between initialization and optimizer behavior. Optimizers like Adam, RMSprop, and SGD with momentum behave differently under various initialization schemes. While adaptive optimizers are less sensitive to poor initialization compared to vanilla SGD, the choice of weight initialization still has a substantial impact on learning dynamics, especially when training time is constrained. A well-initialized model can lead to lower loss plateaus and significantly reduce the number of epochs required for convergence, a crucial advantage in computationally intensive RS workflows.

Recent advances in weight initialization have also begun exploring meta-initialization, where models learn to generate optimal initial weights through meta-learning algorithms. Though promising, these techniques require additional training steps and are computationally intensive, thus less suited for large-scale RS applications in their current form. Nevertheless, hybrid strategies combining data-driven initialization (e.g., K-means-based Laor initialization) with conventional analytical methods are beginning to show advantages in niche RS problems like small object segmentation or spatio-temporal prediction.

The growing diversity of RS data types—optical, SAR, LiDAR, multispectral, and hyperspectral—also introduces modality-specific challenges for initialization.

For instance, initializing models that process SAR images (which contain phase information and speckle noise) demands different strategies than those designed for RGB or multispectral inputs. In such cases, tailored initializations based on domain knowledge or spectral priors can help the model focus its capacity on learning discriminative features instead of compensating for poorly scaled initial parameters.

In summary, weight initialization is not merely a technical prerequisite but a crucial design decision that directly impacts learning efficiency, convergence speed, and final model performance. In CNNs applied to RS tasks, especially when trained from scratch, initialization governs the flow of information through layers and determines whether meaningful features can be extracted from noisy or high-dimensional data. The widespread success of He initialization underscores its robustness, particularly in ReLU-based architectures, but future progress in RS modeling will require more context-aware, data-sensitive, and adaptive initialization schemes.

Ultimately, researchers and practitioners in the RS community should no longer treat weight initialization as a fixed recipe but rather as a tunable component of model design. As RS expands into real-time disaster detection, environmental monitoring, and infrastructure assessment, the demand for fast, accurate, and stable models will continue to grow. In this context, the development of novel weight initialization techniques—whether grounded in theory, driven by data, or learned via meta-models—will remain a fertile area for innovation. The journey from random weights to strategically initialized models reflects the broader evolution of deep learning from an experimental science to a principled engineering discipline, one layer at a time.

REFERENCES

Adam, K. D. B. J. (2014). A method for stochastic optimization. *arXiv preprint arXiv:1412.6980, 1412*(6).

Alsubaie, M. G., Luo, S., & Shaukat, K. (2024). ConvADD: Exploring a novel CNN architecture for Alzheimer's disease detection. *International Journal of Advanced Computer Science and Applications, 15*(4). Advance online publication. DOI: 10.14569/IJACSA.2024.0150431

An, F.-P. (2019). Medical Image Classification Algorithm Based on Weight Initialization-Sliding Window Fusion Convolutional Neural Network. *complexity, 2019*(1), 9151670.

Boongasame, L., Muangprathub, J., & Thammarak, K. (2025). Laor Initialization: A New Weight Initialization Method for the Backpropagation of Deep Learning. *Big Data and Cognitive Computing, 9*(7), 181. DOI: 10.3390/bdcc9070181

Boulila, W., Alshanqiti, E., Alzahem, A., Koubaa, A., & Mlaiki, N. (2024). An effective weight initialization method for deep learning: Application to satellite image classification. *Expert Systems with Applications, 254*, 124344. DOI: 10.1016/j.eswa.2024.124344

Boulila, W., Driss, M., Alshanqiti, E., Al-Sarem, M., Saeed, F., & Krichen, M. (2022). Weight initialization techniques for deep learning algorithms in remote sensing: Recent trends and future perspectives. *Advances on Smart and Soft Computing*, 477-484.

Boulila, W., Sellami, M., Driss, M., Al-Sarem, M., Safaei, M., & Ghaleb, F. A. (2021). RS-DCNN: A novel distributed convolutional-neural-networks based-approach for big remote-sensing image classification. *Computers and Electronics in Agriculture, 182*, 106014. DOI: 10.1016/j.compag.2021.106014

Chen, G., Li, Y., & Lin, Q. (2024). On the impacts of the random initialization in the neural tangent kernel theory. *Advances in Neural Information Processing Systems, 37*, 35909–35944. DOI: 10.52202/079017-1132

Dauphin, Y. N., & Schoenholz, S. (2019). Metainit: Initializing learning by learning to initialize. *Advances in Neural Information Processing Systems*, 32.

Deng, Z., Cao, Y., Zhou, X., Yi, Y., Jiang, Y., & You, I. (2020). Toward efficient image recognition in sensor-based IoT: A weight initialization optimizing method for CNN based on RGB influence proportion. *Sensors (Basel), 20*(10), 2866. DOI: 10.3390/s20102866 PMID: 32443591

El Moudden, T., & Amnai, M. (2023). Building an efficient convolution neural network from scratch: A case study on detecting and localizing slums. *Scientific African*, *20*, e01612. DOI: 10.1016/j.sciaf.2023.e01612

Emara, A.-H. M., Atteia, G., & Alkhateeb, J. H. (2025). Fine Tuning Hyperparameters of Deep Learning Models Using Metaheuristic Accelerated Particle Swarm Optimization Algorithm. *IEEE Access : Practical Innovations, Open Solutions*, *13*, 134506–134518. DOI: 10.1109/ACCESS.2025.3591403

He, K., Zhang, X., Ren, S., & Sun, J. (2015). Delving deep into rectifiers: Surpassing human-level performance on imagenet classification. Proceedings of the IEEE international conference on computer vision.

He, K., Zhang, X., Ren, S., & Sun, J. (2016). Deep residual learning for image recognition. Proceedings of the IEEE conference on computer vision and pattern recognition.

Hlav, E. (2022). Xavier glorot initialization in neural networks—math proof. *Towards Data Science*.

Huang, G., Liu, Z., Van Der Maaten, L., & Weinberger, K. Q. (2017). Densely connected convolutional networks. Proceedings of the IEEE conference on computer vision and pattern recognition.

Ikotun, A. M., Ezugwu, A. E., Abualigah, L., Abuhaija, B., & Heming, J. (2023). K-means clustering algorithms: A comprehensive review, variants analysis, and advances in the era of big data. *Information Sciences*, *622*, 178–210.

Ioffe, S., & Szegedy, C. (2015). Batch normalization: Accelerating deep network training by reducing internal covariate shift. International conference on machine learning.

Jia, Y., Shelhamer, E., Donahue, J., Karayev, S., Long, J., Girshick, R., Guadarrama, S., & Darrell, T. (2014). Caffe: Convolutional architecture for fast feature embedding. Proceedings of the 22nd ACM international conference on Multimedia.

Kampffmeyer, M., Salberg, A.-B., & Jenssen, R. (2016). Semantic segmentation of small objects and modeling of uncertainty in urban remote sensing images using deep convolutional neural networks. Proceedings of the IEEE conference on computer vision and pattern recognition workshops.

Lguensat, R., Sun, M., Fablet, R., Tandeo, P., Mason, E., & Chen, G. (2018). EddyNet: A deep neural network for pixel-wise classification of oceanic eddies. IGARSS 2018-2018 IEEE International Geoscience and Remote Sensing Symposium.

Mol, E. N., & Kumar, M. S. (2024). End-to-end framework for agricultural entity extraction–A hybrid model with transformer. *Computers and Electronics in Agriculture*, *225*, 109309.

Moudden, T. E., Amnai, M., Choukri, A., Fakhri, Y., & Noreddine, G. (2024). New unfreezing strategy of transfer learning in satellite imagery for mapping the diversity of slum areas: A case study in Kenitra city—Morocco. *Scientific African*, *24*, e02135. DOI: 10.1016/j.sciaf.2024.e02135

Narkhede, M. V., Bartakke, P. P., & Sutaone, M. S. (2022). A review on weight initialization strategies for neural networks. *Artificial Intelligence Review*, *55*(1), 291–322. DOI: 10.1007/s10462-021-10033-z

Oshri, B., Hu, A., Adelson, P., Chen, X., Dupas, P., Weinstein, J., Burke, M., Lobell, D., & Ermon, S. (2018). Infrastructure quality assessment in africa using satellite imagery and deep learning. Proceedings of the 24th ACM SIGKDD international conference on knowledge discovery & data mining.

Ruder, S. (2016). An overview of gradient descent optimization algorithms. *arXiv preprint arXiv:1609.04747*. DOI: 10.1145/3219819.3219924

Saxe, A. M., McClelland, J. L., & Ganguli, S. (2013). Exact solutions to the nonlinear dynamics of learning in deep linear neural networks. *arXiv preprint arXiv:1312.6120*.

Simonyan, K., & Zisserman, A. (2014). Very deep convolutional networks for large-scale image recognition. *arXiv preprint arXiv:1409.1556*.

Wilmanski, M., Kreucher, C., & Lauer, J. (2016). Modern approaches in deep learning for SAR ATR. Algorithms for synthetic aperture radar imagery XXIII, Zagoruyko, S., & Komodakis, N. (2016). Wide residual networks. *arXiv preprint arXiv:1605.07146*.

Zhang, H., Feng, L., Zhang, X., Yang, Y., & Li, J. (2022). Necessary conditions for convergence of CNNs and initialization of convolution kernels. *Digital Signal Processing*, *123*, 103397. DOI: 10.1016/j.dsp.2022.103397

Zhu, C., Ni, R., Xu, Z., Kong, K., Huang, W. R., & Goldstein, T. (2021). Gradinit: Learning to initialize neural networks for stable and efficient training. *Advances in Neural Information Processing Systems*, *34*, 16410–16422.

Chapter 9
Assessing the Reliability of Large Language Models in Radiological Scenarios:
Error Typology and Mitigation Strategies

Ikram Gouri
https://orcid.org/0009-0005-6589-3529
University Hassan II, Morocco

Rachid Dehbi
University Hassan II, Morocco

Amine Dehbi
University Hassan II, Morocco

ABSTRACT

Large language models (LLMs), such as GPT-4 or BioGPT, offer us attractive prospects for automatic natural language processing in the medical field, particularly in the field of radiology. However, their use raises important questions regarding the reliability of the results they provide us. This study comprehensively examines the errors generated by these models in simulated radiological scenarios, analyzing their types, origins, and potential clinical repercussions. To reduce these errors, we explored strategies such as prompt reformulation and the addition of clinical

DOI: 10.4018/979-8-3373-8011-7.ch009

context. Our initial results show that structured approaches can significantly reduce factual errors and hallucinations. Two scientific articles resulting from this work are currently being submitted.

I. INTRODUCTION

Large language models (LLMs) have revolutionized natural language processing through the application of transformer architectures that enable large-scale and efficient processing of human language. These models, trained on massive and diverse text datasets, are adept at understanding and generating human language. Their applications cross many fields, among them medicine where precise documentation, good communication, and top-level decision-making are vital. Radiology, a field full of imaging information as well as verbose text reports, is particularly a promising field for LLM integration.

Radiology reports provide a critical channel for the communication between radiologists and ordering clinicians, indicating diagnoses, treatment regimens, and patient outcomes. Unlike other structured clinical data, such as laboratory values, radiology information is usually recorded in free text, a challenging format for automation but holding potential for natural language processing. LLMs can transform this unstructured information into structured, clinically relevant findings. Applications could be initial report creation, clinical report translation, findings summarization, and diagnostic support. Computational modeling is further facilitated by the normalized imaging protocols, reporting templates, and robust digital stores in radiology.

Despite their remarkable language abilities, LLMs are vulnerable to generating factually incorrect or misleading material a kind of occurrence referred to as "hallucination." In clinical contexts like radiology, these kinds of errors can be harmful, e.g., providing incorrect diagnoses and treatments, ultimately creating patient safety concerns and eroding clinician trust. This issue partially stems from the probabilistic nature of LLMs, which generate text by extrapolating the most likely subsequent word based on context. With unclear or unknown inputs, they can generate plausible but unsubstantiated statements, a serious hazard in a clinical environment.

Radiology reports also very much rely on concise idiomatized terms that presuppose shared clinical knowledge and temporal information regarding patient history and disease course. Extended linguistic shades that is, distinctions like those between "no abnormal findings" and "abnormal findings not excluded" are hard for LLMs to distinguish. Furthermore, insufficiencies in medical terminology coverage, domain vagueness, and word polysemy make it difficult for the models to fully appreciate clinical subtlety and meaning.

The second key challenge that needs to be addressed is the interpretability of LLMs. Their mechanisms for decision-making are typically not transparent, and it becomes difficult to understand why given outputs are generated. This "black-box" behavior prevents error detection, explanation, and accountability, all of which are imperative for clinical adoption. Transparency and interpretability are thus the primary building blocks to enabling trust among clinicians and patients and ensuring patient safety.

Aspects of LLM performance tend to be grounded in general natural language metrics such as accuracy or BLEU scores, which value linguistic similarity over clinical accuracy. It is necessary to construct evaluation protocols that are peculiar to medical and radiological environments, with assessments of diagnostic accuracy, clinical concordance, and impact of error. Multimodal AI systems that integrate language understanding and medical imaging need to be developed in the future, as they can render richer, clinically consistent outputs.

For successful integration of LLMs in radiology practice, creation of realistic simulation environments and involving clinicians in participatory design will play a critical role. Understanding human factors such as trust, cognitive workload, and interaction dynamics will guide effective collaboration between AI tools and healthcare professionals. Regulatory frameworks, ethical principles, and ongoing education on AI literacy will be crucial ingredients in responsible deployment.

Integration of LLMs into radiology is full of hopeful potential as well as intimidating challenges. Progress will require not only technological advancements in models but also advancements in standards of assessment, interpretability, human-centered design, and policy. Addressing these intricate demands can enable the realization of LLMs as reliable assistants that improve radiological practice, enable improved care for patients, and safeguard the essential role of human expertise.

II. BACKGROUND AND RELATED WORK ON AI IN MEDICAL IMAGING

Current studies highlight the promise of artificial intelligence (AI) to revolutionize the diagnosis and treatment of complicated clinical disorders, such as those of colorectal cancer and radiologic interpretation Figure 1. AI supports more accurate, patient-specific diagnoses and optimizes clinical workflow in a range of specialties.

Figure 1. Background and related work on AI Medical Imaging

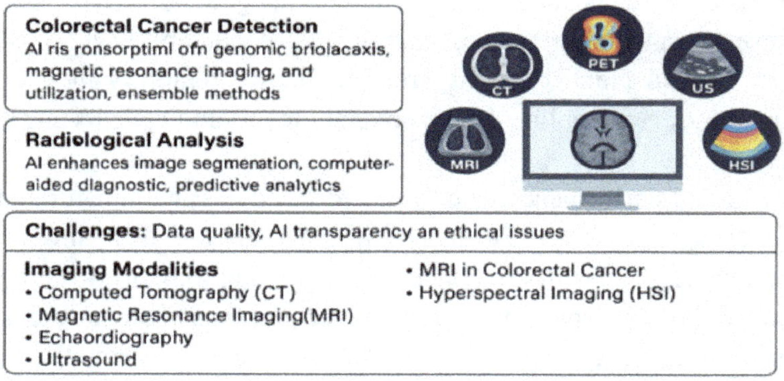

In colorectal cancer, artificial intelligence (AI) has supported early detection through the use of genomic biomarkers and advanced imaging tools like magnetic resonance imaging (MRI) and hyperspectral imaging (HSI), (Ardila et al., 2019; Weikert et al., 2020; Palaniappan, Lin, & Vogel, 2024; Weikert et al., 2020). Neural networks and deep learning algorithms have been effective for analyzing high-dimensional datasets and identifying cancer markers, while ensemble methods in the guise of majority voting algorithms have improved diagnostic accuracy. However, there are built-in problems in the quality of data, transparency of the algorithm (the "black box" problem), and ethical uptake within clinical environments, (Khanna et al., 2020; Zhu et al., 2019; Shen, Wu, & Suk, 2017; Mazurowski et al., 2019; Esteva et al., 2019).

Radiology too has been helped by AI-powered developments, notably image segmentation, computer-aided diagnosis, and workflow optimization. While improving diagnostic accuracy, AI is transforming the practice of radiology by providing quicker, more streamlined image analysis capabilities. There are multiple studies illustrating the wide applicability of AI across medical specialties, such as oncology, cardiology, and neurology. However, data heterogeneity, technical complexity, and the need for transparent and ethical AI deployment continue to challenge the field, (Bera et al., 2024; Panayides et al., 2020).

Despite these limitations, AI can continue to transform medical practice from early diagnosis to personalized treatment regimens. Effective application in clinical environments is contingent on tight collaboration between computer scientists and clinicians, emphasis on data quality, algorithm interpretability, and ethical design, (Gerke, Minssen, & Cohen, 2020; Kim et al., 2019; Roberts et al., 2021; Zahra Sadeghi et al., 2024).

All imaging modalities have been explored extensively in AI-aided research:

- Computed Tomography (CT): Applied in lung nodule detection, image reconstruction, and cerebral lesion identification.
- Magnetic Resonance Imaging (MRI): Used for brain tumor diagnosis, as well as detection of early neurodegenerative diseases.
- Echocardiography: Allows detection and quantification of cardiac pathology.
- Ultrasound Imaging: Allows real-time anatomical analysis.
- Positron Emission Tomography (PET): Enhances diagnostic performance, generally combined with CT (PET/CT).
- Hybrid Imaging: Techniques like PET/CT allow for the combination of metabolic and anatomical information.
- MRI for Colorectal Cancer: Aids rectal tumor staging and segmentation.
- Hyperspectral Imaging (HSI): Optical property-based non-invasive tissue analysis across the spectrum.
- PET and PET/CT in Oncology: Indispensible for tumour localization and tracking, especially if complemented by AI.

Parallel to the evolution of image-based AI, large language models (LLMs) have emerged as powerful instruments for computerized reasoning, knowledge generation, and language comprehension. Their potential to generate reports automatically, optimize clinical workflows, and support decision-making in radiology has ignited the imagination of the scientific world. However, their application must be weighed against rigorous scrutiny of how these models function in clinical environments.

While linguistically sophisticated, LLMs are typically trained on general-use datasets and not extensively rooted in specialist medicine. This disconnection has the potential to cause issues of reliability, especially in high-consequence fields like radiology, where errors can have a direct relationship with patient outcome. Linguistically acceptable errors or omissions can compromise care. Standard NLP metrics such as BLEU or accuracy are not assessing clinical relevance or risk of such errors in real-world use. For example, a properly phrased radiology report can be grammatically correct but fail to mention the significant pathological findings, exposing significant risk,. (Bera et al., 2024).

Benchmark data also have a tendency to lose the nuance and richness of clinical language or the fuzzy, piecemeal nature of real patient information. Aside from correctness, clinicians require transparent reasoning: not just correct answers, but traceable decisions. LLMs most often today do little to shed light on their inner workings, remaining black boxes whose responses could be artifacts of shallow linguistic associations rather than medically sound deliberation.

Such limitations highlight the need for context-sensitive, clinically grounded, and error-sensitive evaluation methods, e.g., to hallucinations, omissions, or factual error. Addressing this, our work adopts a simulation-based, qualitative methodology.

Rather than relying on single use of automated benchmarks, we simulate clinical environments through purpose-built prompts, radiological vignettes, and expert ratings to assess model behavior in real-world conditions.

By combining expert critique along the evaluation pipeline, we can bring to the surface not just the models' strengths but also their blind spots, bias, and failure modes. This reflects a more human-centered approach, which both tests formal correctness as well as contextual utility of model outputs. It challenges and builds upon existing paradigms in AI evaluation in medicine, (Arora et al., 2023; Xie et al., 2023).

Before we outline our approach, we emphasize two related points: first, measuring LLM performance in sound clinically, simulated radiology settings; and second, developing an evaluation process that is rigorous, open, and in harmony with the ethical and practical necessities of healthcare. The following section outlines how we went about these goals.

I. Data Privacy and Ethical Considerations in LLM-Driven Radiology

Large Language Models (LLMs) represent a tremendous leap forward in revolutionizing radiology by enabling the automation of report writing, streamlining diagnostic workflows, and enhancing multilingual communication among professionals and patients. Their integration, however, raises significant privacy and ethical challenges due to the sensitive nature of the health data used. To control the use of such technologies, several global regulatory bodies, such as the Health Insurance Portability and Accountability Act (HIPAA) in the US and the General Data Protection Regulation (GDPR) in Europe, impose strict rules on the collection, processing, and distribution of personal data. These frameworks aim to protect patient privacy while enabling technological progress, but they require increased vigilance when deploying LLMs in clinical settings.

The differences between these regulatory frameworks lie primarily in their specific approaches and obligations. HIPAA requires, in particular, the complete de-identification of health data before any secondary use, accompanied by strict access control and IT security measures. The GDPR, which focuses more on individual rights, establishes principles such as informed consent, minimization of data collection, and the ability for patients to request the erasure of their data. Furthermore, in 2021, the World Health Organization (WHO) published ethical guidelines recommending transparent and responsible governance of artificial intelligence in healthcare, including the need for regular audits and human oversight of automated systems. The table below summarizes these key elements, (Lekadir et al., 2021).

Table 1. Summary of Key Regulatory Frameworks and Their Application to LLMs in Radiology

Regulatory Framework	Main Objective	Key Principles	Application to LLM in Radiology
HIPAA (USA)	Confidentiality and security of health information	De-identification, access control, secure storage	Mandatory prior anonymization, restricted access to data
RGPD (UE)	Protection of individuals rights over their personal data	Consent, data limitation, right to erasure	Ability for patients to control and delete their data
Directives OMS (2021)	Ethical governance of AI in health	Transparency, accountability, inclusiveness	Human supervision, periodic audits, risk management

This Table 1 compares major regulatory frameworks HIPAA, GDPR, and WHO guidelines highlighting their objectives, key principles, and specific applications to the deployment of large language models (LLMs) in radiology.

Beyond the legal requirements, several major ethical concerns arise with the use of LLMs in the field of radiology. The first revolves around the issue of algorithmic bias, stemming in many cases from learning on unrepresentative or unbalanced data, and leading to differential diagnostic errors based on patient profiles. Ensuring equity of the outcomes generated by such models is thus imperative in order not to dig deep into health inequalities. Furthermore, the transparent and opaque nature of LLMs, regularly described as "black boxes," raises questions regarding the feasibility of testing them and explaining their decisions. The implementation of intelligibility tools, such as attention maps or localized explanations, is crucial to enable radiologists to understand and validate automated analyses.

Another critical point concerns the risk of sensitive data leakage. LLMs, trained on large corpora of medical texts, can inadvertently memorize and retrieve confidential information, thus exposing patients to violations of their privacy. To mitigate this risk, several privacy-preserving methods have been developed. Differential privacy superimposes controlled noise on the data, limiting the information it can reveal to the individual, and federated learning is the process of training multiple models in multiple decentralized databases without directly streaming sensitive data.

These practices and principles are illustrated in Figure 2, which describes the secure flow of data in a radiology LLM framework. This diagram shows the entire process, from medical image acquisition to the final integration of validated reports into the patient record, including phases of anonymization, encrypted storage, controlled inference, and human supervision.

Figure 2. secure data flow for the deployment of LLM in radiology

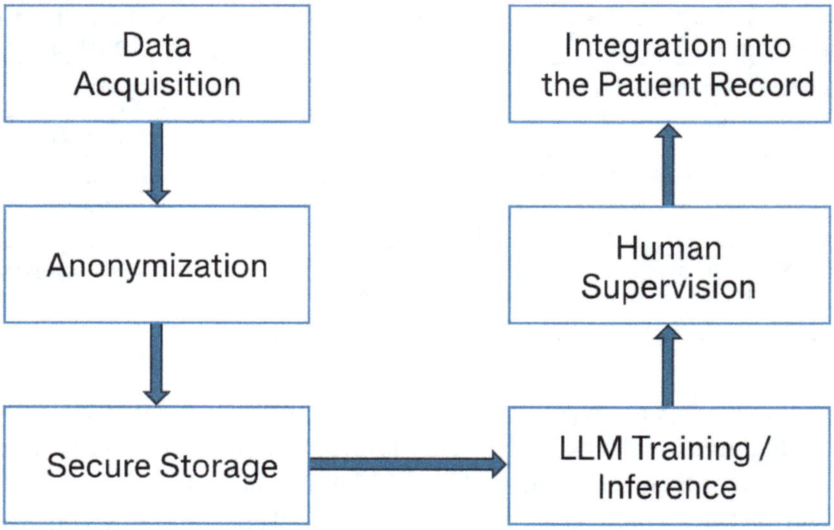

For effective and responsible deployment, radiology departments have to take an integrated strategy involving multiple levers: automatic pipelines of anonymization automation, secure storage with encryption and robust access control, systematic human validation of results produced by the models, and frequent audits to catch any bias or malfunction. All these practices are in line with international recommendations, such as those of the OMS, and support patient and professional confidence.

In summary, l'adoption des LLM dans la radiologie offre de nouvelles perspectives pour améliorer la qualité et la rapidité des diagnostics mais doit être nécessairement doublée d'un cadre strict de protection des données et de respect des principes éthiques fondamentaux. La participation de chercheurs, médecins, philosophes et régulateurs est essentielle afin de préserver que ces technologies profitent pleinement à la santé publique tout en préservant les droits et la dignité des patients.

III. METHODOLOGY

The precipitous rise and deployment of large language models (LLMs) in numerous domains necessitate rigorous methodological approaches that can replicate their advanced behaviors, especially in high-stakes domains like radiology in medicine. Traditional quantitative metrics most commonly used in natural language processing, such as accuracy, BLEU scores, or perplexity, while helpful, do not always present an entirely complete picture of the advanced types of errors and context-specific failures that can occur when LLMs are applied to specialized clinical use cases. Specialized clinical practice, such as in radiology, demands both linguistic competence and accuracy, contextual awareness, and clinical acuity. This raises a unique challenge: how do researchers rigorously evaluate and interpret the quality of LLM responses beyond sheer numeric measures, with attention paid to their practical implications for patient care and safety?

To respond to this challenge, this research adopts a qualitative and experiential methodology aimed at investigating in depth the nature of LLM-generated errors in simulation radiology contexts. This approach allows us to move past the shallow assessment of model outputs and into a finer-grained, richer analysis of the behavior of systems like these in realistic clinical contexts and under real-world linguistic input. Through controlled radiology vignettes and targeted clinical prompts, we create an environment that mimics true real-world clinical workflows without stifling the exact monitoring and annotation of outputs so generated. This system informs a systematic classification of errors starting with hallucinations and fact inaccuracies and concluding with omission of important clinical information illuminating the conditions under which such difficulties arise and how they may be remediated through established mechanisms.

Figure 3. Workflow of the Qualitative Evaluation Methodology in Simulated Radiology Contexts

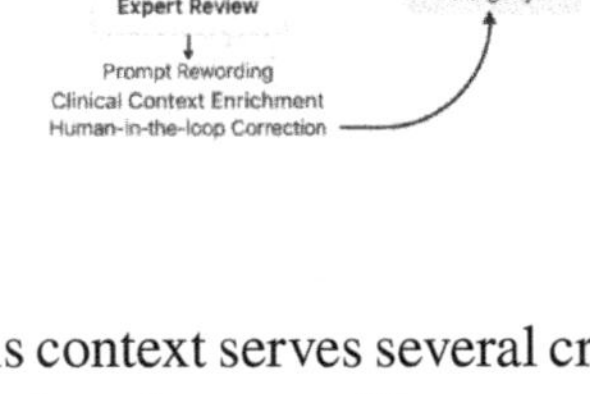

Qualitative analysis in this context serves several crucial purposes. It first makes it possible to identify typologies of errors of interest to clinical stakeholders, such as radiologists and doctors, so that assessment criteria are matched according to their priorities. For instance, a language error that may be inconsequential in a day-to-day language situation can be catastrophic if it covers up a diagnostic aspect or alters clinical interpretation. By categorizing errors based on clinical importance, we harmonize our assessment with the real-world impacts of LLM responses on patient treatment and clinical precision, as illustrated in Figure 3 and Figure 4, which maps each error type to appropriate mitigation strategies, (Xu et al., 2025).

Figure 4. Typology of LLM Errors in Radiology Simulation and Corresponding Mitigation Strategies

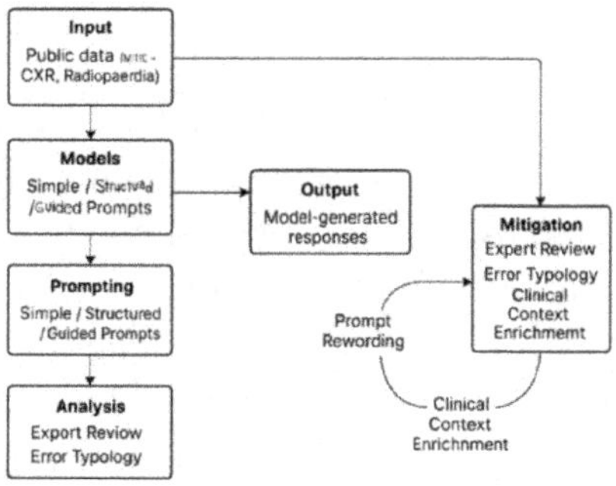

Second, our experiential dimension acknowledges the pivotal and contextual nature of clinical decision-making. Radiologic interpretation often involves integration of disparate strands of evidence, with consideration of patient background, imaging method, and dynamic clinical status. Our methodology emulates this complexity by crafting prompts that incorporate pertinent clinical information, enabling us to see how LLMs approach the creation of multi-dimensional data. This offers a more realistic test of the models' abilities, showing not only where they excel but also where their thought processes might fall short or become too simplistic.

The rapid advent of large language models (LLMs) and their deployment in high-stakes domains such as radiology requires rigorous and transparent evaluation mechanisms. Traditional NLP metrics such as BLEU scores or perplexity are not adequate to meaningfully capture the depth, nuance, and potential danger of LLM-generated output in clinical settings. Accordingly, this study employs a hybrid qualitative-experiential methodology, augmented by quantitative validation, to evaluate LLM performance in controlled, clinically relevant conditions.

A. Dataset and Corpus Creation

We constructed our prompt corpus from labeled data of the SIPaKMeD dataset (available on Kaggle). The dataset has 4049 single cervical cell images manually cropped from 966 cluster images of Pap smear slides. Images were captured using a CCD camera attached to an optical microscope. All images are classified into one of five diagnostic classes (including normal, benign, and abnormal classes). For these cases, we mimicked radiological cases by creating textual vignettes for each image that mirrored actual diagnostic workflows.

These vignettes were subsequently used to develop 60 clinical prompts 3 for each of 20 representative cases that reflected a variety of complexity and diagnostic settings.

Figure 5. Example of a SIPaKMeD cytology image used for LLM evaluation

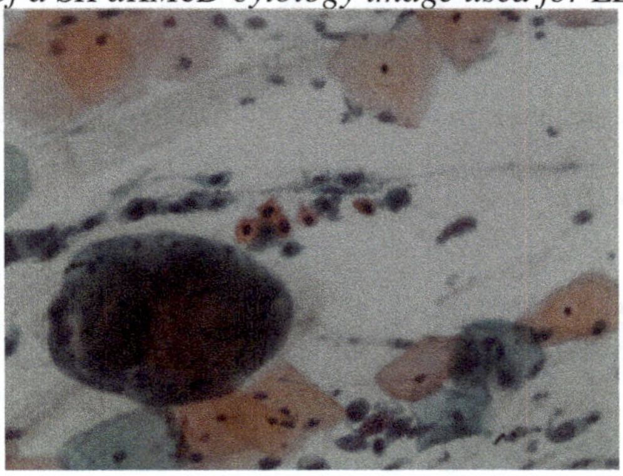

This representative cytology image (figure 5) from the SIPaKMeD dataset used in this study, showing squamous epithelial cells with Papanicolaou staining (orange: superficial cells; green: intermediate cells; purple/blue: nuclei). These images formed the foundation for the development of clinical vignettes and the evaluation of LLM responses in simulated radiological reporting tasks.

B. Model Selection

To lend breadth to our comparative evaluation, we selected four leading LLMs:

- GPT-3.5 (OpenAI)
- GPT-4 (OpenAI)
- BioGPT (Microsoft)
- LLaMA-2 (Meta)

These models were chosen based on availability, clinical or biomedical specialty, and architectural diversity. Each prompt was administered to every model, and responses were inventoried systematically.

C. Prompt Design

Prompts were designed in three structural types to examine the influence of formulation on model reliability:

- Simple Prompts: Open-ended interpretive or diagnostic questions.
- Structured Prompts: Included targeted clinical information (e.g., age, symptomatology, imaging modality).
- Guided Prompts: Chain-of-thought prompts that added intermediate reasoning steps to encourage reflection and process transparency.

D. Evaluation and Error Analysis

LLM responses were reviewed and annotated independently by a panel of domain experts, comprising radiologists and computational linguists. Reviewers scored each response based on a preestablished taxonomy of clinically relevant errors:

- Hallucinations: Invented or fabricated findings not present in the source vignette.
- Factual Errors: Misinterpretation of accepted clinical facts.
- Omissions: Failing to mention important clinical points.
- Ambiguities: Vague or ill-defined statements that undermine clinical interpretability.

A subset of samples was cross-annotated for consistency. Inter-annotator agreement (Cohen's Kappa = 0.78) was calculated, indicating substantial reliability in classification.

E. Quantitative Support

While predominantly qualitative, the analysis included basic frequency counts of each error type per model and prompt type. These results are summarized in Table 2.

Table 2. Error Frequency by Type (n = 60 prompts)

Model	Hallucinations	Factual Errors	Omissions	Ambiguities
GPT-4	3	2	4	1
GPT-3.5	5	3	6	2
BioGPT	8	5	9	4
LLaMA-2	10	6	11	6

This basic quantitative summary supports the more nuanced qualitative findings and helps establish performance trends across models.

F. Mitigation Strategies

To reduce error occurrence, the following corrective techniques were iteratively tested:

- Prompt Refinement: Rewriting prompts for clarity, specificity, or contextual enrichment.
- Contextual Injection: Providing structured patient metadata (age, history, imaging modality).
- Human-in-the-Loop Validation: Adding expert review to validate and edit generated outputs.

These methods were evaluated for their impact on output quality, with refined prompts consistently producing more accurate and clinically appropriate responses.

Table 3. Overview of the methodology steps

STEPS	DESCRIPTION
Corpus creation	Collection of anonymized or synthetic radiology reports from public data
Model selection	Selection of multiple LLMs (GPT-3.5, GPT-4, BioGPT, LLaMA-2) for comparison
Prompt design	Designing different types of prompts: simple, structured, and chain-of-thought
Error annotation	Manual classification of model outputs into hallucinations, factual errors
Mitigation strategies	Application of prompt engineering, clinical context injection, and human validation

As illustrated in Table 3, this enables systematic and clinically grounded evaluation of LLM reliability in radiological use. By integrating synthetic yet realistic case presentations, expert-driven error classification, and remedial feedback loops, the method facilitates safer and more ethical deployment of LLMs in medicine. The combination of qualitative depth and quantitative underpinning addresses limitations of prior work and provides a template for future cross-disciplinary AI-clinical evaluation activities.

IV. RESULTS

We identified some broad categories of errors made by large language models (LLMs) in the interpretation of radiological and clinical data. It is not just important to know these errors for assessing current model capabilities, but also to guide the development of safer and more reliable AI healthcare technologies.

The most frequent and serious error type observed was hallucination, where the model generates information without basis in the input data. These invented facts tend to be delivered in authoritative terms, which might cause clinicians to make incorrect diagnoses or inappropriate interventions. This risk is especially pressing when hallucinations fill evidentiary or clinical reasoning gaps. In radiology, where precision is critical, hallucinations undermine both patient safety and trust in AI-augmented workflows.

Fact errors were also common, including incorrect information extraction, left-right anatomical side confusion, failure to read negations (e.g., “no fracture” interpreted as “fracture present”), and omission of crucial clinical information like patient history or imaging protocol. These are repercussions of the model's foundation in pattern recognition rather than deep semantic understanding, resulting in oversimplification of intricate clinical terminology. Distortions or exclusions of important information may lead to inaccurate or incomplete summaries, with potential negative implications for clinical decision-making, (Ting et al., 2018; Gunning et al., 2019).

Linguistic ambiguity was another frequent issue. Phrases like “possible abnormality” or “findings suggestive of” were encountered without adequate context or qualification, which made them hard to interpret for clinicians. Interestingly, the amount of ambiguity was directly proportional to the specificity of input prompts. Open and vague prompts yielded more equivocal responses, whereas framed, context-rich prompts with clear clinical information and well-defined goals greatly reduced ambiguity and improved relevance. Initial qualitative evaluation by radiologists supported these results, indicating that better prompt design significantly improves the readability and clinical utility of LLM-generated reports.

Figure 6. Comparison of Error Types Generated by LLMs Before and After Mitigation Strategies

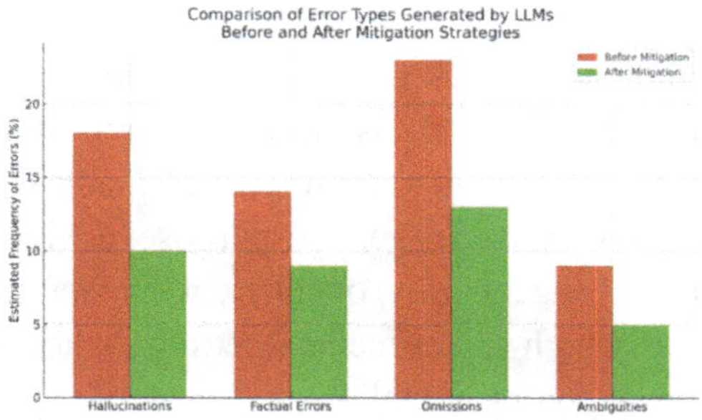

The experimental setup in Table 1 held constant a representative subset of radiological cases and employed various LLM architectures and prompt styles. All the outputs were manually annotated by domain specialists according to an extensive error taxonomy, allowing for fine-grained analysis of error types and frequency. Figure 6 visually captures these findings with a clear reduction in hallucinations, factual errors, and omissions upon implementation of structured, context-sensitive prompting methods. This quantitative information is complemented by qualitative feedback from clinical experts, confirming direct engineering to be an effective mechanism for improving LLM reliability within healthcare settings.

In conclusion, while LLMs demonstrate tremendous promise as supportive tools in radiology, their output must be scrutinized carefully. Errors, particularly hallucinations and factual inaccuracies, can have serious consequences if uncontrolled. The partnership of systematic prompt engineering, continuous human curation, and inter-disciplinary collaboration appears a promising approach for maximizing the utility of LLMs while minimizing damage. These results also underscore the need for standardized testing protocols and clinical simulation platforms to rigorously test model performance before deployment into real-world environments.

In the end, secure integration of LLMs into clinical care will require a marriage of domain expertise, methodological sophistication, and technical ingenuity. The mitigation strategies tested here, particularly the use of structured and context-sensitive prompts, offer a practical and effective solution for model calibration and clinical trust enhancement. However, ongoing surveillance, research, and tuning must continue to guarantee these advanced AI tools achieve their promise without compromising patient safety or the quality of care.

V. ADAPTIVE DECODING STRATEGIES FOR NOISE-RESILIENT LLMS IN MEDICAL IMAGING

The use of large language models (LLMs) in radiology workflows holds huge potential for enhancing diagnostic decision-making, report writing, and patient communication. But the delicacy and sensitivity of medical image data present unique challenges not well addressed in general-purpose LLM architectures. Of these challenges, hallucinations the generation of coherent but factually incorrect content are of particular concern in high-stakes medical settings, where false statements can lead to misdiagnosis or inappropriate follow-up treatment.

Hallucinations of LLM output typically are the consequences of model overconfidence, undercoverage of training material, or misunderstanding specialty-specific vocabulary. In radiology, all of these issues are compounded by the heterogeneity of imaging results, the abundance of subtle diagnostic vocabulary, and the concurrence of multiple comorbidities in a single patient. Furthermore, clinical narratives in radiology reports are rich in structured redundancy and nuanced context dependence; typical noise-removal techniques risk discarding useful confirmatory information. This necessitates decoding machinery that is selectively discriminative in the sense that it can penalize miscontent and context-preserving in the sense that it can retain clinically significant but redundant information, (Qu et al., 2025).

a) Dual-Assisted LLM Architecture

Recently, the advancement in retrieval-augmented generation (RAG) has demonstrated that additional domain-specific data sources can notably improve the factual precision of LLM. In line with this principle, a two-assisted architecture has been suggested that takes advantage of two assisting LLM components: an expert LLM and a non-expert LLM, both operating in conjunction with a base radiology-focused model.

Figure 7. Dual-Assisted LLM Architecture

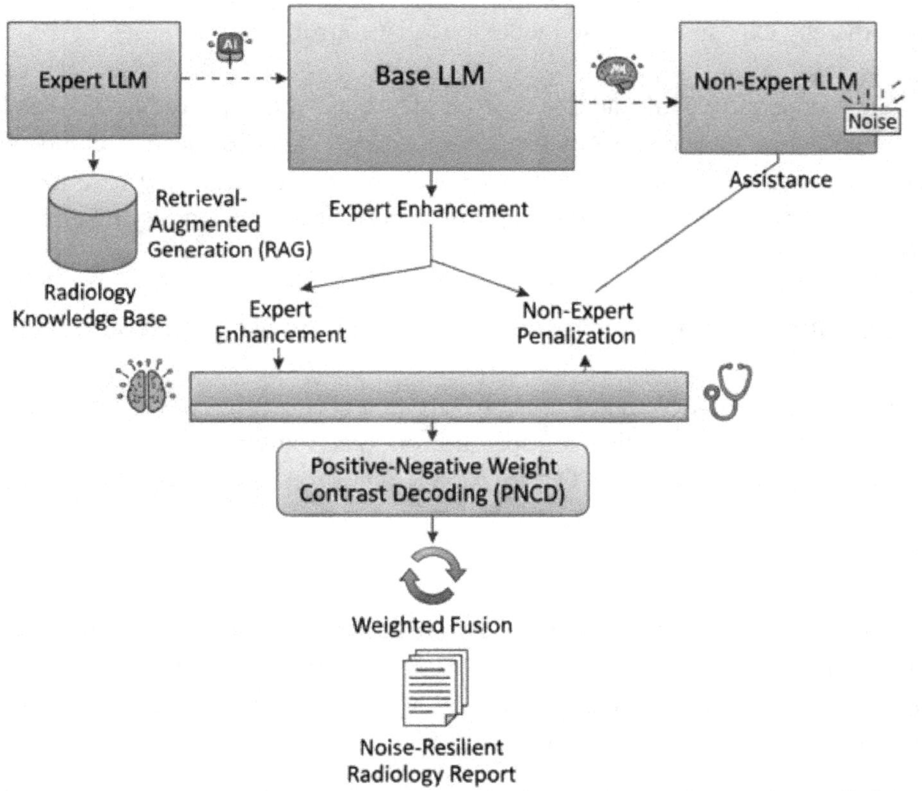

The figure 7 shows the dual-assisted LLM model designed for noise-robust performance on medical imaging downstream tasks. The model incorporates three modules: an expert LLM, trained on authoritative radiology datasets; a non-expert LLM, with intentional noise added to simulate real-world uncertainty; and a base radiology LLM, the base model. Predictions from all the models are combined by the Positive–Negative Weight Contrast Decoding (PNCD) mechanism, which improves factual accuracy by boosting correct predictions and deactivating hallucinated or misleading ones. The flow shows how each model contributes to the final decision, highlighting the adaptive fusion method trading reliability and robustness off for clinical use.

- **Expert LLM**: Fine-tuned or augmented via RAG with authoritative radiology corpora such as annotated imaging datasets, peer-reviewed case reports, and standardized lexicons (e.g., RadLex) to enhance factual reliability and domain precision.

- **Non-expert LLM**: Calibrated to simulate common sources of noise, including outdated guidelines, incomplete findings, or irrelevant imaging artifacts, thereby exposing the base model to realistic error patterns.

This cooperative configuration is inspired by but distinct from adversarial architectures such as Generative Adversarial Networks (GANs). Instead of competing, the expert and non-expert LLMs work collaboratively to adjust the base model's token-level probabilities, suppressing error tendencies while amplifying clinically valid reasoning.

b) Positive–Negative Weight Contrast Decoding (PNCD)

Positive–Negative Weight Contrast Decoding (PNCD) lies at the heart of this architecture, an adaptive balancing operation of expert reinforcement and non-expert penalization at inference time, (Qu et al., 2025). PNCD operates in the following way:

- Expert Enhancement:

With RAG, the expert LLM extracts contextually insightful verifiable radiology facts. An information entropy-based dynamic uncertainty boost factor increases probability weights of tokens that resemble trusted content, thereby producing evidence-based predictions that are stronger.

- Non-Expert Penalization:

The non-expert LLM adds controlled interference when there is noisy or deceptive content. A penalty factor that adapts dynamically, with fixed constraints and dynamic thresholds, brings down token probabilities related to observed hallucinatory behaviors or low-confidence inferences.

- Weighted Fusion:

The predictions from the expert-augmented and non-expert-penalized distributions are combined linearly with the native predictions of the base LLM. The produced probability distribution is still accurate and well-supported but actively penalizes unsupported hypotheses.

c) Consequences for Medical Imaging

In radiology, PNCD has several significant advantages:

- Ambiguity Robustness: When image evidence is uncertain (e.g., indeterminate pulmonary nodules), PNCD limits the conjectural hallucinations but maintains the qualified probabilistic terms that one can find in standard radiology reports, (Simon et al., 2024; Weikert et al., 2020).
- Integration with Dynamic Knowledge Bases: Radiology best practices and interpretation guidelines continually shift. PNCD can be integrated with regularly updated imaging repositories such that produced outputs continue to draw upon the latest in diagnostic standards.
- Redundant Evidence Preservation: In radiology, redundant descriptors too often redundantly repeat important findings (e.g., "ill-defined opacity" reported both in impression and findings). Unlike conventional denoising methods, PNCD separates redundant noise and clinically important repetition as two distinct entities.

d) Potential Deployment Process

An example of a real-world deployment application would be to use PNCD in a pipeline for radiology report generation:

1. Image Analysis Stage: Medical image information is first processed using a vision–language model to get preliminary results.
2. Knowledge Enrichment Stage: Case-related literature, prior imaging comparisons, and formal clinical information are retrieved through RAG for the domain specialist LLM.
3. Contrasting Decoding Phase: The beginning LLM appends standard confounders (e.g., wrongly marked anatomical regions, outdated measurement boundaries) to challenge the reasoning of the underlying model.
4. Final Report Generation: The PNCD algorithm merges the three probability distributions, producing an evidence-aligned and noise-robust radiology report.

e) Future Research Directions

While promising, PNCD needs to be further adapted for large-scale radiology deployment. Main research directions are:

- Entropy-weighted optimization to avoid underrepresentation of rare but valuable imaging observations.
- Expansion of domain coverage to subspecialty imaging (e.g., neuroradiology, cardiac MRI) without compromising inference speed.

- Conducting human-in-the-loop evaluations with radiologists to iteratively tune penalty thresholds and boost factors.

With the combination of retrieval-augmented expert reinforcement and noise-sensitivity penalization, PNCD is a hopeful path toward safer, more dependable LLM deployments in radiology. Its two-aided mechanism not only resolves the hallucination issue but also guarantees higher interpretive accuracy of AI-generated imaging narratives, ultimately allowing for better patient care standards, (Qu et al., 2025).

VI. DISCUSSION

The results of this study show strong limitations of large language models (LLMs) in radiological environments. Although such models have the enormous potential to generate language that is close to human communication, they remain prone to ill effects that make them unsuitable for clinic usage. Via controlled simulation based on SIPaKMeD-derived vignettes and evaluation of 60 clinical prompts, we identified prevalent categories of errors including hallucinations (invented results not supported by input data), factual errors, and omission to report clinically significant information. These findings confirm the fact that linguistic fluency alone does not guarantee clinical reliability and safety.

Our hybrid qualitative-quantitative methodology, constructed by virtue of integrating a thoughtfully crafted prompt corpus with specialist manual annotation and inter-annotator agreement estimates (Cohen's Kappa = 0.78), provided a solid platform to examine model behavior across four LLMs: GPT-3.5, GPT-4, BioGPT, and LLaMA-2, (Kim et al., 2023). The evaluation of simple, structured, and guided prompt classes validated that mitigation strategies, particularly systematic prompt engineering augmented with clinical context, radically improve output accuracy and error frequency reduction. For example, prompted queries that included patient demographics, clinical indications, and imaging findings produced substantial hallucination and factual error reductions. These findings are consistent with the recent literature that strongly emphasizes prompt design as a determinant of LLM tuning, especially in high-stakes medical applications, (Ohde, Rost, & Overgaard, 2025; Ray, 2024; Nakaura et al., 2024).

One of the most important findings of this study is that the value of LLMs relies greatly on how they are queried. Detailed, precise, and context-sensitive inputs yield clinically more appropriate and less vague answers, whereas vague or inadequate inputs produce generic or wrong responses. This is practically relevant to clinical interface design enabled by LLMs: people may require training or prompting to generate useful inputs with a reduction of risk and an enhancement of model value.

Despite the robustness of our methodology, several limitations warrant consideration. Our experiments were conducted on a relatively small, synthetic dataset of clinical vignettes, which, while enabling controlled error tracking, may not fully capture the complexity and heterogeneity of real-world radiological practice. Additionally, the manual and qualitative nature of error annotation, although performed by domain experts, introduces some degree of subjectivity. Future research would have to examine automated or semi-automated measures of assessment, possibly involving clinical NLP metrics like BLEU, ROUGE, or accuracy of clinical concept extraction to enhance reproducibility and scalability.

Our focus on non-fee-paying general-purpose (GPT-3.5, GPT-4) and biomedical-specialized models (BioGPT) precluded radiology-dedicated or multimodal designs combining textual and imaging information. Such next-generation hybrid systems can integrate linguistic generation and domain-level radiological reasoning and warrant more dedicated research, (Kim et al., 2023; Xu et al., 2025).

Conceptually, our findings reinforce the necessity for LLMs to be viewed as assistance tools complementing, rather than replacing, human knowledge. Their maximum utility is to accelerate routine documentation, provide preliminary interpretation, and summarize enormous datasets. Final diagnosis cannot fall to LLMs because of the risk of error and resultant ethical and legal liabilities of misdiagnosis. Effective and safe deployment of LLMs in clinical workflows requires intense collaboration among AI researchers, clinicians, and regulatory authorities.

Trust and safety are built on transparency, interpretability, and accountability. Systems must clearly articulate model limitations, provide traceability of information sources, and maintain human oversight. Our interdisciplinary evaluation approach exemplifies this principle by combining clinical understanding with computational exactness.

Continuous learning through feedback mechanisms offers a potential route to improving model performance in medical environments. Feedback from radiologists in marking errors could be employed to improve continuous retraining of the model, enabling it to cope with evolving medical knowledge and domain requirements, in turn bringing about convergence between general-purpose abilities and expert-level radiological operations.

Top priority to ethical and data governance problems is needed by future LLM deployment. Public datasets may not reflect population heterogeneity or imaging quality variations, with scope for biased output, most notably in the case of underrepresented groups or rare pathologies. Deployment paradigms need to be fair, private, and compliant with medical regulations.

Finally, interdisciplinary education consolidating clinical and AI professions is required. Radiologists must be aware of the strengths and limitations of AI technologies, while developers must be aware of medical workflow and clinical risks.

Shared knowledge in this context is essential for the creation of trustworthy, safe, and effective AI-aided clinical systems.

Finally, this study presents meaningful information on the practical and methodological concerns of applying LLMs in radiology. Although current models exhibit remarkable generative power, they still fall short of the reliability threshold for unsupervised clinical application. Carefully designed mitigation strategies, testbeds with high strength, and clear knowledge of model limitations will be necessary before practice can be regarded as safe to deploy. Eventually, LLMs have the potential to serve as useful adjuncts to radiological practice entities that, with oversight, can simplify reports, aid clinical decision-making, and improve access to medical information, (Jha & Topol, 2016).

VII. LIMITATIONS AND FUTURE OUTLOOK

The use of Large Language Models (LLMs) in diagnostic radiology, although promising, hinges on surmounting the tall technical, operational, and ethical challenges. The proposed Positive-Negative Weight Contrast Decoding (PNCD) paradigm offers a robust solution to countering model hallucinations, but its performance is intrinsically linked to a broader system of issues that must be addressed to achieve safe, reliable, and fair clinical deployment. This chapter separates the principal limitations of current approaches and presents a strategic perspective for further research and development.

1. Architectural and Computational Constraints

The dual-assisted architecture, even though effective in minimizing noise, comes with computational overhead that can prove to be restrictive in the environment of real-time clinical application in resource-poor settings. The three parallel models (base, expert, and non-expert) computational demands at inference time are high, which can limit scalability. Model optimization techniques, such as knowledge distillation, parameter pruning, or quantization, must be focused on in future research to create more lightweight but equally effective architectures without loss of diagnostic accuracy.

Moreover, the functioning of the PNCD mechanism itself hinges on the completeness and immediacy of the external knowledge base. A short or outdated corpus used in Retrieval-Augmented Generation (RAG) could inadvertently contribute to the expert LLM propagating suboptimal or outdated diagnostic criteria. Such reliance places a high requirement on dynamic, dynamically updated, and rigorously validated knowledge bases that support the evolving standards of radiological practice, (Qu et al., 2025).

2. Scarcity, Heterogeneity, and Bias of Data

The achievement of high-performance, domain-specific LLMs is constrained by a proven lack of large-scale, high-quality, richly annotated medical imaging data. Challenges for anonymization of data, patient confidentiality (e.g., GDPR, HIPAA), and the proprietary nature of institutional data complicate sharing data and training models enormously. Consequently, models are often trained on small, homogeneous data sets, which have two critical implications:

- Underperformance on Rare Pathologies: Models can fail to detect or characterize rare illnesses or exotic presentations of common conditions underrepresented in training data.
- Bias Amplification: Demographically imbalanced training data (e.g., race, sex, age) or technical heterogeneity (e.g., scanner model, imaging protocol) can be learned and propagated by the model. This may result in algorithms that are inequitable among diverse patient groups, possibly expanding health disparities.

Future research will need to concentrate on creating federated learning platforms to support multi-institution model training without direct sharing of sensitive patient data. Additionally, data augmentation and synthetic data generation technique development plays a key role in enriching training sets and model generalizability.

3. Limitations of Domain-Specific Evaluation Metrics

The assessment of LLMs in radiology now relies on metrics directly borrowed from general Natural Language Processing (NLP), such as BLEU or ROUGE. These are inadequate for assessing clinical feasibility since they primarily measure textual similarity rather than diagnostic accuracy, clinical judgment, or preservation of semantic nuance. For instance, an LLM can generate a textually identical ground-truth report lacking some key finding (e.g., a minute but suspicious nodule), a form of failure not indicated by typical NLP metrics.

Paradigm shift towards the development and testing of clinically informed assessment frameworks is required. They must incorporate metrics that assess:

- Factual Accuracy: Finding accuracy with regard to imaging findings.
- Clinical Reasoning: Logical coherence of the diagnostic impression.

- Risk Stratification: The model's ability to correctly identify and rank high-risk findings.
- Safety and Failure Analysis: Rigorous testing for clinically significant error modes, such as overlooked findings or incorrect anatomical labeling.

4. Human-Computer Interaction and Workflow Integration

The successful deployment of LLMs from the lab to the clinic is as much a sociotechnical as a technical challenge. The "black box" nature of much current-model AI often discourages trust and adoption by radiologists, who are legally and ethically accountable for patient results. Therefore, constructing methods for maximizing model XAI is a top priority.

In addition, integration with widely established clinical workflows like Picture Archiving and Communication Systems (PACS) and Radiology Information Systems (RIS) is imperative. In the absence of human factor consideration, automation bias has high chances of being perpetrated, wherein clinicians will tend to over-depend on AI output, which can lead to a decline in their own interpretive abilities or insensitivity to subtle model mistakes.

The innovation of LLMs for radiology will be a multi-dimensional, interdisciplinary process. The long-term aim is not to replace the radiologist but to create a synergistic man-machine system that enhances diagnostic quality and productivity. High-priority research areas are:

- Multimodal Fusion: Beyond text-only analysis to create true multimodal systems that can reason on each other about imaging data (e.g., CT, MRI), electronic health records (EHR), genomic data, and clinical notes. Such an inclusive approach is required to incorporate imaging findings into the broader clinical context, (Xie et al., 2023; Mekala Srinivasa Rao et al., 2022).
- Regulatory Science and Adaptive AI: Developing new regulations in collaboration with bodies like the FDA and the EMA. Such regulations need to be capable of controlling adaptive AI systems that learn continuously over time and make sure that changes to the models increase, rather than decrease, performance and safety.
- Human-in-the-Loop Validation: Beyond research like the retrospective study noted above, to prospective, multi-site clinical trials that measure the real-world impact of such tools on diagnostic performance, workflow efficiency, and patient outcomes. Practicing radiologists' continuous feedback will be essential to iterative refinement.

Finally, the journey from technically competent models to clinically useful tools is predicated on a foundation of trust, transparency, and rigorous scientific calibration. By proactively engaging the constraints of the moment while strategically envisioning future innovations, the discipline can ethically unlock the transformational potential of LLMs to improve the standard of care in medical imaging, (Erickson et al., 2017).

VIII. CONCLUSION

The growing application of large language models (LLMs) in medicine, and more particularly in radiology, is a paradigm shift in the near future of clinical documentation, semantic processing, and decision-support systems. No longer limited to theoretical tracts or experimental pilots, these technologies are now assuming their role as authoritative tools in real medical practice. Their potential for natural language understanding and generation makes them phenomenally powerful across a wide variety of clinical activities. From their use in the transformation of unstructured text-based data into actionable forms to their contribution towards facilitating big data summarization, their extent of influence is large and still increasing. The practical application of LLMs is particularly potent in the discipline of radiology, one which habitually generates extensive volumes of text and data in the form of imaging reports and clinical notes. As the medical sector continues to rely more on digital infrastructures, the integration of tools capable of handling such complex and advanced linguistic information is not only desirable but obligatory. These models hold out the promise of resolving entrenched problems of documentation efficiency, system interoperability, and access to specialist medical content. They have the theoretical capability of enabling easier communication between the many stakeholders within the healthcare ecosystem, from radiologists and clinicians to patients and administrative staff. Despite this promise, however, such systems are not devoid of significant limitations and hazards.

Throughout our evaluation of LLM responses to mock radiological vignettes, a theme of shortcomings has been consistent. These include factual inaccuracies, hallucinations, exclusion of critical clinical information, and the use of overly vague terminology of restricted diagnostic usefulness. The frequency of such errors raises fundamental questions about the safety, reliability, and overall trustworthiness of LLMs in high-stakes medical settings. While certain mistakes are easy to spot and correct, others are insidious and may elude cursory inspection a genuine menace to patient safety and diagnostic integrity. That these issues are insidious in character makes detection and mitigation all the more difficult, and underscores the need to develop effective guardrails. These considerations underscore the need for thoughtful and judicious introduction of LLMs into radiology. Over-reliance on

AI-generated content, especially without critical human oversight, can take away from instead of adding value to clinical workflows. While automation can conserve workload, the margin for error must be infinitesimally small when human lives are at stake. The current generation of LLMs, despite all their linguistic proficiency and astounding contextual grasp, lacks a sense of clinical nuance and causality. This absence of domain-sensitive reasoning can produce superficially credible but clinically erroneous or incomplete outputs. Despite these limitations, our findings indicate that targeted mitigation strategies can go far in enhancing model reliability. Techniques for constructing structured prompts, embedding contextual constraints, and embedding domain-specific knowledge in the input process have been shown to reduce the frequency and seriousness of errors. The incorporation of human oversight, particularly from domain specialists with a particular expertise, remains an indispensable aspect of any workflow using LLMs. It is this collaborative effort between machine and human that brings about a new paradigm of clinical decision support: one where AI augments and not replaces human judgment.

Prompt engineering and contextualization of the input data cannot be overemphasized. These are levers for optimizing the quality and clinical usefulness of LLM outputs. Prompt design is not merely a technicality but a basic methodological tool in the management of how models interpret and respond to questions. Our findings are harmonious with recent advances in the field that accentuate how well-designed prompts, informed by domain insight, can serve as a strong filter to refine the clinical utility of AI-generated content. This suggests a shift in focus from solely model-centric development to more application-aware engineering, in which user-model interaction becomes a source of output quality.

Notably, our study contributes not only empirical but also philosophical and ethical contributions to the growing debate on AI in medicine. As we get nearer to the deployment of LLMs in radiology, it is increasingly necessary to develop frameworks that prioritize explainability, transparency, and evaluability. These are crucial in gaining the trust of clinicians and in enabling AI systems to function in predictable and accountable ways. An AI development strategy that is ethical must include enough well-defined standards of error detection, model auditing, and performance benchmarking. This ethical emphasis extends beyond the technical deployment and includes policy, education, and clinical culture.

LLMs must be designed as support tools and not as replacements for medical judgment. The value of a radiologist lies not only in the ability to describe what is visible on a scan, but in the nuanced interpretation of clinical context, history, and evolving condition. AI systems lack experiential judgment that characterizes medical professionals and must thus be confined to a protocol where their output is critically evaluated. Their correct role is one of augmentation: workflow optimization, reduction of administrative workload, and facilitating education and training, but always under close human supervision. This indicates the requirement for interdisciplinary collaboration between radiologists, data scientists, ethicists, engineers, and health policymakers.

Our research has already led to two scientific contributions. The first article provides an overarching methodology for the assessment of LLMs in radiology, along with a taxonomy for the most frequent error types encountered. The second article takes a more technical approach, discussing prompt optimization and its impact on different model architectures and vendor-implemented models. The articles are designed to be informative but also templates for ongoing assessment and development of AI in medicine. Looking forward, we anticipate a number of directions for continued research and development. First and foremost, there is a pressing need to establish consensus evaluation standards for LLM performance in radiology. Such benchmarks need to go beyond generic language testing to include domain-specific measures such as clinical accuracy, diagnostic sensitivity, and interpretive relevance. These standards need to be supplemented by automated evaluation tools that have the capacity to rapidly and systematically identify potential model failures or areas of concern.

Second, future work must address the development of hybrid systems that combine natural language processing-based capabilities with imaging analytics. By combining text and image modalities, it is possible to generate richer, context-dependent outputs that better reflect the complexity of real clinical scenarios. Such systems may leverage the complementary strengths of different AI elements towards a more unified comprehension of patient data. A second critical direction is the creation of realistic clinical simulation environments in which LLMs can be tested before they are deployed in live settings. These simulations would enable experimentation and verification safely under controlled conditions, with developers and clinicians collaborating to identify weaknesses and iteratively improve system performance. Simulated testing is a fundamental step towards a rigorous understanding of AI boundaries and performance in real-world settings.

Further research is also needed to explore the long-term interaction dynamics between clinicians and AI systems. As LLMs become more integrated into day-to-day workflows, there will be a necessity to study how trust, reliance, and user behavior evolve over time. Insights from human-computer interaction research will be especially crucial in maintaining AI systems as instruments of empowerment and not sources of distraction or mistakes. This line of inquiry must consider cognitive load, alert fatigue, and the subtle psychological influences that affect decision-making in the clinical environment.

Moreover, training and education programs must evolve to prepare clinicians for this new reality. As AI assumes its position as a defining feature of modern radiology, medical curricula will require inclusion of fundamental knowledge in data science, AI ethics, and algorithmic reasoning. Clinicians will not only need to be able to use these tools but also to question, interpret, and audit their outputs. Professional development programs and continuing education activities will be key to radiologists' confidence and competency in an AI-augmented practice. Governance and regulatory policy will also be a deciding influence on the future of LLMs in radiology. Policymakers must develop guidelines that encourage innovation while safeguarding patient safety and ethical considerations. This includes developing standards for model validation, defining liability boundaries, and transparency of vendor claims and system performance. Cross-institutional coordination and international harmonization of regulatory standards will be important, given the globalized state of both healthcare and AI technology development. More broadly, the responsible integration of LLMs into radiology is symptomatic of a more fundamental transformation in the way knowledge, technology, and human expertise are interwoven in medicine. These advancements necessitate a rethinking of the roles, responsibilities, and relations between clinicians and computational systems. Rather than diminishing the role of the radiologist, LLMs can, in fact, augment it liberating professionals to focus on tasks demanding deep interpretation, human empathy, and ethical judgment, and ceding only routine or repetitive tasks to intelligent systems.

In conclusion, the integration of LLMs into radiology represents both an enormous opportunity and an enormous challenge. While their technical promise offers exciting new possibilities for documentation, workflow, and decision support, their current limitations demand guarded and critical integration. The path to successful and safe use is via formalized prompt engineering, domain-specific model tuning, interprofessional collaboration, and strong commitment to transparency and oversight. Future research should aim to develop rigorous testing protocols, hybrid platforms combining language and image analysis, and real-world simulation environments. The long-term goal, nevertheless, is not the development of autonomous systems that replace clinicians, but the creation of intelligent assistants that can continuously enhance the skills of radiology professionals, advance patient care, and uphold the moral underpinnings of medical practice.

REFERENCES

Ardila, D., Kiraly, A. P., Bharadwaj, S., Choi, B., Reicher, J. J., Peng, L., Tse, D., Etemadi, M., Ye, W., Corrado, G., Naidich, D. P., & Shetty, S. (2019). End-to-end lung cancer screening with three-dimensional deep learning on low-dose chest computed tomography. *Nature Medicine, 25*(6), 954–961. DOI: 10.1038/s41591-019-0447-x PMID: 31110349

Arora, A., Alderman, J. E., Palmer, J., Ganapathi, S., Laws, E., Mccradden, M. D., ... & Liu, X. (2023). The value of standards for health datasets in artificial intelligence-based applications.

Bera, K., O'Connor, G., Jiang, S., Tirumani, S. H., & Ramaiya, N. (2024). Analysis of ChatGPT publications in radiology: Literature so far. *Current Problems in Diagnostic Radiology, 53*(2), 215–225. DOI: 10.1067/j.cpradiol.2023.10.013 PMID: 37891083

Erickson, B. J., Korfiatis, P., Akkus, Z., & Kline, T. L. (2017). Machine learning for medical imaging. *radiographics, 37(2)*, 505-515.

Esteva, A., Robicquet, A., Ramsundar, B., Kuleshov, V., DePristo, M., Chou, K., Cui, C., Corrado, G., Thrun, S., & Dean, J. (2019). A guide to deep learning in healthcare. *Nature Medicine, 25*(1), 24–29. DOI: 10.1038/s41591-018-0316-z PMID: 30617335

Gerke, S., Minssen, T., & Cohen, G. (2020). Ethical and legal challenges of artificial intelligence-driven healthcare. In *Artificial intelligence in healthcare* (pp. 295–336). Academic Press. DOI: 10.1016/B978-0-12-818438-7.00012-5

Gunning, D., & Aha, D. W.DW. (2019). DARPA's explainable artificial intelligence program. *AI Magazine, 40*(2), 44–58. DOI: 10.1609/aimag.v40i2.2850

Jha, S., & Topol, E. J. (2016). Adapting to artificial intelligence: Radiologists and pathologists as information specialists. *Journal of the American Medical Association, 316*(22), 2353–2354. DOI: 10.1001/jama.2016.17438 PMID: 27898975

Khanna, S., Srivastava, S., Khanna, I., & Pandey, V. (2020). Current Challenges and Opportunities in Implementing AI/ML in Cancer Imaging: Integration, Development, and Adoption Perspectives. *Journal of Advanced Analytics in Healthcare Management, 4*(10), 1–25.

Kim, D. W., Jang, H. Y., Kim, K. W., Shin, Y., & Park, S. H. (2019). Design characteristics of studies reporting the performance of artificial intelligence algorithms for diagnostic analysis of medical images: Results from recently published papers. *Korean Journal of Radiology, 20*(3), 405–410. DOI: 10.3348/kjr.2019.0025 PMID: 30799571

Kim, J. K., Chua, M., Rickard, M., & Lorenzo, A. (2023). ChatGPT and large language model (LLM) chatbots: The current state of acceptability and a proposal for guidelines on utilization in academic medicine. *Journal of Pediatric Urology, 19*(5), 598–604. DOI: 10.1016/j.jpurol.2023.05.018 PMID: 37328321

Lekadir, K., Osuala, R., Gallin, C., Lazrak, N., Kushibar, K., Tsakou, G., ... & Martí-Bonmatí, L. (2021). FUTURE-AI: guiding principles and consensus recommendations for trustworthy artificial intelligence in medical imaging.

Mazurowski, M. A., Buda, M., Saha, A., & Bashir, M. R. (2019). Deep learning in radiology: An overview of the concepts and a survey of the state of the art with focus on MRI. *Journal of Magnetic Resonance Imaging, 49*(4), 939–954. DOI: 10.1002/jmri.26534 PMID: 30575178

Nakaura, T., Ito, R., Ueda, D., Nozaki, T., Fushimi, Y., Matsui, Y., Yanagawa, M., Yamada, A., Tsuboyama, T., Fujima, N., Tatsugami, F., Hirata, K., Fujita, S., Kamagata, K., Fujioka, T., Kawamura, M., & Naganawa, S. (2024). The impact of large language models on radiology: A guide for radiologists on the latest innovations in AI. *Japanese Journal of Radiology, 42*(7), 685–696. DOI: 10.1007/s11604-024-01552-0 PMID: 38551772

Ohde, J. W., Rost, L. M., & Overgaard, J. D. (2025). The Burden of Reviewing LLM-Generated Content. *NEJM AI, 2*(2), AIp2400979. DOI: 10.1056/AIp2400979

Palaniappan, K., Lin, E. Y. T., & Vogel, S. (2024). *Global regulatory frameworks for the use of artificial intelligence (AI) in the healthcare services sector.* MDPI. DOI: 10.3390/healthcare12050562

Panayides, A. S., Amini, A., Filipovic, N. D., Sharma, A., Tsaftaris, S. A., Young, A., Foran, D., Do, N., Golemati, S., Kurc, T., Huang, K., Nikita, K. S., Veasey, B. P., Zervakis, M., Saltz, J. H., & Pattichis, C. S. (2020). AI in medical imaging informatics: Current challenges and future directions. *IEEE Journal of Biomedical and Health Informatics, 24*(7), 1837–1857. DOI: 10.1109/JBHI.2020.2991043 PMID: 32609615

Panayides, A. S., Amini, A., Filipovic, N. D., Sharma, A., Tsaftaris, S. A., Young, A., Foran, D., Do, N., Golemati, S., Kurc, T., Huang, K., Nikita, K. S., Veasey, B. P., Zervakis, M., Saltz, J. H., & Pattichis, C. S. (2020). AI in medical imaging informatics: Current challenges and future directions. *IEEE Journal of Biomedical and Health Informatics, 24*(7), 1837–1857. DOI: 10.1109/JBHI.2020.2991043 PMID: 32609615

Qu, J., Liu, J., Liu, X., Chen, M., Li, J., & Wang, J. (2025). PNCD: Mitigating LLM Hallucinations in Noisy Environments A Medical Case Study. *Information Fusion*, *123*, 103328. DOI: 10.1016/j.inffus.2025.103328

Mekala Srinivasa Rao, Sagenela Vijaya Kumar, Rambabu Pemula, Anil Kumar Prathipati (2022).Change detection of pulmonary embolism using isomeric cluster and computer vision.

Ray, P. P. (2024). Integrating AI in radiology: Insights from GPT-generated reports and multimodal LLM performance on European Board of Radiology examinations. *Japanese Journal of Radiology*, *42*(9), 1083–1084. DOI: 10.1007/s11604-024-01576-6 PMID: 38647884

Roberts, M., Driggs, D., Thorpe, M., Gilbey, J., Yeung, M., Ursprung, S., Aviles-Rivero, A. I., Etmann, C., McCague, C., Beer, L., Weir-McCall, J. R., Teng, Z., Gkrania-Klotsas, E., Ruggiero, A., Korhonen, A., Jefferson, E., Ako, E., Langs, G., Gozaliasl, G., & Schönlieb, C. B. (2021). Common pitfalls and recommendations for using machine learning to detect and prognosticate for COVID-19 using chest radiographs and CT scans. *Nature Machine Intelligence*, *3*(3), 199–217. DOI: 10.1038/s42256-021-00307-0

Zahra Sadeghi, Roohallah Alizadehsani, Mehmet Akif CIFCI, Samina Kausar, Rizwan Rehman, Priyakshi Mahanta, Pranjal Kumar Bora, Ammar Almasri, Rami S. Alkhawalde, Sadiq Hussain, Bilal Alatas, Afshin Shoeibi l, Hossein Moosaei, Milan Hladík, Saeid Nahavandi, Panos M. Pardalos. (2024). A review of Explainable Artificial Intelligence in healthcare.

Shen, D., Wu, G., & Suk, H. I. (2017). Deep learning in medical image analysis. *Annual Review of Biomedical Engineering*, *19*(1), 221–248. DOI: 10.1146/annurev-bioeng-071516-044442 PMID: 28301734

Simon, B. D., Ozyoruk, K. B., Gelikman, D. G., Harmon, S. A., & Türkbey, B (2024). The future of multimodal artificial intelligence models for integrating imaging and clinical metadata: a narrative review. Diagnostic and interventional radiology (Ankara, Turkey).

Ting, D. S., Liu, Y., Burlina, P., Xu, X., Bressler, N. M., & Wong, T. Y. (2018). AI for medical imaging goes deep. *Nature Medicine*, *24*(5), 539–540. DOI: 10.1038/s41591-018-0029-3 PMID: 29736024

Weikert, T., Winkel, D. J., Bremerich, J., Stieltjes, B., Parmar, V., Sauter, A. W., & Sommer, G. (2020). Automated detection of pulmonary embolism in CT pulmonary angiograms using an AI-powered algorithm. *European Radiology*, *30*(12), 6545–6553. DOI: 10.1007/s00330-020-06998-0 PMID: 32621243

Weikert, T., Winkel, D. J., Bremerich, J., Stieltjes, B., Parmar, V., Sauter, A. W., & Sommer, G. (2020). Automated detection of pulmonary embolism in CT pulmonary angiograms using an AI-powered algorithm. *European Radiology*, *30*(12), 6545–6553. DOI: 10.1007/s00330-020-06998-0 PMID: 32621243

Xie, J., Luo, X., Deng, X., Tang, Y., Tian, W., Cheng, H., ... & Xie, X. (2023). Advances in artificial intelligence to predict cancer immunotherapy efficacy.
Xie, J., Luo, X., Deng, X., Tang, Y., Tian, W., Cheng, H., ... & Xie, X. (2023). Advances in artificial intelligence to predict cancer immunotherapy efficacy.
Xu, Q., Wu, T., Wang, Y., Li, X., Yu, H., Cen, S., & Li, Z. (2025). A comprehensive review of Intelligent Question-Answering Systems in Traditional Chinese Medicine Based on LLMs. *Journal of Pharmaceutical Analysis*, 101406. DOI: 10.1016/j.jpha.2025.101406

Zhu, W., Huang, Y., Zeng, L., Chen, X., Liu, Y., Qian, Z., Du, N., Fan, W., & Xie, X. (2019). AnatomyNet: Deep learning for fast and fully automated whole-volume segmentation of head and neck anatomy. *Medical Physics*, *46*(2), 576–589. DOI: 10.1002/mp.13300 PMID: 30480818

Chapter 10
Safeguarding Digital Transformation:
Cybersecurity for Digital Twin and IoT Ecosystems

Kirti Jain
School of Computer Technology, Sanjeev Agrawal Global Educational University, Bhopal, India

Shital Gupta
https://orcid.org/0000-0002-6647-9195
Bansal Institute of Science and Technology, India

Nitesh Behare
https://orcid.org/0000-0002-9338-8563
Balaji Institute of International Business, Sri Balaji University, Pune, India

ABSTRACT

The convergence of Digital Twins and the Internet of Things (IoT) is transforming industrial ecosystems by facilitating real-time intelligence, predictive analytics, and data-driven decision-making. However, this integration also amplifies cybersecurity vulnerabilities, necessitating robust and adaptive security frameworks. This chapter critically examines the cybersecurity imperatives associated with Digital Twin–IoT environments, highlighting threats such as ransomware, data breaches, and supply chain attacks. It underscores the role of secure communication protocols, identity and access management, and blockchain-based solutions in mitigating risks. Regulatory frameworks—including GDPR, NIST, and ISO/IEC 27001—are analyzed to elucidate compliance complexities in transnational contexts. Through empirical case studies,

DOI: 10.4018/979-8-3373-8011-7.ch010

the chapter illustrates past cyber incidents and identifies strategic mitigation practices. Finally, it explores emerging challenges posed by quantum computing and edge security, advocating for dynamic, future-ready cybersecurity architectures.

1. INTRODUCTION

The rapid advancement of digital technologies is transforming industries at an unprecedented pace. Among these technologies, Digital Twins and the Internet of Things (IoT) are at the forefront of this transformation, enabling businesses to simulate, analyze, and optimize real-world operations in real time (Rajora et al., 2023). Digital Twins—virtual representations of physical assets, processes, or systems—are increasingly used in manufacturing, healthcare, smart cities, and logistics to improve efficiency, reduce costs, and drive innovation. When combined with IoT, which facilitates continuous data exchange between physical and digital environments, these technologies create highly interconnected ecosystems that power predictive analytics, automation, and intelligent decision-making (Tsintotas et al., 2024). However, as organizations accelerate their digital transformation initiatives, cybersecurity emerges as a critical challenge that must be addressed to ensure the integrity, reliability, and security of these interconnected systems (Swain et al., 2022).

The integration of Digital Twins and IoT introduces a complex security landscape (Abdullahi et al., 2024). These technologies rely on vast amounts of real-time data collected from IoT sensors, industrial control systems, and cloud-based platforms. While this connectivity offers significant advantages, it also expands the attack surface, making Digital Twin and IoT environments prime targets for cyber threats (Nguyen et al., 2025). Cybercriminals exploit vulnerabilities in connected devices, communication networks, and cloud infrastructures to launch attacks such as data breaches, ransomware, denial-of-service (DoS) attacks, and industrial espionage. The consequences of these cyber threats can be severe, leading to financial losses, operational disruptions, compromised data integrity, and reputational damage for businesses (Sandhu, 2021).

One of the biggest challenges in securing Digital Twin and IoT ecosystems is the heterogeneous nature of devices and platforms. Unlike traditional IT systems, IoT devices often have limited computational power, weak security mechanisms (Saeed et al., 2024) and outdated firmware, making them susceptible to exploitation. Many organizations also deploy IoT solutions from multiple vendors, leading to inconsistencies in security protocols and integration challenges (Rawajbeh et al., 2023). Furthermore, legacy systems that were not designed with cybersecurity in mind are often connected to modern IoT infrastructures, increasing the risk of cyber intrusions. As a result, a comprehensive cybersecurity strategy is essential to protect Digital Twin and IoT deployments from emerging threats.

Another major concern is data security and privacy. Digital Twins continuously process large volumes of sensitive information, including proprietary business data, customer records, and real-time operational insights (Sijan et al., 2022). If this data falls into the wrong hands, it can lead to corporate espionage, regulatory violations, or manipulation of critical infrastructure. Ensuring end-to-end encryption, secure authentication, and access controls is crucial to safeguarding data integrity and preventing unauthorized access (Saeed et al., 2024). Additionally, compliance with international cybersecurity standards, such as the General Data Protection Regulation (GDPR), National Institute of Standards and Technology (NIST) guidelines, and ISO/IEC 27001, plays a vital role in strengthening security frameworks and maintaining trust in digital ecosystems (Al-Dalati, 2022).

Beyond technical vulnerabilities, the human factor remains a significant cybersecurity risk. Employees, suppliers, and third-party vendors often have access to Digital Twin and IoT systems, creating potential entry points for cyberattacks. Phishing attacks, insider threats, and poor security practices can expose critical infrastructures to malicious actors (Flores Ccanto et al., 2021). Organizations must invest in cybersecurity awareness training, strong identity and access management (IAM), and zero-trust security architectures to minimize human-related risks.

As the digital landscape evolves, emerging technologies AI, ML and Blockchain are playing a crucial role in enhancing cybersecurity for Digital Twin and IoT environments (Soudan, 2024). AI-powered threat detection systems can analyze behavioral patterns and identify anomalies in real time, while blockchain technology provides tamper-proof data integrity and secure transaction management. Implementing these advanced security measures will be essential for organizations to stay ahead of cyber threats and build resilient digital ecosystems (Nguyen et al., 2025).

2. UNDERSTANDING DIGITAL TWINS AND IOT

Digital transformation is reshaping industries by leveraging cutting-edge technologies such as Digital Twins and the Internet of Things (IoT). These innovations enable businesses to optimize performance, improve decision-making, and enhance operational efficiency by creating a seamless bridge between the physical and digital worlds. Digital Twins, in particular, serve as dynamic virtual models that replicate real-world objects, processes, or systems (Rajora et al., 2023). When integrated with IoT devices, they continuously collect, process, and analyze real-time data, providing valuable insights into performance, predictive maintenance, and system optimization. However, as the complexity and interconnectivity of these technologies increase, so do the security challenges, making it essential to adopt robust cybersecurity frameworks to protect against emerging threats (Taherdoost et al., 2021).

2.1 The Role of Digital Twins in Modern Industries

A Digital Twin is essentially a virtual representation of a physical asset that simulates its behavior and operational conditions in real time. These models are created using historical data, real-time sensor inputs, and advanced analytics, allowing organizations to test different scenarios (Vaczi et al., 2020), predict failures, and optimize processes without disrupting real-world operations. Digital Twins have found applications in various industries, including:

- Manufacturing: Factories use Digital Twins to monitor equipment health, predict failures, and streamline production. By analyzing sensor data from IoT-enabled machinery, manufacturers can prevent costly downtime and improve efficiency (Priya & A., 2024).
- Healthcare: In medical applications, Digital Twins are used for patient monitoring, personalized treatment planning, and surgical simulations. For example, a Digital Twin of a human organ can help doctors assess potential risks before performing surgeries (Priya & A., 2024).
- Smart Cities: Digital Twins are transforming urban infrastructure by optimizing traffic management, energy consumption, and emergency response systems. Cities use real-time IoT data to simulate various urban planning scenarios and enhance public services (Priya & A., 2024).

By providing real-time visibility and predictive capabilities, Digital Twins enable organizations to make informed decisions, enhance productivity, and reduce operational costs.

2.2 IoT: The Backbone of Digital Twin Technology

IoT plays a fundamental role in enabling Digital Twins by providing real-time data collection, transmission, and analysis. IoT refers to a vast network of interconnected devices—ranging from industrial sensors to smart appliances (Chen et al., 2021) —that collect and share data over the internet. These devices continuously communicate with Digital Twins, feeding them live operational data that ensures accurate simulations and predictions (Rajora et al., 2023). IoT-powered Digital Twins rely on various communication protocols and cloud-based infrastructures to function efficiently. Some key components of an IoT-integrated Digital Twin ecosystem include:

- IoT Sensors: Devices embedded in machinery, vehicles, or medical equipment that collect real-time data such as temperature, pressure, vibration, and motion (Chandhana et al., 2023).
- Edge Computing: A distributed computing model that processes IoT data closer to the source, reducing latency and improving real-time analytics.
- Cloud & AI Integration: Digital Twins leverage cloud computing and artificial intelligence (AI) to analyse massive datasets, detect patterns and generate predictive insights (Yang et al., 2023).

With IoT's ability to seamlessly connect digital and physical environments, businesses can achieve unprecedented levels of automation, efficiency, and innovation.

2.3 The Convergence of Digital Twins, IoT and AI

The true potential of Digital Twins is unlocked when combined with IoT and AI-powered analytics. AI enhances Digital Twin technology by enabling self-learning algorithms, pattern recognition, and intelligent decision-making (Redelinghuys et al., 2020). Some key benefits of this convergence include:

- Predictive Maintenance: AI analyzes IoT sensor data to forecast equipment failures and trigger preventive maintenance actions before issues arise (Rai et al., 2025).
- Autonomous Operations: AI-driven Digital Twins enable machines and industrial systems to self-adjust based on real-time conditions, reducing human intervention (Redelinghuys et al., 2020).
- Enhanced Cybersecurity: AI-powered anomaly detection helps identify suspicious activities and cyber threats within IoT-connected Digital Twin environments (Bhaskar, 2023).

By integrating AI, Digital Twins evolve from static digital replicas to dynamic, intelligent systems that continuously learn and adapt to changing conditions.

3. CYBERSECURITY CHALLENGES IN DIGITAL TWIN AND IOT ECOSYSTEMS

The integration of Digital Twin (DT) technology with the Internet of Things (IoT) ecosystems is revolutionizing industries by enabling real-time monitoring, predictive analytics, and automation. However, the complex, interconnected, and dynamic nature of these systems introduces significant cybersecurity challenges.

The fusion of IoT, Cyber-Physical Systems (CPS), and Digital Twins expands the attack surface (Correia et al., 2023), making it increasingly difficult to safeguard against evolving threats. In this context, ensuring the security, integrity, and resilience of DT-based IoT ecosystems demands a proactive approach that addresses multiple vulnerabilities.

3.1. Distributed and Heterogeneous Nature: Expanding the Attack Surface

Digital Twin and IoT ecosystems consist of diverse and distributed components, including sensors, industrial controllers, cloud platforms, and edge devices. The heterogeneity of these systems—spanning multiple vendors, protocols, and security standards—makes it challenging to implement uniform security measures (Nguyen et al., 2025). Attackers can exploit inconsistencies in device configurations, unpatched software, or outdated firmware, leading to unauthorized access, data manipulation, or system disruptions. The lack of centralized control in distributed IoT environments further complicates the detection and mitigation of cyber threats (Sciullo et al., 2024).

3.2. Evolving Security Threats: The Growing Complexity of Attacks

As Digital Twin and IoT ecosystems become more advanced, the nature of cyber threats continues to evolve. Distributed Denial-of-Service (DDoS) attacks, tampered data injections, ransomware, and AI-driven cyber threats pose significant risks to critical infrastructure, smart cities, and industrial networks. Attackers leverage botnets of compromised IoT devices to launch large-scale DDoS attacks, disrupting services and crippling operations (Stuma & Mathonsi, 2024). Furthermore, data poisoning attacks can corrupt Digital Twin models, leading to inaccurate simulations and flawed decision-making processes. Traditional security methods are often inadequate to address these emerging threats, necessitating AI-driven anomaly detection and real-time threat intelligence (Malakuti & Grüner, 2018).

3.3. Unauthorized Access and Data Manipulation

Unauthorized access remains one of the most critical risks in Digital Twin-based IoT environments. Many IoT devices rely on default passwords, insecure APIs, or weak authentication mechanisms, making them vulnerable to cyber intrusions. Attackers who gain access to these systems can manipulate real-time sensor data, falsify Digital Twin models, or disrupt critical services (Nguyen et al., 2025). In smart city infrastructures, unauthorized access to transportation, energy grids, or emergency response systems can lead to public safety risks and severe economic losses. Implementing robust identity and access management (IAM), multi-factor authentication (MFA), and zero-trust security architectures is essential to mitigating these threats (Maleshkova & Seydoux, 2020).

3.4. Integration with AI and 6G Networks: New Security Concerns

The convergence of 6G networks, AI, and IoT in Digital Twin ecosystems introduces new cybersecurity vulnerabilities. While these technologies enhance automation and efficiency, they also create potential risks related to data integrity, confidentiality, and system availability (Padmapriya & Srivenkatesh, 2024). AI-driven cybersecurity solutions must be integrated with secure authentication, access control, encryption, and anomaly detection mechanisms to safeguard Digital Twin models from adversarial attacks. Additionally, 6G-enabled ultra-low latency connections could be exploited by attackers to disrupt real-time data transmission, leading to incorrect decision-making in mission-critical applications (Maheshwari et al., 2024).

3.5. Increased Attack Surface in Industrial IoT (IIoT)

In Industrial IoT (IIoT) environments, Digital Twins serve as high-fidelity representations of physical assets, enabling real-time monitoring and predictive maintenance. However, their integration with networked IIoT infrastructures exposes them to cyber threats such as industrial espionage, insider threats, and ransomware attacks. Compromised Digital Twins can be used to simulate fraudulent operational data, leading to misinformed business decisions (Soudan, 2024). Securing IIoT-based Digital Twins requires continuous monitoring, segmentation of operational networks, and encrypted data exchanges to prevent unauthorized access and data leaks (Lo et al., 2023).

3.6. Proactive Security Management with Digital Twins

Digital Twins themselves can play a proactive role in cybersecurity management by enabling real-time monitoring and threat detection in IoT networks. Cybersecurity Digital Twins (CDTs) can simulate potential cyberattacks, assess the impact of security vulnerabilities, and test security patches before deploying them in real-world environments (Empl et al., 2023). This approach enhances incident response strategies, allowing organizations to anticipate and mitigate cyber risks before they escalate (Malakuti & Grüner, 2018).

3.7. Federated Learning and AI-Driven Threat Detection

The integration of Federated Learning (FL) in Digital Twins can improve real-time threat detection by enabling distributed cybersecurity intelligence across multiple IoT devices. Unlike traditional centralized machine learning models, Federated Learning trains AI models locally on edge devices, reducing the risk of data exposure and enhancing privacy (Akpabio et al., 2024). This decentralized approach is particularly effective in detecting zero-day attacks, where conventional signature-based security solutions often fail. By leveraging AI-powered threat detection, Digital Twins can identify anomalous patterns, predict cyber threats, and automate security responses (Wang et al., 2024).

3.8. Secure Data Transmission and Access Control

Ensuring secure data transmission, access control, and encryption is fundamental to protecting Digital Twin ecosystems. As IoT devices continuously exchange real-time data with cloud and edge computing platforms, any weakness in data encryption or access policies could lead to eavesdropping, data breaches, or unauthorized manipulations. Key security measures include:

- End-to-end encryption (E2EE): Encrypting data from source to destination to prevent interception (Balpande et al., 2024).
- Role-based access control (RBAC): Restricting data access based on pre-defined user roles and privileges (Cheng et al., 2013).
- Blockchain-based authentication: Using decentralized identity management to enhance trust and transparency in Digital Twin ecosystems (Bigiotti et al., 2025).

3.9. Trust and Privacy in Human-Machine Collaboration

In sectors like biopharma manufacturing and smart healthcare, the integration of AI, machine learning, and Digital Twins raises trust and privacy concerns between human-machine teams. Patient data, drug formulations (Balpande et al., 2024), and biomedical research models stored in Digital Twins must be protected against cyberattacks and unauthorized access. A biosecurity Digital Twin (BDT) framework can enhance data privacy, ensure compliance with regulations (such as GDPR and HIPAA), and foster trust in human-machine interactions (Jørgensen et al., 2024).

3.10. Dynamic Security Policies for IoT Ecosystems

Traditional static security policies are inadequate for the dynamic and resource-constrained nature of IoT ecosystems. Adaptive security frameworks, driven by AI and machine learning, are essential for creating responsive, self-healing cybersecurity measures. These frameworks dynamically adjust security configurations based on real-time threat intelligence, ensuring continuous protection against evolving cyber risks (Mylrea, 2024).

4. KEY CYBERSECURITY STRATEGIES AND BEST PRACTICES

As Digital Twin (DT) and Internet of Things (IoT) ecosystems continue to revolutionize industries, ensuring robust cybersecurity becomes imperative. The interconnected nature of these technologies expands the attack surface, making them vulnerable to various cyber threats such as data breaches, ransomware, unauthorized access, and system manipulation. To safeguard these ecosystems, organizations must adopt a multi-layered cybersecurity strategy that combines advanced encryption, strong authentication, real-time threat detection, and proactive risk managemen (Heydari et al., 2019)t.

4.1. Implementing Secure Communication Protocols

Digital Twins and IoT devices rely on continuous data exchange between physical assets, cloud platforms, and edge computing systems. Transport Layer Security (TLS) and Secure Sockets Layer (SSL) protocols ensure encrypted communication channels, protecting data from man-in-the-middle (MITM) attacks and eavesdropping (Song, 2023). Secure communication mechanisms must also include Virtual Private Networks (VPNs), Zero Trust Network Access (ZTNA), and software-defined perimeters (SDP) to prevent unauthorized network intrusions (Li et al., 2019). Additionally, adopting lightweight encryption protocols for resource-constrained IoT devices, such as Lightweight Cryptographic Protocols (LCP) and Datagram Transport Layer Security (DTLS), ensures secure communication without excessive computational overhead (Ananda et al., 2014).

4.2. Strengthening Identity and Access Management (IAM)

Unauthorized access to Digital Twin and IoT environments can lead to data manipulation, operational disruptions, and industrial espionage. Implementing Identity and Access Management (IAM) frameworks helps enforce stringent authentication and authorization measures. Key IAM strategies include:

- Multi-Factor Authentication (MFA): Requiring multiple credentials (e.g., passwords, biometrics, one-time codes) to verify user identities (Soudan, 2024).
- Role-Based Access Control (RBAC): Granting access privileges based on user roles to minimize exposure to sensitive data. (Padmapriya & Srivenkatesh, 2024)
- Zero Trust Architecture (ZTA): Enforcing the principle of "never trust, always verify" by continuously authenticating users and devices before granting access (Padmapriya & Srivenkatesh, 2024).
- Blockchain-Based Identity Management: Using decentralized digital identities to reduce the risk of identity theft and unauthorized credential use (Sciullo et al., 2024).

4.3. Leveraging Blockchain for Data Integrity

Blockchain technology provides immutable, tamper-proof transaction records, enhancing the security and trustworthiness of Digital Twin environments. By storing data in a decentralized ledger, blockchain ensures that data modifications are transparent and traceable, reducing the risk of data manipulation, fraud, and insider threats (Charanya et al., 2025).

4.4. AI-Driven Threat Detection and Anomaly Monitoring

Artificial Intelligence (AI) and Machine Learning (ML) play a crucial role in identifying cyber threats in real-time. Traditional rule-based security systems often fail to detect zero-day attacks, insider threats, and sophisticated malware. AI-driven cybersecurity solutions use behavioral analytics, predictive modeling, and anomaly detection to proactively identify threats before they escalate (Simran et al., 2024). Key AI-driven security applications include:

- Anomaly Detection Algorithms: Monitoring device behavior to detect suspicious patterns (e.g., unusual data transmissions, unauthorized access attempts) (Sengupta et al., 2024).
- Federated Learning for Cybersecurity: Enhancing distributed threat detection while preserving data privacy (S. et al., 2024).

- AI-Powered Security Information and Event Management (SIEM) Systems: Aggregating and analyzing security logs to detect, classify, and respond to threats in real-time (Sengupta et al., 2024).

4.5. Encryption for Data Protection

Encrypting data at rest, in transit, and during processing is fundamental to safeguarding Digital Twin ecosystems from cyberattacks. Without proper encryption, attackers can intercept and manipulate sensitive data, leading to security breaches. Best practices for encryption include:

- End-to-End Encryption (E2EE): Protecting data as it moves between IoT devices, cloud systems, and Digital Twin models (Balpande et al., 2024).
- Advanced Encryption Standard (AES-256): Encrypting stored data to prevent unauthorized access (Sridevi & Santhanalakshmi, 2022).
- Homomorphic Encryption: Enabling data processing without decrypting it, enhancing security in AI-driven analytics and cloud computing (Havard et al., 2021).
- Quantum-Safe Cryptography: Preparing for post-quantum security threats by implementing lattice-based cryptography and quantum-resistant encryption algorithms (Gulomov et al., 2024).

4.6. Securing IoT Supply Chains

Digital Twins and IoT ecosystems depend on multi-vendor supply chains, where vulnerabilities in third-party components can introduce security risks. Supply chain attacks, such as malicious firmware updates, counterfeit hardware, and backdoor exploits, can compromise entire IoT networks (Kieras et al., 2021). Mitigation strategies include:

- Vendor Risk Assessments: Evaluating security practices of third-party vendors before integration (Bhaskar, 2023).
- Secure Software Development Lifecycle (SDLC): Ensuring that software updates and patches are free from malicious code or hidden vulnerabilities.
- Hardware Security Modules (HSMs): Using tamper-resistant hardware to secure cryptographic keys and protect sensitive data. (Nguyen et al., 2025)

4.7. Adaptive Security Policies for IoT and Digital Twins

Traditional static security frameworks are inadequate for dynamic IoT environments. Organizations must adopt adaptive, AI-driven security policies that adjust in real-time based on changing cyber threats (Sauerwein et al., 2024). Key elements of adaptive security include:

- Automated Patch Management: Deploying real-time security updates to IoT devices and Digital Twins without requiring manual intervention (Ting et al., 2023).
- Threat Intelligence Sharing: Collaborating with industry cybersecurity forums to share insights on emerging attack vectors (Dunnett et al., 2022).
- Software-Defined Security (SDS): Implementing dynamic security controls that adapt to new threats and operational changes (Basu et al., 2024).

4.8. Proactive Incident Response and Recovery Plans

Despite robust cybersecurity measures, organizations must be prepared for potential security breaches. A well-defined incident response plan (IRP) ensures rapid detection, containment, and mitigation of cyber threats (Kumar Jain et al., 2024). Essential components of an effective IRP include:

- Cyber Resilience Testing: Conducting regular penetration testing and security audits to identify weaknesses (Padmapriya & Srivenkatesh, 2024).
- Automated Threat Containment: Isolating compromised IoT devices or DT environments to prevent the spread of attacks (Jørgensen et al., 2024).
- Backup and Disaster Recovery: Implementing secure, encrypted backups to restore operations quickly in case of ransomware or data loss (Ke & Sudhir, 2023).

5. REGULATORY AND COMPLIANCE FRAMEWORKS

The integration of Digital Twin (DT) and Internet of Things (IoT) ecosystems is transforming industries by enabling real-time monitoring, predictive analytics, and automation. However, these benefits come with significant cybersecurity challenges, requiring organizations to align with international regulatory frameworks to mitigate risks (Răileanu et al., 2024). Ensuring compliance with cybersecurity regulations and standards is crucial to protecting data integrity, privacy, and system security.

However, achieving compliance in cross-border digital operations is complex due to varying national standards and industry-specific regulations.

5.1. Key Regulations and Standards

Several international standards provide structured frameworks for risk assessment, data protection, and incident response in Digital Twin and IoT ecosystems. These include:

5.1.1. General Data Protection Regulation (GDPR) – Europe

GDPR focuses on data protection and privacy for individuals within the European Union (EU). It enforces stringent measures for data collection, processing, and storage, ensuring organizations handle personal data responsibly. Key principles include:

- Lawful Processing: Organizations must have clear consent or a legitimate reason for data collection (Ke & Sudhir, 2023).
- Right to Erasure: Individuals can request data deletion to protect their privacy.
- Data Breach Notification: Organizations must report security incidents within 72 hours (Ke & Sudhir, 2023).

GDPR compliance is particularly relevant for IoT applications that collect user data, such as smart cities, healthcare devices, and industrial systems.

5.1.2. National Institute of Standards and Technology (NIST) Guidelines – USA

The NIST Cybersecurity Framework (CSF) provides a risk-based approach to managing cybersecurity. It is widely adopted in critical infrastructure sectors like maritime, aviation, and industrial automation (Dickinson, 2016). The framework consists of five core functions (Charanya et al., 2025):

- Identify: Assess cybersecurity risks in IoT and DT ecosystems.
- Protect: Implement safeguards such as encryption and multi-factor authentication (MFA).
- Detect: Monitor systems for anomalies and cyber threats.
- Respond: Take immediate action to contain security breaches.
- Recover: Ensure business continuity and resilience after an attack.

NIST is especially useful for sectors with highly interconnected systems, such as aviation and maritime industries, where securing communication networks and control systems is critical (Correia et al., 2023).

5.1.3. ISO/IEC 27001 – Global Standard for Information Security

ISO/IEC 27001 is an internationally recognized standard for Information Security Management Systems (ISMS). It provides organizations with a framework to (Vakhula et al., 2024):

- Secure sensitive information through encryption and access control.
- Ensure continuous monitoring to detect cyber threats.
- Implement risk management policies tailored to industry needs.

Many organizations integrate ISO/IEC 27001 with other cybersecurity frameworks to create a unified approach to regulatory compliance.

5.2. Challenges in Cross-Border Compliance

Ensuring compliance in global Digital Twin and IoT operations presents significant challenges due to variations in national standards, sector-specific regulations, and the complexity of IoT environments.

5.2.1. Varying National Standards

Different countries impose distinct cybersecurity requirements, making compliance difficult for multinational organizations.

For example:

- Saudi Arabia's NCA-ECC framework requires specific security controls that differ from ISO/IEC 27001, necessitating additional compliance efforts (Alfaadhel et al., 2023) (Marotta & Madnick, 2021).
- China's Cybersecurity Law imposes strict data localization policies, affecting cross-border data transfers (Alfaadhel et al., 2023) (Marotta & Madnick, 2021)..

Organizations must align with multiple regulatory frameworks, increasing compliance costs and complexity.

5.2.2. Sector-Specific Regulations

Certain industries have unique cybersecurity requirements that must be integrated with general standards like NIST and ISO/IEC 27001.

For instance:

- The maritime industry follows the IMO's Maritime Cyber Risk Management Resolution alongside NIST guidelines to secure ships, ports, and communication networks (Alfaadhel et al., 2023) (Marotta & Madnick, 2021).
- The aviation sector requires compliance with FAA and ICAO cybersecurity guidelines to protect aircraft communication systems from cyber threats.

Balancing sector-specific regulations with global compliance frameworks is essential for maintaining cybersecurity across different industries (Alfaadhel et al., 2023) (Marotta & Madnick, 2021).

5.2.3. Complexity of IoT Environments

The proliferation of IoT devices increases the complexity of managing cybersecurity. Digital Twins can enhance real-time monitoring and threat detection, but they also introduce new vulnerabilities, such as:

- Unauthorized Access: IoT endpoints are susceptible to hacking and data manipulation.
- Supply Chain Risks: Third-party vendors can introduce security gaps in interconnected systems (Ke & Sudhir, 2023).
- Dynamic Attack Surfaces: The continuous evolution of IoT networks makes traditional static security policies inadequate.

Organizations need adaptive security frameworks that integrate Artificial Intelligence (AI) and Machine Learning (ML) for real-time anomaly detection and proactive threat mitigation.

5.3. Strategies for Effective Compliance

To overcome these challenges, organizations must adopt strategic approaches to ensure compliance while maintaining strong cybersecurity defenses.

5.3.1. Unified Mapping Approach

A unified compliance strategy involves integrating multiple cybersecurity frameworks to identify common security requirements (Wang et al., 2024). Key steps include:

- Mapping different regulations to find overlapping security controls.
- Implementing a centralized compliance framework that aligns with multiple standards (Marotta & Madnick, 2021).
- Automating compliance reporting to reduce manual efforts (Malakuti & Grüner, 2018).

This approach streamlines regulatory adherence while reducing complexity and redundancies.

5.3.2. Proactive Security Management with Digital Twins

Digital Twins can play a crucial role in proactive cybersecurity management (Luzzi et al., 2024)by:

- Simulating cyber threats in a virtual environment before they affect real systems.
- Providing continuous monitoring to detect vulnerabilities in real-time (Dunnett et al., 2022).
- Enhancing predictive analytics to prevent cyberattacks before they escalate.

By leveraging AI-driven threat detection and behavioral analysis, Digital Twins improve security resilience while ensuring compliance with evolving regulatory standards.

5.3.3. Collaborative Efforts and Shared Responsibility Models

Given the interconnected nature of Digital Twin and IoT ecosystems, cybersecurity should be treated as a shared responsibility among (Nguyen et al., 2025):

- Technology providers (e.g., cloud service providers, IoT manufacturers).
- Regulatory bodies that establish and update security standards.
- Industry stakeholders who adopt best practices and compliance measures.

For example, in critical infrastructure sectors, collaboration between government agencies, private firms, and cybersecurity experts can enhance threat intelligence sharing and incident response capabilities (Alfaadhel et al., 2023) (Marotta & Madnick, 2021).

6. CASE STUDIES AND REAL-WORLD APPLICATIONS

The convergence of Digital Twins (DT) and Internet of Things (IoT) has transformed industries by enabling real-time data analysis, predictive maintenance, and automation. However, cybersecurity remains a critical challenge as cyber threats evolve. Here are three real-world applications showcasing how cybersecurity is being implemented in manufacturing, healthcare, and smart cities to protect Digital Twin and IoT environments.

6.1. Secure Digital Twins in Smart Manufacturing – General Electric (GE) and Predictive Maintenance

Use Case:

General Electric (GE) has pioneered the use of Digital Twins in industrial manufacturing to optimize performance, improve efficiency, and predict equipment failures before they occur. Their Predix platform, a cloud-based Industrial IoT (IIoT) solution, integrates real-time sensor data from factory machines to generate a Digital Twin that simulates production processes (Zorchenko et al., 2024).

Cybersecurity Measures Implemented:

- End-to-End Data Encryption: Ensures secure data transmission between IoT devices, cloud storage, and Digital Twins to prevent cyberattacks (Li et al., 2019).
- AI-Driven Intrusion Detection Systems (IDS): Detects anomalies in network traffic that could indicate cyber threats such as ransomware attacks or unauthorized access (Suresh & Jose, 2023).
- Zero Trust Security Model: Restricts system access using multi-factor authentication (MFA) and role-based access control (RBAC), ensuring only authorized personnel can modify Digital Twin models (Lv et al., 2023).

Impact:

- Reduced downtime by 20% through predictive maintenance, avoiding costly machine failures.

- Enhanced resilience against cyber threats targeting industrial control systems (ICS) and factory automation.

6.2. Securing IoT-Connected Medical Devices – Medtronic and Remote Patient Monitoring

Use Case:

Medtronic, a global leader in medical devices, uses IoT-connected pacemakers and insulin pumps to provide remote patient monitoring. These devices transmit real-time health data to doctors, enabling them to track patient conditions and intervene before emergencies arise (Medtronic, 2025).

Cybersecurity Challenges & Measures Implemented:

- End-to-End Encryption & Secure Communication Protocols (TLS 1.2/1.3): Prevents unauthorized interception of sensitive health data during transmission.
- Firmware Security Updates & Patch Management: Medtronic continuously updates device firmware to fix vulnerabilities and prevent exploits like the Medtronic pacemaker hack (2018) (Medtronic, 2025).
- Biometric Authentication & Blockchain for Patient Data: Strengthens identity verification and prevents tampering of patient records in hospital systems.

Impact:

- Improved patient safety by securing life-critical IoT medical devices from cyberattacks.
- Increased regulatory compliance with HIPAA (Health Insurance Portability and Accountability Act) and GDPR (General Data Protection Regulation).

6.3. Cyber-Resilient Smart Cities – Singapore's Smart Nation Initiative

Use Case:

Singapore's Smart Nation Initiative leverages Digital Twins to simulate urban environments, optimize city infrastructure, and enhance public safety. The government integrates IoT sensors into traffic systems, energy grids, and public buildings to manage resources efficiently (Babin, 2024).

Cybersecurity Measures Implemented:

- AI-Powered Threat Detection in Public Infrastructure: AI continuously scans for anomalies in IoT-enabled surveillance cameras and traffic control systems.
- Blockchain for Secure Public Data Sharing: Ensures tamper-proof, decentralized records for government transactions, land registries, and citizen services (Wang et al., 2021).
- Cybersecurity Operations Center (SOC): Monitors cyber threats in real-time, detecting and mitigating attacks on critical infrastructure such as power grids and transport systems.

Impact:

- Reduced cyber threats by 40% through real-time security monitoring (Babin, 2024).
- Increased efficiency in urban management, improving traffic flow, energy consumption, and emergency response.

6.4. Cybersecurity in Digital Twin and IoT for Smart Grids – India's National Smart Grid Mission (NSGM)

Use Case:

India's National Smart Grid Mission (NSGM) aims to modernize the country's power infrastructure by integrating IoT-enabled smart meters, automated substations, and Digital Twin simulations (Ananda et al., 2014). These technologies help optimize energy distribution, reduce transmission losses, and enhance grid resilience.

Cybersecurity Challenges & Measures Implemented:

- Threats to Smart Meters & Grid Control Systems:
  - Cyberattacks on IoT-enabled smart meters can result in power theft, incorrect billing, or large-scale outages.
  - Digital Twins that simulate grid performance must be protected from data manipulation and unauthorized access (Medtronic, 2025).
- Cybersecurity Strategies Adopted:
  - End-to-End Encryption: Secure communication channels for real-time energy data transmission between smart meters and control centers.
  - AI-Based Intrusion Detection Systems (IDS): Identifies anomalies in grid activity, preventing cyberattacks on substations (Priya & A., 2024).
  - Blockchain for Secure Transactions: Used for tamper-proof energy trading in peer-to-peer (P2P) electricity exchange models.

Impact:

- Enhanced grid reliability by detecting and mitigating cyber threats in real time.
- Reduced energy losses and theft, improving revenue for electricity distribution companies (DISCOMs).
- Improved compliance with India's cybersecurity regulations, including CERT-In guidelines and the Personal Data Protection Act (PDPA).

India's NSGM showcases how Digital Twins and IoT can transform power management, but also highlights the need for robust cybersecurity frameworks to prevent threats to critical infrastructure.

7. FUTURE TRENDS AND EMERGING THREATS

As Digital Twin (DT) and Internet of Things (IoT) technologies continue to evolve, so too do the cybersecurity challenges associated with them. The increasing integration of artificial intelligence (AI), edge computing, blockchain, and quantum computing brings both opportunities and risks. Emerging threats will require advanced security frameworks, proactive defense mechanisms, and industry-wide collaboration to mitigate risks.

7.1. Quantum Computing and the Need for Quantum-Resistant Cryptography

One of the most significant future threats is quantum computing, which has the potential to revolutionize data processing and problem-solving. However, it also poses a serious risk to traditional encryption methods such as RSA and ECC (Elliptic Curve Cryptography), which secure IoT and DT communications today (Sahu & Mazumdar, 2024). Malicious actors could leverage quantum algorithms like Shor's Algorithm to break encryption keys in a fraction of the time required by classical computers, leading to data breaches, espionage, and system takeovers.

To counter this, cybersecurity researchers are actively developing quantum-resistant cryptographic techniques, such as lattice-based, hash-based, and code-based cryptography. Organizations must begin adopting post-quantum cryptography (PQC) standards to future-proof their security architectures against quantum-enabled cyber threats (Alfaadhel et al., 2023) (Marotta & Madnick, 2021).

7.2. Edge Computing and Decentralized Security Challenges

The proliferation of edge computing, where data processing occurs closer to IoT devices rather than in centralized cloud systems, introduces new security challenges. While edge computing reduces latency and improves efficiency, it also increases the attack surface by creating multiple entry points for cybercriminals (Heydari et al., 2019). Key threats in edge computing environments include:

- Weak Authentication and Access Controls – Without robust identity management, unauthorized access to edge nodes could lead to data leaks and system manipulation.
- Compromised IoT Devices as Attack Vectors – Hackers can exploit vulnerabilities in smart sensors, wearables, and industrial IoT devices to infiltrate the network (Abdullahi et al., 2024).
- Data Integrity Risks – Since data is processed at multiple edge locations, ensuring the integrity and authenticity of information becomes a challenge.

To address these risks, organizations must implement Zero Trust Architecture (ZTA), AI-driven anomaly detection, and robust endpoint security to monitor and protect decentralized IoT and DT environments.

7.3. AI-Powered Cyber Threats and Autonomous Attacks

While AI enhances cybersecurity defenses through automated threat detection, self-healing networks, and predictive analytics, it also empowers cybercriminals to launch more sophisticated attacks (Dontu et al., 2024). AI-powered malware and adversarial machine learning attacks can:

- Bypass traditional security measures by mimicking legitimate system behavior.
- Exploit vulnerabilities in real-time using AI-driven reconnaissance techniques.
- Disrupt Digital Twins and IoT systems by injecting false data, leading to incorrect predictions and system failures (Dontu et al., 2024).

To counter these AI-driven threats, organizations must adopt AI-powered cybersecurity solutions that leverage behavioral analysis, federated learning, and adversarial AI detection to identify and mitigate evolving risks.

7.4. 5G and 6G Networks: Expanding the Cyber Threat Landscape

The rollout of 5G networks has significantly improved IoT connectivity, enabling seamless data exchange between Digital Twins and smart devices. However, wider network coverage, increased bandwidth, and lower latency also mean greater exposure to cyber threats (Kaur & Gupta, 2024). Future 6G networks, expected to integrate AI, blockchain, and ultra-fast communications, will introduce even more cybersecurity challenges, such as:

- Increased DDoS Attack Risks – Higher speeds and more connected devices could amplify Distributed Denial-of-Service (DDoS) attacks.
- Vulnerabilities in Network Slicing – Segmented 5G/6G networks, used for specialized IoT applications, may be exploited by attackers if not properly secured.
- New Encryption Standards Required – Data security frameworks must evolve to protect the vast amount of real-time IoT and Digital Twin data flowing through 5G/6G networks (You et al., 2024).

Implementing secure network protocols, AI-driven threat monitoring, and adaptive encryption mechanisms will be essential to safeguarding next-generation digital infrastructures.

7.5. Cybersecurity Regulations and Compliance Evolution

As cyber threats grow, global regulatory bodies will introduce stricter cybersecurity laws for IoT and Digital Twin ecosystems. Governments and industry groups are already working on compliance frameworks to ensure the security of critical infrastructure (Padmapriya & Srivenkatesh, 2024). Future trends in cybersecurity regulations include:

- Mandated Cyber Resilience Testing – Organizations may be required to conduct frequent cybersecurity stress tests for their DT and IoT systems.
- Expanded IoT Device Certification Standards – New standards may emerge to ensure IoT devices are manufactured with built-in security features (Bhaskar, 2023).
- Cross-Border Data Protection Agreements – With IoT systems generating massive amounts of cross-border data, international agreements will be necessary to address jurisdictional cybersecurity concerns.

Companies must stay ahead of regulatory changes, invest in compliance automation, and integrate security-by-design approaches to meet evolving legal requirements.

7.6. Digital Twin Security Enhancements: Moving Towards Proactive Cyber Defence

With the increasing complexity of Digital Twin ecosystems, cybersecurity strategies will shift from reactive to proactive defence mechanisms. Emerging security enhancements for Digital Twins include:

- Cyber-Resilient Digital Twins (CRDTs): Digital Twins equipped with AI-based self-healing mechanisms that detect and neutralize cyber threats autonomously (Flammini, 2021).
- Blockchain for Secure DT Transactions: Using blockchain-ledger systems to ensure data integrity, traceability, and authenticity in Digital Twin environments.
- Federated Learning for Cyber Threat Intelligence: AI-driven federated learning models can enable real-time cyber threat analysis across multiple Digital Twins without compromising privacy.

8. CONCLUSION

As technologies like DT and IoT evolved, cybersecurity must remain a top priority to mitigate emerging threats. Organizations should implement multi-layered security measures, proactive risk management, and compliance with evolving regulations to protect digital infrastructures. The rise of quantum computing, AI-powered cyberattacks, and edge computing risks necessitates next-generation security frameworks, Zero Trust architectures, and real-time anomaly detection. Moving forward, cyber-resilient Digital Twins, blockchain integration, and federated learning will play a crucial role in enhancing security, trust, and system integrity. To ensure sustainable cybersecurity, businesses must embrace innovation, collaborate on industry standards, and invest in advanced cybersecurity solutions to build resilient and secure digital ecosystems.

REFERENCES

Abdullahi, S. M., Zare, A., & Lazarova-Molnar, S. (2024). Cybersecurity in Distributed Industrial Digital Twins: Threats, Defenses, and Key Takeaways. *1st International Workshop on Distributed Digital Twins, DiDit 2024*. Groningen: CEUR-WS. Retrieved Beb 16, 2025, from https://www.scopus.com/record/display.uri?eid=2-s2.0-85204377211&origin=scopusAI

Akpabio, E., Narad, S., Akpabio, I., & Akpabio, I. (2024). Securing the Connected World: Federated Learning and IoT Cybersecurity. In *Federated Learning for Smart Communication using IoT Application* (pp. 178-195). CRC Press. DOI: 10.1201/9781003489368-9

Al-Dalati, I. (2022). Digital twins and cybersecurity in healthcare systems. In *Digital Twin for Healthcare: Design, Challenges, and Solutions* (pp. 195-221). Elsevier. DOI: 10.1016/B978-0-32-399163-6.00015-9

Alfaadhel, A., Almomani, I., & Ahmed, M. (2023, May). Risk-Based Cybersecurity Compliance Assessment System (RC2AS). *Applied Sciences (Basel, Switzerland), 13*(10), 6145. Advance online publication. DOI: 10.3390/app13106145

Ananda, K. V., Pandey, K. K., & Punia, D. K. (2014, February). Cyber security threats in the power sector: Need for a domain specific regulatory framework in India. *Energy Policy, 65*, 126–133. DOI: 10.1016/j.enpol.2013.10.025

Babin, N. (2024, Mar 26). *Harnessing the Power of AI and Digital Twins: Lessons from Singapore's Smart Nation Initiative*. Retrieved Feb 11, 2025, from https://www.linkedin.com: https://www.linkedin.com/pulse/harnessing-power-ai-digital-twins-lessons-from-singapores-babin-0bi3e/

Balpande, V. P., Aher, U. B., Borkar, P., Bhanarkar, P., Chavan, G. T., & Sairise, R. M. (2024, March). Implementing end-to-end encryption strategist for strengthening data security across network communication. *Journal of Discrete Mathematical Sciences and Cryptography, 27*(02), 465–476. DOI: 10.47974/JDMSC-1902

Basu, S., Raun, N. F., Ghosal, A., Chatterjee, D., Maitra, D., & Mazumdar, C. (2024). A Novel Software Defined Security Framework for SDN. *18th International Conference on Risks and Security of Internet and Systems, CRiSIS 2023. 14529 LNCS*, pp. 216-230. Rabat: Springer Science and Business Media Deutschland GmbH. DOI: 10.1007/978-3-031-61231-2_14

Bhaskar, A. (2023). Industrial IoT Condition Monitoring using Wireless IoT Sensor. *International Conference on Artificial Intelligence and Smart Communication, AISC 2023* (pp. 831-837). Greater Noida: IEEE. DOI: 10.1109/AISC56616.2023.10085613

Bigiotti, A., Shah, P., & Trestian, R. (2025). Blockchain and Digital Twin Integration for Remote Control of Cyber-Physical Systems. In *Lecture Notes on Data Engineering and Communications Technologies* (Vol. 232, pp. 258–269). Springer Science and Business Media Deutschland GmbH., DOI: 10.1007/978-3-031-76462-2_23

Chandhana, T., Balija, A., Kumaran, S. R., & Singh, B. (2023). Digital twins-enabling technologies including AI, sensors, cloud, and edge computing. In *Handbook of Research on Applications of AI, Digital Twin, and Internet of Things for Sustainable Development* (pp. 306-331). IGI Global. DOI: 10.4018/978-1-6684-6821-0.ch018

Charanya, J., Abinaya, P., Aadhavan, G., & Duraisamy, P. (2025). Blockchain and Digital Twin for Enhancing Personal Security in Modern Cities. In *Digital Twin and Blockchain for Smart Cities* (pp. 59-80). wiley. DOI: 10.1002/9781394303564.ch4

Chen, J., Schluse, M., & Rossmann, J. (2021). Enabling a Secured Communication in Distributed IoT Using the Smart Systems Service Infrastructure. *2021 IEEE International Conference on Pervasive Computing and Communications Workshops and other Affiliated Events, PerCom Workshops 2021* (pp. 674 - 679). Kassel: Institute of Electrical and Electronics Engineers Inc. DOI: 10.1109/PerComWorkshops51409.2021.9431124

Cheng, J., Kang, R., & Zhao, X. (2013). Role based Access Control and its application in high speed railway. *6th International Conference on Advanced Computational Intelligence, ICACI 2013* (pp. 362-364). IEEE Computer Society. DOI: 10.1109/ICACI.2013.6748531

Correia, J. B., Abel, M., & Becker, K. (2023, August). Data management in digital twins: A systematic literature review. *Knowledge and Information Systems*, *65*(08), 3165–3196. DOI: 10.1007/s10115-023-01870-1

Dickinson, D. (2016). Cybersecurity, going beyond protection. *Water/Wastewater and Automatic Controls Symposium 2016, WWAC 2016* (pp. 90-101). Orlando: International Society of Automation (ISA). https://doi.org/DOI: 978-151083849-9

Dontu, S., Addula, S. R., Kumar Pareek, P., Vallabhaneni, R., & Adnan, M. M. (2024). Attack Detection from Internet of Things using TPE based Self-Attention based Bidirectional Long-Short Term Memory. *International Conference on Intelligent Algorithms for Computational Intelligence Systems, IACIS 2024*. Hassan: IEEE. DOI: 10.1109/IACIS61494.2024.10722002

Dunnett, K., Pal, S., Putra, G. D., & Jadidi, Z. (2022). A Trusted, Verifiable and Differential Cyber Threat Intelligence Sharing Framework using Blockchain. *21st IEEE International Conference on Trust, Security and Privacy in Computing and Communications, TrustCom 2022* (pp. 1107-1114). Virtual, Online: IEEE. DOI: 10.1109/TrustCom56396.2022.00152

Empl, P., Hager, H., & Pernul, G. (2023). Digital Twins for IoT Security Management. *37th Annual IFIP WG 11.3 Conference on Data and Applications Security and Privacy, DBSec 2023. 13942 LNCS*, pp. 141-149. Sophia Antipolis: Springer Science and Business Media Deutschland GmbH. DOI: 10.1007/978-3-031-37586-6_9

Flammini, F. (2021, October 04). Digital twins as run-time predictive models for the resilience of cyber-physical systems: A conceptual framework. *Philosophical Transactions. Series A, Mathematical, Physical, and Engineering Sciences, 379*(2207), 20200369. Advance online publication. DOI: 10.1098/rsta.2020.0369 PMID: 34398658

Flores Ccanto, F., Pozo Curo, C., Flores Conislla, L. D., & Adauto Medina, W. A. (2021). Challenges of transformational leadership in organizational cybersecurity matters. *Revista Venezolana de Gerencia, 26*, 417–429. DOI: 10.52080/rvgluz.26.e5.27

Gulomov, S. R., Khudayberganov, T. R., Ravshanova, M. X., Turdiev, T. T., & Atabayev, S. S. (2024). Exploring Post-Quantum Cryptographic Algorithms for Secure Data Transmission. *3rd IEEE International Conference on Problems of Informatics, Electronics and Radio Engineering, PIERE 2024* (pp. 1480-1483). Novosibirsk: IEEE. DOI: 10.1109/PIERE62470.2024.10805050

Havard, V., Sahnoun, M., Bettayeb, B., Duval, F., & Baudry, D. (2021, December). Data architecture and model design for Industry 4.0 components integration in cyber-physical production systems. *Proceedings of the Institution of Mechanical Engineers. Part B, Journal of Engineering Manufacture, 235*(14), 2338–2349. DOI: 10.1177/0954405420979463

Heydari, M., Mylonas, A., Katos, V., Balaguer-Ballester, E., Tafreshi, V. H., & Benkhelifa, E. (2019). Uncertainty-aware authentication model for fog computing in IoT. *4th International Conference on Fog and Mobile Edge Computing, FMEC 2019* (pp. 52-59). Rome: IEEE. DOI: 10.1109/FMEC.2019.8795332

Jørgensen, C. S., Shukla, A., & Katt, B. (2024). Digital Twins in Healthcare: Security, Privacy, Trust and Safety Challenges. *International Workshops which were held in conjunction with 28th European Symposium on Research in Computer Security, ESORICS 2023. 14399 LNCS*, pp. 140-153. The Hague: Springer Science and Business Media Deutschland GmbH. DOI: 10.1007/978-3-031-54129-2_9

Kaur, N., & Gupta, L. (2024). Enhancing IoT Security in 6G Environment With Transparent AI: Leveraging XGBoost, SHAP and LIME. *0th IEEE International Conference on Network Softwarization, NetSoft 2024* (pp. 180-184). Saint Louis: IEEE. DOI: 10.1109/NetSoft60951.2024.10588922

Ke, T. T., & Sudhir, K. (2023, August). Privacy Rights and Data Security: GDPR and Personal Data Markets. *Management Science*, *68*(08), 4399–4412. DOI: 10.1287/mnsc.2022.4614

Kieras, T., Farooq, J., & Zhu, Q. (2021). I-SCRAM: A Framework for IoT Supply Chain Risk Analysis and Mitigation Decisions. *IEEE Access : Practical Innovations, Open Solutions*, *09*, 29827–29840. DOI: 10.1109/ACCESS.2021.3058338

Kumar Jain, Y., C.A., D. S., Johrawanshi, A., Gupta, M., Choudhary, D. K., & Pandey, A. (2024). Cybersecurity Frameworks: A Roadmap for Business Resilience. *International Conference on Cybernation and Computation, CYBERCOM 2024* (pp. 102-108). Dehradun: IEEE. DOI: 10.1109/CYBERCOM63683.2024.10803234

Li, P., Su, J., & Wang, X. (2019). *ITLS/iDTLS: Lightweight end-to-end security protocol for iot through minimal latency. ACM SIGCOMM Conference Posters and Demos, SIGCOMM 2019*. Association for Computing Machinery, Inc., DOI: 10.1145/3342280.3342347

Lo, C., Win, T. Y., Rezaeifar, Z., Khan, Z., & Legg, P. (2023). Digital Twins in Industry 4.0 Cyber Security. *9th IEEE Smart World Congress, SWC 2023*. Portsmouth: IEEE. DOI: 10.1109/SWC57546.2023.10449147

Luzzi, J., Naha, R., Arulappan, A., & Mahanti, A. (2024). SoK: A Holistic View of Cyberattacks Prediction with Digital Twins. *2nd International Conference on Emerging Trends in Information Technology and Engineering, ic-ETITE 2024*. Vellore: IEEE. DOI: 10.1109/ic-ETITE58242.2024.10493514

Lv, P., Sun, C., & Li, Q. (2023). Research and Application of Grid Cloud Service Security Access Control Technology Based on Zero Trust Model. *International Conference on Data Science and Network Security, ICDSNS 2023*. Tiptur: IEEE. DOI: 10.1109/ICDSNS58469.2023.10245681

Maheshwari, R. U., Shankar, P. R., Chandrasekaran, G., & Mahendrakhan, K. (2024, October 02). Assessment of Cybersecurity Risks in Digital Twin Deployments in Smart Cities. *International Journal of Computational and Experimental Science and Engineering, 10*(04), 695–700. DOI: 10.22399/ijcesen.494

Malakuti, S., & Grüner, S. (2018). Architectural aspects of digital twins in IIoT systems. *12th European Conference on Software Architecture, ECSA 2018.* Madrid: Association for Computing Machinery. DOI: 10.1145/3241403.3241417

Maleshkova, M., & Seydoux, N. (2020). Data representation and reasoning. In *The Internet of Things: From Data to Insight* (pp. 79 - 90). wiley. DOI: 10.1002/9781119545293.ch7

Marotta, A., & Madnick, S. (2021). Convergence and divergence of regulatory compliance and cybersecurity. *Issues in Information Systems, 22*(01), 10–50. DOI: 10.48009/1_iis_2021_10-50

Medtronic. (2025, Feb 05). *Medtronic: Enterprise Architecture for IoT-Enabled Remote Patient Monitoring*. Retrieved Feb 09, 2025, from https://www.linkedin.com: https://www.linkedin.com/pulse/medtronic-enterprise-architecture-iot-enabled-remote-patient-suf6e/

Mylrea, M. (2024). Building a trustworthy digital twin: A brave new world of human machine teams and autonomous biological internet of things (BIoT). In *Putting AI in the Critical Loop: Assured Trust and Autonomy in Human-Machine Teams* (pp. 219-243). Elsevier. DOI: 10.1016/B978-0-443-15988-6.00005-4

Nguyen, P. H., Rauniyar, A., & Niemi, T. V. (2025). Digital Twin-Based Security Orchestration, Automation and Response for IoT and CPS. *7th IFIP WG 5.5 International Cross-Domain Conference on Internet of Things, IFIPIoT 2024. 737 IFIPAICT*, pp. 243-260. Nice: Springer Science and Business Media Deutschland GmbH. DOI: 10.1007/978-3-031-81900-1_15

Padmapriya, V., & Srivenkatesh, M. (2024, February 02). IoT Network based Cyber Attack Mitigation in Digital Twin with Multi Level Key Management Using Enhanced KNN Model. *International Journal of Intelligent Systems and Applications in Engineering, 12*(14s), 49–62. Retrieved February 07, 2025, from https://www.scopus.com/record/display.uri?eid=2-s2.0-85184694434&origin=scopusAI

Priya, P. K., & A., R. (2024). A Review of Digital Twin Applications in Various Sectors. In *Transforming Industry using Digital Twin Technology* (pp. 239-258). Springer Nature. https://doi.org/DOI: 10.1007/9783031585234_12

Rai, A., Shastri, J., & Bansal, H. (2025). Artificial Intelligence Techniques in Predictive Maintenance, Their Applications, Challenges, and Prospects. In *Artificial Intelligence-Enabled Digital Twin for Smart Manufacturing* (pp. 565-579). wiley. DOI: 10.1002/9781394303601.ch24

Răileanu, S., Borangiu, T., Len oiu, I., Anton, F., & Negoiţă, R. (2024). Data Acquisition System for Developing Digital Twin Solutions: A Practical Guide. *13th International Workshop on Service Orientation in Holonic and Multi-Agent Manufacturing, SOHOMA 2023. 1136 SCI*, pp. 38-49. Annecy: Springer Science and Business Media Deutschland GmbH. DOI: 10.1007/978-3-031-53445-4_4

Rajora, R., Rajora, A., Sharma, B., & Aggarwal, P. (2023). Unveiling the Synergy: IoT and Digital Twins in Transforming Industries. *3rd International Conference on Smart Generation Computing, Communication and Networking, SMART GENCON 2023*. Bangalore: Institute of Electrical and Electronics Engineers Inc. DOI: 10.1109/SMARTGENCON60755.2023.10442175

Rajora, R., Rajora, A., Sharma, B., Aggarwal, P., & Thapliyal, S. (2023). Unveiling the Synergy: IoT and Digital Twins in Transforming Industries. *3rd International Conference on Smart Generation Computing, Communication and Networking, SMART GENCON 2023*. Bangalore: IEEE. DOI: 10.1109/SMARTGENCON60755.2023.10442175

Rawajbeh, M. A., Alzu'bi, S., & Alkhatib, A. (2023). IoT-Paradigm: Evolution Challenges and Proposed Solutions. *9th IEEE International Smart Cities Conference, ISC2 2023*. Bucharest: Institute of Electrical and Electronics Engineers Inc. DOI: 10.1109/ISC257844.2023.10293646

Redelinghuys, A., Basson, A., & Kruger, K. (2020, August 01). A six-layer architecture for the digital twin: A manufacturing case study implementation. *Journal of Intelligent Manufacturing, 31*(06), 1383–1402. DOI: 10.1007/s10845-019-01516-6

Saeed, M. M., Saeed, R. A., & Ahmed, Z. E. (2024). Data security and privacy in the age of AI and digital twins. In *Digital Twin Technology and AI Implementations in Future-Focused Businesses* (pp. 99–124). IGI Global., DOI: 10.4018/979-8-3693-1818-8.ch008

Saeed, S., Gull, H., Aldossary, M. M., Altamimi, A. F., Alshahrani, M. S., Saqib, M., Zafar Iqbal, S., & Almuhaideb, A. M. (2024, December). Digital Transformation in Energy Sector: Cybersecurity Challenges and Implications. *Information (Basel), 15*(12), 764. Advance online publication. DOI: 10.3390/info15120764

Sahu, S. K., & Mazumdar, K. (2024). State-of-the-art analysis of quantum cryptography: Applications and future prospects. *Frontiers in Physics (Lausanne), 12*, 1456491. Advance online publication. DOI: 10.3389/fphy.2024.1456491

Sandhu, K. (2021). Advancing cybersecurity for digital transformation: Opportunities and challenges. In *Handbook of Research on Advancing Cybersecurity for Digital Transformation* (pp. 01-17). IGI Global. DOI: 10.4018/978-1-7998-6975-7.ch001

Sauerwein, C., Wenzl, C., & Breu, R. (2024). Uncovering Critical Resources and Factors Influencing the Use of Threat Intelligence Sharing Platforms. *57th Annual Hawaii International Conference on System Sciences, HICSS 2024* (pp. 1921-1930). Honolulu: IEEE Computer Society. DOI: 10.24251/HICSS.2024.241

Sciullo, L., De Marchi, A., Trotta, A., Montori, F. L., & Di Felice, M. (2024). APr). Relativistic Digital Twin: Bringing the IoT to the future. *Future Generation Computer Systems, 153*, 521–536. DOI: 10.1016/j.future.2023.12.016

Sengupta, A., Kundu, A., & Mukhopadhyay, A. (2024). An Approach to Detect and Classify Potentially Suspicious Activity from Real-Time Log Data using Anomaly Detection Methods. *3rd International Conference for Innovation in Technology, INOCON 2024.* Bangalore: IEEE. DOI: 10.1109/INOCON60754.2024.10511679

Sijan, M. A., Shahoriar, A., Salimullah, M., Islam, A. S., & Khan, R. H. (2022). A Review on E-Banking Security in Bangladesh: An Empirical Study. *2nd International Conference on Computing Advancements: Age of Computing and Augmented Life, ICCA 2022* (pp. 330-336). Dhaka: Association for Computing Machinery. DOI: 10.1145/3542954.3543002

Simran, K., S., & Hans, A. (2024). The AI Shield and Red AI Framework: Machine Learning Solutions for Cyber Threat Intelligence(CTI). *International Conference on Intelligent Systems for Cybersecurity, ISCS 2024.* Gurugram: IEEE. DOI: 10.1109/ISCS61804.2024.10581195

Song, Y. (2023, December 01). Human Digital Twin, the Development and Impact on Design. *Journal of Computing and Information Science in Engineering, 23*(06), 060819. Advance online publication. DOI: 10.1115/1.4063132

Soudan, B. (2024). Cybersecurity of Digital Twins in Industrial IoT Environments. *Advances in Science and Engineering Technology International Conferences, ASET 2024.* Abu Dhabi: Institute of Electrical and Electronics Engineers Inc. DOI: 10.1109/ASET60340.2024.10708640

Sridevi, K., & Santhanalakshmi, M. (2022). An Efficient Implementation of AES algorithm using Custom Key. *International Conference on Intelligent Innovations in Engineering and Technology, ICIIET 2022* (pp. 268-272). Coimbatore: IEEE. DOI: 10.1109/ICIIET55458.2022.9967508

Stuma, V. S., & Mathonsi, T. E. (2024). A Security Algorithm to Prevent Denial of Service Attacks in the Internet of Things Devices. *4th IEEE International Conference on Electrical, Computer, and Energy Technologies, ICECET 2024.* Sydney: IEEE. DOI: 10.1109/ICECET61485.2024.10698594

Suresh, A., & Jose, A. C. (2023). Detection of Malicious Activities by AI-Supported Anomaly-Based IDS. In *Artificial Intelligence for Intrusion Detection Systems* (pp. 79–93). CRC Press., DOI: 10.1201/9781003346340-4

Swain, A., Swain, K., Pattnaik, S., Samal, S., & Das, J. (2022). Cybersecurity in Digital Transformations. *4th International Conference Intelligent Computing and Communication, ICAC 2021.* 430, pp. 247-252. Virtual, Online: Springer Science and Business Media Deutschland GmbH. DOI: 10.1007/978-981-19-0825-5_26

Taherdoost, H., Madanchian, M., & Ebrahimi, M. (2021). Advancement of cybersecurity and information security awareness to facilitate digital transformation: Opportunities and challenges. In *Handbook of Research on Advancing Cybersecurity for Digital Transformation* (pp. 99–117). IGI Global., DOI: 10.4018/978-1-7998-6975-7.ch006

Ting, V., Chou, H.-Y., & Wang, J.-H. (2023). Securing Manufacturing through Patch Management for IoT Devices. *3rd IEEE International Conference on Electronic Communications, Internet of Things and Big Data, ICEIB 2023* (pp. 479-482). Taichung: IEEE. DOI: 10.1109/ICEIB57887.2023.10170074

Tsintotas, K. A., Moutsis, S. N., Konstantinidis, F. K., & Gasteratos, A. (2024). Toward Smart Supply Chain: Adopting Internet of Things and Digital Twins. *6th International Conference Series on ICT, Entertainment Technologies, and Intelligent Information Management in Education and Industry, ETLTC 2024. 3220.* Hybrid, Aizuwakamatsu: American Institute of Physics. DOI: 10.1063/5.0235214

Vaczi, D., Toth-Laufer, E., & Szadeczky, T. (2020). Fuzzy-based Cybersecurity Risk Analysis of the Human Factor from the Perspective of Classified Information Leakage. *18th IEEE International Symposium on Intelligent Systems and Informatics, SISY 2020* (pp. 113-118). Institute of Electrical and Electronics Engineers Inc. DOI: 10.1109/SISY50555.2020.9217053

Vakhula, O., Kurii, Y., Opirskyy, I., & Susukailo, V. (2024). Security-as-Code Concept for Fulfilling ISO/IEC 27001:2022 Requirements. *Workshop Cybersecurity Providing in Information and Telecommunication Systems, CPITS 2024. 3654.* Virtual, Online: CEUR-WS. Retrieved Feb 13, 2025, from https://www.scopus.com/record/display.uri?eid=2-s2.0-85189135508&origin=scopusAI

Wang, H., Wang, X., Wu, H., Wang, H., Zhang, L., Zhang, Q., & Wang, J. (2021). Design and Research of Network Security Threat Detection and Traceability System Based on AI. *2nd IYSF Academic Symposium on Artificial Intelligence and Computer Engineering. 12079.* Xi'an: SPIE. DOI: 10.1117/12.2622727

Wang, W., Sadjadi, S. M., & Rishe, N. (2024). A Survey of Major Cybersecurity Compliance Frameworks. *10th IEEE Conference on Big Data Security on Cloud, BigDataSecurity 2024* (pp. 23-34). New York City: IEEE. DOI: 10.1109/BigDataSecurity62737.2024.00013

Yang, X., Yang, L., & Li, S. (2023). A Digital Twin Application Framework in the Field of Industry. *18th IEEE Conference on Industrial Electronics and Applications, ICIEA 2023* (pp. 1615-1619). Ningbo: Institute of Electrical and Electronics Engineers Inc. DOI: 10.1109/ICIEA58696.2023.10241448

You, I., Kim, J., Pawana, I. W., & Ko, Y. (2024, November). Mitigating Security Vulnerabilities in 6G Networks: A Comprehensive Analysis of the DMRN Protocol Using SVO Logic and ProVerif. *Applied Sciences (Basel, Switzerland), 14*(21), 9726. Advance online publication. DOI: 10.3390/app14219726

Zorchenko, N. V., Tyupina, T. G., & Parshutin, M. E. (2024). Technologies Used by General Electric to Create Digital Twins for Energy Industry. *Power Technology and Engineering*. https://doi.org/https://doi.org/10.1007/s10749-024-01839-2

Chapter 11

Securing IoT With Advanced Machine and Deep Learning for Multi-Class Intrusion Detection:

Leveraging AI for Robust Multi-Class Intrusion Detection in IoT Systems

Idriss Moumen
https://orcid.org/0000-0002-9981-6370
Hassan II University, Morocco

Youssef Oukassou
Independent Researcher, Morocco

Jaafar Abouchabaka
Independent Researcher, Morocco

Najat Rafalia
Independent Researcher, Morocco

ABSTRACT

This study presents an AI-powered solution addressing three critical challenges in IoT security: Class imbalance in intrusion datasets, limited diversity in attack patterns, and the need for real-time analysis of network traffic. Our hybrid approach combines optimized machine learning models (Logistic Regression, Random Forest with One-vs-Rest strategy) with advanced deep learning architectures (FNN, LSTM, GRU) to

DOI: 10.4018/979-8-3373-8011-7.ch011

handle complex multi-class classification of network intrusions. We developed an end-to-end detection system featuring a user-friendly Streamlit interface that supports PCAP file analysis, real-time traffic visualization, and interactive threat reporting. The system achieved 98.56% detection accuracy in our evaluations, significantly outperforming conventional methods. Practical implementation features include automated firewall configuration recommendations and dynamic IP blocking for high-risk threats. This research demonstrates how AI-driven security solutions can provide adaptive protection for IoT ecosystems, offering both technical innovation and practical utility.

1. INTRODUCTION

Industries have undergone a revolution thanks to the Internet of Things (IoT), which has made the globe hyperconnected and enabled smooth network communication between billions of gadgets. This connectedness does, however, have some serious concerns (Tyagi & Kumar, 2021a). Networks are now vulnerable to a wide range of cyberthreats, including man-in-the-middle and Distributed Denial of Service (DDoS) assaults, as a result of the rapid proliferation of the Internet of Things, which is bringing over a million new devices online every day. Since they frequently lack built-in security features, many IoT devices are naturally unsafe due to their low processing and memory capacities, making them prime targets for hackers (Bukhari et al., 2023a). Industrial IoT devices like sensors and machine controllers, wearable technology like fitness trackers and smartwatches, and smart home appliances like lighting, thermostats, and security systems are examples of common gadgets (Zhou et al., 2021). Because these devices usually use antiquated protocols and are unable to incorporate strong encryption or authentication, they are susceptible to risks like code injection, replay assaults, and botnet formation, which have the potential to compromise entire networks. The confluence of IoT and OT exacerbates these problems by obfuscating the distinctions between traditional IT environments and industrial control systems, rendering them more vulnerable to intrusions (Alzahrani et al., 2022). The use of artificial intelligence (AI) and machine learning (ML) technologies to strengthen IoT security is developing in response to these mounting concerns. Because of these sophisticated methods' exceptional ability to recognize intricate threat patterns and counteract dynamic threats, AI-driven solutions are an essential feature of next-generation intrusion detection systems (IDS). In order to detect a wide variety of cyberattacks, we use ML and deep learning (DL) techniques in this study to investigate the use of AI to improve IoT security (Moumen, Rafalia, et al., 2023). To protect IoT ecosystems from new threats, this work attempts to create a strong multi-class IDS by tackling issues including class imbalance, data diversity, and the requirement for efficient analysis of stored network traffic data (Moumen, Abouchabaka, et al., 2023). In addition, we introduce an easy-to-use Streamlit platform for uploading, converting, and displaying pcap files of network traffic that can be used as an analysis tool and as a feed dataset for our classification model, leading to practical suggestions to improve cybersecurity.

2. LITERATURE REVIEW

The landscape of Internet of Things (IoT) security is complex, characterized by interconnected systems facing diverse cyber threats. Current security approaches heavily rely on various datasets that encapsulate different attack scenarios, including denial-of-service attacks, malware infections, and unauthorized data access. The most prominent datasets include UNSW-NB15 (Moustafa & Slay, 2015), NSL-KDD (Tavallaee et al., 2009), CICIDS2017 (Sharafaldin et al., 2018), IoTID20 (Ullah & Mahmoud, 2020), and the recent CICIoT2023 (Neto et al., 2023), each offering unique challenges and opportunities for security research.

Table 1. Attacks & Potential Problems in various Datasets.

Dataset	Targeted Environment	Attacks Identified	Potential Studies or Focus Areas
UNSW-NB15 (Moustafa & Slay, 2015)	IoT Networks	Malicious vs. Benign Traffic, Network Intrusions (uzzers, Analysis, Backdoors, DoS, Exploits, Generic, Reconnaissance, Shellcode, and Worms)	Enhancing traffic classification, improving intrusion detection reliability, scalability of security solutions
NSL-KDD (Tavallaee et al., 2009)	IoT & Network Data	Intrusions, DDoS Attacks (DoS, U2R, and R2L Probe)	Generalization across different intrusion scenarios, robust detection of DDoS attacks
CICIDS2017 (Sharafaldin et al., 2018)	IoT & Smart City Frameworks	Variety of Attacks (Bot, DDoS, DoS GoldenEye, DoS Hulk, DoS Slowhttptest, DoS slowlorFTPPatator, Heartbleed, Infiltration, PortSca, SSH-Patator, and Web Attack)	Benchmarking security solutions, evaluating ensemble techniques, comparative analysis of intrusion detection

continued on following page

Table 1. Continued

Dataset	Targeted Environment	Attacks Identified	Potential Studies or Focus Areas
IoTID20 (Ullah & Mahmoud, 2020)	IoT Environments	DoS Attacks (DoS and spoofing)	Addressing large dataset challenges, improving feature selection techniques, enhancing DoS attack detection
CICIoT2023 (Neto et al., 2023)	IoT Environments, Networks, Extensive Topology (>100 Devices)	Execution of 33 Attacks Divided into 7 Classes (DDoS, Dos, Recon, Web-based, Brute Force, Mirai, Spoofing)	Real-Time Dataset and Benchmark for Large-Scale Attacks in IoT Environment.

In recent years, traditional ML approaches have shown promising results in IoT security. Support Vector Machine (SVM) algorithms demonstrated a precision of 92.6% with an F1-score of 0.65 in differentiating between malicious and benign traffic (Tyagi & Kumar, 2021b). Similarly, when applied to smart city frameworks, SVM achieved approximately 90.5% accuracy, while Artificial Neural Networks (ANN) reached 79.5% (Bukhari et al., 2023b). DL applications have also made significant strides in IoT security. A Variational LSTM model achieved 86% precision on testing data and 96.7% on validation data (Zhou et al., 2021). Genetic Algorithm-enhanced SVM approaches yielded an accuracy of 88.2922% (Kim et al., 2005), while a comprehensive study using multiple algorithms showed varying success rates (Mhawi et al., 2022). However, some implementations showed limitations in their effectiveness. A Deep Neural Network with three hidden layers only achieved 75.75% accuracy (Tang et al., 2020), while a Convolutional Neural Network approach using transformed network data reached 79% accuracy (Wu et al., 2018). Deep autoencoders combined with multilayer perceptrons showed better results at 87% accuracy, though they struggled with specific attack types (Ieracitano et al., 2020). A self-taught learning approach using sparse autoencoders achieved 88.39% accuracy (Niyaz et al., 2017).

More recent studies have explored innovative approaches. Principal Component Analysis (PCA) and Linear Discriminant Analysis (LDA) achieved 84.82% accuracy (Pajouh et al., 2019), while a DL-based system for routing attacks showed impressive results with 95% precision and 96% recall (Yavuz et al., 2018). Standard ML classifiers demonstrated 94% accuracy (Anthi et al., 2019), though Logistic Regression showed limitations in multiclass classification with only 34% precision (Tyagi & Kumar, 2021a). Several studies highlighted the challenges in real-world applications. A Deep Recurrent Neural Network implementation achieved 92% accuracy but struggled with complex attacks (Almiani et al., 2020). DL Artificial Neural Networks showed around 89% accuracy but faced challenges with high-dimensional data (Sumathi & Karthikeyan, 2021). DDoS attack detection using Deep Neural Networks reached 93% accuracy but showed reduced effectiveness in diverse environments (Tama & Rhee, 2017). Multiple ML techniques evaluated together achieved approximately 90% accuracy but highlighted challenges with heterogeneous IoT devices (Chatterjee et al., 2019). Recent advancements utilizing the CICIoT2023 dataset have shown promising results in IoT security. He et al. proposed a transferable and adaptable framework combining reinforcement learning with network intrusion detection, achieving a remarkable 95.60% accuracy in multi-class classification (He et al., 2024). (Abbas et al., 2023), introduced a novel federated edge learning approach, demonstrating exceptional performance with 99.00% accuracy in binary classification using DNN-based federated learning. Additionally, (Jaradat et al., 2023), explored genetic optimization techniques for web attack classification, achieving 95.00% accuracy through an ensemble approach combining Gradient Boost, MLP, Logistic Regression, and KNN algorithms.

Table 2. Findings and limitations from various studie.

Author(s)	Dataset	Detection Model	Evaluation Metrics	Limitations/Gaps
(Tyagi & Kumar, 2021a)	UNSW-NB15	SVM	92.6% Precision, F1-score of 0.65	Small sample size, lack of real-world implementation
(Bukhari et al., 2023a) P.	CICIDS2017	SVM, KNN, ANN	90.5% for SVM, 79.5% for ANN	Restricted dataset, absence of comparative analysis
(Zhou et al., 2021)	UNSW-NB15	Decision Trees, RF, ANN	70.4% for DT, 91% for RF	Dataset size not representing real-world network variability
(Altulaihan et al., 2024)	IoTID20	SVM with Genetic Algorithm (GA)	88.2922%	Poor performance on large datasets with correlated features
(Tang et al., 2020)	NSL-KDD	Deep Neural Network	75.75%	Inability to generalize across different network scenarios
(Wu et al., 2018)	NSL-KDD	CNN (data transformed into 11x11 array)	79%	Misalignment between model architecture and dataset characteristics
(Ieracitano et al., 2020)	UNSW-NB15	Deep autoencoders, Multilayer Perceptron	87%	Underperformance in detecting R2L attacks
(Alzahrani et al., 2022)	UNSW-NB15	VLSTM	86% Testing Precision, 96.7% Validation Precision	Lack of real-world validation

continued on following page

Table 2. Continued

Author(s)	Dataset	Detection Model	Evaluation Metrics	Limitations/Gaps
(Niyaz et al., 2017)	NSL-KDD	Sparse Autoencoder	88.39%	Limited robustness in detecting various attack types
(Pajouh et al., 2019)	NSL-KDD	PCA, LDA, two-tier classification system	Accuracy: 84.82%	Feature reduction techniques altered core meaning of variables, impacting detection accuracy
(Yavuz et al., 2018)	COOJA Simulator	Deep learning-based system	Precision: 95%, Recall: 96%, F1-score: 94%	Dependence on specific routing attacks, simulation-based dataset might not capture complexities of real-world environments
(Anthi et al., 2019)	Not specified	Standard ML classifiers	Accuracy: 94%	Low precision due to high false positive rate, low recall due to high false negative rate, limited reliability and practical applicability in real-world IoT environments
(Tyagi & Kumar, 2021a)	Bot-IoT dataset	Logistic Regression (LR)	Binary classification accuracy: 92.2%, Multiclass precision: 34%, Recall: 46%, F1-score: 17%, AUROC: 0.45	High false alarm rates, low precision and recall values, unsuitable for attack type detection in IoT environments
(Almiani et al., 2020)	Simulation data in IoT environments	Deep RNN	Accuracy: 92%, Recall: 91%, Precision: 90%, FPR: 8%	Struggles with detecting complex, multi-step attacks; limited complexity of training data
(Sumathi & Karthikeyan, 2021)	Standard IoT datasets	DLANNs	Accuracy: 89%, Precision: 88%, Recall: 88%, FPR: 10%	High dimensionality and noise in datasets; computational overhead for real-time data
(Tama & Rhee, 2017)	Simulation data for DDoS attacks	DNN	Accuracy: 93%, Recall: 90%, Precision: 88%, FPR: 7%	Variability in attack patterns affecting generalization; diminished effectiveness in diverse real-world settings

continued on following page

Table 2. Continued

Author(s)	Dataset	Detection Model	Evaluation Metrics	Limitations/Gaps
(Chatterjee et al., 2019)	Multiple IoT security datasets	SVM, k-NN, Decision Trees	Accuracy: 90%, Precision: 88%, Recall: 87%, F1-score: 87%, FPR: 9%	Heterogeneous nature of IoT devices; varying data quality; need for robust preprocessing techniques
(He et al., 2024)	CIC-IoT2023	Transferable and Adaptable Network Intrusion Detection System (TA-NIDS) using Deep Reinforcement Learning	Detection Accuracy: 95.6%	Limited exploration of multi-class detection accuracy; computational cost during training phase

Based on this comprehensive review of existing literature, several critical gaps emerge that require urgent attention. First, while various ML and DL approaches show promising results, most studies struggle with class imbalance issues in multi-class attack detection, leading to reduced accuracy for less frequent attack types. Second, there is a notable lack of practical, user-friendly implementations that can handle real-world network traffic data effectively - particularly in processing and analyzing stored pcap files. Third, existing solutions often focus on either traditional ML or DL approaches in isolation, rather than leveraging the strengths of both through comprehensive model integration. Fourth, while many studies achieve reasonable detection accuracy, they often fail to provide actionable insights or recommendations for proactive security measures. Finally, there is a significant gap between theoretical model development and practical deployment, with few solutions offering interactive visualization and analysis capabilities for network traffic patterns. These limitations highlight the need for a more comprehensive, practical, and user-centric approach to IoT security that can effectively bridge the gap between sophisticated AI-driven detection and real-world application.

3. METHODOLOGY

The methodology depicted in the Figure 1 outlines a structured approach for processing and analyzing network traffic data to enhance threat classification and intrusion detection. It begins with the CICIoT2023 Dataset, which consists of PCAP (Packet Capture) traffic data, and utilizes a pipeline transformer to generate CSV chunks. This raw data undergoes several preprocessing steps including data merging from 169 CSV files, feature selection, data normalization, balancing, encoding, and segmentation to prepare it for effective model training. Training and evaluation are critical components of this methodology, where the data is divided into training, validation, and testing sets. The training set is specifically used to reshape data to suit three ML models and a feed-forward neural network, as well as four RNN (Recurrent Neural Network) models. Hyperparameter tuning is conducted to refine model parameters, followed by the evaluation of models based on predefined metrics. The final phase involves practical deployment, where the best-performing model is selected for deployment in a real-world environment. This includes integration with a Streamlit-based IDS platform and comprehensive threat management, ensuring robust security measures are implemented and maintained. This methodology underscores a meticulous, data-driven approach to enhance the detection and classification of network threats.

Figure 1. Methodology Diagram.

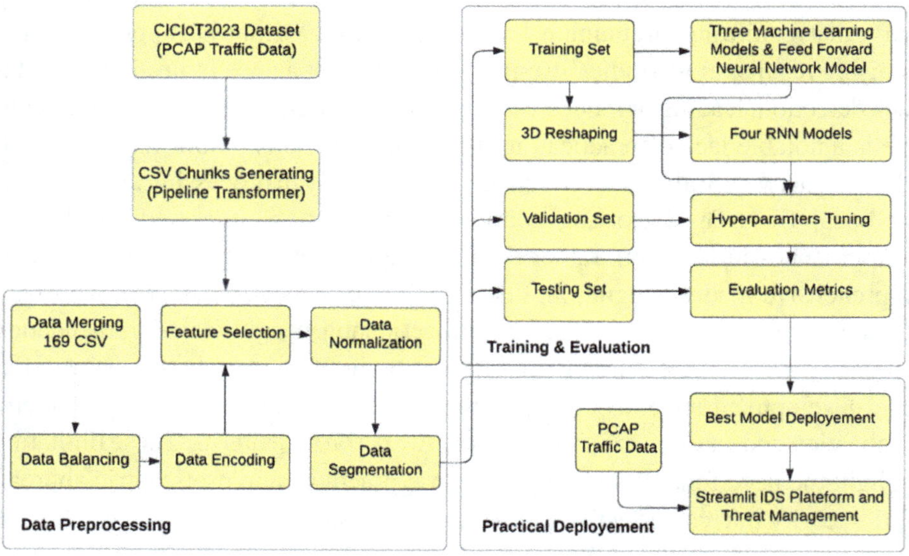

3.1. Dataset Overview

A vast collection of data, the CICIoT2023 dataset is intended to assess cybersecurity risks in Internet of Things (IoT) contexts. 105 different IoT devices make up the network topology it simulates, covering a broad range of applications such as wearable technology like fitness trackers and smartwatches, industrial IoT devices like sensors and microcontrollers used in manufacturing processes, and smart home devices like thermostats, security cameras, and smart lights. This diversity reflects the complexity of real-world IoT networks by allowing the investigation of both benign and malicious communications under realistic conditions. There are 33 different types of attacks in the dataset, which are divided into seven major categories: Denial of Service (DoS), Distributed Denial of Service (DDoS), reconnaissance, web-based assaults, brute force attacks, spoofing attacks, and Mirai-based attacks. Malicious IoT devices carried out these attacks, simulating real-world situations in which gadgets target one another, the following table presents a comprehensive overview of various network threat types and their respective data points in the dataset.

Table 3. Labels Distribution.

Label 1	Quantity	Label 2	Quantity	Label 3	Quantity
DDoS-ICMP_ Flood	7,200,504	Mirai-greeth_ flood	991,866	Vulnerability Scan	37,382
DDoS-UDP_ Flood	5,412,287	Mirai-udpplain	890,576	DDoS-SlowLoris	23,246
DDoS-TCP_ Flood	4,497,667	Mirai-greip_ flood	751,682	DictionaryBruteForce	13,064
DDoSPSHACK_ Flood	4,094,755	DDoSICMP_ Fragmentation	452,489	BrowserHijacking	5,859
DDoS-SYN_ Flood	4,059,190	MITM- ArpSpoofing	307,593	CommandInjection	5,409
DDoS-RSTFIN_ Flood	4,045,190	DDoSUDP_ Fragmentation	286,925	SQL Injection	5,245
DDoSSynonymousIP_ Flood	3,598,138	DDoSACK_ Fragmentation	285,104	XSS	3,946
DoS-UDP_ Flood	3,318,595	Recon- HostDiscovery	178,911	Backdoor_Malware	3,218
DoS-TCP_ Flood	2,671,445	Recon- OSScan	134,378	Recon-PingSweep	2,262
DoS-SYN_ Flood	2,028,834	Recon- PortScan	98,259	Uploading_Attack	1,252
Benign	1,098,195	DoS-HTTP_ Flood	71,864	None	None

In order to obtain the data, network taps and traffic monitors were used to record 548 GB of traffic in pcap format. With more than 5 million labelled records, this extensive dataset includes important characteristics like traffic rate, protocol type, header length, flow duration, and different TCP flags. Additionally, because of the dataset's versatility in feature extraction, researchers can design new features that are customized to meet their unique analytical requirements. Notably, it fills a major research vacuum in IoT security by offering data from a range of IoT devices, which improves the creation and assessment of ML and DL models for IoT network intrusion detection.

3.2. Feature Engineering and Selection

In the context of IoT network security analysis, the selection and engineering of appropriate features play a crucial role in developing effective ML models. This section details our systematic approach to feature engineering and selection, emphasizing both statistical relationships and domain-specific knowledge.

a. Domain-Specific Feature Engineering

The feature engineering process for IoT network security analysis requires careful consideration of various network behavior aspects and potential security threats. We developed a comprehensive approach that encompasses temporal patterns, protocol-specific characteristics, and statistical measures to effectively capture both obvious and subtle patterns in network traffic.

Table 4. Feature Categories, Descriptions, and Security Applications.

Category	Features	Description	Security Applications
Temporal Features	Flow Metrics:	Temporal characteristics of packet flows and their intervals	DDoS Detection, Timing Attack Identification, Traffic Anomaly Detection
	Flow Duration		
	Inter-Arrival Time		
	Transmission Rates (Total, Source, Destination)		
Protocol Features	Flag Indicators	TCP connection states and behavior patterns Multi-layer protocol identification	Protocol Manipulation Detection, Scanning Activity Identification Service Abuse Detection, Protocol Anomaly Identification
	TCP Flags (FIN, SYN, RST, PSH, ACK, ECE, CWR)		
	Flag Counts		
	Protocol Types		
	Application Layer (HTTP, HTTPS, DNS)		
	Transport Layer (TCP, UDP)		
	Network Layer (ICMP, IPv)		

continued on following page

Table 4. Continued

Category	Features	Description	Security Applications
Statistical Features	Size Statistics	Packet size distribution metrics Advanced flow behavior metrics	Data Exfiltration Detection, Payload Anomaly Identification Complex Attack Pattern Detection, Traffic Behavior Profiling
	Total Sum/Size		
	Min/Max/Average		
	Standard Deviation		
	Flow Statistics		
	Magnitude		
	Radius		
	Covariance		
	Weight		

This comprehensive feature set enables effective detection and classification of various IoT network behaviors and security threats while maintaining computational efficiency and real-time processing capabilities.

b. Correlation-Based Feature Selection

Feature selection through correlation analysis serves two primary purposes: identifying the most informative features for model training and eliminating redundant features that could introduce noise or computational overhead. Our correlation analysis methodology employed both Pearson correlation coefficients and visual correlation matrix analysis to ensure comprehensive feature evaluation. We implemented a systematic correlation analysis approach (Figure 2 presents the correlation matrix of the most significantly correlated features in our dataset) using the following steps:

1. Calculation of pairwise correlations between all features
2. Generation of a correlation matrix
3. Identification of features with significant correlations (threshold > 0.7)
4. Assessment of multicollinearity among selected features

Figure 2. Correlation Matrix for Multicollinearity Features

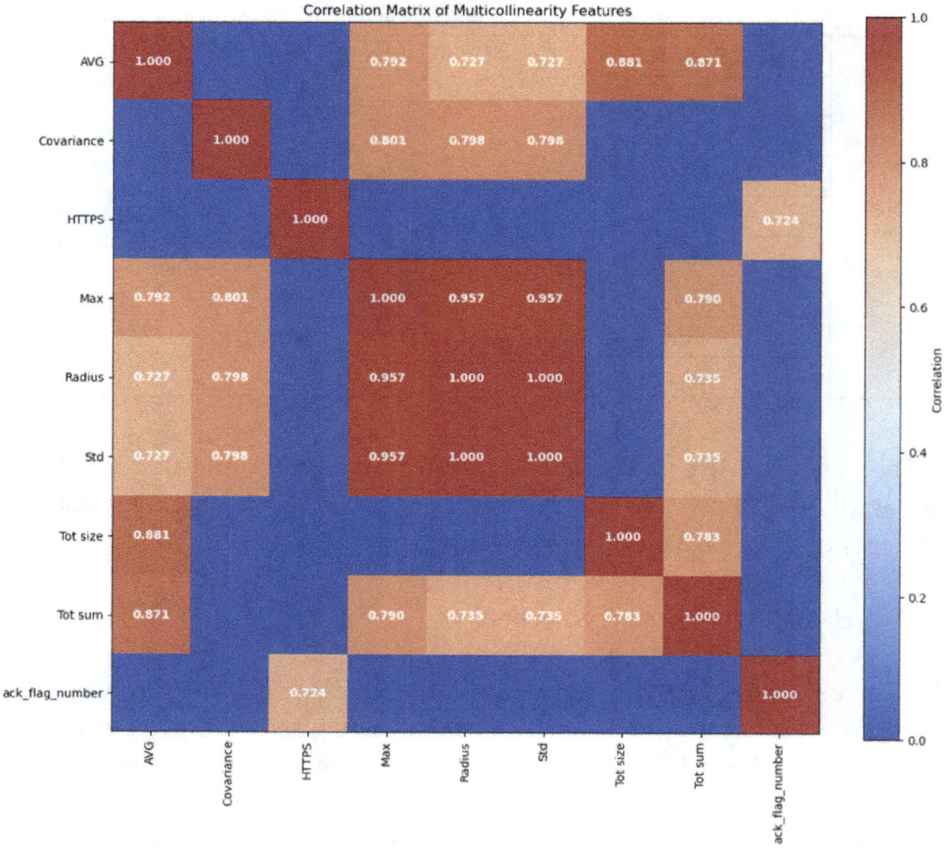

The correlation matrix reveals several important relationships among features: Size-Related Metrics Cluster:

- Total sum demonstrates strong positive correlations with multiple size-related features (Tot size: 0.783, AVG: 0.871, Max: 0.790)
- This cluster suggests that these metrics capture related aspects of packet size distributions

Statistical Measures Group:

- Perfect correlation (1.000) between Radius and Standard Deviation
- Very strong correlation (0.957) between Max and Radius
- These relationships indicate potential redundancy in statistical descriptors

Protocol-Specific Correlations:

- HTTPS shows significant correlation with ack_flag_number (0.724)
- This relationship aligns with expected HTTPS protocol behavior in establishing secure connections

To address multicollinearity concerns, we established a threshold of 0.7 for correlation coefficients, above which features were subjected to careful evaluation. The following criteria guided our feature retention decisions:

- Information Value: Features providing unique information despite high correlations were retained
- Computational Efficiency: Among highly correlated features, those with lower computational complexity were preferred
- Domain Relevance: Features with direct security implications were prioritized over derived metrics

3.3. Data Merging

In the data processing workflow, "Data Merging" is a critical initial step aimed at consolidating multiple datasets into a single, cohesive unit to facilitate comprehensive analysis. Specifically, the process involves the integration of 169 CSV files, each representing different segments or captures of network traffic data, into a unified dataset. This step is essential for ensuring that the subsequent feature selection and data normalization phases have a complete set of data to work from, thereby enhancing the reliability and accuracy of the threat detection models. By aggregating the data in this manner, we can address potential biases or gaps in the analysis, while also streamlining the computational processing during the feature engineering stages.

3.4. Data Balancing

Managing imbalanced data sets is crucial for developing robust predictive models. The dataset in question, CIC-IoT-2023, which is noted as the most extensive collection derived from real IoT devices, comprises data from various IoT device types and documents 33 different attack vectors. This dataset stands out not only for its diversity but also for its unbalanced nature, where the class distribution shows a substantial skewness towards benign traffic, which far outnumbers the instances of various types of attacks . To address this imbalance, it is essential to implement strategic preprocessing techniques that aid in mitigating bias towards the majority class, thereby enhancing model performance across less frequent but critical categories of cyber threats. Our approach involves a combination of downsampling the majority class and applying Synthetic Minority Over-sampling Technique (SMOTE) in a hierarchical fashion to incrementally balance the classes up to the majority class (benign traffic), as illustrated in Figure 3, which depicts the class imbalance distribution before preprocessing.

Figure 3. Class Imbalance Distribution

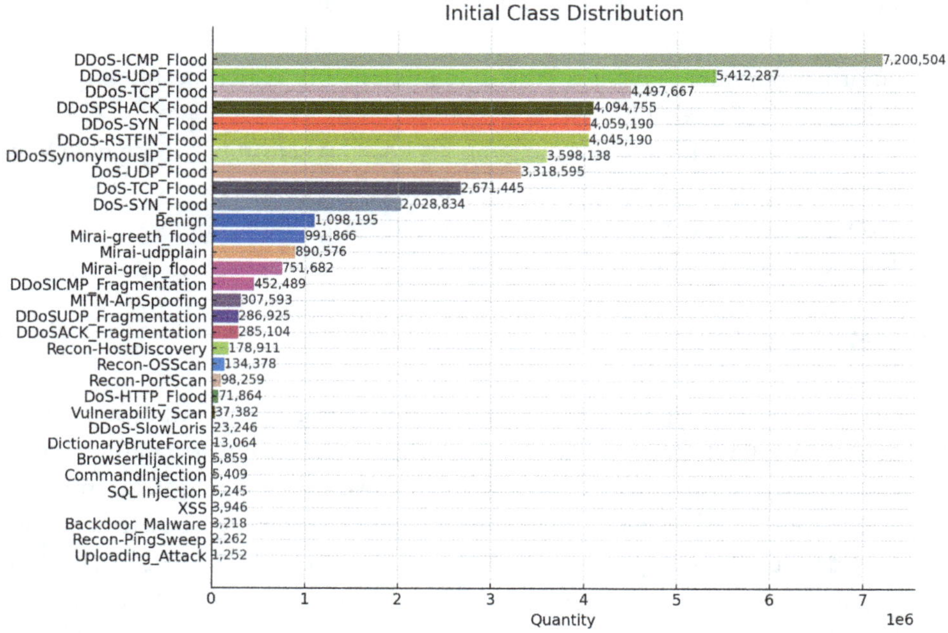

- Downsampling: Initially, the most frequent classes which significantly overshadows others, are downsized to a predefined target. This step helps to prevent the model from being overwhelmingly biased towards predicting the majority classes.
- Hierarchical SMOTE: SMOTE is employed to increase the representation of minority classes. However, instead of uniformly increasing all minority classes to match the majority class directly, we use a hierarchical approach. We progressively over-sample the minority classes towards a series of escalating targets, starting from the smallest class up to the predefined threshold below the majority class. This technique enables a more balanced dataset while maintaining a realistic distribution of attack types, reflecting real-world scenarios more accurately.

3.5. Data Encoding

After balancing the classes, Data Encoding is applied to transform categorical labels into numerical values, which is a necessary step for ML models, as they operate on numerical data. This is done through Label Encoding, which assigns a unique integer to each category within a categorical feature, allowing the model to interpret and process categorical information. By converting categories into numbers, label encoding ensures that the model can utilize categorical data without any loss of information or interpretability.

3.6. Data Normalization

Following data encoding, Data Normalization is performed to bring all features within a standardized range. This step is crucial because it prevents the model from being disproportionately influenced by features with larger numerical scales, ensuring an equitable impact of each feature on the model's learning process. Normalization techniques, such as scaling data to a specific range or standardizing to a zero-mean and unit variance, make the features comparable and stabilize the learning process. This standardized range across features allows the model to converge faster and improves its predictive accuracy by reducing bias towards certain variables.

3.7. Data Reshaping

With Recurrent Neural Networks (RNNs), especially suited for time-series and sequence-based data, data reshaping is a critical preprocessing step. RNNs require input in a 3-dimensional format (samples, time steps, features) to capture the sequential dependencies in the data. Therefore, the dataset is reshaped to accommodate this structure, allowing the RNN model to recognize patterns across time steps and capture temporal dependencies. This reshaping is particularly valuable for capturing trends and sequential nuances, making the data suitable for the recurrent nature of the RNN model, which "remembers" past inputs to inform future predictions.

3.8. Data Splitting (Segmentation)

In the final stage of preprocessing, Data Splitting divides the dataset into training, validation and testing subsets. This split is typically done using a stratified approach based on the label distribution, ensuring that all the sets reflect the overall dataset's class proportions accurately. Stratified sampling maintains the balance of classes in both subsets, preventing bias in model evaluation. This step is crucial for reliable model performance assessment and subsequent tuning of parameters, as it allows the model to be evaluated on data it has not seen during training, providing an unbiased estimate of its effectiveness.

3.9. Machine Learning Models

In the development of efficient IDS for categorizing network traffic in multi-class classification scenarios, we investigated a variety of ML models. This section discusses the models selected—Logistic Regression, Decision Trees, and Random Forest—their parameterization, and the rationale behind their use as foundational models before exploring more complex DL techniques.

Model Overview and Rationale

The models were specifically chosen for their ability to handle class imbalances and their effectiveness in multi-class classification, crucial for the accurate and robust categorization of network threats. Table 5 summarizes the models and their key parameters:

Table 5. Overview of ML Models Used.

Model	Key Parameters	Purpose
Logistic Regression	- Balanced class weight - Max iterations: 1000 - Parallel processing	Establishes a baseline with efficient binary classification adaptability to multi-class via OvR technique.
Decision Trees	- Max depth: 10 - Random state: fixed - Balanced class weight	Prevents overfitting, ensures reproducibility, and manages class imbalance.
Random Forest	- Estimators: 100 - Random state: fixed - Balanced class weight - Parallel processing	Increases accuracy and robustness, suitable for large datasets with complex decision boundaries.

The selection of Logistic Regression, Decision Trees, and Random Forest as starting models was strategic. Their established methodologies provide a solid benchmark against which the performance of more sophisticated models can be compared. Moreover, these models allow for a clearer understanding of the IDS landscape, making them invaluable for initial explorations into the domain of network security. Their simplicity and robustness enable us to dissect the challenges in network traffic categorization thoroughly, which is crucial before transitioning to more complex DL models. This progression ensures a methodical enhancement in model sophistication, aligned with our research goals to not only address but also deeply understand the nuances of intrusion detection.

3.10. ML Models Hyperparameters Tuning

Hyperparameter tuning is integral to optimizing the predictive performance of ML models. We employed Grid Search, a comprehensive hyperparameter optimization technique that systematically explores a range of configurations, focusing on maximizing cross-validated model accuracy. This approach is detailed in Table 6:

Table 6. Hyperparameter Tuning with Grid Search.

Model	Parameters Tuned	Grid Search Strategy	Best Parameters Found
Logistic Regression	- C (Regularization strength) - Solver (Optimization algorithm)	Explores logarithmic scale of C, multiple solvers.	- C: 1.0 - Solver: 'liblinear'
Decision Trees	- Max depth - Min samples split	Ranges from shallow depths to more complex trees.	- Max depth: 10 - Min samples split: 2
Random Forest	- Number of estimators - Max features	Evaluates various levels of tree complexity and ensemble size.	- Estimators: 100 - Max features: 'auto'

3.11. Deep Learning Models

The challenges posed by IoT network traffic, characterized by high-dimensional data and intricate temporal dependencies, demand analytical capabilities beyond traditional ML approaches. While baseline ML models provided initial insights, they lacked the depth required to capture the complex, evolving patterns inherent in network traffic data. This section explores the DL architectures implemented in our study, namely Feedforward Neural Networks (FNN), Gated Recurrent Units (GRU), Long Short-Term Memory (LSTM), Bidirectional LSTM (Bi-D LSTM), and a Hybrid Bidirectional LSTM-GRU model, each progressively enhancing the model's capacity for handling sequential data. Our choice of architectures reflects a methodical progression from simpler to more sophisticated structures, each serving a specific purpose in enhancing model performance on multi-class classification tasks within an IDS framework. Table 7 outlines the core architectures and their primary design elements.

Table 7. Overview of DL Models and Architectures.

Model	Architectural Highlights	Purpose
FNN	Dense layers with dropout and class weighting for balancing	Establishes baseline performance, identifies initial classification trends
GRU	Streamlined RNN with fewer gates	Reduces computational complexity while maintaining sequential learning efficiency
LSTM	Sequential layers with memory cells for long-term dependencies	Captures evolving attack patterns over longer sequences in IoT data
Bi-D LSTM	Processes sequences in both forward and backward directions for comprehensive context awareness	Enhances context-based learning, crucial for identifying bidirectional dependencies in data
Hybrid Bi-Directional LSTM-GRU	Combined Bidirectional LSTM and GRU layers with dropout for multi-level sequence analysis and efficiency	Balances computational efficiency and accuracy, maximizing pattern recognition in temporal contexts

Each architecture was carefully selected based on its ability to capture distinct aspects of the dataset, from simpler non-temporal relationships to complex, bidirectional dependencies. The reasoning behind layer sizes, dropout rates, and model complexity is outlined below:

1. As a starting point, we used a Feedforward Neural Network (FNN) model, which was constructed using a simple yet efficient architecture tailored for our dataset. The architecture depicted in Figure 4, begins with an input layer that matches the dimensionality of our features, followed by a 128-neuron dense layer equipped with ReLU activation. This layer is designed to capture complex relationships within the data effectively. Following this, a 64-neuron layer is added with a dropout rate of 0.2 for additional regularization, ensuring that the model does not overly rely on any specific neurons and thus helps mitigate the risk of overfitting. To further enhance model robustness, a softmax activation function is applied at the output layer, enabling the network to perform multi-class classification across the various categories present in our dataset.

Figure 4. Feed Forward Neural Network Model's Architecture

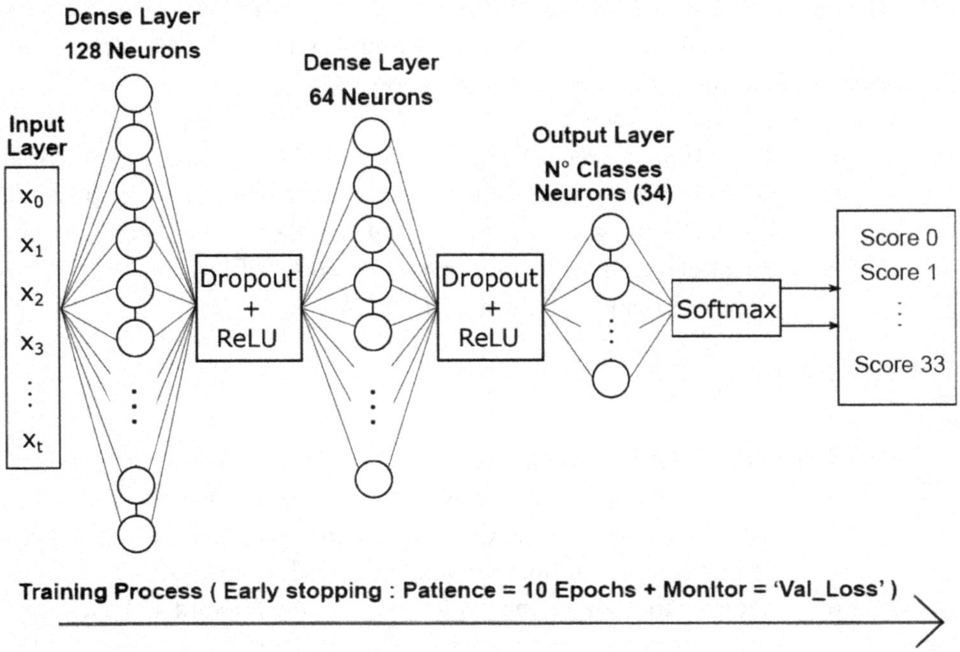

2. LSTMs were introduced to handle the sequential nature of IoT data more effectively. The architecture's memory cells allowed the retention of long-term dependencies across time steps, addressing evolving attack patterns. The model used a 64-unit LSTM layer with a dropout rate of 0.2, balancing memory retention with regularization to prevent overfitting while capturing temporal dependencies.
3. GRUs were incorporated to simplify the RNN architecture while maintaining sequence-learning capabilities. This model was structured with 64 GRU units and a 0.2 dropout rate, which streamlined the learning process and reduced computational requirements compared to LSTM, offering an efficient alternative for scenarios with resource constraints.
4. To further enhance the model's context-awareness, we introduced a Bi-D LSTM. By processing sequences in both forward and backward directions, this architecture could interpret events in context—vital for identifying bidirectional dependencies in IoT data. This bidirectional processing proved valuable in scenarios where the order and context of events significantly influence the interpretation of attacks.

5. Hybrid Bidirectional LSTM-GRU Model: This Model integrates Bidirectional LSTM and Bidirectional GRU layers to capture complex temporal dependencies in both forward and backward directions within IoT network data, addressing the demands of multi-class intrusion detection.
   - Bidirectional LSTM Layers:
     - o Two Bidirectional LSTM Layers with 128 neurons each: These layers capture forward and backward dependencies in the data.
     - o For each time step *t*, the hidden states in the forward and backward directions are represented as $h_t^{\rightarrow LSTM}$ and $h_t^{\leftarrow LSTM}$.
     - o Combined hidden state at *t* for LSTM:

$$h_t^{LSTM} = \left[h_t^{\rightarrow LSTM} \; ; h_t^{\leftarrow LSTM}\right]$$

   - Bidirectional GRU Layers:
     - o Two Bidirectional GRU Layers with 64 neurons each: Following the LSTM layers, these GRU layers further capture sequential dependencies in both forward and backward directions.
     - o For each time step *t*, the hidden states in the forward and backward directions are represented as $h_t^{\rightarrow GRU}$ and $h_t^{\leftarrow GRU}$.
     - o Combined hidden state at *t* for GRU:

$$h_t^{GRU} = \left[h_t^{\rightarrow GRU} \; ; h_t^{\leftarrow GRU}\right]$$

   - Dropout Layer:
     - o Dropout Layer with a 50% rate: Applied after the GRU layers to prevent overfitting by randomly deactivating 50% of the neurons during training.
     - o Fully Connected and Softmax Layer:
     - o Dense Layer with output neurons equal to the number of classes: The final hidden representation is fed into a dense layer for classification.
     - o Softmax Activation: Converts the output into probabilities for each class *j* (for *C* classes):

$$P(y = jx) = \frac{e^{(W_j \, . \, h + b_j)}}{\sum_{K=1}^{C} e^{(W_k \, . \, h + b_k)}}$$

Where W_j and W_k represent the weights associated with each class in the fully connected (Dense) layer, where *j* and *k* denote different classes.

- Leveraging Bidirectional Processing: In complex IoT traffic, patterns are often contextual, requiring both past and future information for accurate interpretation. By employing a Bidirectional LSTM, this model can access both preceding and succeeding contexts in a sequence, enhancing its capacity to detect subtle patterns that might only be evident when viewed in both temporal directions.
- Combining LSTM and GRU for Temporal Flexibility and Computational Efficiency: While both LSTM and GRU are specialized in handling sequential data, each has distinct advantages. LSTMs retain long-term dependencies but can be computationally intensive, while GRUs streamline the learning process with fewer gates, achieving comparable performance with faster computation and lower memory requirements. By combining these two types of layers, the hybrid architecture achieves a balance between LSTM's detailed temporal information retention and GRU's computational efficiency.
- Enhanced Pattern Recognition through Sequential Layering: The 128-unit Bidirectional LSTM layer captures prolonged patterns, while the 64-unit Bidirectional GRU refines this information by focusing on shorter-term dependencies. This layered approach enhances adaptability, enabling the model to recognize intricate linkages that single-layer or unidirectional models might miss.
- Optimizing for Multi-Class Classification Tasks in IDS: The bidirectional architecture of this model, as shown in Figure 5, combined with LSTM-GRU layering, enables effective differentiation of subtle class-specific patterns, thereby enhancing performance in multi-class intrusion detection tasks.

Figure 5. Hybrid Bidirectional LSTM-GRU Model's Architecture

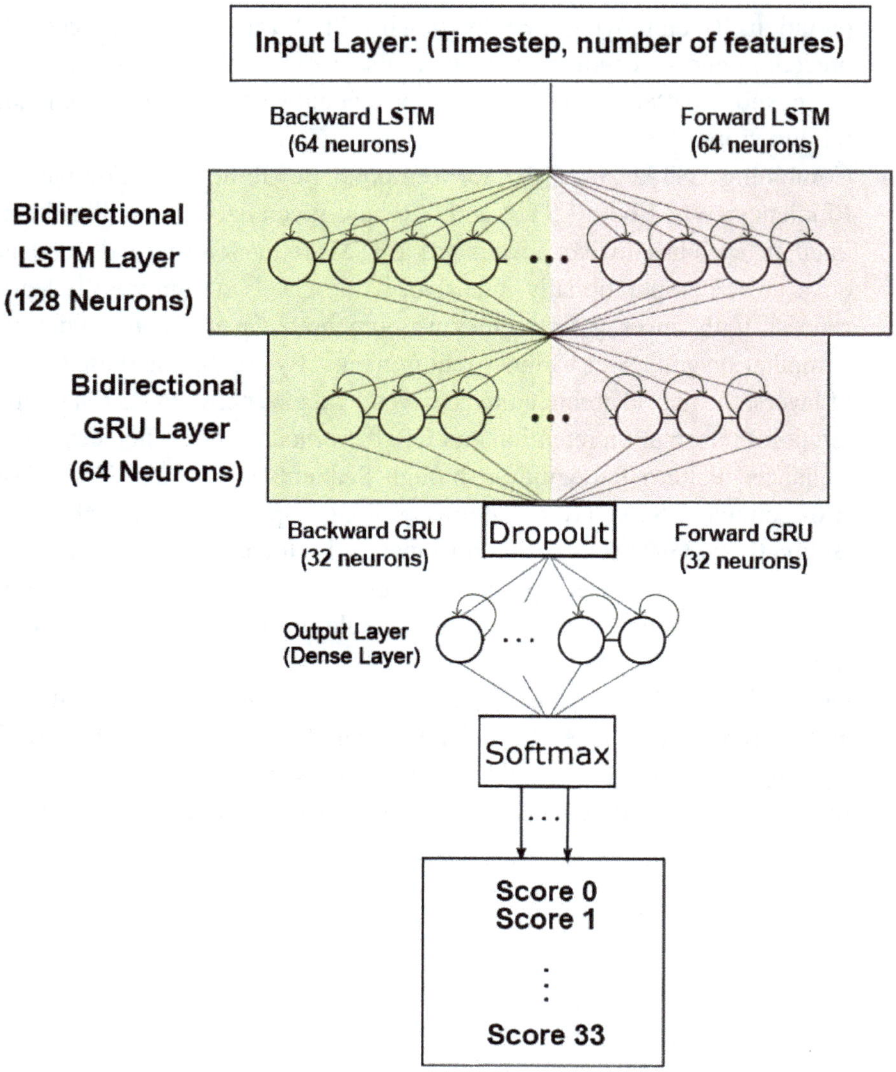

3.12. DL Models Hyperparameters Tuning

Hyperparameter tuning is essential in refining DL models to achieve optimal performance. We implemented random search as our tuning method, which, compared to exhaustive grid search, allows for more extensive exploration across a broader parameter space with lower computational costs. Key hyperparameters such as layer units, dropout rates, batch size, and learning rate were fine-tuned using random search with cross-validation. Table 8 provides details on the best configurations identified through this process.

Table 8. Random Search Hyperparameter Tuning Results.

Model	Optimized Hyperparameters	Random Search Ranges
FNN	- Dense layer: 128 and 64 neurons - Dropout: 0.3 (layer 1), 0.2 (layer 2) - Batch size: 32 - Learning rate: 0.001	Dropout (0.1–0.5), Batch size (64–128), LR (0.0001–0.01)
LSTM	- LSTM units: 64 - Dropout: 0.2 - Batch size: 64 - Learning rate: 0.001	Units (32–128), Dropout (0.1–0.5), Batch size (16–128)
GRU	- GRU units: 64 - Dropout: 0.2 - Batch size: 64 - Learning rate: 0.001	Units (32–128), Dropout (0.1–0.5), Batch size (16–128)
Bi-D LSTM	- LSTM units: 128 - Dropout: 0.3 - Batch size: 32 - Learning rate: 0.001	Units (64–128), Dropout (0.1–0.5), Batch size (16–64)
Hybrid Bi-Directional LSTM-GRU	- Bi-D LSTM units: 128 - Bi-D GRU units: 64 - Dropout: 0.3 - Batch size: 32 - Learning rate: 0.001	LSTM/GRU units (32–64–128), Dropout (0.1–0.5), Batch size (16–64)

Cross-Validation Strategy: To ensure model robustness, we employed k-fold cross-validation during the random search process, dividing the data into subsets for training and validation to reduce overfitting and enhance generalizability. Accuracy was used as the primary metric, ensuring model performance across classes.

1. RandomizedSearchCV: We implemented RandomizedSearchCV with specific configurations to systematically evaluate predefined parameter combinations. Key parameters were set to:
    - LSTM units: (64, 128) - configured for specific pairings
    - GRU units: (32, 64, 128) - matched to corresponding LSTM units
    - Learning rate: (0.001, 0.01) - paired strategically with network architectures The number of iterations (n_iter=4) and folds (cv=2) were set

to ensure complete evaluation of all configurations while maintaining computational efficiency.

2. Resource Monitoring: A custom ResourceMonitor callback tracked memory usage, CPU usage, and training time per epoch. This helped optimize settings like batch size and training epochs, ensuring efficient resource usage and balanced performance.
3. Model Architecture with Early Stopping: The KerasClassifier class integrated the Bidirectional LSTM-GRU architecture, including:
    - Bidirectional LSTM layer with either 64 or 128 units for capturing dependencies in both directions.
    - Bidirectional GRU layer with 32, 64, or 128 units for streamlined sequence processing.
    - Softmax output layer for multi-class predictions. EarlyStopping monitored validation loss with a patience of 2 epochs, restoring best weights to prevent overfitting.
4. Performance Evaluation: After RandomizedSearchCV, the optimal parameters were chosen based on cross-validation scores. The final evaluation provided:
    - Best parameters: Indicating the optimal configuration from the predefined set.
    - Best cross-validation score: Offering an accuracy measure for generalizability. This integrated approach combined specific configuration testing, cross-validation, and early stopping with resource monitoring, ensuring high accuracy and computational efficiency, essential for effective IDS deployment in real-world environments.

The DL models presented have shown marked improvements in handling the complexities of IoT network traffic data. By leveraging a range of architectures—from FNN to Bidirectional LSTM-GRU—and optimizing each through random search with cross-validation, we achieved an efficient and accurate IDS model capable of adapting to various attack patterns. This systematic exploration provides a foundation for robust IDS implementations and lays the groundwork for future enhancements using even more sophisticated DL architectures.

4. EXPERIMENTAL RESULTS

4.1. Experimental Metrics

To thoroughly assess the performance of our ML and DL models in the context of an IDS, we utilized several evaluation metrics tailored to each model type:

1. ML Models: Logistic Regression, Decision Trees, and Random Forest—we evaluated performance using accuracy, precision, recall, and F1 score. Each of these metrics provides specific insights essential for IDS applications:
   - Accuracy: Represents the overall proportion of correct predictions. For a model with predictions $\hat{y}$ and true labels y, accuracy is defined as:

$$Accuracy = \frac{TP + TN}{TP + TN + FP + FN}$$

This metric provides a broad view of the model's effectiveness, especially in cases where attack types are relatively balanced.

- Precision: Reflects how accurately the model identifies true attacks among all instances labeled as attacks. Precision is calculated as:

$$Precision = \frac{TP}{TP + FP}$$

High precision is crucial for reducing false alarms in IDS, which helps avoid alarm fatigue.

- Recall: Indicates the model's ability to detect actual threats or true positives, thus measuring its sensitivity to various attack types. Recall is given by:

$$Recall = \frac{TP}{TP + FN}$$

High recall is essential to ensure that genuine threats are not overlooked, minimizing security risks.

- F1 Score: Provides a balance between precision and recall, combining them into a single metric that captures both accuracy in threat identification and sensitivity to all threats. F1 score is calculated as:

$$F1\ Score = 2 \cdot \frac{Precision \cdot Recall}{Precision + Recall}$$

Table 9 presents detailed metrics for each ML model, with ensemble-based models (e.g., Random Forest) achieving higher performance than simpler models, emphasizing the benefit of ensemble techniques for complex, multi-class IDS tasks.

2. DL Models: we focused on accuracy and loss, which are widely used in DL to evaluate both performance and model learning efficiency:

- Accuracy: As with ML models, accuracy provides an overall measure of the model's correctness in classifying network traffic. It helps determine the general reliability of DL models in distinguishing between normal and attack types.
- Loss: Represents the difference between the predicted and actual values, capturing the model's learning progress over epochs. For a multi-class classification problem, categorical cross-entropy loss is commonly used:

$$Loss = -\frac{1}{N}\sum_{i=1}^{N}\sum_{j=1}^{C} y_{i,j}\log\left(\hat{y}_{i,j}\right)$$

Where N: Number of samples, C: Number of classes, $y_{i,j}$: Binary indicator (0 or 1) if class label j is the correct classification for sample i, $\hat{y}_{i,j}$: Predicted probability of sample i belonging to class j

Table 9. Summarized Performance Metrics For all Models.

Model	Accuracy	Precision	Recall	F1 Score	Loss
Logistic Regression	71.99%	0.6619	0.7199	0.6586	-
Decision Tree	82.30%	0.8163	0.8230	0.8145	-
Random Forest	85.72%	0.8459	0.8572	0.8400	-
FNN	92.98%	-	-	-	0.2084
GRU	93.97%	-	-	-	0.1990
LSTM	93.64%	-	-	-	0.1947
Bi-D LSTM	95.13%	-	-	-	0.1399
Hybrid Bi-D LSTM + GRU	98.56%	-	-	-	0.0391

4.2. Training and Validation Analysis

The accuracy plot shows a steady increase in training accuracy, stabilizing around 92.5%, with validation accuracy following a similar trend but with minor fluctuations, hinting at slight overfitting. Figure 6, both training and validation loss decrease rapidly within the first few epochs, stabilizing near 0.2. The close alignment between training and validation loss suggests reasonable generalization, though periodic fluctuations in validation loss indicate the model's sensitivity to data variability. Overall, the FNN achieves high accuracy but exhibits some instability in validation performance, possibly due to limited capacity for complex patterns.

Figure 6. FNN Accuracy & Loss

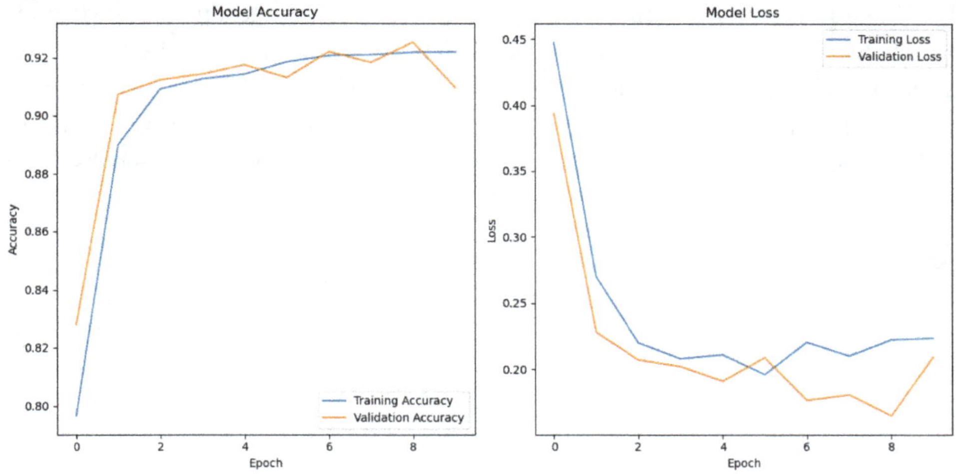

Figure 7, both training and validation accuracy rise quickly, stabilizing around 93.9%, with validation accuracy slightly higher, suggesting strong generalization. The loss plot shows a rapid drop in both training and validation loss, converging around 0.189 by the final epochs. The close alignment between the two curves indicates that the GRU model learns efficiently with minimal overfitting. The GRU achieves high accuracy with stable loss, reflecting effective learning and generalization.

Figure 7. GRU Accuracy & Loss

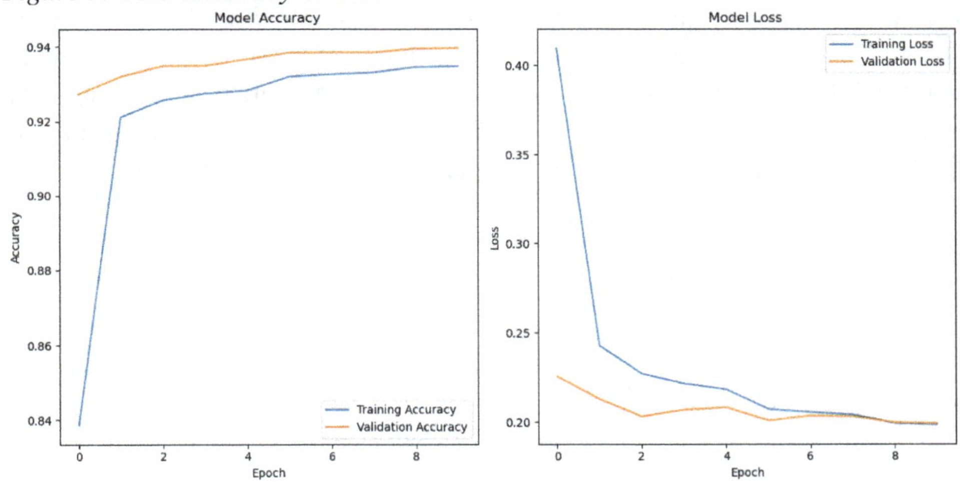

Figure 8, shows both training and validation accuracy quickly reaching around 93.5%, with validation accuracy slightly higher and stable, suggesting robust generalization. In the loss plot, both training and validation loss decrease rapidly, converging around 0.189. The minimal gap between the curves indicates efficient learning with good stability and low overfitting. Overall, the LSTM model demonstrates strong performance with high accuracy and consistent loss reduction across epochs.

Figure 8. LSTM Accuracy & Loss

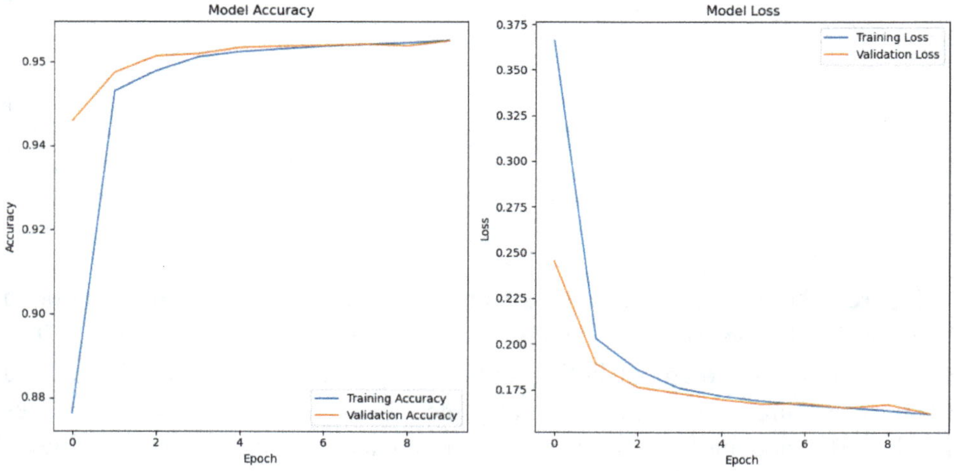

Figure 9, shows both training and validation accuracy quickly reaching around 95%, with minimal fluctuation, indicating strong learning and excellent generalization. In the loss plot, both training and validation loss decrease sharply, converging near 0.15. The close alignment of the curves demonstrates effective learning with minimal overfitting. Overall, the Bi-D LSTM model achieves high accuracy and stable loss, highlighting its robustness in capturing sequential dependencies.

Figure 9. Bi-D LSTM Accuracy & Loss

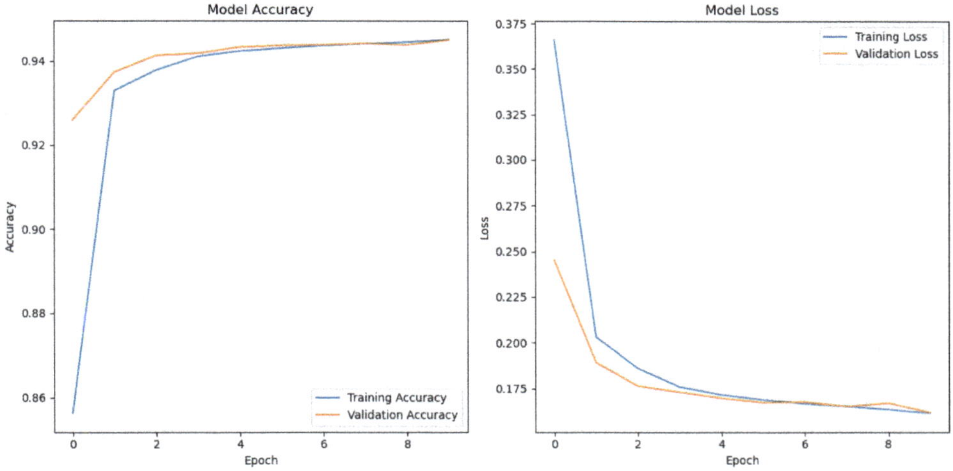

In Figure 10, The hybrid model achieves rapid convergence, with training and validation accuracy reaching approximately 98% by the second epoch. The close alignment and minimal fluctuations between these curves indicate strong generalization, suggesting that the model effectively handles unseen data without overfitting. This stability is particularly impressive given the dataset's diversity, which includes 34 distinct attack classes, each representing unique network intrusion scenarios. The high validation accuracy across such a broad dataset demonstrates the model's capability to capture complex attack patterns and adapt to varied threat scenarios. Both training and validation loss decline sharply, stabilizing at low values by the second epoch and maintaining consistency throughout. This low and steady loss reflects the model's robustness and indicates effective learning without significant error accumulation. Such stability in loss is crucial for the model's reliability, especially when applied to complex, multi-class datasets, ensuring it remains accurate and responsive for real-time deployment scenarios.

Figure 10. Hybrid Bi-D LSTM-GRU Accuracy & Loss

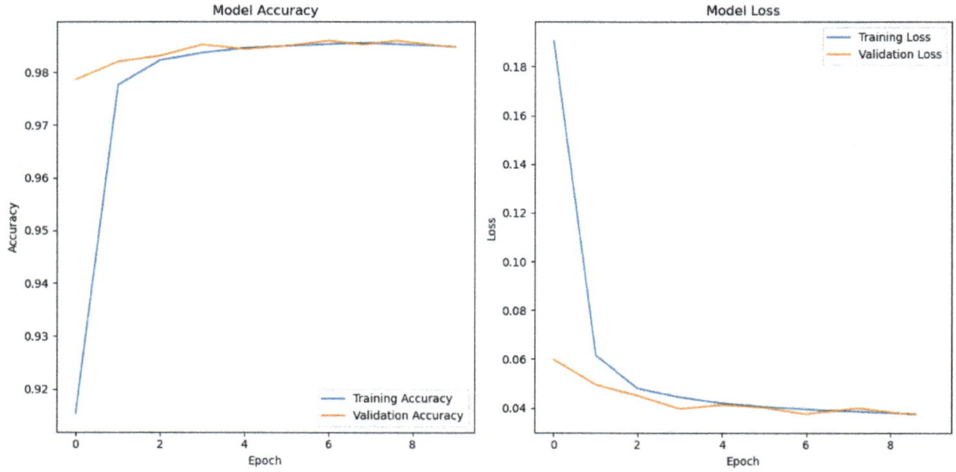

4.3. Adaptability Across Diverse Attack Types

- Comprehensive Dataset: The dataset used in training encompasses 34 different classes of attacks, covering a wide spectrum of potential intrusion scenarios. Each class represents a unique threat profile, including both common and complex attack types that span different temporal and behavioral characteristics. By training on this diverse set of classes, the model is exposed to a broad variety of attack patterns, equipping it with the ability to generalize across a wide range of known threat vectors. This diversity serves as an extensive "training ground," preparing the model to recognize and respond to variations in attack types without needing anomaly detection for unseen threats within this scope.
- Ability to Generalize Within a Complex Threat Landscape: The high accuracy and low loss on the validation data demonstrate that the model has effectively learned the distinguishing features of each attack class without overfitting to specific patterns within the training set. This capacity to generalize is essential in the context of intrusion detection, where network traffic often varies in structure and timing. The inclusion of multiple classes ensures that the model learns from a spectrum of potential scenarios, making it well-suited to handle both frequent and rare attack types, as well as subtle variations in behavior within known categories.
- Robustness Against Overfitting: The alignment between training and validation metrics indicates that the model's performance is not limited to mem-

orizing training data but instead reflects a deeper understanding of attack patterns. This robustness is key for IDS applications, where the model must reliably detect intrusions in real-world traffic that may differ slightly from training data but still fit within the broad classes it has learned. This broad generalization ability makes the model resilient in identifying nuanced deviations within known attack classes, thereby reducing the likelihood of false negatives and enhancing detection reliability.

- Minimal Need for Anomaly Detection: Given the extensive range of attack classes represented in the dataset, the model is effectively trained to recognize a variety of known threat patterns. While anomaly detection can be useful in identifying completely novel attacks, the wide scope of the dataset suggests that the model is already well-prepared to handle many variations in known attack behaviors. The comprehensive training on 34 classes reduces the necessity for anomaly detection, as the model can adaptively respond to diverse threats within this established framework. This positions the model as a robust and flexible solution for detecting known and evolving attacks within the scope of the dataset.

In summary, the high accuracy, low loss, and stability observed in the model's performance on a diverse dataset of 34 attack classes collectively demonstrate its adaptability and robustness. The model's ability to generalize across such a wide range of known threats underscores its suitability for real-world IDS applications, where it must handle varying attack types with minimal reliance on additional anomaly detection methods. This adaptability positions the hybrid Bi-D LSTM-GRU model as an effective solution for real-time intrusion detection in complex and dynamic IoT environments.

4.4. Cross-Validation

To ensure the robustness of our findings, we used cross-validation to evaluate model consistency across different data splits. Figure 11 shows the cross-validation test scores across multiple configurations, summarizing the average accuracy and variance for each configuration:

Figure 11. cross-validation test scores across multiple configurations

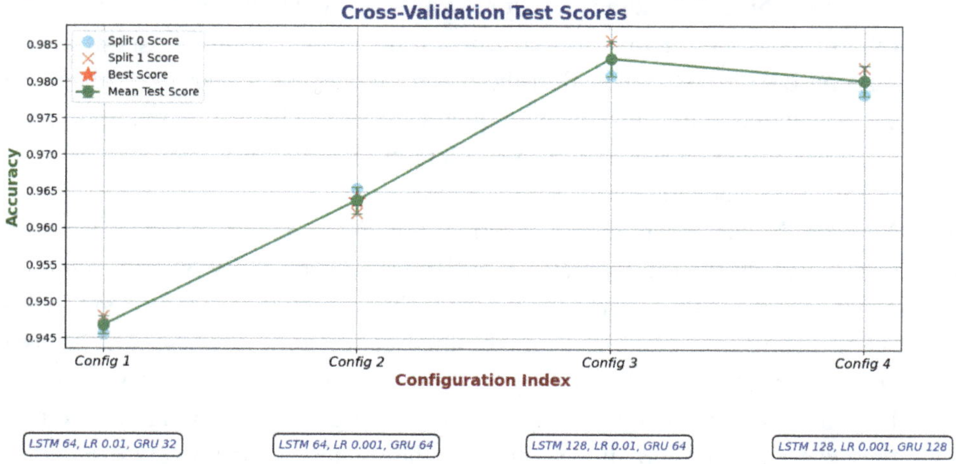

- Configuration Performance: The hybrid Bi-D LSTM-GRU model consistently outperformed alternative configurations, achieving the highest mean accuracy, with minimal variance across splits.
- Best Configuration: The model configuration with 128 LSTM units, 64 GRU units, and a learning rate of 0.001 demonstrated the most reliable performance across all validation splits, confirming the robustness of this architecture for multi-class IDS.

Cross-validation provided valuable insights into the model's ability to generalize to new data, underscoring the stability of the hybrid model's performance and confirming its suitability for complex IDS tasks.

4.5. False Positives and Negatives

The Hybrid Bidirectional LSTM-GRU model achieved an impressive 98.56% accuracy in classifying network traffic, as confirmed by the confusion matrix and detailed error analysis. Despite this high accuracy, a closer examination of false positives (FP) and false negatives (FN) reveals insights into specific patterns of misclassification. The following table summarizes the FP and FN counts for each class, along with the most common misclassified classes, providing a focused view of the model's strengths and areas for improvement:

Table 10. False Positive & Negative Summary.

Class	False Positives	Common False Positive Class	False Negatives	Common False Negative Class
Backdoor_Malware	925	DDoS-TCP_Flood	330	DDoS-TCP_Flood
BenignTraffic	20	BrowserHijacking	15	BrowserHijacking
BrowserHijacking	451	DDoS-RSTFINFlood	219	BenignTraffic
CommandInjection	112	BenignTraffic	85	BenignTraffic
DDoS-ACK_Fragmentation	135	DDoS-UDP_Fragmentation	200	DDoS-UDP_Fragmentation
DDoS-HTTP_Flood	280	DDoS-SYN_Flood	300	DDoS-SYN_Flood
DDoS-ICMP_Flood	240	DDoS-SynonymousIP_Flood	160	DDoS-SYN_Flood
DDoS-ICMP_Fragmentation	190	DDoS-UDP_Fragmentation	180	DDoS-SYN_Flood
DDoS-PSHACK_Flood	160	DDoS-SlowLoris	150	DDoS-SYN_Flood
DDoS-RSTFINFlood	310	DDoS-SYN_Flood	241	DDoS-SYN_Flood
DDoS-SYN_Flood	292	DDoS-HTTP_Flood	211	DDoS-HTTP_Flood
DDoS-SlowLoris	118	DDoS-ICMP_Fragmentation	52	DDoS-ICMP_Fragmentation
DDoS-SynonymousIP_Flood	140	DDoS-PSHACK_Flood	150	DDoS-TCP_Flood
DDoS-TCP_Flood	330	Backdoor_Malware	924	Backdoor_Malware
DDoS-UDP_Flood	811	DDoS-UDP_Fragmentation	1196	DDoS-UDP_Fragmentation
DDoS-UDP_Fragmentation	1150	DDoS-UDP_Flood	938	DDoS-UDP_Flood
DNS_Spoofing	85	DDoS-UDP_Flood	113	DDoS-SYN_Flood
DictionaryBruteForce	924	SqlInjection	347	SqlInjection
DoS-HTTP_Flood	294	DoS-SYN_Flood	223	DoS-SYN_Flood
DoS-SYN_Flood	424	Recon-HostDiscovery	236	DoS-HTTP_Flood
DoS-TCP_Flood	114	DoS-HTTP_Flood	135	DoS-HTTP_Flood
DoS-UDP_Flood	102	DoS-SYN_Flood	115	DoS-HTTP_Flood
MITM-ArpSpoofing	140	Recon-OSScan	199	Recon-OSScan
Mirai-greeth_flood	97	Recon-PingSweep	100	Recon-OSScan
Mirai-greip_flood	67	Recon-PortScan	87	Recon-OSScan
Mirai-udpplain	75	Recon-PingSweep	99	Recon-PortScan
Recon-HostDiscovery	293	DoS-SYN_Flood	221	DoS-SYN_Flood
Recon-OSScan	294	MITM-ArpSpoofing	203	MITM-ArpSpoofing
Recon-PingSweep	122	Mirai-greip_flood	155	Recon-OSScan

continued on following page

Table 10. Continued

Class	False Positives	Common False Positive Class	False Negatives	Common False Negative Class
Recon-PortScan	100	Mirai-udpplain	113	Recon-OSScan
SqlInjection	349	DictionaryBruteForce	226	DictionaryBruteForce
Uploading_Attack	133	VulnerabilityScan	109	VulnerabilityScan
VulnerabilityScan	125	Uploading_Attack	113	Uploading_Attack
XSS	79	VulnerabilityScan	115	Uploading_Attack

4.6. Key Observations from the Table

1. BenignTraffic Misclassification:
   - The BenignTraffic class, representing normal traffic, maintains a very low rate of FPs (20) and FNs (15), with minor confusion involving BrowserHijacking.
   - Significance: This low FP rate is crucial in reducing false alarms and ensuring that benign traffic is not mistaken for high-risk attacks, thus maintaining the IDS's reliability in real-world applications.
2. Intra-Family Misclassifications in Attack Classes:
   - Misclassifications within attack families are frequent, especially among DDoS, DoS, and Recon categories. For instance:
     - o DDoS classes like DDoS-HTTP_Flood and DDoS-SYN_Flood often misclassify each other, with FP rates of 280 and 292, respectively, indicating shared characteristics within these attack types.
     - o Recon classes such as Recon-PingSweep and Recon-OSScan also exhibit intra-family confusion, reflecting similarities in reconnaissance behaviors.
     - o Significance: These intra-family misclassifications are consistent with the similar behavioral signatures within each attack category. While they may affect the specificity of the model in distinguishing exact attack types, they still allow for effective malicious traffic detection.
3. Mutual Misclassifications Between Certain Classes:
   - o Certain attack types, such as DictionaryBruteForce and SqlInjection, mutually misclassify each other (with 924 FPs for DictionaryBruteForce and 349 for SqlInjection). This mutual confusion is likely due to common characteristics in brute-force or injection techniques.

- Significance: Although these classes are occasionally confused, the IDS accurately identifies them as malicious. For enhanced specificity, further feature engineering may help distinguish these similar attack types.

4. Low-Risk Misclassifications:
   - Some minor classes, like CommandInjection and XSS, exhibit low misclassification rates, with FPs and FNs involving benign traffic or other low-severity classes.
   - Significance: These low-risk misclassifications have minimal impact on overall security, further supporting the robustness of the model in differentiating critical threats from benign traffic.

4.7. Insights from False Positives and Negatives

The confusion matrix visualization, Figure 12, reflects a strong diagonal pattern with minimal off-diagonal entries, underscoring the model's high accuracy. However, certain FP and FN patterns emerge:

Figure 12. Confusion Matrix

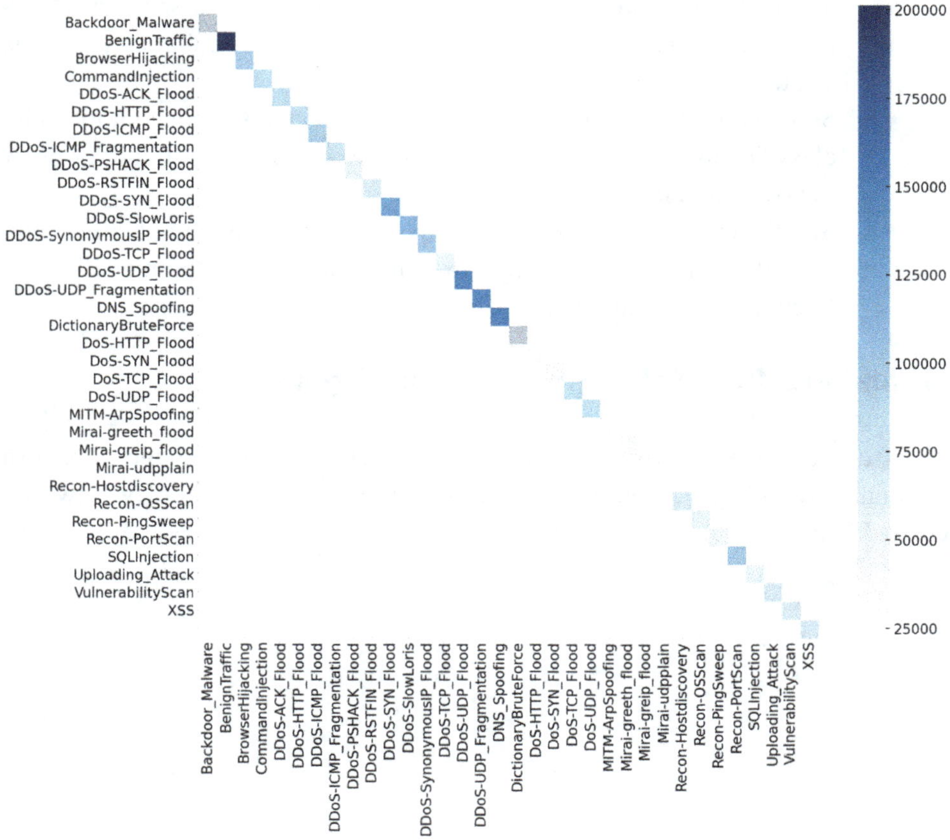

- Intra-Family Confusion: Misclassifications among DDoS, DoS, and Recon classes suggest intra-family similarities in traffic patterns, making precise differentiation challenging. Nevertheless, the model still correctly identifies these as malicious.
- Class-Specific Challenges: High FP rates in classes like DictionaryBruteForce and SqlInjection suggest areas where additional feature engineering or threshold adjustments could reduce misclassification.

The error analysis confirms that the model is effective at minimizing false alarms for benign traffic and maintaining accurate detection for malicious traffic, even when precise attack classification varies within families. This balance of high accuracy and low false alarm rate demonstrates the model's robustness and practical suitability for IDS.

4.8. Computational Efficiency

As researchers, we were tasked with developing a ML/DL model that could be efficiently deployed in IoT environments, where resources like memory, CPU, and processing time are often limited. To address these constraints, we implemented several optimization techniques aimed at reducing the computational load while maintaining high model accuracy. Our evaluation encompassed resource monitoring, model compression, and quantization.

4.9. Model Compression Techniques

To further enhance computational efficiency, we applied model pruning and quantization techniques. These methods reduce model size and improve inference speed, making the model more suitable for deployment on resource-limited devices.

- Selective Pruning: Using TensorFlow Model Optimization Toolkit (TFMOT), we applied layer-specific pruning to reduce the number of parameters in dense and convolutional layers. This selective pruning slightly reduced accuracy from 98.56% to 97.46%, but the minor trade-off was deemed acceptable given the substantial gains in computational efficiency.
- Quantization with TFLite: The pruned model was further converted into a TensorFlow Lite (TFLite) format with quantization enabled. This reduced the model's size to just 0.15 MB, making it suitable for real-time processing on IoT devices with limited storage and processing power.

Table 11. Model Optimization Results

Optimization	Result
Pruned Model	Achieved a loss of 0.0671 and accuracy of 97.46%, with a slight reduction in accuracy compared to the original 98.56%.
Quantized Model Size	Reduced to 0.15 MB, significantly decreasing memory footprint and enhancing deployment feasibility in edge IoT environments.

These optimization techniques were essential for balancing accuracy with computational efficiency. By implementing resource monitoring, selective pruning, and quantization, we ensured the final model not only achieved high predictive performance but also met the computational constraints inherent in IoT systems. This approach allowed for a streamlined and efficient model capable of supporting real-time intrusion detection in resource-limited environments.

5. LIMITATIONS AND FUTURE PERSPECTIVES

While this study provides significant insights into the effectiveness of hybrid Bi-D LSTM-GRU architectures for intrusion detection in IoT environments, certain limitations must be acknowledged. Addressing these limitations can enhance the model's applicability and scalability in real-world deployments.

- Dataset Generalization: Although the dataset used for training includes 34 different attack types, it may not fully capture the wide variability present in real-world IoT ecosystems. Many IoT networks consist of highly heterogeneous devices, operating on distinct protocols and often experiencing unique attack patterns. The current model's performance, while robust within the scope of the available dataset, may not fully generalize to the diverse and evolving threat landscape in all IoT networks. Expanding the dataset to include additional protocols, device types, and region-specific threat profiles would provide a more comprehensive representation, enhancing the model's adaptability and robustness in broader settings.
- Computational Requirements for DL Models: The hybrid Bi-D LSTM-GRU architecture, while highly effective, is computationally intensive. Training and deploying such models in real-time IDS or intrusion prevention systems (IPS) can be challenging, especially in resource-constrained IoT environments. High computational and memory requirements could limit the model's applicability in edge-based IDS solutions, where low latency and minimal resource usage are critical. To mitigate this, deployment in cloud-based environments might be considered; however, this approach introduces latency and potential data privacy concerns. Future work on optimizing model efficiency through lightweight design or model compression would be essential to ensure real-time processing capabilities.
- Challenges in Real-World Deployment of AI-based IDS/IPS: Implementing AI-driven models in operational IDS/IPS systems poses additional challenges, particularly with the need for real-time processing and quick response to threats. Real-world IoT systems often have constraints such as low bandwidth, limited power, and heterogeneous devices. Deploying complex DL models like Bi-D LSTM-GRU in such ecosystems may not be feasible without further optimization. Moreover, the reliance on centralized learning raises concerns about data privacy and processing delays. Moving toward more distributed architectures, such as edge-based or federated learning approaches, could help address these deployment challenges.
- Computational Demands of Transformer-based Models: While Transformer-based architectures, such as large language models (LLMs), offer potential

for enhanced pattern recognition and adaptability, their high computational and memory requirements make them impractical for many IoT applications. These models are typically large in size, necessitating substantial computational resources that may only be feasible through cloud-based solutions. This dependency on cloud infrastructure can introduce latency and raise privacy concerns, especially when processing sensitive network traffic. Developing smaller, domain-specific pre-trained models or adapting lightweight versions of Transformer architectures could provide a pathway to harnessing their capabilities while minimizing resource constraints.

- Lack of Continuous Learning Capability: The current model operates in a static learning environment, meaning it does not have mechanisms to continuously learn and adapt based on newly encountered data. As IoT threats evolve rapidly, this limitation may reduce the model's effectiveness over time. Implementing continual learning techniques, where the model incrementally updates its knowledge with new data, or federated learning, which enables decentralized model training across devices while maintaining data privacy, would allow the model to remain relevant and responsive to emerging threats. These approaches would improve the model's long-term adaptability and make it more suitable for deployment in dynamic IoT ecosystems.

To address these limitations and further advance the adaptability and efficiency of AI-driven IDS solutions, several research directions are recommended:

- Enhancing Dataset Diversity: Future studies should aim to expand the diversity and size of datasets used for training and validation. This expansion should include a broader variety of device types, protocols, and threat scenarios that reflect the complexity of real-world IoT ecosystems. Collaborative efforts to build publicly accessible, comprehensive IoT attack datasets would be valuable for advancing the field. Moreover, incorporating real-time data from operational IoT environments could help simulate real-world conditions more accurately, improving the model's ability to generalize across different network settings.
- Designing Lightweight and Efficient Models: Given the computational constraints of many IoT devices, developing lightweight models that maintain high detection accuracy while reducing resource demands is a crucial area for future work. Techniques such as model pruning, quantization, and distillation can help reduce model size and improve inference speed. Additionally, exploring lightweight versions of Transformer architectures, such as MobileBERT or TinyBERT, may provide a balance between advanced pattern recognition

and resource efficiency, allowing for more practical deployment in edge-based IoT environments.

- Implementing Continual and Federated Learning: To improve adaptability to emerging threats, integrating continual and federated learning capabilities into IDS models is recommended. Continual learning would allow the model to incrementally learn from new data, ensuring it remains relevant as attack patterns evolve. Federated learning could enable the distributed training of models across multiple devices or nodes, preserving data privacy and reducing the need for centralized data aggregation. These techniques would support a dynamic, decentralized approach to IDS, enhancing responsiveness to novel threats without requiring constant retraining from scratch.
- Exploring Transformer-based Architectures for Enhanced Adaptability: Transformer-based architectures hold promise for more sophisticated sequence modeling in IDS applications, especially with the rise of more complex and persistent IoT threats. Future research could investigate adapting smaller, task-specific Transformer models for IDS, or employing techniques to fine-tune pre-trained Transformer models on specific IoT traffic data. Self-supervised pre-training could also be explored as a way to enable models to learn from large volumes of unlabeled IoT data, preparing them for more effective fine-tuning on labeled datasets. These approaches could leverage the rich feature extraction capabilities of Transformers while addressing the computational challenges they pose.
- Developing Cloud-Edge Hybrid Solutions: For applications requiring both high computational power and low latency, hybrid solutions that combine cloud and edge computing could be a promising direction. Cloud servers could handle resource-intensive processing tasks, such as model training and large-scale inference, while edge devices could perform real-time anomaly detection using lightweight model versions. This approach would allow IoT networks to benefit from advanced IDS capabilities without compromising on speed or data privacy. Future research could focus on optimizing the interaction between cloud and edge components to achieve seamless and efficient IDS deployment in IoT environments.

In summary, while the current hybrid Bi-D LSTM-GRU model demonstrates substantial potential for IoT network security, addressing its limitations through expanded datasets, model optimization, and adaptive learning techniques is essential for real-world application. By pursuing these future research directions—particularly in lightweight model design, continual and federated learning, and Transformer-based architectures—the field can move closer to developing scalable, high-performance IDS solutions tailored to the dynamic needs of IoT environments. These advancements will be crucial to sustaining robust, adaptable, and responsive protection for the evolving landscape of IoT security.

6. CONCLUSION

This study demonstrates the effectiveness of ML and DL architectures for intrusion detection in IoT environments, where diverse and evolving threats challenge traditional security frameworks. Among the models evaluated, the hybrid Bi-Directional LSTM-GRU architecture proved to be the most effective, achieving high accuracy (98.56%) and robust performance across a dataset comprising 34 distinct attack types. The training and validation analysis indicated the model's strong generalization capability, with minimal overfitting, suggesting its adaptability to unseen variations in IoT traffic. By leveraging both bidirectional LSTM and GRU layers, the hybrid model capitalizes on the strengths of each architecture, offering an optimal balance between memory retention for long-term dependencies and computational efficiency. This sequential learning capability allowed the model to effectively capture complex patterns within IoT traffic, addressing both short- and long-term dependencies across diverse network scenarios. Furthermore, the inclusion of varied attack types in the dataset enabled the model to handle a broad spectrum of intrusion patterns, reducing the need for additional anomaly detection techniques in recognizing known attack variations.

This research contributes significantly to the field of IoT security through the development of an adaptive, high-performance IDS tailored for the dynamic nature of IoT environments. The hybrid Bi-Directional LSTM-GRU model represents a major advancement in IDS design, balancing sequence learning with computational efficiency to meet the resource constraints of IoT devices. This model's high accuracy and adaptability underscore its potential as a reliable solution for real-time intrusion detection. Additionally, the study provides valuable insights into the adaptability of DL models, demonstrating how architectures like Bi-Directional LSTM-GRU can generalize across varied attack types and respond to evolving traffic patterns. The exploration of continual, transfer, and federated learning as future enhancements offers a roadmap for developing IDS systems that remain effective in rapidly evolving IoT networks.

Furthermore, this study establishes a practical framework for deploying AI-driven IDS solutions within IoT ecosystems, where constraints such as low latency, bandwidth, and power consumption must be addressed. By discussing cloud-edge hybrid architectures, model compression techniques, and adaptive learning methods, the study provides a blueprint for transitioning high-performance models into real-world applications. This approach ensures that IoT networks can benefit from advanced

IDS capabilities without compromising on speed, privacy, or resource efficiency. The discussion on integrating Transformer-based models and self-supervised learning techniques opens further avenues for enhancing IDS adaptability and precision. Although these advanced models currently pose computational challenges, exploring smaller, domain-specific Transformers or cloud-based solutions could make them viable for IoT security applications, paving the way for future research.

The findings and contributions of this study have significant implications for IoT security. The hybrid model's performance in handling diverse attack types demonstrates that adaptive ML and DL architectures can enhance intrusion detection capabilities, providing robust protection against a wide range of known threats. The need for IDS solutions that can adapt to the evolving nature of IoT networks—where new devices, protocols, and attack types continuously emerge—is evident. By incorporating adaptable learning frameworks, AI-driven IDS solutions can respond dynamically to this evolving landscape, fortifying IoT networks against both current and future threats.

In conclusion, this study underscores the critical role of advanced DL architectures in enhancing IoT security, demonstrating how a carefully chosen hybrid model can balance accuracy, adaptability, and efficiency. By addressing both the limitations and future potential of AI-driven IDS systems, this research offers valuable insights for developing resilient and scalable IoT security solutions. Through continued advancements in model efficiency, adaptability, and deployment strategies, AI-based IDS systems hold immense promise for securing the future of IoT networks in an increasingly complex and interconnected world.

7. REFERENCES

Abbas, S., Al Hejaili, A., Sampedro, G. A., Abisado, M., Almadhor, A. S., Shahzad, T., & Ouahada, K. (2023). A Novel Federated Edge Learning Approach for Detecting Cyberattacks in IoT Infrastructures. *IEEE Access : Practical Innovations, Open Solutions*, *11*, 112189–112198. DOI: 10.1109/ACCESS.2023.3318866

Almiani, M., AbuGhazleh, A., Al-Rahayfeh, A., Atiewi, S., & Razaque, A. (2020). Deep recurrent neural network for IoT intrusion detection system. *Simulation Modelling Practice and Theory*, *101*, 102031. DOI: 10.1016/j.simpat.2019.102031

Altulaihan, E., Almaiah, M. A., & Aljughaiman, A. (2024). Anomaly Detection IDS for Detecting DoS Attacks in IoT Networks Based on Machine Learning Algorithms. Sensors 2024, Vol. 24, Page 713, 24(2), 713. DOI: 10.3390/s24020713

Alzahrani, A. I. A., Al-Rasheed, A., Ksibi, A., Ayadi, M., Asiri, M. M., & Zakariah, M. (2022). Anomaly Detection in Fog Computing Architectures Using Custom Tab Transformer for Internet of Things. Electronics 2022, Vol. 11, Page 4017, 11(23), 4017. DOI: 10.3390/electronics11234017

Anthi, E., Williams, L., Slowinska, M., Theodorakopoulos, G., & Burnap, P. (2019). A Supervised Intrusion Detection System for Smart Home IoT Devices. *IEEE Internet of Things Journal*, *6*(5), 9042–9053. DOI: 10.1109/JIOT.2019.2926365

Bukhari, O., Agarwal, P., Koundal, D., & Zafar, S. (2023a). Anomaly detection using ensemble techniques for boosting the security of intrusion detection system. *Procedia Computer Science*, *218*, 1003–1013. DOI: 10.1016/j.procs.2023.01.080

Bukhari, O., Agarwal, P., Koundal, D., & Zafar, S. (2023b). Anomaly detection using ensemble techniques for boosting the security of intrusion detection system. *Procedia Computer Science*, *218*, 1003–1013. DOI: 10.1016/j.procs.2023.01.080

Chatterjee, R., Maitra, T., Hafizul Islam, S. K., Hassan, M. M., Alamri, A., & Fortino, G. (2019). A novel machine learning based feature selection for motor imagery EEG signal classification in Internet of medical things environment. *Future Generation Computer Systems*, *98*, 419–434. DOI: 10.1016/j.future.2019.01.048

He, M., Wang, X., Wei, P., Yang, L., Teng, Y., & Lyu, R. (2024). Reinforcement Learning Meets Network Intrusion Detection: A Transferable and Adaptable Framework for Anomaly Behavior Identification. *IEEE Transactions on Network and Service Management*, *21*(2), 2477–2492. DOI: 10.1109/TNSM.2024.3352586

Ieracitano, C., Adeel, A., Morabito, F. C., & Hussain, A. (2020). A novel statistical analysis and autoencoder driven intelligent intrusion detection approach. *Neurocomputing*, *387*, 51–62. DOI: 10.1016/j.neucom.2019.11.016

Jaradat, A. S., Nasayreh, A., Al-Na'amneh, Q., Gharaibeh, H., & Al Mamlook, R. E. (2023). Genetic Optimization Techniques for Enhancing Web Attacks Classification in Machine Learning. 2023 IEEE Intl Conf on Dependable, Autonomic and Secure Computing, Intl Conf on Pervasive Intelligence and Computing, Intl Conf on Cloud and Big Data Computing, Intl Conf on Cyber Science and Technology Congress (DASC/PiCom/CBDCom/CyberSciTech), 0130–0136. DOI: 10.1109/DASC/PiCom/CBDCom/Cy59711.2023.10361399

Kim, D. S., Nguyen, H. N., & Park, J. S. (2005). Genetic algorithm to improve SVM based network intrusion detection system. Proceedings - International Conference on Advanced Information Networking and Applications, AINA, 2, 155–158. DOI: 10.1109/AINA.2005.191

Mhawi, D. N., Aldallal, A., & Hassan, S. (2022). Advanced Feature-Selection-Based Hybrid Ensemble Learning Algorithms for Network Intrusion Detection Systems. Symmetry 2022, Vol. 14, Page 1461, 14(7), 1461. DOI: 10.3390/sym14071461

Moumen, I., Abouchabaka, J., & Rafalia, N. (2023). Enhancing urban mobility: Integration of IoT road traffic data and artificial intelligence in smart city environment. *Indonesian Journal of Electrical Engineering and Computer Science*, *32*(2), 985–993. DOI: 10.11591/ijeecs.v32.i2.pp985-993

Moumen, I., Rafalia, N., Abouchabaka, J., & Chatoui, Y. (2023). AODV-based Defense Mechanism for Mitigating Blackhole Attacks in MANET. E3S Web of Conferences, 412. DOI: 10.1051/e3sconf/202341201094

Moustafa, N., & Slay, J. (2015). UNSW-NB15: A comprehensive data set for network intrusion detection systems (UNSW-NB15 network data set). 2015 Military Communications and Information Systems Conference, MilCIS 2015 - Proceedings. DOI: 10.1109/MilCIS.2015.7348942

Neto, E. C. P., Dadkhah, S., Ferreira, R., Zohourian, A., Lu, R., & Ghorbani, A. A. (2023). CICIoT2023: A Real-Time Dataset and Benchmark for Large-Scale Attacks in IoT Environment. Sensors 2023, Vol. 23, Page 5941, 23(13), 5941. DOI: 10.3390/s23135941

Niyaz, Q., Sun, W., & Javaid, A. Y. (2017). A Deep Learning Based DDoS Detection System in Software-Defined Networking (SDN). EAI Endorsed Transactions on Security and Safety, "4"(12), 153515. DOI: 10.4108/eai.28-12-2017.153515

Pajouh, H. H., Javidan, R., Khayami, R., Dehghantanha, A., & Choo, K. K. R. (2019). A Two-Layer Dimension Reduction and Two-Tier Classification Model for Anomaly-Based Intrusion Detection in IoT Backbone Networks. *IEEE Transactions on Emerging Topics in Computing*, *7*(2), 314–323. DOI: 10.1109/TETC.2016.2633228

Sharafaldin, I., Lashkari, A. H., & Ghorbani, A. A. (2018). Toward generating a new intrusion detection dataset and intrusion traffic characterization. ICISSP 2018 - Proceedings of the 4th International Conference on Information Systems Security and Privacy, 2018-January, 108–116. DOI: 10.5220/0006639801080116

Sumathi, S., & Karthikeyan, N. (2021). Detection of distributed denial of service using deep learning neural network. *Journal of Ambient Intelligence and Humanized Computing*, *12*(6), 5943–5953. DOI: 10.1007/s12652-020-02144-2

Tama, B. A., & Rhee, K.-H. (2017). Attack Classification Analysis of IoT Network via Deep Learning Approach. *Research Briefs on Information and Communication Technology Evolution*, *3*, 150–158. DOI: 10.56801/rebicte.v3i.54

Tang, T. A., Mhamdi, L., McLernon, D., Zaidi, S. A. R., Ghogho, M., & Moussa, F. El. (2020). DeepIDS: Deep Learning Approach for Intrusion Detection in Software Defined Networking. Electronics 2020, Vol. 9, Page 1533, 9(9), 1533. DOI: 10.3390/electronics9091533

Tavallaee, M., Bagheri, E., Lu, W., & Ghorbani, A. A. (2009). A detailed analysis of the KDD CUP 99 data set. *IEEE Symposium on Computational Intelligence for Security and Defense Applications, CISDA 2009*. DOI: 10.1109/CISDA.2009.5356528

Tyagi, H., & Kumar, R. (2021a). Attack and anomaly detection in IoT networks using supervised machine learning approaches. *Revue d'Intelligence Artificielle*, *35*(1), 11–21. DOI: 10.18280/ria.350102

Tyagi, H., & Kumar, R. (2021b). Attack and anomaly detection in IoT networks using supervised machine learning approaches. *Revue d'Intelligence Artificielle*, *35*(1), 11–21. DOI: 10.18280/ria.350102

Ullah, I., & Mahmoud, Q. H. (2020). A Scheme for Generating a Dataset for Anomalous Activity Detection in IoT Networks. Lecture Notes in Computer Science (Including Subseries Lecture Notes in Artificial Intelligence and Lecture Notes in Bioinformatics), 12109 LNAI, 508–520. DOI: 10.1007/978-3-030-47358-7_52

Wu, K., Chen, Z., & Li, W. (2018). A Novel Intrusion Detection Model for a Massive Network Using Convolutional Neural Networks. *IEEE Access : Practical Innovations, Open Solutions*, *6*, 50850–50859. DOI: 10.1109/ACCESS.2018.2868993

Yavuz, F. Y., Ünal, D., & Gül, E. (2018). Deep learning for detection of routing attacks in the internet of things. *International Journal of Computational Intelligence Systems, 12*(1), 39–58. DOI: 10.2991/ijcis.2018.25905181

Zhou, X., Hu, Y., Liang, W., Ma, J., & Jin, Q. (2021). Variational LSTM Enhanced Anomaly Detection for Industrial Big Data. *IEEE Transactions on Industrial Informatics, 17*(5), 3469–3477. DOI: 10.1109/TII.2020.3022432

Compilation of References

Abbas, S., Al Hejaili, A., Sampedro, G. A., Abisado, M., Almadhor, A. S., Shahzad, T., & Ouahada, K. (2023). A Novel Federated Edge Learning Approach for Detecting Cyberattacks in IoT Infrastructures. *IEEE Access : Practical Innovations, Open Solutions*, *11*, 112189–112198. DOI: 10.1109/ACCESS.2023.3318866

Abd-Alrazaq, A. A., Rababeh, A., Alajlani, M., Bewick, B. M., & Househ, M. (2020). Effectiveness and Safety of Using Chatbots to Improve Mental Health: Systematic Review and Meta-Analysis. *Journal of Medical Internet Research*, *22*(7), e16021. DOI: 10.2196/16021 PMID: 32673216

Abdollahpouri, H., Mansoury, M., Burke, R., Mobasher, B., & Malthouse, E. (2021). User-centered evaluation of popularity bias in recommender systems. Proceedings of the 29th ACM conference on user modeling, adaptation and personalization.

Abdullahi, S. M., Zare, A., & Lazarova-Molnar, S. (2024). Cybersecurity in Distributed Industrial Digital Twins: Threats, Defenses, and Key Takeaways. *1st International Workshop on Distributed Digital Twins, DiDit 2024*. Groningen: CEUR-WS. Retrieved Beb 16, 2025, from https://www.scopus.com/record/display.uri?eid=2-s2.0-85204377211&origin=scopusAI

Ackermans, K., Bakker, M., van Loon, A. M., Kral, M., & Camp, G. (2025). Young learners' motivation, self-regulation and performance in personalized learning. *Computers & Education*, *226*, 105208. DOI: 10.1016/j.compedu.2024.105208

Adam, K. D. B. J. (2014). A method for stochastic optimization. *arXiv preprint arXiv:1412.6980, 1412*(6).

Adamopoulou, E., & Moussiades, L. (2020). An overview of Chatbot technology. In *IFIP advances in information and communication technology* (pp. 373–383). DOI: 10.1007/978-3-030-49186-4_31

Adomavicius, G., & Tuzhilin, A. (2005). Toward the next generation of recommender systems: A survey of the state-of-the-art and possible extensions. *IEEE Transactions on Knowledge and Data Engineering*, *17*(6), 734–749.

Afsar, M. M., Crump, T., & Far, B. (2022). Reinforcement learning based recommender systems: A survey. *ACM Computing Surveys*, *55*(7), 1–38. DOI: 10.1145/3543846

Ahmed, Y., Ahmed, T., Raza, A., & Jan, I. (2025). Harnessing AI for Personalized Learning, Equity, and Administrative Efficiency in Transnational Higher Education. *Bridging Global Divides for Transnational Higher Education in the AI Era*, 191-204. DOI: DOI: 10.4018/979-8-3693-7016-2.ch009

Aïmeur, E., Amri, S., & Brassard, G. (2023). Fake news, disinformation and misinformation in social media: A review. *Social Network Analysis and Mining*, *13*(1), 30. DOI: 10.1007/s13278-023-01028-5 PMID: 36789378

Airen, S., & Agrawal, J. (2022). Movie recommender system using k-nearest neighbors variants. *National Academy Science Letters*, *45*(1), 75–82. DOI: 10.1007/s40009-021-01051-0

Ajao, O., Bhowmik, D., & Zargari, S. (2019). *Sentiment aware fake news detection on online social networks.* Paper presented at the ICASSP 2019-2019 IEEE International Conference on Acoustics, Speech and Signal Processing (ICASSP). DOI: 10.1109/ICASSP.2019.8683170

Akpabio, E., Narad, S., Akpabio, I., & Akpabio, I. (2024). Securing the Connected World: Federated Learning and IoT Cybersecurity. In *Federated Learning for Smart Communication using IoT Application* (pp. 178-195). CRC Press. DOI: 10.1201/9781003489368-9

Al-Abri, A. (2025). Exploring ChatGPT as a virtual tutor: A multi-dimensional analysis of large language models in academic support. *Education and Information Technologies*, *30*(12), 1–36. DOI: 10.1007/s10639-025-13484-x

AlAli, R., & Wardat, Y. (2024, May). Opportunities and challenges of integrating generative artificial intelligence in education. *International Journal of Religion.*, *5*(7), 784–793. DOI: 10.61707/8y29gv34

Al-Amin, M., Ali, M. S., Salam, A., Khan, A., Ali, A., Ullah, A., Alam, M. N., & Chowdhury, S. K. (2024). History of generative Artificial Intelligence (AI) chatbots: past, present, and future development. *arXiv (Cornell University).* /arxiv.2402.05122DOI: 10.48550

Al-Dalati, I. (2022). Digital twins and cybersecurity in healthcare systems. In *Digital Twin for Healthcare: Design, Challenges, and Solutions* (pp. 195-221). Elsevier. DOI: 10.1016/B978-0-32-399163-6.00015-9

Alderton, J., & Pratt, N. (2025). The construction of mathematical reasoning as a pedagogical object. *Educational Studies in Mathematics, 120*(2), 1–17. DOI: 10.1007/s10649-025-10420-1

Alfaadhel, A., Almomani, I., & Ahmed, M. (2023, May). Risk-Based Cybersecurity Compliance Assessment System (RC2AS). *Applied Sciences (Basel, Switzerland), 13*(10), 6145. Advance online publication. DOI: 10.3390/app13106145

Alier, M., García-Peñalvo, F., & Camba, J. D. (2024). Generative artificial intelligence in Education: From deceptive to disruptive. *International Journal of Interactive Multimedia and Artificial Intelligence, 8*(5), 5. DOI: 10.9781/ijimai.2024.02.011

Allison, J. (2025). *Digital equity in the age of generative AI: Bridging the divide in educational technology. British Educational Research Association.* BERA.

Almeida, F., & Xexéo, G. (2019). Word embeddings: A survey. *arXiv preprint arXiv:1901.09069.*

Almiani, M., AbuGhazleh, A., Al-Rahayfeh, A., Atiewi, S., & Razaque, A. (2020). Deep recurrent neural network for IoT intrusion detection system. *Simulation Modelling Practice and Theory, 101*, 102031. DOI: 10.1016/j.simpat.2019.102031

Alonso, R. R., Carvajal, K. A., & Acevedo, N. R. (2025). Role of Artificial Intelligence in the personalization of distance education: A systematic review. *Revista Iberoamericana de Educación a Distancia, 28*(1), 9–32. DOI: 10.5944/ried.28.1.41538

Alsayed, W. O., Al-Hafdi, F. S., & Alhalafawy, W. S. (2025). Chatbots in Education. In *Empowering STEM Educators With Digital Tools* (pp. 137–154). IGI Global Scientific Publishing., DOI: 10.4018/979-8-3693-9806-7.ch006

Alsubaie, M. G., Luo, S., & Shaukat, K. (2024). ConvADD: Exploring a novel CNN architecture for Alzheimer's disease detection. *International Journal of Advanced Computer Science and Applications, 15*(4). Advance online publication. DOI: 10.14569/IJACSA.2024.0150431

Altulaihan, E., Almaiah, M. A., & Aljughaiman, A. (2024). Anomaly Detection IDS for Detecting DoS Attacks in IoT Networks Based on Machine Learning Algorithms. Sensors 2024, Vol. 24, Page 713, 24(2), 713. DOI: 10.3390/s24020713

Alwazzan, M. S. (2024). Investigating the Effectiveness of Artificial Intelligence Chatbots in Enhancing Digital Dialogue Skills for Students. *European Journal of Educational Research, 13*(2), 573–584. Advance online publication. DOI: 10.12973/eu-jer.13.2.573

Alzahrani, A. I. A., Al-Rasheed, A., Ksibi, A., Ayadi, M., Asiri, M. M., & Zakariah, M. (2022). Anomaly Detection in Fog Computing Architectures Using Custom Tab Transformer for Internet of Things. Electronics 2022, Vol. 11, Page 4017, 11(23), 4017. DOI: 10.3390/electronics11234017

Ammar, N., & Shaban-Nejad, A. (2020). Explainable artificial intelligence recommendation system by leveraging the semantics of adverse childhood experiences: Proof-of-concept prototype development. *JMIR Medical Informatics, 8*(11), e18752. DOI: 10.2196/18752 PMID: 33146623

An, F.-P. (2019). Medical Image Classification Algorithm Based on Weight Initialization-Sliding Window Fusion Convolutional Neural Network. *complexity, 2019*(1), 9151670.

Ananda, K. V., Pandey, K. K., & Punia, D. K. (2014, February). Cyber security threats in the power sector: Need for a domain specific regulatory framework in India. *Energy Policy, 65*, 126–133. DOI: 10.1016/j.enpol.2013.10.025

An, B. (2023, June 20). AI-generated text detection: Challenges and future directions. *International Journal of Asian Language Processing., 33*(02), 2330002. DOI: 10.1142/S2717554523300025

Anthi, E., Williams, L., Slowinska, M., Theodorakopoulos, G., & Burnap, P. (2019). A Supervised Intrusion Detection System for Smart Home IoT Devices. *IEEE Internet of Things Journal, 6*(5), 9042–9053. DOI: 10.1109/JIOT.2019.2926365

Antonova, A., & Dankov, Y. (2022). Smart services in education: facilitating teachers to deliver personalized learning experiences. In *Proceedings of the Computational Methods in Systems and Software* (pp. 108-117). Cham: Springer International Publishing. DOI: 10.1007/978-3-031-21438-7_9

Anwar, T., Uma, V., Hussain, M. I., & Pantula, M. (2022). Collaborative filtering and kNN based recommendation to overcome cold start and sparsity issues: A comparative analysis. *Multimedia Tools and Applications, 81*(25), 35693–35711. DOI: 10.1007/s11042-021-11883-z

Arantes, J. (2024). Digital twins and the terminology of "personalization" or "personalized learning" in educational policy: A discussion paper. *Policy Futures in Education, 22*(4), 524–543. DOI: 10.1177/14782103231176357

Archana, R., & Jeevaraj, P. E. (2024). Deep learning models for digital image processing: A review. *Artificial Intelligence Review, 57*(1), 11. DOI: 10.1007/s10462-023-10631-z

Ardila, D., Kiraly, A. P., Bharadwaj, S., Choi, B., Reicher, J. J., Peng, L., Tse, D., Etemadi, M., Ye, W., Corrado, G., Naidich, D. P., & Shetty, S. (2019). End-to-end lung cancer screening with three-dimensional deep learning on low-dose chest computed tomography. *Nature Medicine, 25*(6), 954–961. DOI: 10.1038/s41591-019-0447-x PMID: 31110349

Arora, A., Alderman, J. E., Palmer, J., Ganapathi, S., Laws, E., Mccradden, M. D., ... & Liu, X. (2023). The value of standards for health datasets in artificial intelligence-based applications.

Ashcroft, C., & Whitaker, K. (2024). Evaluation of domain-specific prompt engineering attacks on large language models. *ESS Open Arch. Eprints, 362*, 36267312. DOI: DOI: 10.22541/au.172252453.36267312/v1

Ayeni, O. O., Al Hamad, N. M., Chisom, O. N., Osawaru, B., & Adewusi, O. E. (2024). AI in education: A review of personalized learning and educational technology. *GSC Advanced Research and Reviews, 18*(2), 261–271. DOI: 10.30574/gscarr.2024.18.2.0062

Babin, N. (2024, Mar 26). *Harnessing the Power of AI and Digital Twins: Lessons from Singapore's Smart Nation Initiative*. Retrieved Feb 11, 2025, from https://www.linkedin.com: https://www.linkedin.com/pulse/harnessing-power-ai-digital-twins-lessons-from-singapores-babin-0bi3e/

Baccianella, S., Esuli, A., & Sebastiani, F. (2010). *Sentiwordnet 3.0: an enhanced lexical resource for sentiment analysis and opinion mining*. Paper presented at the Lrec.

Baek, G., Cha, C., & Han, J. (2025). AI Chatbots for Psychological Health for Health Professionals: A Scoping Review (Preprint). *JMIR Human Factors, 12*, e67682. DOI: 10.2196/67682 PMID: 40106346

Balpande, V. P., Aher, U. B., Borkar, P., Bhanarkar, P., Chavan, G. T., & Sairise, R. M. (2024, March). Implementing end-to-end encryption strategist for strengthening data security across network communication. *Journal of Discrete Mathematical Sciences and Cryptography, 27*(02), 465–476. DOI: 10.47974/JDMSC-1902

Balwant, M. K. (2019). *Bidirectional LSTM based on POS tags and CNN architecture for fake news detection.* Paper presented at the 2019 10th International conference on computing, communication and networking technologies (ICCCNT). DOI: 10.1109/ICCCNT45670.2019.8944460

Barreda, M., Cantarero-Prieto, D., Coca, D., Delgado, A., Lanza-León, P., Lera, J., Montalbán, R., & Pérez, F. (2025). Transforming healthcare with chatbots: Uses and applications—A scoping review. *Digital Health, 11,* 20552076251319174. Advance online publication. DOI: 10.1177/20552076251319174 PMID: 40103640

Basri, W. S. (2024). Effectiveness of AI-powered Tutoring Systems in Enhancing Learning Outcomes. [EJER]. *Eurasian Journal of Educational Research,* (110). Advance online publication. DOI: 10.14689/ejer.2024.110.003

Basu, S., Raun, N. F., Ghosal, A., Chatterjee, D., Maitra, D., & Mazumdar, C. (2024). A Novel Software Defined Security Framework for SDN. *18th International Conference on Risks and Security of Internet and Systems, CRiSIS 2023. 14529 LNCS,* pp. 216-230. Rabat: Springer Science and Business Media Deutschland GmbH. DOI: 10.1007/978-3-031-61231-2_14

Bayes, T. (1968). Naive bayes classifier. *Article Sources and Contributors,* 1-9.

Beel, J., Gipp, B., Langer, S., & Breitinger, C. (2016). Paper recommender systems: A literature survey. *International Journal on Digital Libraries, 17*(4), 305–338. DOI: 10.1007/s00799-015-0156-0

Behforouz, B., & Al Ghaithi, A. (2024). The Impact of Using Interactive Chatbots on Self-Directed Learning. *Studies in Self-Access Learning Journal, 15*(3), 317–344. Advance online publication. DOI: 10.37237/150302

Bera, K., O'Connor, G., Jiang, S., Tirumani, S. H., & Ramaiya, N. (2024). Analysis of ChatGPT publications in radiology: Literature so far. *Current Problems in Diagnostic Radiology, 53*(2), 215–225. DOI: 10.1067/j.cpradiol.2023.10.013 PMID: 37891083

Bernacki, M. L., Greene, M. J., & Lobczowski, N. G. (2021). A systematic review of research on personalized learning: Personalized by whom, to what, how, and for what purpose (s)? *Educational Psychology Review, 33*(4), 1675–1715. DOI: 10.1007/s10648-021-09615-8

Bernal, M. E. (2024). Revolutionizing eLearning assessments: The role of GPT in crafting dynamic content and feedback. *Journal of Artificial Intelligence and Technology, 4*(3), 188–199. https://orcid.org/0009-0009-7642-8090

Bharadhwaj, H., Park, H., & Lim, B. Y. (2018). RecGAN: Recurrent generative adversarial networks for recommendation systems. Proceedings of the 12th ACM Conference on Recommender Systems.

Bhaskar, A. (2023). Industrial IoT Condition Monitoring using Wireless IoT Sensor. *International Conference on Artificial Intelligence and Smart Communication, AISC 2023* (pp. 831-837). Greater Noida: IEEE. DOI: 10.1109/AISC56616.2023.10085613

Bhattacharya, P., Prasad, V. K., Verma, A., Gupta, D., Sapsomboon, A., Viriyasitavat, W., & Dhiman, G. (2024). Demystifying ChatGPT: An in-depth survey of OpenAI's robust large language models. *Archives of Computational Methods in Engineering*, *31*(8), 1–44. DOI: 10.1007/s11831-024-10115-5

Bhoyar M. (n.d.). Enhancing Conversational Agents with Generative AI: A Framework for Creating More Adaptive and Context-aware chatbots.

Bigiotti, A., Shah, P., & Trestian, R. (2025). Blockchain and Digital Twin Integration for Remote Control of Cyber-Physical Systems. In *Lecture Notes on Data Engineering and Communications Technologies* (Vol. 232, pp. 258–269). Springer Science and Business Media Deutschland GmbH., DOI: 10.1007/978-3-031-76462-2_23

Bird, S. (2006). *NLTK: the natural language toolkit.* Paper presented at the Proceedings of the COLING/ACL 2006 interactive presentation sessions. DOI: 10.3115/1225403.1225421

Bobadilla, J., Ortega, F., Hernando, A., & Gutiérrez, A. (2013). Recommender systems survey. *Knowledge-Based Systems*, *46*, 109–132.

Bode, S. P., & Satpute, R. S. (2024, November). Natural Language Processing in Education System. In *2024 2nd DMIHER International Conference on Artificial Intelligence in Healthcare, Education and Industry (IDICAIEI)* (pp. 1-5). IEEE. **DOI:** DOI: 10.1109/IDICAIEI61867.2024.10842725

Boongasame, L., Muangprathub, J., & Thammarak, K. (2025). Laor Initialization: A New Weight Initialization Method for the Backpropagation of Deep Learning. *Big Data and Cognitive Computing*, *9*(7), 181. DOI: 10.3390/bdcc9070181

Boulila, W., Driss, M., Alshanqiti, E., Al-Sarem, M., Saeed, F., & Krichen, M. (2022). Weight initialization techniques for deep learning algorithms in remote sensing: Recent trends and future perspectives. *Advances on Smart and Soft Computing*, 477-484.

Boulila, W., Alshanqiti, E., Alzahem, A., Koubaa, A., & Mlaiki, N. (2024). An effective weight initialization method for deep learning: Application to satellite image classification. *Expert Systems with Applications*, *254*, 124344. DOI: 10.1016/j.eswa.2024.124344

Boulila, W., Sellami, M., Driss, M., Al-Sarem, M., Safaei, M., & Ghaleb, F. A. (2021). RS-DCNN: A novel distributed convolutional-neural-networks based-approach for big remote-sensing image classification. *Computers and Electronics in Agriculture*, *182*, 106014. DOI: 10.1016/j.compag.2021.106014

Breiman, L. (2001). Random forests. *Machine Learning*, *45*(1), 5–32. DOI: 10.1023/A:1010933404324

Briganti, G., & Le Moine, O. (2020). Artificial intelligence in medicine: Today and tomorrow. *Frontiers in Medicine*, *7*, 509744. DOI: 10.3389/fmed.2020.00027 PMID: 32118012

Buijsman, S. (2024). Transparency for AI systems: A value-based approach. *Ethics and Information Technology*, *26*(2), 34. DOI: 10.1007/s10676-024-09770-w

Bukhari, O., Agarwal, P., Koundal, D., & Zafar, S. (2023a). Anomaly detection using ensemble techniques for boosting the security of intrusion detection system. *Procedia Computer Science*, *218*, 1003–1013. DOI: 10.1016/j.procs.2023.01.080

Burke, R. (2002). Hybrid recommender systems: Survey and experiments. *User Modeling and User-Adapted Interaction*, *12*(4), 331–370. DOI: 10.1023/A:1021240730564

Burke, R., Felfernig, A., & Göker, M. H. (2011). Recommender systems: An overview. *AI Magazine*, *32*(3), 13–18. DOI: 10.1609/aimag.v32i3.2361

Cai, D., Hu, J., Zhao, Q., Qian, S., Fang, Q., & Xu, C. (2021). Grecx: An efficient and unified benchmark for GNN-based recommendation. *arXiv preprint arXiv:2111.10342*.

Caldarini, G., Jaf, S., & McGarry, K. (2022). A literature survey of recent advances in chatbots. *Information (Basel)*, *13*(1), 41. DOI: 10.3390/info13010041

Calders, T., & Verwer, S. (2010). Three naive bayes approaches for discrimination-free classification. *Data Mining and Knowledge Discovery*, *21*(2), 277–292. DOI: 10.1007/s10618-010-0190-x

Carreño, I. D. V. G. (2025). Reflections on ChatGPT in the Field of Social Sciences: A Bibliometric Study. *European Educational Researcher*, *8*(1), 5–28. DOI: 10.31757/euer.812

Chakraborty, C., Pal, S., Bhattacharya, M., Dash, S., & Lee, S. (2023). Overview of Chatbots with special emphasis on artificial intelligence-enabled ChatGPT in medical science. *Frontiers in Artificial Intelligence*, *6*, 1237704. Advance online publication. DOI: 10.3389/frai.2023.1237704 PMID: 38028668

Challagundla, B. C., & Challagundla, S. (2024). Dynamic Adaptation and Synergistic Integration of Genetic Algorithms and Deep Learning in Advanced Natural Language Processing. DOI: DOI: 10.21203/rs.3.rs-4300654/v1

Chandhana, T., Balija, A., Kumaran, S. R., & Singh, B. (2023). Digital twins-enabling technologies including AI, sensors, cloud, and edge computing. In *Handbook of Research on Applications of AI, Digital Twin, and Internet of Things for Sustainable Development* (pp. 306-331). IGI Global. DOI: 10.4018/978-1-6684-6821-0.ch018

Chandir, H. (2022). Student responses on the survey of global competence in PISA 2018. *Discourse (Abingdon)*, *43*(4), 526–542. DOI: 10.1080/01596306.2020.1844153

Charanya, J., Abinaya, P., Aadhavan, G., & Duraisamy, P. (2025). Blockchain and Digital Twin for Enhancing Personal Security in Modern Cities. In *Digital Twin and Blockchain for Smart Cities* (pp. 59-80). wiley. DOI: 10.1002/9781394303564.ch4

Chatterjee, R., Maitra, T., Hafizul Islam, S. K., Hassan, M. M., Alamri, A., & Fortino, G. (2019). A novel machine learning based feature selection for motor imagery EEG signal classification in Internet of medical things environment. *Future Generation Computer Systems*, *98*, 419–434. DOI: 10.1016/j.future.2019.01.048

Chen, Z., Huang, H., Hrinchuk, O., Puvvada, K. C., Koluguri, N. R., Żelasko, P., . . . Ginsburg, B. (2024, December). Bestow: Efficient and streamable speech language model with the best of two worlds in gpt and t5. In *2024 IEEE Spoken Language Technology Workshop (SLT)* (pp. 147-154). IEEE. DOI: DOI: 10.1109/SLT61566.2024.10832146

Chen, C. H., & Chang, C. L. (2024). Effectiveness of AI-assisted game-based learning on science learning outcomes, intrinsic motivation, cognitive load, and learning behavior. *Education and Information Technologies*, *29*(14), 18621–18642. DOI: 10.1007/s10639-024-12553-x

Chen, G., Li, Y., & Lin, Q. (2024). On the impacts of the random initialization in the neural tangent kernel theory. *Advances in Neural Information Processing Systems*, *37*, 35909–35944. DOI: 10.52202/079017-1132

Cheng, J., Kang, R., & Zhao, X. (2013). Role based Access Control and its application in high speed railway. *6th International Conference on Advanced Computational Intelligence, ICACI 2013* (pp. 362-364). IEEE Computer Society. DOI: 10.1109/ICACI.2013.6748531

Chen, J., Dong, H., Wang, X., Feng, F., Wang, M., & He, X. (2023). Bias and debias in recommender system: A survey and future directions. *ACM Transactions on Information Systems*, *41*(3), 1–39. DOI: 10.1145/3564284

Chen, J., Schluse, M., & Rossmann, J. (2021). Enabling a Secured Communication in Distributed IoT Using the Smart Systems Service Infrastructure. *2021 IEEE International Conference on Pervasive Computing and Communications Workshops and other Affiliated Events, PerCom Workshops 2021* (pp. 674 - 679). Kassel: Institute of Electrical and Electronics Engineers Inc. DOI: 10.1109/PerComWorkshops51409.2021.9431124

Chen, L., Chen, P., & Lin, Z. (2020). Artificial intelligence in education: A review. *IEEE Access : Practical Innovations, Open Solutions*, *8*, 75264–75278. DOI: 10.1109/ACCESS.2020.2988510

Chen, X., Yao, L., McAuley, J., Zhou, G., & Wang, X. (2023). Deep reinforcement learning in recommender systems: A survey and new perspectives. *Knowledge-Based Systems*, *264*, 110335. DOI: 10.1016/j.knosys.2023.110335

Chen, Y. C., Jordan, M., Park, J., & Starrett, E. (2024). Navigating student uncertainty for productive struggle: Establishing the importance for and distinguishing types, sources, and desirability of scientific uncertainties. *Science Education*, *108*(4), 1099–1133. DOI: 10.1002/sce.21864

Chen, Z. (2023). Ethics and discrimination in artificial intelligence-enabled recruitment practices. *Humanities & Social Sciences Communications*, *10*(1), 567. Advance online publication. DOI: 10.1057/s41599-023-02079-x

Cheong, B. C. (2024). Transparency and accountability in AI systems: Safeguarding wellbeing in the age of algorithmic decision-making. *Frontiers in Human Dynamics*, *6*, 1421273. DOI: 10.3389/fhumd.2024.1421273

Cheong, K. X., Zhang, C., Tan, T., Fenner, B. J., Wong, W. M., Teo, K. Y., Wang, Y. X., Sivaprasad, S., Keane, P. A., Lee, C. S., Lee, A. Y., Cheung, C. M. G., Wong, T. Y., Cheong, Y., Song, S. J., & Tham, Y. C. (2024). Comparing generative and retrieval-based chatbots in answering patient questions regarding age-related macular degeneration and diabetic retinopathy. *The British Journal of Ophthalmology*, *108*(10), 1443–1449. DOI: 10.1136/bjo-2023-324533 PMID: 38749531

Choi, W. C., & Chang, C. I. (2025). A Survey of Techniques, Design, Applications, Challenges, and Student Perspective of Chatbot-Based Learning Tutoring System Supporting Students to Learn in Education. DOI: 10.20944/preprints202503.1134.v1

Chumakov, S., Kovantsev, A., & Surikov, A. (2023, January 1). Generative approach to aspect based sentiment analysis with GPT language models. *Procedia Computer Science*, *229*, 284–293. DOI: 10.1016/j.procs.2023.12.030

Correia, J. B., Abel, M., & Becker, K. (2023, August). Data management in digital twins: A systematic literature review. *Knowledge and Information Systems*, *65*(08), 3165–3196. DOI: 10.1007/s10115-023-01870-1

Coscrato, V., & Bridge, D. (2023). Estimating and evaluating the uncertainty of rating predictions and top-n recommendations in recommender systems. *ACM Transactions on Recommender Systems*, *1*(2), 1–34. DOI: 10.1145/3584021

Cui, L., & Lee, D. (2020). Coaid: Covid-19 healthcare misinformation dataset. *arXiv preprint arXiv:2006.00885.*

Da'u, A., & Salim, N. (2020). Recommendation system based on deep learning methods: A systematic review and new directions. *Artificial Intelligence Review*, *53*(4), 2709–2748. DOI: 10.1007/s10462-019-09744-1

Dang, N. C., Moreno-García, M. N., & De la Prieta, F. (2020). Sentiment analysis based on deep learning: A comparative study. *Electronics (Basel)*, *9*(3), 483. DOI: 10.3390/electronics9030483

Dauphin, Y. N., & Schoenholz, S. (2019). Metainit: Initializing learning by learning to initialize. *Advances in Neural Information Processing Systems*, 32.

Davar, N. F., Dewan, M. A. A., & Zhang, X. (2025). AI chatbots in education: Challenges and opportunities. *Information (Basel)*, *16*(3), 235. DOI: 10.3390/info16030235

De-Arteaga, M., Jeanselme, V., Dubrawski, A., & Chouldechova, A. (2025). Leveraging expert consistency to improve algorithmic decision support. *Management Science*, mnsc.2022.01576. Advance online publication. DOI: 10.1287/mnsc.2022.01576

Deldjoo, Y., Jannach, D., Bellogin, A., Difonzo, A., & Zanzonelli, D. (2024). Fairness in recommender systems: Research landscape and future directions. *User Modeling and User-Adapted Interaction*, *34*(1), 59–108. DOI: 10.1007/s11257-023-09364-z

Deng, Z., Cao, Y., Zhou, X., Yi, Y., Jiang, Y., & You, I. (2020). Toward efficient image recognition in sensor-based IoT: A weight initialization optimizing method for CNN based on RGB influence proportion. *Sensors (Basel)*, *20*(10), 2866. DOI: 10.3390/s20102866 PMID: 32443591

Desai, H. (2025). Reimagining Compliance: Explainable AI models for financial regulatory Audits. SSRN *Electronic Journal*. DOI: 10.2139/ssrn.5230527

Dhelim, S., Aung, N., Bouras, M. A., Ning, H., & Cambria, E. (2022). A survey on personality-aware recommendation systems. *Artificial Intelligence Review*, •••, 1–46.

Dickinson, D. (2016). Cybersecurity, going beyond protection. *Water/Wastewater and Automatic Controls Symposium 2016, WWAC 2016* (pp. 90-101). Orlando: International Society of Automation (ISA). https://doi.org/DOI: 978-151083849-9

Ding, A.-C. E., Shi, L., Yang, H., & Choi, I. (2024). Enhancing Teacher AI Literacy and Integration Through Different Types of Cases in Teacher Professional Development. *Computers and Education Open*, *6*(100), 178. DOI: 10.1016/j.caeo.2024.100178

Dodds, M., Guo, J., Löhr, T., Tibo, A., Engkvist, O., & Janet, J. P. (2024). Sample efficient reinforcement learning with active learning for molecular design. *Chemical Science (Cambridge)*, *15*(11), 4146–4160. DOI: 10.1039/D3SC04653B PMID: 38487235

Dontu, S., Addula, S. R., Kumar Pareek, P., Vallabhaneni, R., & Adnan, M. M. (2024). Attack Detection from Internet of Things using TPE based Self-Attention based Bidirectional Long-Short Term Memory. *International Conference on Intelligent Algorithms for Computational Intelligence Systems, IACIS 2024*. Hassan: IEEE. DOI: 10.1109/IACIS61494.2024.10722002

Dorner, C., Ableitinger, C., & Krammer, G. (2025). Revealing the nature of mathematical procedural knowledge by analysing students' deficiencies and errors. *International Journal of Mathematical Education in Science and Technology*, 1–22. DOI: 10.1080/0020739X.2024.2445666

Dumont, H., & Ready, D. D. (2023). On the promise of personalized learning for educational equity. *NPJ Science of Learning*, *8*(1), 26. DOI: 10.1038/s41539-023-00174-x PMID: 37542046

Dunnett, K., Pal, S., Putra, G. D., & Jadidi, Z. (2022). A Trusted, Verifiable and Differential Cyber Threat Intelligence Sharing Framework using Blockchain. *21st IEEE International Conference on Trust, Security and Privacy in Computing and Communications, TrustCom 2022* (pp. 1107-1114). Virtual, Online: IEEE. DOI: 10.1109/TrustCom56396.2022.00152

Dwivedi, Y. K., Hughes, L., Ismagilova, E., Aarts, G., Coombs, C., Crick, T., Duan, Y., Dwivedi, R., Edwards, J., Eirug, A., Galanos, V., Ilavarasan, P. V., Janssen, M., Jones, P., Kar, A. K., Kizgin, H., Kronemann, B., Lal, B., Lucini, B., & Williams, M. D. (2019). Artificial Intelligence (AI): Multidisciplinary perspectives on emerging challenges, opportunities, and agenda for research, practice and policy. *International Journal of Information Management, 57*, 101994. DOI: 10.1016/j.ijinfomgt.2019.08.002

Dziugaite, G. K., & Roy, D. M. (2015). Neural network matrix factorization. *arXiv preprint arXiv:1511.06443.*

Egara, F. O., & Mosimege, M. (2024). Exploring the integration of artificial intelligence-based ChatGPT into mathematics instruction: Perceptions, challenges, and implications for educators. *Education Sciences, 14*(7), 742. DOI: 10.3390/educsci14070742

El Moudden, T., & Amnai, M. (2023). Building an efficient convolution neural network from scratch: A case study on detecting and localizing slums. *Scientific African, 20*, e01612. DOI: 10.1016/j.sciaf.2023.e01612

Eliyas, S., & Ranjana, P. (2022). Recommendation systems: Content-based filtering vs collaborative filtering. 2022 2nd International Conference on Advance Computing and Innovative Technologies in Engineering (ICACITE).

Emara, A.-H. M., Atteia, G., & Alkhateeb, J. H. (2025). Fine Tuning Hyperparameters of Deep Learning Models Using Metaheuristic Accelerated Particle Swarm Optimization Algorithm. *IEEE Access : Practical Innovations, Open Solutions, 13*, 134506–134518. DOI: 10.1109/ACCESS.2025.3591403

Empl, P., Hager, H., & Pernul, G. (2023). Digital Twins for IoT Security Management. *37th Annual IFIP WG 11.3 Conference on Data and Applications Security and Privacy, DBSec 2023. 13942 LNCS*, pp. 141-149. Sophia Antipolis: Springer Science and Business Media Deutschland GmbH. DOI: 10.1007/978-3-031-37586-6_9

Erickson, B. J., Korfiatis, P., Akkus, Z., & Kline, T. L. (2017). Machine learning for medical imaging. *radiographics, 37(2)*, 505-515.

Ernst, D., & Louette, A. (2024). Introduction to reinforcement learning.

Esteva, A., Robicquet, A., Ramsundar, B., Kuleshov, V., DePristo, M., Chou, K., Cui, C., Corrado, G., Thrun, S., & Dean, J. (2019). A guide to deep learning in healthcare. *Nature Medicine, 25*(1), 24–29. DOI: 10.1038/s41591-018-0316-z PMID: 30617335

Eustaquio-Jiménez, R., Durand-Azurza, M., Gamboa-Cruzado, J., Morales, M. L., Ruiz, N. P., De Montoya, R. L., & Céliz, N. M. O. (2024). Chatbots for customer service in financial entities—A comprehensive systematic review. *Journal of Infrastructure Policy and Development, 8*(16), 10122. DOI: 10.24294/jipd10122

Fagbohun, O., Iduwe, N. P., Abdullahi, M., Ifaturoti, A., & Nwanna, O. M. (2024). Beyond traditional assessment: Exploring the impact of large language models on grading practices. *Journal of Artificial Intelligence. Machine Learning and Data Science, 2*(1), 1–8. DOI: 10. 51219/ JAIMLD/19fagbohun-oluwole/19

Fayyaz, Z., Ebrahimian, M., Nawara, D., Ibrahim, A., & Kashef, R. (2020). Recommendation systems: Algorithms, challenges, metrics, and business opportunities. *applied sciences, 10*(21), 7748.

Feldman, J., Gilchrist, C., & Leung, F. H. (2025). Artificial Intelligence can transform formative assessment in medical education. *Canadian Medical Education Journal.* Feldman, J., Gilchrist, C., & Leung, F. H. (2025). Artificial Intelligence can transform formative assessment in medical education. *Canadian Medical Education Journal.* Advance online publication. DOI: 10.36834/cmej.79759

Fellbaum, C. (2010). WordNet. In *Theory and applications of ontology: computer applications* (pp. 231–243). Springer. DOI: 10.1007/978-90-481-8847-5_10

Feng, S., Magana, A. J., & Kao, D. (2021, October). *A systematic review of literature on the effectiveness of intelligent tutoring systems in STEM. In 2021 IEEE frontiers in education conference (fie).* IEEE., DOI: 10.1109/FIE49875.2021.9637240

Flammini, F. (2021, October 04). Digital twins as run-time predictive models for the resilience of cyber-physical systems: A conceptual framework. *Philosophical Transactions. Series A, Mathematical, Physical, and Engineering Sciences, 379*(2207), 20200369. Advance online publication. DOI: 10.1098/rsta.2020.0369 PMID: 34398658

Flores Ccanto, F., Pozo Curo, C., Flores Conislla, L. D., & Adauto Medina, W. A. (2021). Challenges of transformational leadership in organizational cybersecurity matters. *Revista Venezolana de Gerencia, 26*, 417–429. DOI: 10.52080/rvgluz.26.e5.27

Fountaine, T., McCarthy, B., & Saleh, T. (2019). Building the AI-powered organization. *Harvard Business Review, 97*(4), 62–73.

Frankford, E., Sauerwein, C., Bassner, P., Krusche, S., & Breu, R. (2024, April). Ai-tutoring in software engineering education. In *Proceedings of the 46th International Conference on Software Engineering: Software Engineering Education and Training* (pp. 309-319). https://doi.org/DOI: 10.1145/3639474.3640061

Gabrani, G., Sabharwal, S., & Singh, V. K. (2017). Artificial intelligence based recommender systems: A survey. Advances in Computing and Data Sciences: First International Conference, ICACDS 2016, Ghaziabad, India, November 11-12, 2016, Revised Selected Papers 1.

Gao, C., Zheng, Y., Li, N., Li, Y., Qin, Y., Piao, J., Quan, Y., Chang, J., Jin, D., & He, X. (2023). A survey of graph neural networks for recommender systems: Challenges, methods, and directions. *ACM Transactions on Recommender Systems, 1*(1), 1-51. DOI: 10.1007/978-981-10-5427-3_6

Gao, Y., Xiong, Y., Gao, X., Jia, K., Pan, J., Bi, Y., . . . Wang, H. (2023). Retrieval-augmented generation for large language models: A survey. *arXiv preprint arXiv:2312.10997, 2*(1). https://arxiv.org/pdf/2312.10997

Gerke, S., Minssen, T., & Cohen, G. (2020). Ethical and legal challenges of artificial intelligence-driven healthcare. In *Artificial intelligence in healthcare* (pp. 295–336). Academic Press. DOI: 10.1016/B978-0-12-818438-7.00012-5

Gill, S. S., Xu, M., Ottaviani, C., Patros, P., Bahsoon, R., Shaghaghi, A., Golec, M., Stankovski, V., Wu, H., Abraham, A., Singh, M., Mehta, H., Ghosh, S. K., Baker, T., Parlikad, A. K., Lutfiyya, H., Kanhere, S. S., Sakellariou, R., Dustdar, S., & Uhlig, S. (2022). AI for next generation computing: Emerging trends and future directions. *Internet of Things : Engineering Cyber Physical Human Systems, 19*, 100514. DOI: 10.1016/j.iot.2022.100514

Gökçearslan, S., Tosun, C., & Erdemir, Z. G. (2024). Benefits, challenges, and methods of artificial intelligence (AI) chatbots in education: A systematic literature review. *International Journal of Technology in Education, 7*(1), 19–39. DOI: 10.46328/ijte.600

Goksel, N., & Bozkurt, A. (2019). Artificial intelligence in education: Current insights and future perspectives. In *Handbook of Research on Learning in the Age of Transhumanism* (pp. 224–236). IGI Global. DOI: 10.4018/978-1-5225-8431-5.ch014

Goldberg, Y., & Levy, O. (2014). word2vec Explained: deriving Mikolov et al.'s negative-sampling word-embedding method. *arXiv preprint arXiv:1402.3722.*

Gopalan, P. K., Charlin, L., & Blei, D. (2014). Content-based recommendations with Poisson factorization. *Advances in Neural Information Processing Systems*, 27.

Granik, M., & Mesyura, V. (2017). *Fake news detection using naive Bayes classifier.* Paper presented at the 2017 IEEE first Ukraine conference on electrical and computer engineering (UKRCON). DOI: 10.1109/UKRCON.2017.8100379

Graves, A. (2012). Long short-term memory. *Supervised sequence labelling with recurrent neural networks*, 37-45.

Guan, R., Raković, M., Chen, G., & Gašević, D. (2025). How educational chatbots support self-regulated learning? A systematic review of the literature. *Education and Information Technologies*, *30*(4), 4493–4518. DOI: 10.1007/s10639-024-12881-y

Gujar, V. (2024). New age marketing: AI personalization strategies in digital world. International Advanced Research Journal in Science, Engineering and Technology, 11(3).

Gulomov, S. R., Khudayberganov, T. R., Ravshanova, M. X., Turdiev, T. T., & Atabayev, S. S. (2024). Exploring Post-Quantum Cryptographic Algorithms for Secure Data Transmission. *3rd IEEE International Conference on Problems of Informatics, Electronics and Radio Engineering, PIERE 2024* (pp. 1480-1483). Novosibirsk: IEEE. DOI: 10.1109/PIERE62470.2024.10805050

Gunning, D., & Aha, D. W.DW. (2019). DARPA's explainable artificial intelligence program. *AI Magazine*, *40*(2), 44–58. DOI: 10.1609/aimag.v40i2.2850

Günther, E., & Quandt, T. (2018). Word counts and topic models: Automated text analysis methods for digital journalism research. In *Rethinking research methods in an age of digital journalism* (pp. 75–88). Routledge. DOI: 10.4324/9781315115047-6

Günther, F., Dudschig, C., & Kaup, B. (2016). Latent semantic analysis cosines as a cognitive similarity measure: Evidence from priming studies. *Quarterly Journal of Experimental Psychology*, *69*(4), 626–653. DOI: 10.1080/17470218.2015.1038280 PMID: 25952009

Guo, C., Liu, J., Gao, W., Lu, Z., Li, Y., Wang, C., & Yang, J. (2025). A large language model driven knowledge graph construction scheme for semantic communication. *Applied Sciences (Basel, Switzerland)*, *15*(8), 4575. DOI: 10.3390/app15084575

Gu, R. (2025). Personalized learning path based on graph attention mechanism deep reinforcement learning research on recommender systems. *Journal of Computational Methods in Sciences and Engineering*, *14727978241313260*(3), 2411–2426. Advance online publication. DOI: 10.1177/14727978241313260

Hakak, S., Alazab, M., Khan, S., Gadekallu, T. R., Maddikunta, P. K. R., & Khan, W. Z. (2021). An ensemble machine learning approach through effective feature extraction to classify fake news. *Future Generation Computer Systems*, *117*, 47–58. DOI: 10.1016/j.future.2020.11.022

Haque, M. D. R., & Rubya, S. (2023). An overview of Chatbot-Based mobile mental health apps: Insights from app description and user reviews. *JMIR mHealth and uHealth*, *11*, e44838. DOI: 10.2196/44838 PMID: 37213181

Harper, F. M., & Konstan, J. A. (2015). The movielens datasets: History and context. [tiis]. *ACM Transactions on Interactive Intelligent Systems*, *5*(4), 1–19. DOI: 10.1145/2827872

Havard, V., Sahnoun, M., Bettayeb, B., Duval, F., & Baudry, D. (2021, December). Data architecture and model design for Industry 4.0 components integration in cyber-physical production systems. *Proceedings of the Institution of Mechanical Engineers. Part B, Journal of Engineering Manufacture*, *235*(14), 2338–2349. DOI: 10.1177/0954405420979463

Havrlant, L., & Kreinovich, V. (2017). A simple probabilistic explanation of term frequency-inverse document frequency (tf-idf) heuristic (and variations motivated by this explanation). *International Journal of General Systems*, *46*(1), 27–36. DOI: 10.1080/03081079.2017.1291635

He, K., Zhang, X., Ren, S., & Sun, J. (2015). Delving deep into rectifiers: Surpassing human-level performance on imagenet classification. Proceedings of the IEEE international conference on computer vision.

He, K., Zhang, X., Ren, S., & Sun, J. (2016). Deep residual learning for image recognition. Proceedings of the IEEE conference on computer vision and pattern recognition.

He, M., Wang, X., Wei, P., Yang, L., Teng, Y., & Lyu, R. (2024). Reinforcement Learning Meets Network Intrusion Detection: A Transferable and Adaptable Framework for Anomaly Behavior Identification. *IEEE Transactions on Network and Service Management*, *21*(2), 2477–2492. DOI: 10.1109/TNSM.2024.3352586

Heydari, M., Mylonas, A., Katos, V., Balaguer-Ballester, E., Tafreshi, V. H., & Benkhelifa, E. (2019). Uncertainty-aware authentication model for fog computing in IoT. *4th International Conference on Fog and Mobile Edge Computing, FMEC 2019* (pp. 52-59). Rome: IEEE. DOI: 10.1109/FMEC.2019.8795332

Himeur, Y., Sayed, A., Alsalemi, A., Bensaali, F., Amira, A., Varlamis, I., Eirinaki, M., Sardianos, C., & Dimitrakopoulos, G. (2022). Blockchain-based recommender systems: Applications, challenges and future opportunities. *Computer Science Review, 43*, 100439. DOI: 10.1016/j.cosrev.2021.100439

Hlav, E. (2022). Xavier glorot initialization in neural networks—math proof. *Towards Data Science.*

Hong, W., Zhang, H., & Zhu, J. (2022). FedHD: A Privacy-Preserving Recommendation System with Homomorphic Encryption and Differential Privacy. International Conference on Computer Science and Education.

Hossain, I., Puppala, S., Alam, M. J., & Talukder, S. (2025). EVOLVE: Predicting user evolution and network dynamics in social media using fine-tuned GPT-like model. In *International Conference on Advances in Social Networks Analysis and Mining* (pp. 379-395). Springer, Cham. DOI: 10.1007/978-3-031-85386-9_27

Huang, G., Liu, Z., Van Der Maaten, L., & Weinberger, K. Q. (2017). Densely connected convolutional networks. Proceedings of the IEEE conference on computer vision and pattern recognition.

Huang, D., Yan, C., Li, Q., & Peng, X. (2024). From large language models to large multimodal models: A literature review. *Applied Sciences (Basel, Switzerland), 14*(12), 5068. DOI: 10.3390/app14125068

Huesca, G., Elizondo-García, M. E., Aguayo-González, R., Aguayo-Hernández, C. H., González-Buenrostro, T., & Verdugo-Jasso, Y. A. (2025). Evaluating the Potential of Generative Artificial Intelligence to Innovate Feedback Processes. *Education Sciences, 15*(4), 505. DOI: 10.3390/educsci15040505

Hui, B., Zhang, L., Zhou, X., Wen, X., & Nian, Y. (2022). Personalized recommendation system based on knowledge embedding and historical behavior. *Applied Intelligence*, 1-13.

Idowu, E. (2024). Personalized Learning: Tailoring Instruction to Individual Student Needs. *Preprints*. DOI: 10.20944/preprints202411.0863.v1

Ieracitano, C., Adeel, A., Morabito, F. C., & Hussain, A. (2020). A novel statistical analysis and autoencoder driven intelligent intrusion detection approach. *Neurocomputing, 387*, 51–62. DOI: 10.1016/j.neucom.2019.11.016

Ikotun, A. M., Ezugwu, A. E., Abualigah, L., Abuhaija, B., & Heming, J. (2023). K-means clustering algorithms: A comprehensive review, variants analysis, and advances in the era of big data. *Information Sciences, 622*, 178–210.

Ioffe, S., & Szegedy, C. (2015). Batch normalization: Accelerating deep network training by reducing internal covariate shift. International conference on machine learning.

Iqbal, F., Samsom, F., Kamoun, F., & MacDermott, Á. (2023). When ChatGPT goes rogue: Exploring the potential cybersecurity threats of AI-powered conversational chatbots. *Frontiers in Communications and Networks*, *4*, 1220243. Advance online publication. DOI: 10.3389/frcmn.2023.1220243

Isinkaye, F. O., Folajimi, Y. O., & Ojokoh, B. A. (2015). Recommendation systems: Principles, methods and evaluation. *Egyptian informatics journal, 16*(3), 261-273.

Islek, I., & Oguducu, S. G. (2022). A hierarchical recommendation system for E-commerce using online user reviews. *Electronic Commerce Research and Applications*, *52*, 101131. DOI: 10.1016/j.elerap.2022.101131

Jain, V., Singh, I., Syed, M., Mondal, S., & Palai, D. R. (2024, March). Enhancing educational interactions: A comprehensive review of AI chatbots in learning environments. In *2024 11th international conference on reliability, infocom technologies and optimization (trends and future directions)(ICRITO)* (pp. 1-5). IEEE. DOI: DOI: 10.1109/ICRITO61523.2024.10522392

Jaradat, A. S., Nasayreh, A., Al-Na'amneh, Q., Gharaibeh, H., & Al Mamlook, R. E. (2023). Genetic Optimization Techniques for Enhancing Web Attacks Classification in Machine Learning. 2023 IEEE Intl Conf on Dependable, Autonomic and Secure Computing, Intl Conf on Pervasive Intelligence and Computing, Intl Conf on Cloud and Big Data Computing, Intl Conf on Cyber Science and Technology Congress (DASC/PiCom/CBDCom/CyberSciTech), 0130–0136. DOI: 10.1109/DASC/PiCom/CBDCom/Cy59711.2023.10361399

Javed, U., Shaukat, K., Hameed, I. A., Iqbal, F., Alam, T. M., & Luo, S. (2021). A review of content-based and context-based recommendation systems. [iJET]. *International Journal of Emerging Technologies in Learning*, *16*(3), 274–306. DOI: 10.3991/ijet.v16i03.18851

Jawaheer, G., Weller, P., & Kostkova, P. (2014). Modeling user preferences in recommender systems: A classification framework for explicit and implicit user feedback. [tiis]. *ACM Transactions on Interactive Intelligent Systems*, *4*(2), 1–26. DOI: 10.1145/2512208

Jeevamol, J., & Renumol, V. (2021). An ontology-based hybrid e-learning content recommender system for alleviating the cold-start problem. *Education and Information Technologies*, *26*(4), 4993–5022. DOI: 10.1007/s10639-021-10508-0

Jha, S., & Topol, E. J. (2016). Adapting to artificial intelligence: Radiologists and pathologists as information specialists. *Journal of the American Medical Association, 316*(22), 2353–2354. DOI: 10.1001/jama.2016.17438 PMID: 27898975

Jia, Y., Shelhamer, E., Donahue, J., Karayev, S., Long, J., Girshick, R., Guadarrama, S., & Darrell, T. (2014). Caffe: Convolutional architecture for fast feature embedding. Proceedings of the 22nd ACM international conference on Multimedia.

Joe, M. C. V., & Raj, J. S. (2021). Location-based orientation context dependent recommender system for users. [TCSST]. *J. Trends Comput. Sci. Smart Technol., 3*(01), 14–23. DOI: 10.36548/jtcsst.2021.1.002

Jørgensen, C. S., Shukla, A., & Katt, B. (2024). Digital Twins in Healthcare: Security, Privacy, Trust and Safety Challenges. *International Workshops which were held in conjunction with 28th European Symposium on Research in Computer Security, ESORICS 2023. 14399 LNCS*, pp. 140-153. The Hague: Springer Science and Business Media Deutschland GmbH. DOI: 10.1007/978-3-031-54129-2_9

Jui, T. D., & Rivas, P. (2024). Fairness issues, current approaches, and challenges in machine learning models. *International Journal of Machine Learning and Cybernetics, 15*(8), 3095–3125. DOI: 10.1007/s13042-023-02083-2

Kampffmeyer, M., Salberg, A.-B., & Jenssen, R. (2016). Semantic segmentation of small objects and modeling of uncertainty in urban remote sensing images using deep convolutional neural networks. Proceedings of the IEEE conference on computer vision and pattern recognition workshops.

Kasneci, E., Seßler, K., Küchemann, S., Bannert, M., Dementieva, D., Fischer, F., Gasser, U., Groh, G., Günnemann, S., Hüllermeier, E., Krusche, S., Kutyniok, G., Michaeli, T., Nerdel, C., Pfeffer, J., Poquet, O., Sailer, M., Schmidt, A., Seidel, T., & Kasneci, G. (2023). ChatGPT for good? On opportunities and challenges of large language models for education. *Learning and Individual Differences, 103*, 102274. DOI: 10.1016/j.lindif.2023.102274

Kaur, N., & Gupta, L. (2024). Enhancing IoT Security in 6G Environment With Transparent AI: Leveraging XGBoost, SHAP and LIME. *0th IEEE International Conference on Network Softwarization, NetSoft 2024* (pp. 180-184). Saint Louis: IEEE. DOI: 10.1109/NetSoft60951.2024.10588922

Ke, T. T., & Sudhir, K. (2023, August). Privacy Rights and Data Security: GDPR and Personal Data Markets. *Management Science, 68*(08), 4399–4412. DOI: 10.1287/mnsc.2022.4614

Khanal, S. S., Prasad, P., Alsadoon, A., & Maag, A. (2020). A systematic review: Machine learning based recommendation systems for e-learning. *Education and Information Technologies*, *25*(4), 2635–2664. DOI: 10.1007/s10639-019-10063-9

Khanna, S., Srivastava, S., Khanna, I., & Pandey, V. (2020). Current Challenges and Opportunities in Implementing AI/ML in Cancer Imaging: Integration, Development, and Adoption Perspectives. *Journal of Advanced Analytics in Healthcare Management*, *4*(10), 1–25.

Khyani, D., Siddhartha, B., Niveditha, N., & Divya, B. (2021). An interpretation of lemmatization and stemming in natural language processing. *Shanghai Ligong Daxue Xuebao*, *22*(10), 350–357.

Kieras, T., Farooq, J., & Zhu, Q. (2021). I-SCRAM: A Framework for IoT Supply Chain Risk Analysis and Mitigation Decisions. *IEEE Access : Practical Innovations, Open Solutions*, *09*, 29827–29840. DOI: 10.1109/ACCESS.2021.3058338

Kilani, Y., Otoom, A. F., Alsarhan, A., & Almaayah, M. (2018). A genetic algorithms-based hybrid recommender system of matrix factorization and neighborhood-based techniques. *Journal of Computational Science*, *28*, 78–93. DOI: 10.1016/j.jocs.2018.08.007

Kim, D. S., Nguyen, H. N., & Park, J. S. (2005). Genetic algorithm to improve SVM based network intrusion detection system. Proceedings - International Conference on Advanced Information Networking and Applications, AINA, 2, 155–158. DOI: 10.1109/AINA.2005.191

Kim, D. W., Jang, H. Y., Kim, K. W., Shin, Y., & Park, S. H. (2019). Design characteristics of studies reporting the performance of artificial intelligence algorithms for diagnostic analysis of medical images: Results from recently published papers. *Korean Journal of Radiology*, *20*(3), 405–410. DOI: 10.3348/kjr.2019.0025 PMID: 30799571

Kim, J. K., Chua, M., Rickard, M., & Lorenzo, A. (2023). ChatGPT and large language model (LLM) chatbots: The current state of acceptability and a proposal for guidelines on utilization in academic medicine. *Journal of Pediatric Urology*, *19*(5), 598–604. DOI: 10.1016/j.jpurol.2023.05.018 PMID: 37328321

Kohnke, S., & Zaugg, T. (2025). Artificial intelligence: An untapped opportunity for equity and access in STEM education. *Education Sciences*, *15*(1), 68. DOI: 10.3390/educsci15010068

Koren, Y., Rendle, S., & Bell, R. (2021). Advances in collaborative filtering. *Recommender systems handbook*, 91-142.

Kulkarni, P. V., Rai, S., & Kale, R. (2020). Recommender system in elearning: a survey. Proceeding of International Conference on Computational Science and Applications: ICCSA 2019.

Kumar Jain, Y., C.A., D. S., Johrawanshi, A., Gupta, M., Choudhary, D. K., & Pandey, A. (2024). Cybersecurity Frameworks: A Roadmap for Business Resilience. *International Conference on Cybernation and Computation, CYBERCOM 2024* (pp. 102-108). Dehradun: IEEE. DOI: 10.1109/CYBERCOM63683.2024.10803234

Lauriola, I., Lavelli, A., & Aiolli, F. (2022). An introduction to deep learning in natural language processing: Models, techniques, and tools. *Neurocomputing*, *470*, 443–456. DOI: 10.1016/j.neucom.2021.05.103

Lee, I., & Hahn, S. (2024). On the relationship between mind perception and social support of chatbots. *Frontiers in Psychology*, *15*, 1282036. DOI: 10.3389/fpsyg.2024.1282036 PMID: 38510306

Lee, Y. F., Hwang, G. J., & Chen, P. Y. (2025). Technology-based interactive guidance to promote learning performance and self-regulation: A chatbot-assisted self-regulated learning approach. *Educational Technology Research and Development*, *73*(4), 1–26. DOI: 10.1007/s11423-025-10478-x

Lekadir, K., Osuala, R., Gallin, C., Lazrak, N., Kushibar, K., Tsakou, G., ... & Martí-Bonmatí, L. (2021). FUTURE-AI: guiding principles and consensus recommendations for trustworthy artificial intelligence in medical imaging.

Lguensat, R., Sun, M., Fablet, R., Tandeo, P., Mason, E., & Chen, G. (2018). EddyNet: A deep neural network for pixel-wise classification of oceanic eddies. IGARSS 2018-2018 IEEE International Geoscience and Remote Sensing Symposium.

Li, H., & Zhang, R. (2024). Finding love in algorithms: Deciphering the emotional contexts of close encounters with AI chatbots. *Journal of Computer-Mediated Communication*, *29*(5), zmae015. Advance online publication. DOI: 10.1093/jcmc/zmae015

Li, J. (2023). Security implications of AI chatbots in health care. *Journal of Medical Internet Research*, *25*, e47551. DOI: 10.2196/47551 PMID: 38015597

Lin, C. C., Huang, A. Y., & Lu, O. H. (2023). Artificial intelligence in intelligent tutoring systems toward sustainable education: A systematic review. *Smart Learning Environments*, *10*(1), 41. DOI: 10.1186/s40561-023-00260-y

Li, P., Su, J., & Wang, X. (2019). *ITLS/iDTLS: Lightweight end-to-end security protocol for iot through minimal latency. ACM SIGCOMM Conference Posters and Demos, SIGCOMM 2019.* Association for Computing Machinery, Inc., DOI: 10.1145/3342280.3342347

Li, Z., Liu, F., Yang, W., Peng, S., & Zhou, J. (2021). A survey of convolutional neural networks: Analysis, applications, and prospects. *IEEE Transactions on Neural Networks and Learning Systems, 33*(12), 6999–7019. DOI: 10.1109/TNNLS.2021.3084827 PMID: 34111009

Lo, C., Win, T. Y., Rezaeifar, Z., Khan, Z., & Legg, P. (2023). Digital Twins in Industry 4.0 Cyber Security. *9th IEEE Smart World Congress, SWC 2023.* Portsmouth: IEEE. DOI: 10.1109/SWC57546.2023.10449147

Loh, E. (2023). ChatGPT and generative AI chatbots: Challenges and opportunities for science, medicine and medical leaders. *BMJ Leader, 8*(1), 51–54. DOI: 10.1136/leader-2023-000797 PMID: 37192124

Luzzi, J., Naha, R., Arulappan, A., & Mahanti, A. (2024). SoK: A Holistic View of Cyberattacks Prediction with Digital Twins. *2nd International Conference on Emerging Trends in Information Technology and Engineering, ic-ETITE 2024.* Vellore: IEEE. DOI: 10.1109/ic-ETITE58242.2024.10493514

Lv, P., Sun, C., & Li, Q. (2023). Research and Application of Grid Cloud Service Security Access Control Technology Based on Zero Trust Model. *International Conference on Data Science and Network Security, ICDSNS 2023.* Tiptur: IEEE. DOI: 10.1109/ICDSNS58469.2023.10245681

Lytras, M. D., Serban, A. C., Alkhaldi, A., Aldosemani, T., & Malik, S. (2024). Digital transformation in higher education in times of artificial intelligence: Setting the emerging landscape. In *Digital Transformation in Higher Education, Part A* (pp. 1-22). Emerald Publishing Limited. https://doi.org/DOI: 10.1108/978-1-83549-480-620241001

M, V. (2023). The use of natural language processing in virtual assistants and chatbots. *IJERT.* DOI: 10.17577/NCRTCA-PID-075

Madaan, G., Asthana, S. K., & Kaur, J. (2024). Generative AI: Applications, models, challenges, opportunities, and future directions. Generative AI and implications for ethics, security, and data management, 88-121.

Madupati, B. (2025). *Assessing bias in AI Chatbot responses.* dzone.com. https://dzone.com/articles/assessing-bias-in-ai-chatbot-responses

Mahesh, B. (2020). Machine learning algorithms-a review. *International Journal of Science and Research (IJSR).[Internet], 9*(1), 381-386.

Maheshwari, R. U., Shankar, P. R., Chandrasekaran, G., & Mahendrakhan, K. (2024, October 02). Assessment of Cybersecurity Risks in Digital Twin Deployments in Smart Cities. *International Journal of Computational and Experimental Science and Engineering, 10*(04), 695–700. DOI: 10.22399/ijcesen.494

Mahmoud, C. F., & Sørensen, J. T. (2024). Artificial Intelligence in Personalized Learning with a Focus on Current Developments and Future Prospects. *Research and Advances in Education, 3*(8), 25–31. DOI: 10.56397/RAE.2024.08.04

Malakuti, S., & Grüner, S. (2018). Architectural aspects of digital twins in IIoT systems. *12th European Conference on Software Architecture, ECSA 2018*. Madrid: Association for Computing Machinery. DOI: 10.1145/3241403.3241417

Maleshkova, M., & Seydoux, N. (2020). Data representation and reasoning. In *The Internet of Things: From Data to Insight* (pp. 79 - 90). wiley. DOI: 10.1002/9781119545293.ch7

Mammone, A., Turchi, M., & Cristianini, N. (2009). Support vector machines. *Wiley Interdisciplinary Reviews: Computational Statistics, 1*(3), 283–289. DOI: 10.1002/wics.49

Mansur, F., Patel, V., & Patel, M. (2017). A review on recommender systems. 2017 International Conference on Innovations in Information, Embedded and Communication Systems (ICIIECS).

Marotta, A., & Madnick, S. (2021). Convergence and divergence of regulatory compliance and cybersecurity. *Issues in Information Systems, 22*(01), 10–50. DOI: 10.48009/1_iis_2021_10-50

Martinovic, D., & Danesi, M. (Eds.). (2025). *Mathematics and Education in an AI Era: Cognitive Science, Technological, and Semiotic Perspectives*. Springer Nature. DOI: 10.1007/978-3-031-80696-4

Maulud, D. H., Zeebaree, S. R., Jacksi, K., Sadeeq, M. A. M., & Sharif, K. H. (2021). State of art for semantic analysis of natural language processing. *Qubahan academic journal, 1*(2), 21-28. DOI: .DOI: 10.48161/qaj.v1n2a44

Mazurowski, M. A., Buda, M., Saha, A., & Bashir, M. R. (2019). Deep learning in radiology: An overview of the concepts and a survey of the state of the art with focus on MRI. *Journal of Magnetic Resonance Imaging, 49*(4), 939–954. DOI: 10.1002/jmri.26534 PMID: 30575178

McNee, S. M., Riedl, J., & Konstan, J. A. (2006). Being accurate is not enough: how accuracy metrics have hurt recommender systems. CHI'06 extended abstracts on Human factors in computing systems.

Medhat, M., Ayoub, L. W., Daher, M., & Mohamed, K. M. (2025). Ethical Considerations in AI-Generated Content on Social Media. In *Sustainable Data Management: Navigating Big Data, Communication Technology, and Business Digital Leadership* (Vol. 1, pp. 611–620). Springer Nature Switzerland. DOI: 10.1007/978-3-031-83911-5_52

Medsker, L. R., & Jain, L. (2001). Recurrent neural networks. *Design and applications, 5*(64-67), 2.

Medtronic. (2025, Feb 05). *Medtronic: Enterprise Architecture for IoT-Enabled Remote Patient Monitoring*. Retrieved Feb 09, 2025, from https://www.linkedin.com: https://www.linkedin.com/pulse/medtronic-enterprise-architecture-iot-enabled-remote-patient-suf6e/

Mehmood, T. (2025). Ethical AI in education: Addressing bias, privacy, and equity in ai-driven learning systems. *AI EDIFY Journal*, *2*(1), 38–45.

Mehta, R., & Rana, K. (2017). A review on matrix factorization techniques in recommender systems. 2017 2nd International Conference on Communication Systems, Computing and IT Applications (CSCITA)

Mekala Srinivasa Rao, Sagenela Vijaya Kumar, Rambabu Pemula, Anil Kumar Prathipati (2022).Change detection of pulmonary embolism using isomeric cluster and computer vision.

Merelo, J. J., Castillo, P. A., Mora, A. M., Barranco, F., Abbas, N., Guillén, A., & Tsivitanidou, O. (2024). Chatbots and messaging platforms in the classroom: An analysis from the teacher's perspective. *Education and Information Technologies*, *29*(2), 1903–1938. DOI: 10.1007/s10639-023-11703-x PMID: 37361787

Merino-Campos, C. (2025). The impact of artificial intelligence on personalized learning in higher education: A systematic review. *Trends in Higher Education*, *4*(2), 17. DOI: 10.3390/higheredu4020017

Meyer, D. (2016). How exactly does word2vec work. *Uoregon. Edu, Brocade. Com*, 1-18.

Meyrowitsch, D. W., Jensen, A. K., Sørensen, J. B., & Varga, T. V. (2023). AI chatbots and (mis)information in public health: Impact on vulnerable communities. *Frontiers in Public Health*, *11*, 1226776. Advance online publication. DOI: 10.3389/fpubh.2023.1226776 PMID: 38026315

Mhawi, D. N., Aldallal, A., & Hassan, S. (2022). Advanced Feature-Selection-Based Hybrid Ensemble Learning Algorithms for Network Intrusion Detection Systems. Symmetry 2022, Vol. 14, Page 1461, 14(7), 1461. DOI: 10.3390/sym14071461

Mitra, T., & Gilbert, E. (2015). *Credbank: A large-scale social media corpus with associated credibility annotations.* Paper presented at the Proceedings of the international AAAI conference on web and social media.

Mohallick, I., & Özgöbek, Ö. (2017). Exploring privacy concerns in news recommender systems. Proceedings of the International Conference on Web Intelligence.

Mohamed, B., Abdelhadi, F., Adil, B., & Haytam, H. (2019). *Smart city services monitoring framework using fuzzy logic based sentiment analysis and apache spark.* Paper presented at the 2019 1st International conference on smart systems and data science (ICSSD). DOI: 10.1109/ICSSD47982.2019.9002687

Mohamed, M. H., Khafagy, M. H., & Ibrahim, M. H. (2019). Recommender systems challenges and solutions survey. 2019 international conference on innovative trends in computer engineering (ITCE).

Mohanty, S. N., Chatterjee, J. M., Jain, S., Elngar, A. A., & Gupta, P. (2020). *Recommender system with machine learning and artificial intelligence: practical tools and applications in medical, agricultural and other industries*. John Wiley & Sons. DOI: 10.1145/3106426.3109435

Mol, E. N., & Kumar, M. S. (2024). End-to-end framework for agricultural entity extraction–A hybrid model with transformer. *Computers and Electronics in Agriculture*, *225*, 109309.

Moudden, T. E., Amnai, M., Choukri, A., Fakhri, Y., & Noreddine, G. (2024). New unfreezing strategy of transfer learning in satellite imagery for mapping the diversity of slum areas: A case study in Kenitra city—Morocco. *Scientific African*, *24*, e02135. DOI: 10.1016/j.sciaf.2024.e02135

Moumen, I., Rafalia, N., Abouchabaka, J., & Chatoui, Y. (2023). AODV-based Defense Mechanism for Mitigating Blackhole Attacks in MANET. E3S Web of Conferences, 412. DOI: 10.1051/e3sconf/202341201094

Moumen, I., Abouchabaka, J., & Rafalia, N. (2023). Enhancing urban mobility: Integration of IoT road traffic data and artificial intelligence in smart city environment. *Indonesian Journal of Electrical Engineering and Computer Science*, *32*(2), 985–993. DOI: 10.11591/ijeecs.v32.i2.pp985-993

Moustafa, N., & Slay, J. (2015). UNSW-NB15: A comprehensive data set for network intrusion detection systems (UNSW-NB15 network data set). 2015 Military Communications and Information Systems Conference, MilCIS 2015 - Proceedings. DOI: 10.1109/MilCIS.2015.7348942

Musa, J. M., & Zhihong, X. (2020). Item based collaborative filtering approach in movie recommendation system using different similarity measures. Proceedings of the 2020 6th International Conference on Computer and Technology Applications.

Mylrea, M. (2024). Building a trustworthy digital twin: A brave new world of human machine teams and autonomous biological internet of things (BIoT). In *Putting AI in the Critical Loop: Assured Trust and Autonomy in Human-Machine Teams* (pp. 219-243). Elsevier. DOI: 10.1016/B978-0-443-15988-6.00005-4

Nachiappan B, Rajkumar N, Radha V, Kalpana C, Viji C, Nagarajan G, Mohanraj A. (2026). Fusion of Generative AI and Blockchain Conceptual Framework. In *Fusion of Multimodal Generative AI and Blockchain Technology in Digital Media* (pp. 57–86). IGI Global Scientific Publishing.

Nakaura, T., Ito, R., Ueda, D., Nozaki, T., Fushimi, Y., Matsui, Y., Yanagawa, M., Yamada, A., Tsuboyama, T., Fujima, N., Tatsugami, F., Hirata, K., Fujita, S., Kamagata, K., Fujioka, T., Kawamura, M., & Naganawa, S. (2024). The impact of large language models on radiology: A guide for radiologists on the latest innovations in AI. *Japanese Journal of Radiology*, *42*(7), 685–696. DOI: 10.1007/s11604-024-01552-0 PMID: 38551772

Narayanan, A., & Kapoor, S. (2024). AI snake oil: What artificial intelligence can do, what it can't, and how to tell the difference. In *AI Snake Oil*. Princeton University Press. DOI: 10.2307/jj.14736606

Narkhede, M. V., Bartakke, P. P., & Sutaone, M. S. (2022). A review on weight initialization strategies for neural networks. *Artificial Intelligence Review*, *55*(1), 291–322. DOI: 10.1007/s10462-021-10033-z

Nawrocka, A., Kot, A., & Nawrocki, M. (2018). Application of machine learning in recommendation systems. 2018 19th International carpathian control conference (ICCC).

Naz, I., & Robertson, R. (2024). Exploring the feasibility and efficacy of ChatGPT3 for personalized feedback in teaching. *Electronic Journal of e-Learning*, *22*(2), 98–111. DOI: 10.34190/ejel.22.2.3345

Neto, E. C. P., Dadkhah, S., Ferreira, R., Zohourian, A., Lu, R., & Ghorbani, A. A. (2023). CICIoT2023: A Real-Time Dataset and Benchmark for Large-Scale Attacks in IoT Environment. Sensors 2023, Vol. 23, Page 5941, 23(13), 5941. DOI: 10.3390/s23135941

Nguyen, P. H., Rauniyar, A., & Niemi, T. V. (2025). Digital Twin-Based Security Orchestration, Automation and Response for IoT and CPS. *7th IFIP WG 5.5 International Cross-Domain Conference on Internet of Things, IFIPIoT 2024. 737 IFIPAICT*, pp. 243-260. Nice: Springer Science and Business Media Deutschland GmbH. DOI: 10.1007/978-3-031-81900-1_15

Ni, A., & Cheung, A. (2023). Understanding secondary students' continuance intention to adopt AI-powered intelligent tutoring system for English learning. *Education and Information Technologies*, *28*(3), 3191–3216. DOI: 10.1007/s10639-022-11305-z PMID: 36119127

Ningsih, W., & Akhyar, Y. The Potential of GPT in Education: Opportunities for Students' Feedback. *Buletin Poltanesa, 25*(1), 568949. DOI: 10.51967/tanesa.v25i1.3043

Niyaz, Q., Sun, W., & Javaid, A. Y. (2017). A Deep Learning Based DDoS Detection System in Software-Defined Networking (SDN). EAI Endorsed Transactions on Security and Safety, "4"(12), 153515. DOI: 10.4108/eai.28-12-2017.153515

O, N. (2023). Using retrieval-augmented generation to elevate low-code developer skills. *Artificial Intelligence, 28*(AI.2023.28(3)), 126–130. https://doi.org/DOI: 10.15407/jai2023.03.126

O'Sullivan, M. E., & Hasenstab, K. (2024). Aleks PPL Scores as a Predictor of Success in Calculus. *PRIMUS (Terre Haute, Ind.), 34*(10), 1025–1049. DOI: 10.1080/10511970.2024.2411054

Oghenekaro, L. U., & Okoro, C. O. (2024). Artificial Intelligence-Based chatbot for student mental health support. *OAlib*, *11*(05), 1–16. DOI: 10.4236/oalib.1111511

Ohde, J. W., Rost, L. M., & Overgaard, J. D. (2025). The Burden of Reviewing LLM-Generated Content. *NEJM AI*, *2*(2), AIp2400979. DOI: 10.1056/AIp2400979

Omeh, C. B., Olelewe, C. J., & Hu, X. (2025). Application of artificial intelligence (AI) technology in tvet education: Ethical issues and policy implementation. *Education and Information Technologies*, *30*(5), 5989–6018. DOI: 10.1007/s10639-024-13018-x

Oriola, O. (2021). Exploring N-gram, word embedding and topic models for content-based fake news detection in FakeNewsNet evaluation. *Int. J. Comput. Appl*, *975*, 8887.

Oshikawa, R., Qian, J., & Wang, W. Y. (2018). A survey on natural language processing for fake news detection. *arXiv preprint arXiv:1811.00770.*

Oshri, B., Hu, A., Adelson, P., Chen, X., Dupas, P., Weinstein, J., Burke, M., Lobell, D., & Ermon, S. (2018). Infrastructure quality assessment in africa using satellite imagery and deep learning. Proceedings of the 24th ACM SIGKDD international conference on knowledge discovery & data mining.

Padmapriya, V., & Srivenkatesh, M. (2024, February 02). IoT Network based Cyber Attack Mitigation in Digital Twin with Multi Level Key Management Using Enhanced KNN Model. *International Journal of Intelligent Systems and Applications in Engineering*, *12*(14s), 49–62. Retrieved February 07, 2025, from https://www.scopus.com/record/display.uri?eid=2-s2.0-85184694434&origin=scopusAI

Pajouh, H. H., Javidan, R., Khayami, R., Dehghantanha, A., & Choo, K. K. R. (2019). A Two-Layer Dimension Reduction and Two-Tier Classification Model for Anomaly-Based Intrusion Detection in IoT Backbone Networks. *IEEE Transactions on Emerging Topics in Computing*, *7*(2), 314–323. DOI: 10.1109/TETC.2016.2633228

Palaniappan, K., Lin, E. Y. T., & Vogel, S. (2024). *Global regulatory frameworks for the use of artificial intelligence (AI) in the healthcare services sector*. MDPI. DOI: 10.3390/healthcare12050562

Pamudhurthy PS, Komali R, Panyam AB, Katarukonda A, Raithatha H. Real Time Language Translation Using AI and ML.

Pan, W. (2016). A survey of transfer learning for collaborative recommendation with auxiliary data. *Neurocomputing*, *177*, 447–453.

Panayides, A. S., Amini, A., Filipovic, N. D., Sharma, A., Tsaftaris, S. A., Young, A., Foran, D., Do, N., Golemati, S., Kurc, T., Huang, K., Nikita, K. S., Veasey, B. P., Zervakis, M., Saltz, J. H., & Pattichis, C. S. (2020). AI in medical imaging informatics: Current challenges and future directions. *IEEE Journal of Biomedical and Health Informatics*, *24*(7), 1837–1857. DOI: 10.1109/JBHI.2020.2991043 PMID: 32609615

Papadakis, H., Papagrigoriou, A., Panagiotakis, C., Kosmas, E., & Fragopoulou, P. (2022). Collaborative filtering recommender systems taxonomy. *Knowledge and Information Systems*, *64*(1), 35–74. DOI: 10.1007/s10115-021-01628-7

Papakostas, C., Troussas, C., Krouska, A., & Sgouropoulou, C. (2024, June). A rule-based chatbot offering personalized guidance in computer programming education. In *International Conference on Intelligent Tutoring Systems* (pp. 253-264). Cham: Springer Nature Switzerland. DOIhttps://DOI: 10.1007/978-3-031-63031-6_22

Park, M., Kim, S., Lee, S., Kwon, S., & Kim, K. (2024, May). Empowering personalized learning through a conversation-based tutoring system with student modeling. In *Extended Abstracts of the CHI Conference on Human Factors in Computing Systems* (pp. 1-10). DOI: 10.1145/3613905.3651122

Pasena, R. B., & Gunadi, G. (2025). IMPLEMENTATION OF A CHATBOT BASED ON ARTIFIFICAL INTELLEGENCE MARKUP LANGUANGE FOR ADMINISTRATIF SERVICE INFORMATION AT KELURAHAN NEGERI AGUNG. *Jurnal Disprotek*, *16*(1), 33–46. DOI: 10.34001/jdpt.v16i1.7332

Patel, M. G., Prajapati, H. N., Patel, N. K., Patel, N. S., Patel, A. K., & Brahmbhatt, H. A. (2024). Chatgpt: A double-edged sword in cybersecurity - evaluating risks and recommendations for safer ai integration. *ShodhKosh Journal of Visual and Performing Arts*, *5*(5). Advance online publication. DOI: 10.29121/shodhkosh.v5.i5.2024.1956

Patra, B., & Kumar, M. (2020). Natural Language Processing in Chatbots: A review. *Türk Bilgisayar Ve Matematik Eğitimi Dergisi*, *11*(3), 2890–2894. DOI: 10.61841/turcomat.v11i3.14655

Patwa, P., Sharma, S., Pykl, S., Guptha, V., Kumari, G., Akhtar, M. S., . . . Chakraborty, T. (2021). *Fighting an infodemic: Covid-19 fake news dataset.* Paper presented at the International Workshop on Combating On line Ho st ile Posts in Regional Languages dur ing Emerge ncy Si tuation. DOI: 10.1007/978-3-030-73696-5_3

Pellas, N. (2024). The role of students higher-order thinking skills in the relationship between academic achievements and machine learning using generative AI chatbots. https://doi.org/DOI: 10.21203/rs.3.rs-4627814/v2

Philbin, C. A. (2023). Exploring the potential of artificial intelligence program generators in computer programming education for students. *ACM Inroads*, *14*(3), 30–38. DOI: 10.1145/3610406

Philip, S., Shola, P., & Ovye, A. (2014). Application of content-based approach in research paper recommendation system for a digital library. *International Journal of Advanced Computer Science and Applications*, *5*(10). Advance online publication. DOI: 10.14569/IJACSA.2014.051006

Portugal, I., Alencar, P., & Cowan, D. (2018). The use of machine learning algorithms in recommender systems: A systematic review. *Expert Systems with Applications*, *97*, 205–227. DOI: 10.1016/j.eswa.2017.12.020

Pramod, D. (2023). Privacy-preserving techniques in recommender systems: State-of-the-art review and future research agenda. *Data Technologies and Applications*, *57*(1), 32–55. DOI: 10.1108/DTA-02-2022-0083

Priya, P. K., & A., R. (2024). A Review of Digital Twin Applications in Various Sectors. In *Transforming Industry using Digital Twin Technology* (pp. 239-258). Springer Nature. https://doi.org/DOI: 10.1007/9783031585234_12

Puspowidjono, K., Chiou, A., & Jha, M. (2024, December). Next Level Chatbot: Expert Advisory Solution. In *2024 International Conference on Sustainable Technology and Engineering (i-COSTE)* (pp. 01-06). IEEE. DOI: DOI: 10.1109/i-COSTE63786.2024.11024843

Qu, J., Liu, J., Liu, X., Chen, M., Li, J., & Wang, J. (2025). PNCD: Mitigating LLM Hallucinations in Noisy Environments A Medical Case Study. *Information Fusion*, *123*, 103328. DOI: 10.1016/j.inffus.2025.103328

Rahiman, H. U., & Kodikal, R. (2024). Revolutionizing education: Artificial intelligence empowered learning in higher education. *Cogent Education, 11*(1), 2293431. Rahiman, H. U., & Kodikal, R. (2024). Revolutionizing education: Artificial intelligence empowered learning in higher education. *Cogent Education*, *11*(1), 2293431. DOI: 10.1080/2331186X.2023.2293431

Rahman, M. K., Hossain, M. A., Ismail, N. A., Hossen, M. S., & Sultana, M. (2025). Determinants of students' adoption of AI chatbots in higher education: The moderating role of tech readiness. *Interactive Technology and Smart Education*, *22*(3), 448–480. Advance online publication. DOI: 10.1108/ITSE-12-2024-0312

Rahman, M. K., Ismail, N. A., Hossain, M. A., & Hossen, M. S. (2025). Students' mindset to adopt AI chatbots for effectiveness of online learning in higher education. *Future Business Journal*, *11*(1), 30. DOI: 10.1186/s43093-025-00459-0

Rai, A., Shastri, J., & Bansal, H. (2025). Artificial Intelligence Techniques in Predictive Maintenance, Their Applications, Challenges, and Prospects. In *Artificial Intelligence-Enabled Digital Twin for Smart Manufacturing* (pp. 565-579). wiley. DOI: 10.1002/9781394303601.ch24

Răileanu, S., Borangiu, T., Len oiu, I., Anton, F., & Negoiţă, R. (2024). Data Acquisition System for Developing Digital Twin Solutions: A Practical Guide. *13th International Workshop on Service Orientation in Holonic and Multi-Agent Manufacturing, SOHOMA 2023. 1136 SCI*, pp. 38-49. Annecy: Springer Science and Business Media Deutschland GmbH. DOI: 10.1007/978-3-031-53445-4_4

Rajkumar N, Viji C, Nachiappan B, Mohanraj A, Nagarajan G, Ravi J, et al. (2026). Generative AI in Virtual Media Image, Video, and Animation Generation. In *Fusion of Multimodal Generative AI and Blockchain Technology in Digital Media* (pp. 209–230). IGI Global Scientific Publishing.

Rajora, R., Rajora, A., Sharma, B., & Aggarwal, P. (2023). Unveiling the Synergy: IoT and Digital Twins in Transforming Industries. *3rd International Conference on Smart Generation Computing, Communication and Networking, SMART GENCON 2023*. Bangalore: Institute of Electrical and Electronics Engineers Inc. DOI: 10.1109/SMARTGENCON60755.2023.10442175

Rane, N. (2023). Chatbot-enhanced teaching and learning: Implementation strategies, challenges, and the role of ChatGPT in education. *Challenges, and the Role of ChatGPT in Education (July 21,* 2023*)*. http://dx.doi.org/DOI: 10.2139/ssrn.4603204

Rashid, S. F., Duong-Trung, N., & Pinkwart, N. (2024). Generative AI in education: technical foundations, applications, and challenges. DOI: DOI: 10.5772/intechopen.1005402

Rawajbeh, M. A., Alzu'bi, S., & Alkhatib, A. (2023). IoT-Paradigm: Evolution Challenges and Proposed Solutions. *9th IEEE International Smart Cities Conference, ISC2 2023*. Bucharest: Institute of Electrical and Electronics Engineers Inc. DOI: 10.1109/ISC257844.2023.10293646

Ray, P. P. (2024). Integrating AI in radiology: Insights from GPT-generated reports and multimodal LLM performance on European Board of Radiology examinations. *Japanese Journal of Radiology*, *42*(9), 1083–1084. DOI: 10.1007/s11604-024-01576-6 PMID: 38647884

Redelinghuys, A., Basson, A., & Kruger, K. (2020, August 01). A six-layer architecture for the digital twin: A manufacturing case study implementation. *Journal of Intelligent Manufacturing*, *31*(06), 1383–1402. DOI: 10.1007/s10845-019-01516-6

Rendle, S., Zhang, L., & Koren, Y. (2019). On the difficulty of evaluating baselines: A study on recommender systems. *arXiv preprint arXiv:1905.01395*.

Reusens, M., Lemahieu, W., Baesens, B., & Sels, L. (2017). A note on explicit versus implicit information for job recommendation. *Decision Support Systems*, *98*, 26–35. DOI: 10.1016/j.dss.2017.04.002

Roberts, M., Driggs, D., Thorpe, M., Gilbey, J., Yeung, M., Ursprung, S., Aviles-Rivero, A. I., Etmann, C., McCague, C., Beer, L., Weir-McCall, J. R., Teng, Z., Gkrania-Klotsas, E., Ruggiero, A., Korhonen, A., Jefferson, E., Ako, E., Langs, G., Gozaliasl, G., & Schönlieb, C. B. (2021). Common pitfalls and recommendations for using machine learning to detect and prognosticate for COVID-19 using chest radiographs and CT scans. *Nature Machine Intelligence*, *3*(3), 199–217. DOI: 10.1038/s42256-021-00307-0

Rodrigues, L., Pereira, F. D., Marinho, M., Macario, V., Bittencourt, I. I., Isotani, S., Dermeval, D., & Mello, R. (2024). Mathematics intelligent tutoring systems with handwritten input: A scoping review. *Education and Information Technologies*, *29*(9), 11183–11209. DOI: 10.1007/s10639-023-12245-y

Roy, D., & Dutta, M. (2022). A systematic review and research perspective on recommender systems. *Journal of Big Data*, *9*(1), 59. DOI: 10.1186/s40537-022-00592-5

Ruder, S. (2016). An overview of gradient descent optimization algorithms. *arXiv preprint arXiv:1609.04747*. DOI: 10.1145/3219819.3219924

Russo, J. A., Roche, A., Russo, T., & Kalogeropoulos, P. (2024). Examining primary school educators' preferences for using digital versus non-digital games to support mathematics instruction. *International Journal of Mathematical Education in Science and Technology*, 1–26. DOI: 10.1080/0020739X.2024.2361699

Sadhu, A. K. R., Parfenov, M., Saripov, D., Muravev, M., & Sadhu, A. K. R. (2024, February 15). *Enhancing Customer Service Automation and User Satisfaction: An Exploration of AI-powered Chatbot Implementation within Customer Relationship Management Systems*. Journal of Computational Intelligence and Robotics. https://thesciencebrigade.com/jcir/article/view/249

Saeed, M. M., Saeed, R. A., & Ahmed, Z. E. (2024). Data security and privacy in the age of AI and digital twins. In *Digital Twin Technology and AI Implementations in Future-Focused Businesses* (pp. 99–124). IGI Global., DOI: 10.4018/979-8-3693-1818-8.ch008

Saeed, S., Gull, H., Aldossary, M. M., Altamimi, A. F., Alshahrani, M. S., Saqib, M., Zafar Iqbal, S., & Almuhaideb, A. M. (2024, December). Digital Transformation in Energy Sector: Cybersecurity Challenges and Implications. *Information (Basel)*, *15*(12), 764. Advance online publication. DOI: 10.3390/info15120764

Saha, B. (2025). Generative AI for Text Generation: Advances and Applications in Natural Language Processing. *Journal of Computer Allied Intelligence (JCAI, ISSN: 2584-2676)*, *3*(1), 77-91.

Sahu, S. K., & Mazumdar, K. (2024). State-of-the-art analysis of quantum cryptography: Applications and future prospects. *Frontiers in Physics (Lausanne)*, *12*, 1456491. Advance online publication. DOI: 10.3389/fphy.2024.1456491

Sandhu, K. (2021). Advancing cybersecurity for digital transformation: Opportunities and challenges. In *Handbook of Research on Advancing Cybersecurity for Digital Transformation* (pp. 01-17). IGI Global. DOI: 10.4018/978-1-7998-6975-7.ch001

Santos-Trigo, M. (2024). Problem solving in mathematics education: Tracing its foundations and current research-practice trends. *ZDM Mathematics Education*, *56*(2), 211–222. DOI: 10.1007/s11858-024-01578-8

Sauerwein, C., Wenzl, C., & Breu, R. (2024). Uncovering Critical Resources and Factors Influencing the Use of Threat Intelligence Sharing Platforms. *57th Annual Hawaii International Conference on System Sciences, HICSS 2024* (pp. 1921-1930). Honolulu: IEEE Computer Society. DOI: 10.24251/HICSS.2024.241

Saxe, A. M., McClelland, J. L., & Ganguli, S. (2013). Exact solutions to the nonlinear dynamics of learning in deep linear neural networks. *arXiv preprint arXiv:1312.6120.*

Schuler, L., Jamil, S., & Kühl, N. (2021, May). AI-based resource allocation: Reinforcement learning for adaptive auto-scaling in serverless environments. In *2021 IEEE/ACM 21st international symposium on cluster, cloud and internet computing (CCGrid)* (pp. 804-811). IEEE. DOI: DOI: 10.1109/CCGrid51090.2021.00098

Sciullo, L., De Marchi, A., Trotta, A., Montori, F. L., & Di Felice, M. (2024). APr). Relativistic Digital Twin: Bringing the IoT to the future. *Future Generation Computer Systems*, *153*, 521–536. DOI: 10.1016/j.future.2023.12.016

Sebastian, G. (2023). Exploring ethical implications of ChatGPT and other AI chatbots and regulation of disinformation propagation. SSRN *Electronic Journal.* https://doi.org/DOI: 10.2139/ssrn.4461801

Sengupta, A., Kundu, A., & Mukhopadhyay, A. (2024). An Approach to Detect and Classify Potentially Suspicious Activity from Real-Time Log Data using Anomaly Detection Methods. *3rd International Conference for Innovation in Technology, INOCON 2024.* Bangalore: IEEE. DOI: 10.1109/INOCON60754.2024.10511679

Seo, K., Yoo, M., Dodson, S., & Jin, S. H. (2025). Augmented teachers: K–12 teachers' needs for artificial intelligence's complementary role in personalized learning. *Journal of Research on Technology in Education*, *57*(4), 876–893. DOI: 10.1080/15391523.2024.2330525

Setyawan, S., & Pramudita, R. F. (2025). Enhancing Academic Speaking Skills Through AI Chatbots: A Study on English Language Learning in Higher Education. *International Journal of Applied Educational Research*, *3*(2), 129–140. DOI: 10.59890/ijaer.v3i2.30

Shah, K., Salunke, A., Dongare, S., & Antala, K. (2017). Recommender systems: An overview of different approaches to recommendations. 2017 International Conference on Innovations in Information, Embedded and Communication Systems (ICIIECS).

Shahri, H., Emad, M., Ibrahim, N., Rais, R. N. B., & Al-Fayoumi, Y. (2024, April). Elevating Education through AI Tutor: Utilizing GPT-4 for Personalized Learning. In *2024 15th Annual Undergraduate Research Conference on Applied Computing (URC)* (pp. 1-5). IEEE. DOI: 10.1109/URC62276.2024.10604578

Sharafaldin, I., Lashkari, A. H., & Ghorbani, A. A. (2018). Toward generating a new intrusion detection dataset and intrusion traffic characterization. ICISSP 2018 - Proceedings of the 4th International Conference on Information Systems Security and Privacy, 2018-January, 108–116. DOI: 10.5220/0006639801080116

Sharma, C., Sharma, S., Bhardwaj, V., & Dhaliwal, B. K. (2025, June 4). Generative artificial intelligence for sustainable development: Predictive trend analysis in key sectors using natural language processing. *Discover Applied Sciences*, *7*(6), 596. DOI: 10.1007/s42452-025-07207-7

Shemshack, A., Kinshuk, , & Spector, J. M. (2021). A comprehensive analysis of personalized learning components. *Journal of Computers in Education*, *8*(4), 485–503. DOI: 10.1007/s40692-021-00188-7

Shen, D., Wu, G., & Suk, H. I. (2017). Deep learning in medical image analysis. *Annual Review of Biomedical Engineering*, *19*(1), 221–248. DOI: 10.1146/annurev-bioeng-071516-044442 PMID: 28301734

Shiva, K. (2024). *Natural language processing for customer service chatbots: Enhancing customer experience*. https://www.ijisae.org/index.php/IJISAE/article/view/6405

Shone, N., Ngoc, T. N., Phai, V. D., & Shi, Q. (2018). A deep learning approach to network intrusion detection. *IEEE Transactions on Emerging Topics in Computational Intelligence*, *2*(1), 41–50. DOI: 10.1109/TETCI.2017.2772792

Shu, K., Mahudeswaran, D., Wang, S., Lee, D., & Liu, H. (2020). Fakenewsnet: A data repository with news content, social context, and spatiotemporal information for studying fake news on social media. *Big Data*, *8*(3), 171–188. DOI: 10.1089/big.2020.0062 PMID: 32491943

Siddals, S., Torous, J., & Coxon, A. (2024). "It happened to be the perfect thing": Experiences of generative AI chatbots for mental health. *Npj Mental Health Research*, *3*(1), 48. Advance online publication. DOI: 10.1038/s44184-024-00097-4 PMID: 39465310

Sijan, M. A., Shahoriar, A., Salimullah, M., Islam, A. S., & Khan, R. H. (2022). A Review on E-Banking Security in Bangladesh: An Empirical Study. *2nd International Conference on Computing Advancements: Age of Computing and Augmented Life, ICCA 2022* (pp. 330-336). Dhaka: Association for Computing Machinery. DOI: 10.1145/3542954.3543002

Simon, B. D., Ozyoruk, K. B., Gelikman, D. G., Harmon, S. A., & Türkbey, B (2024). The future of multimodal artificial intelligence models for integrating imaging and clinical metadata: a narrative review. Diagnostic and interventional radiology (Ankara, Turkey).

Simonyan, K., & Zisserman, A. (2014). Very deep convolutional networks for large-scale image recognition. *arXiv preprint arXiv:1409.1556.*

Simran, K., S., & Hans, A. (2024). The AI Shield and Red AI Framework: Machine Learning Solutions for Cyber Threat Intelligence(CTI). *International Conference on Intelligent Systems for Cybersecurity, ISCS 2024.* Gurugram: IEEE. DOI: 10.1109/ISCS61804.2024.10581195

Singh, M. (2020). Scalability and sparsity issues in recommender datasets: a survey. *Knowledge and Information Systems*, *62*(1), 1–43.

Singhal, A., Sinha, P., & Pant, R. (2017). Use of deep learning in modern recommendation system: A summary of recent works. *arXiv preprint arXiv:1712.07525.*

Singh, R. H., Maurya, S., Tripathi, T., Narula, T., & Srivastav, G. (2020). Movie recommendation system using cosine similarity and KNN. *International Journal of Engineering and Advanced Technology*, *9*(5), 556–559. DOI: 10.35940/ijeat.E9666.069520

Singla, S., Thakur, A., Swami, A., Sawarn, U., & Singla, P. (2024, November). Advancements in Natural Language Processing: BERT and Transformer-Based Models for Text Understanding. In *2024 Second International Conference on Advanced Computing & Communication Technologies (ICACCTech)* (pp. 372-379). IEEE. DOI: 10.1109/ICACCTech65084.2024.00068

Song, M.-H. (2022). A study on explainable artificial intelligence-based sentimental analysis system model. *International Journal of Internet. Broadcasting and Communication*, *14*(1), 142–151.

Song, Y. (2023, December 01). Human Digital Twin, the Development and Impact on Design. *Journal of Computing and Information Science in Engineering*, *23*(06), 060819. Advance online publication. DOI: 10.1115/1.4063132

Soudan, B. (2024). Cybersecurity of Digital Twins in Industrial IoT Environments. *Advances in Science and Engineering Technology International Conferences, ASET 2024*. Abu Dhabi: Institute of Electrical and Electronics Engineers Inc. DOI: 10.1109/ASET60340.2024.10708640

Sridevi, K., & Santhanalakshmi, M. (2022). An Efficient Implementation of AES algorithm using Custom Key. *International Conference on Intelligent Innovations in Engineering and Technology, ICIIET 2022* (pp. 268-272). Coimbatore: IEEE. DOI: 10.1109/ICIIET55458.2022.9967508

Steck, H. (2019). Embarrassingly shallow autoencoders for sparse data. The World Wide Web Conference.

Steinert, S., Avila, K. E., Ruzika, S., Kuhn, J., & Küchemann, S. (2024). Harnessing large language models to develop research-based learning assistants for formative feedback. *Smart Learning Environments*, *11*(1), 62. DOI: 10.1186/s40561-024-00354-1

Stöhr, C., Ou, A. W., & Malmström, H. (2024). Perceptions and usage of AI chatbots among students in higher education across genders, academic levels and fields of study. *Computers and Education: Artificial Intelligence*, *7*, 100259. DOI: 10.1016/j.caeai.2024.100259

Stuma, V. S., & Mathonsi, T. E. (2024). A Security Algorithm to Prevent Denial of Service Attacks in the Internet of Things Devices. *4th IEEE International Conference on Electrical, Computer, and Energy Technologies, ICECET 2024*. Sydney: IEEE. DOI: 10.1109/ICECET61485.2024.10698594

Sumathi, S., & Karthikeyan, N. (2021). Detection of distributed denial of service using deep learning neural network. *Journal of Ambient Intelligence and Humanized Computing*, *12*(6), 5943–5953. DOI: 10.1007/s12652-020-02144-2

Sun, Y., Guo, Q., Zhao, S., Chandran, K., & Fathima, G. (2024). Context-aware augmented reality using human–computer interaction models. *Journal of Control and Decision*, *11*(1), 1–14. DOI: 10.1080/23307706.2022.2026260

Suresh, A., & Jose, A. C. (2023). Detection of Malicious Activities by AI-Supported Anomaly-Based IDS. In *Artificial Intelligence for Intrusion Detection Systems* (pp. 79–93). CRC Press., DOI: 10.1201/9781003346340-4

Swain, A., Swain, K., Pattnaik, S., Samal, S., & Das, J. (2022). Cybersecurity in Digital Transformations. *4th International Conference Intelligent Computing and Communication, ICAC 2021*. 430, pp. 247-252. Virtual, Online: Springer Science and Business Media Deutschland GmbH. DOI: 10.1007/978-981-19-0825-5_26

Taherdoost, H., Madanchian, M., & Ebrahimi, M. (2021). Advancement of cybersecurity and information security awareness to facilitate digital transformation: Opportunities and challenges. In *Handbook of Research on Advancing Cybersecurity for Digital Transformation* (pp. 99–117). IGI Global., DOI: 10.4018/978-1-7998-6975-7.ch006

Talha Junaid, M., Barakat, S., Awad, R., & Anwar, N. (2024). Adopting the power of AI chatbots for enriching students learning in civil engineering education: A study on capabilities and limitations. In *Artificial intelligence in education: The power and dangers of ChatGPT in the classroom* (pp. 25–47). Springer Nature Switzerland., DOI: 10.1007/978-3-031-52280-2_3

Tama, B. A., & Rhee, K.-H. (2017). Attack Classification Analysis of IoT Network via Deep Learning Approach. *Research Briefs on Information and Communication Technology Evolution*, *3*, 150–158. DOI: 10.56801/rebicte.v3i.54

Tang, J., & Wang, K. (2018). Ranking distillation: Learning compact ranking models with high performance for recommender system. Proceedings of the 24th ACM SIGKDD international conference on knowledge discovery & data mining.

Tang, T. A., Mhamdi, L., McLernon, D., Zaidi, S. A. R., Ghogho, M., & Moussa, F. El. (2020). DeepIDS: Deep Learning Approach for Intrusion Detection in Software Defined Networking. Electronics 2020, Vol. 9, Page 1533, 9(9), 1533. DOI: 10.3390/electronics9091533

Tang, Y., Yang, W., Xie, Y., & Yang, M. (2024). Domain adaptive knowledge tracing. *International Journal of Machine Learning and Cybernetics*, *15*(11), 5129–5142. DOI: 10.1007/s13042-024-02219-y

Tan, M., & Subramonyam, H. (2024, May). More than model documentation: uncovering teachers' bespoke information needs for informed classroom integration of ChatGPT. In *Proceedings of the 2024 CHI Conference on Human Factors in Computing Systems* (pp. 1-19). https://doi.org/DOI: 10.1145/3613904.3642592

Tavallaee, M., Bagheri, E., Lu, W., & Ghorbani, A. A. (2009). A detailed analysis of the KDD CUP 99 data set. *IEEE Symposium on Computational Intelligence for Security and Defense Applications, CISDA 2009*. DOI: 10.1109/CISDA.2009.5356528

Tayeb, A., Alahmadi, M., Tajik, E., & Haiduc, S. (2024, October). Investigating Developers' Preferences for Learning and Issue Resolution Resources in the ChatGPT Era. In *2024 IEEE International Conference on Software Maintenance and Evolution (ICSME)* (pp. 413-425). IEEE. DOI: DOI: 10.1109/ICSME58944.2024.00045

Tetzlaff, L., Schmiedek, F., & Brod, G. (2021). Developing personalized education: A dynamic framework. *Educational Psychology Review, 33*(3), 863–882. DOI: 10.1007/s10648-020-09570-w

Thorat, S. A., & Jadhav, V. (2020). A review on implementation issues of rule-based chatbot systems. SSRN *Electronic Journal*. DOI: 10.2139/ssrn.3567047

Thota, A., Tilak, P., Ahluwalia, S., & Lohia, N. (2018). Fake news detection: A deep learning approach. *SMU Data Science Review, 1*(3), 10.

Ting, D. S., Liu, Y., Burlina, P., Xu, X., Bressler, N. M., & Wong, T. Y. (2018). AI for medical imaging goes deep. *Nature Medicine, 24*(5), 539–540. DOI: 10.1038/s41591-018-0029-3 PMID: 29736024

Ting, V., Chou, H.-Y., & Wang, J.-H. (2023). Securing Manufacturing through Patch Management for IoT Devices. *3rd IEEE International Conference on Electronic Communications, Internet of Things and Big Data, ICEIB 2023* (pp. 479-482). Taichung: IEEE. DOI: 10.1109/ICEIB57887.2023.10170074

Tjuatja, L., Chen, V., Wu, T., Talwalkwar, A., & Neubig, G. (2024). Do llms exhibit human-like response biases? a case study in survey design. *Transactions of the Association for Computational Linguistics, 12*, 1011–1026. DOI: 10.1162/tacl_a_00685

Truong, T. C., Zelinka, I., Plucar, J., Čandík, M., & Šulc, V. (2020). Artificial intelligence and cybersecurity: Past, presence, and future. Artificial intelligence and evolutionary computations in engineering systems.

Tsintotas, K. A., Moutsis, S. N., Konstantinidis, F. K., & Gasteratos, A. (2024). Toward Smart Supply Chain: Adopting Internet of Things and Digital Twins. *6th International Conference Series on ICT, Entertainment Technologies, and Intelligent Information Management in Education and Industry, ETLTC 2024. 3220.* Hybrid, Aizuwakamatsu: American Institute of Physics. DOI: 10.1063/5.0235214

Tyagi, H., & Kumar, R. (2021a). Attack and anomaly detection in IoT networks using supervised machine learning approaches. *Revue d'Intelligence Artificielle, 35*(1), 11–21. DOI: 10.18280/ria.350102

Uddin, M. M., & Mc Neill, L. (2024). Flipping the traditional classroom in teaching classical literature in higher education: An experiment with oedipus rex by sophocles. *Ubiquitous Learning, 18*(1), 1–26. DOI: 10.18848/1835-9795/CGP/v18i01/1-26

Ullah, I., & Mahmoud, Q. H. (2020). A Scheme for Generating a Dataset for Anomalous Activity Detection in IoT Networks. Lecture Notes in Computer Science (Including Subseries Lecture Notes in Artificial Intelligence and Lecture Notes in Bioinformatics), 12109 LNAI, 508–520. DOI: 10.1007/978-3-030-47358-7_52

Urbani, R., Ferreira, C., & Lam, J. (2024). Managerial framework for evaluating AI chatbot integration: Bridging organizational readiness and technological challenges. *Business Horizons*, *67*(5), 595–606. DOI: 10.1016/j.bushor.2024.05.004

Vaczi, D., Toth-Laufer, E., & Szadeczky, T. (2020). Fuzzy-based Cybersecurity Risk Analysis of the Human Factor from the Perspective of Classified Information Leakage. *18th IEEE International Symposium on Intelligent Systems and Informatics, SISY 2020* (pp. 113-118). Institute of Electrical and Electronics Engineers Inc. DOI: 10.1109/SISY50555.2020.9217053

Vakhula, O., Kurii, Y., Opirskyy, I., & Susukailo, V. (2024). Security-as-Code Concept for Fulfilling ISO/IEC 27001:2022 Requirements. *Workshop Cybersecurity Providing in Information and Telecommunication Systems, CPITS 2024. 3654.* Virtual, Online: CEUR-WS. Retrieved Feb 13, 2025, from https://www.scopus.com/record/display.uri?eid=2-s2.0-85189135508&origin=scopusAI

Vats, D., & vinash Sharma, A. (2022). A Collaborative Filtering Recommender System using Apache Mahout, Ontology and Dimensionality Reduction Technique. 2022 International Conference on Advances in Computing, Communication and Applied Informatics (ACCAI).

Venkatesan, V. K., Ramakrishna, M. T., Batyuk, A., Barna, A., & Havrysh, B. (2023). High-Performance Artificial Intelligence Recommendation of Quality Research Papers Using Effective Collaborative Approach. *Systems*, *11*(2), 81.

Verma, P., & Sharma, S. (2020). Artificial intelligence based recommendation system. 2020 2nd International Conference on Advances in Computing, Communication Control and Networking (ICACCCN)

Villegas-Ch, W., Buenano-Fernandez, D., Navarro, A. M., & Mera-Navarrete, A. (2025). Adaptive intelligent tutoring systems for STEM education: Analysis of the learning impact and effectiveness of personalized feedback. *Smart Learning Environments*, *12*(1), 1–31. DOI: 10.1186/s40561-025-00389-y

Viswanathan, V. K., Jain, V. K., Vaish, A., Jeyaraman, M., Iyengar, K. P., & Vaishya, R. (2024). Chatbots and their applications in medical fields: Current status and future trends: A scoping review. *Apollo Medicine*, *21*(4), 386–392. DOI: 10.1177/09760016241259851

Vozalis, E., & Margaritis, K. G. (2003). Analysis of recommender systems algorithms. The 6th Hellenic European Conference on Computer Mathematics & its Applications.

Wah, J. N. K. (2025). Revolutionizing e-health: The transformative role of AI-powered hybrid chatbots in healthcare solutions. *Frontiers in Public Health*, *13*, 1530799. Advance online publication. DOI: 10.3389/fpubh.2025.1530799 PMID: 40017541

Wang, B. (2025). Human-AI Systems for Creating, Consuming, and Interacting with Digital Content (Doctoral dissertation, University of Toronto (Canada)).

Wang, C., & Blei, D. M. (2011). Collaborative topic modeling for recommending scientific articles. Proceedings of the 17th ACM SIGKDD international conference on Knowledge discovery and data mining.

Wang, W. Y. (2017). " liar, liar pants on fire": A new benchmark dataset for fake news detection. *arXiv preprint arXiv:1705.00648*. DOI: 10.18653/v1/P17-2067

Wang, Y., Ma, W., Zhang, M., Liu, Y., & Ma, S. (2023). A survey on the fairness of recommender systems. *ACM Transactions on Information Systems*, *41*(3), 1–43.

Wang, H., Wang, X., Wu, H., Wang, H., Zhang, L., Zhang, Q., & Wang, J. (2021). Design and Research of Network Security Threat Detection and Traceability System Based on AI. *2nd IYSF Academic Symposium on Artificial Intelligence and Computer Engineering. 12079*. Xi'an: SPIE. DOI: 10.1117/12.2622727

Wang, J., Deng, W., Yue, C., Su, W., & Bai, X. (2025). Joint optimization of cooling parameters and workload distributions based on model predictive control for rack-based data centers. *Journal of Building Engineering*, *100*, 111801. DOI: 10.1016/j.jobe.2025.111801

Wang, M. (2024). Generative AI: A new challenge for cybersecurity. *Journal of Computer Science and Technology Studies*, *6*(2), 13–18. DOI: 10.32996/jcsts.2024.6.2.3

Wang, W., Sadjadi, S. M., & Rishe, N. (2024). A Survey of Major Cybersecurity Compliance Frameworks. *10th IEEE Conference on Big Data Security on Cloud, BigDataSecurity 2024* (pp. 23-34). New York City: IEEE. DOI: 10.1109/BigDataSecurity62737.2024.00013

Weikert, T., Winkel, D. J., Bremerich, J., Stieltjes, B., Parmar, V., Sauter, A. W., & Sommer, G. (2020). Automated detection of pulmonary embolism in CT pulmonary angiograms using an AI-powered algorithm. *European Radiology*, *30*(12), 6545–6553. DOI: 10.1007/s00330-020-06998-0 PMID: 32621243

Williams, R. T. (2024). The ethical implications of using generative chatbots in higher education. *Frontiers in Education*, *8*, 1331607. Advance online publication. DOI: 10.3389/feduc.2023.1331607

Wilmanski, M., Kreucher, C., & Lauer, J. (2016). Modern approaches in deep learning for SAR ATR. Algorithms for synthetic aperture radar imagery XXIII, Zagoruyko, S., & Komodakis, N. (2016). Wide residual networks. *arXiv preprint arXiv:1605.07146*.

Wilson, L., & Marasoiu, M. (2022). The Development and Use of Chatbots in Public Health: Scoping review. *JMIR Human Factors*, *9*(4), e35882. DOI: 10.2196/35882 PMID: 36197708

Windfont, C. M. (2024). *Secondary special education teachers' perception of technology integration and its use in classroom instructions*. Walden University.

Wollny, S., Schneider, J., Di Mitri, D., Weidlich, J., Rittberger, M., & Drachsler, H. (2021). Are we there yet? - A Systematic Literature review on chatbots in education. *Frontiers in Artificial Intelligence*, *4*, 654924. Advance online publication. DOI: 10.3389/frai.2021.654924 PMID: 34337392

Wong, M. F., Guo, S., Hang, C. N., Ho, S. W., & Tan, C. W. (2023). Natural language generation and understanding of big code for AI-assisted programming: A review. *Entropy (Basel, Switzerland)*, *25*(6), 888. DOI: 10.3390/e25060888 PMID: 37372232

Wu, C., Wu, F., Huang, Y., & Xie, X. (2023). Personalized news recommendation: Methods and challenges. *ACM Transactions on Information Systems*, *41*(1), 1–50. DOI: 10.1145/3530257

Wu, K., Chen, Z., & Li, W. (2018). A Novel Intrusion Detection Model for a Massive Network Using Convolutional Neural Networks. *IEEE Access : Practical Innovations, Open Solutions*, *6*, 50850–50859. DOI: 10.1109/ACCESS.2018.2868993

Xie, J., Luo, X., Deng, X., Tang, Y., Tian, W., Cheng, H., ... & Xie, X. (2023). Advances in artificial intelligence to predict cancer immunotherapy efficacy.

Xue, H.-J., Dai, X., Zhang, J., Huang, S., & Chen, J. (2017). Deep matrix factorization models for recommender systems. IJCAI.

Xu, Q., Wu, T., Wang, Y., Li, X., Yu, H., Cen, S., & Li, Z. (2025). A comprehensive review of Intelligent Question-Answering Systems in Traditional Chinese Medicine Based on LLMs. *Journal of Pharmaceutical Analysis*, 101406. DOI: 10.1016/j.jpha.2025.101406

Yamijala, S. M. S., Chodisetty, R. M., Chakravorty, C., & Sai, K. P. (2025). AI-Powered Learning Revolutionizing Smart Education With Personalized Learning Styles. In *Internet of Behavior-Based Computational Intelligence for Smart Education Systems* (pp. 191–212). IGI Global., DOI: 10.4018/979-8-3693-8151-9.ch007

Yang, X., Yang, L., & Li, S. (2023). A Digital Twin Application Framework in the Field of Industry. *18th IEEE Conference on Industrial Electronics and Applications, ICIEA 2023* (pp. 1615-1619). Ningbo: Institute of Electrical and Electronics Engineers Inc. DOI: 10.1109/ICIEA58696.2023.10241448

Yavuz, F. Y., Ünal, D., & Gül, E. (2018). Deep learning for detection of routing attacks in the internet of things. *International Journal of Computational Intelligence Systems*, *12*(1), 39–58. DOI: 10.2991/ijcis.2018.25905181

Ye, J., & Morris, G. (2025). Promoting Inclusive Practices in Transnational Higher Education Through Staff Training and Development. In *Innovative Approaches to Staff Development in Transnational Higher Education* (pp. 119–138). IGI Global Scientific Publishing., DOI: 10.4018/979-8-3693-9102-0.ch005

Yetişensoy, O., & Karaduman, H. (2024). The effect of AI-powered chatbots in social studies education. *Education and Information Technologies*, *29*(13), 17035–17069. DOI: 10.1007/s10639-024-12485-6

You, I., Kim, J., Pawana, I. W., & Ko, Y. (2024, November). Mitigating Security Vulnerabilities in 6G Networks: A Comprehensive Analysis of the DMRN Protocol Using SVO Logic and ProVerif. *Applied Sciences (Basel, Switzerland)*, *14*(21), 9726. Advance online publication. DOI: 10.3390/app14219726

Yu, D., Zhang, H., Huang, Y., & Xie, Z. (2025). Data distribution inference attack in federated learning via reinforcement learning support. *High-Confidence Computing*, *5*(1), 100235. DOI: 10.1016/j.hcc.2024.100235

Yusuf, H., Money, A., & Daylamani-Zad, D. (2025). Pedagogical AI conversational agents in higher education: A conceptual framework and survey of the state of the art. *Educational Technology Research and Development*, *73*(2), 1–60. DOI: 10.1007/s11423-025-10447-4

Zadeh, L. A. (1972). A fuzzy-set-theoretic interpretation of linguistic hedges.

Zadeh, L. A. (1988). Fuzzy logic. *Computer*, *21*(4), 83–93. DOI: 10.1109/2.53

Zaeem, R. N., Li, C., & Barber, K. S. (2020). *On sentiment of online fake news.* Paper presented at the 2020 IEEE/ACM international conference on advances in social networks analysis and mining (ASONAM).

Zahra Sadeghi, Roohallah Alizadehsani, Mehmet Akif CIFCI, Samina Kausar, Rizwan Rehman, Priyakshi Mahanta, Pranjal Kumar Bora, Ammar Almasri, Rami S. Alkhawalde, Sadiq Hussain, Bilal Alatas, Afshin Shoeibi l, Hossein Moosaei, Milan Hladík, Saeid Nahavandi, Panos M. Pardalos. (2024). A review of Explainable Artificial Intelligence in healthcare.

Zakaria, R., Hadhoum, B., Mourad, E., & Mustapha, M. (2025). *Dynamic Adaptation in an Intelligent Multi-Tutoring System: A Multi-Agent Approach*. IEEE., DOI: 10.1109/ACCESS.2025.3576651

Zalte, S. M. (2023). REVOLUTIONIZING EDUCATION. *LEVERAGING AI-ML TECHNOLOGIES TO ENHANCE TEACHING AND LEARNING OUTCOMES.*, *12*(12), 679–688. DOI: 10.48047/ecb/2023.12.si12.058

Zawacki-Richter, O., Marín, V. I., Bond, M., & Gouverneur, F. (2019). Systematic review of research on artificial intelligence applications in higher education – where are the educators? *International Journal of Educational Technology in Higher Education*, *16*(1), 39. Advance online publication. DOI: 10.1186/s41239-019-0171-0

Zhang, G., Liu, Y., & Jin, X. (2020). A survey of autoencoder-based recommender systems. *Frontiers of Computer Science*, *14*(2), 430–450. DOI: 10.1007/s11704-018-8052-6

Zhang, H., Feng, L., Zhang, X., Yang, Y., & Li, J. (2022). Necessary conditions for convergence of CNNs and initialization of convolution kernels. *Digital Signal Processing*, *123*, 103397. DOI: 10.1016/j.dsp.2022.103397

Zhang, K., & Aslan, A. B. (2021). AI technologies for education: Recent research & future directions. Computers and education. *Artificial Intelligence*, *2*, 100025.

Zhang, Q., Lu, J., & Jin, Y. (2021). Artificial intelligence in recommender systems. *Complex & Intelligent Systems*, *7*(1), 439–457. DOI: 10.1007/s40747-020-00212-w

Zhang, S., Yao, L., Sun, A., & Tay, Y. (2019). Deep learning based recommender system: A survey and new perspectives. *ACM Computing Surveys*, *52*(1), 1–38. DOI: 10.1145/3158369

Zhao, Q., Harper, F. M., Adomavicius, G., & Konstan, J. A. (2018). Explicit or implicit feedback? Engagement or satisfaction? A field experiment on machine-learning-based recommender systems. Proceedings of the 33rd Annual ACM symposium on applied computing.

Zhou, T., Zeng, Y., Li, Y., Jiang, Z., Liu, Z., & Li, T. (2021). Cold-start recommendation method based on homomorphic encryption. 2021 International Conference on Networking and Network Applications (NaNA)

Zhou, J., Zhang, Y., Luo, Q., Parker, A. G., & De Choudhury, M. (2023). Synthetic Lies: Understanding AI-Generated Misinformation and Evaluating Algorithmic and Human Solutions. *In Proceedings of the 2023 CHI Conference on Human Factors in Computing Systems (CHI '23)*, 1–20. DOI: 10.1145/3544548.3581318

Zhou, X., Hu, Y., Liang, W., Ma, J., & Jin, Q. (2021). Variational LSTM Enhanced Anomaly Detection for Industrial Big Data. *IEEE Transactions on Industrial Informatics*, *17*(5), 3469–3477. DOI: 10.1109/TII.2020.3022432

Zhu, C., Ni, R., Xu, Z., Kong, K., Huang, W. R., & Goldstein, T. (2021). Gradinit: Learning to initialize neural networks for stable and efficient training. *Advances in Neural Information Processing Systems*, *34*, 16410–16422.

Zhu, W., Huang, Y., Zeng, L., Chen, X., Liu, Y., Qian, Z., Du, N., Fan, W., & Xie, X. (2019). AnatomyNet: Deep learning for fast and fully automated whole-volume segmentation of head and neck anatomy. *Medical Physics*, *46*(2), 576–589. DOI: 10.1002/mp.13300 PMID: 30480818

Zorchenko, N. V., Tyupina, T. G., & Parshutin, M. E. (2024). Technologies Used by General Electric to Create Digital Twins for Energy Industry. *Power Technology and Engineering*. https://doi.org/https://doi.org/10.1007/s10749-024-01839-2

About the Contributors

Bahaa Eddine Elbaghazaoui is a professor at ENSA Beni Mellal and a PhD holder in Computer Science and Artificial Intelligence. With extensive experience in software engineering, he specializes in full-stack development, microservices, AI integration, and cloud computing. As a project manager and trainer, he has led and contributed to innovative solutions in telecommunications, insurance, and government sectors. His research focuses on data profiling and predictive analytics, with numerous publications in high-impact journals. Passionate about technology and education, he actively mentors, reviews scientific work, and advances cutting-edge software solutions. He can be reached at elbaghazaoui.bahaa@gmail.com and b.elbaghazaoui@usms.as.ma.

Mohamed Amnai is a Full Professor at the Faculty of Sciences, Ibn Tofail University, specializing in Computer Science and Telecommunications. With a Ph.D. in Quality of Service Management and Mobility Control in Ad Hoc Networks, his expertise spans big data, AI-driven decision support systems, machine learning, and network security. Dr. Amnai has contributed extensively to academia as a researcher, supervisor, and journal reviewer, with numerous publications in high-impact journals and conferences. His work focuses on advancing AI applications in data profiling, recommendation systems, and network optimization. He can be reached at mohamed.amnai@uit.ac.ma.

Noreddine Gherabi is a Full Professor of Computer Science at ENSA Khouribga, Sultan Moulay Slimane University. With a Ph.D. in Database Migration and Semantic Web, he specializes in data science, artificial intelligence, semantic technologies, and cybersecurity. He has led significant research on machine learning, recommendation systems, and big data integration, contributing to high-impact publications, books, and conferences. Dr. Gherabi is actively involved in academic leadership, Ph.D. supervision, and scientific committees worldwide. He can be reached at n.gherabi@usms.ma and gherabi@gmail.com.

Prabhu Shankar B, Department of Computer Science and Engineering, Vel Tech Rangarajan Dr Sagunthala R&D Institute of Science and Technology, Chennai, Tamil Nadu, India

Mohamed Bahra is a researcher and software engineer specializing in Natural Language Processing (NLP), artificial intelligence, and misinformation detection. He holds a position at the Faculty of Sciences and Techniques in Tangier, Morocco, where he contributes to the LIST research team. His academic work focuses on the intersection of fuzzy logic, deep learning, and sentiment analysis, particularly in the context of detecting fake news and health-related misinformation. He has co-authored peer-reviewed publications on the application of fuzzy logic and neural networks in sentiment analysis and is actively engaged in exploring hybrid AI models that enhance interpretability and robustness in critical NLP tasks.

Nitesh Behare is an accomplished author with a wealth of knowledge and 16 years of experience in the academic field. He currently holds the position of Associate Professor at the Balaji Institute of International Business (BIIB), Sri Balaji University Pune (SBUP). Throughout his career, Dr. Behare has made significant contributions to the academic world through the publication of numerous research papers and book chapters, establishing himself as a recognized authority in his field.

Kashvi Chaturvedi, is studying B.Tech, specialisation in Artificial Intelligence and Data Science at Ajeenkya DY Patil University. She started solidifying her programming skills by completing various certification courses like Data Structures in C, Tableau functions and Operating Systems along with doing few projects using languages like Python, C, C++ and creating Web Page using HTML, CSS and Java Script. She had also attended an Arduino-Based Automation course at Dolphin Labs to enhance her software knowledge. There, she learned how to work with sensors, microcontrollers, and circuit design. She has also written multiple review papers on topics such as Geographic Information Systems, Comparative Analysis of BJT Configurations, Swiss Bank vs. European Central Bank: Data Analysis. She is also researching on and learning many topics such as Small Modular Reactors, Bibliometric Analysis, UNSDGs etc. Because of her interest in latest technologies, she also participated in Global Hyperloop Competition hosted by IIT Madras representing her college as team Vac-Vectoor where she learnt more about various subtopics from the mentors.

Susanta Das is a seasoned educator with a proven record of teaching and mentoring diverse students, working at multiple institutions, and providing service to the various initiatives of organizations. He received his Ph.D. and M.A. degrees from Western Michigan University (WMU), USA, and M.Sc. degree from Banaras

Hindu University (BHU), India all in Physics. He continued his research as a Marie-Curie post-doctoral fellow at Stockholm University, Stockholm, Sweden on beam diagnostics for the DESIREE (Double ElectroStatic Ion Ring ExpEriment) in the project DITANET (Diagnostic Techniques for particle Accelerators – a Marie-Curie initial training NETwork), at the Indian Institute of Science Education and Research-Kolkata, India on high-pressure physics as a Project Scientist-B, and at the University of Electro-Communications, Tokyo, Japan on ion-surface interactions as a Post-doctoral fellow. Throughout his career, Dr. Das worked and collaborated with many researchers, Ph.D., master, and visiting students from different countries. He further visited many countries to discuss research and an international conference participant (UK, Italy, Germany, Greece, Belgium, Bulgaria, Romania, Brazil etc.). He worked at several institutions before assuming his current role at Ajeenkya D Y Patil University. He received the Marie-Curie post-doctoral fellowship in Sweden, Science Academies' Summer Research Fellowship in India, Gwen Frostic Doctoral Fellowship, Department Graduate Research and Creative Scholar Award by WMU, and Leo R. Parpart Doctoral Fellowship by Dept. of Physics, WMU, among many others, throughout his academic journey. He co-authored several research articles in WoS/Scopus indexed international journals, conference proceedings, and scholarly book chapters and co-edited several books published by renowned international publishing houses (IGI-Global, Springer Nature, Nova Science Publishers, Wiley, & Scrivener-Wiley, Notion Press). At present, Dr. Das continues to delve into cutting-edge fields, with a keen interest in nanotechnology, UN SDGs, and data science. His multifaceted contributions, spanning teaching, research, and administrative leadership, showcase a dedicated professional who is instrumental in advancing the vision and mission of the institutions he serves.

Amine Dehbi, received a Ph.D. in computer science from the Faculty of Sciences Ben M'Sick, Laboratory of Information Processing (LTI) at Hassan II University of Casablanca, Morocco. His ability lies in the intersection of information and communication technology (ICT) in education. He is deeply engaged in exploring how smart technologies can contribute to the development of smart learning environments across various educational levels and fields. His extensive research portfolio spans a range of cutting-edge topics, including smart education, e-learning, interoperability, big data, cloud computing, artificial intelligence, internet of things, engineering education and sustainable development.

Rachid Dehbi is a Full Professor and a prominent researcher at the Laboratory of Computer and Sciences (LIS) within the Faculty of Sciences Ain Chock, Hassan II University of Casablanca, Morocco. With over 24 years of experience in higher education and research, he is a recognized expert in intelligent systems, the Internet of Things (IoT), and advanced technologies. He plays a strategic role in overseeing research policies and doctoral training programs at the university. His work focuses on innovative fields such as E-learning, M-learning, E-health, M-health, Model-Driven Engineering, Database Security, Big Data, and intelligent systems. Professor Dehbi's contributions through his research and publications have significantly enriched the academic and technological landscape, solidifying his reputation as an authority in his field.

Salma El Omari is a PhD student in Computer Science and an Associate Professor at EMSI Casablanca, Morocco. She is affiliated with the Computer Science Department at the Faculty of Sciences and Techniques of Beni Mellal, where she contributes to both teaching and research. Her work focuses on machine learning, computer vision, classification, data clustering, and unsupervised learning, with recent efforts oriented toward applications in the education field. In particular, she is developing recommender systems for personalized learning paths that leverage advanced AI techniques to adapt educational content to individual learner needs. Through her academic and professional roles, Salma combines theoretical research with practical implementation, aiming to improve the effectiveness of intelligent educational systems and contribute to the growing body of knowledge at the intersection of artificial intelligence and education.

Tarik El Moudden is a researcher and educator in the fields of artificial intelligence, deep learning, and geospatial data analysis. He earned his Ph.D. in Computer Science in 2025 from the Faculty of Sciences at Ibn Tofail University, Kenitra, with a dissertation titled "Advances in Deep Learning for Image Classification and Hypothesis Testing with Geospatial Data". His research contributes to remote sensing applications, satellite image analysis, and predictive modeling using advanced deep learning techniques. Dr. El Moudden holds a DESA (Diplôme d'Études Supérieures Approfondies) in Computer Science and Telecommunications (2008) from the same university, with a focus on image indexing by content. He also earned a Bachelor's degree in Physics (2000), specializing in electronic physics, and holds an earlier certification in computer science education from the Regional Pedagogical Center of Rabat (2003). He has obtained numerous certifications from prestigious institutions, including NASA, IBM, Coursera, Packt, and HP Foundation, in topics such as machine learning, sports analytics, concurrent programming, project management with AI, and remote sensing applications. Dr. El Moudden has published widely in peer-reviewed Scopus-indexed journals, including Scientific African, International Journal of Electrical and Computer Engineering, and Journal of Geodynamics. His notable works explore slum detection using transfer learning, convolutional neural networks from scratch, and earthquake prediction via planetary alignment modeling. He has also co-authored papers on wastewater treatment optimization and federated learning in IoT environments. A frequent contributor to international conferences, Dr. El Moudden has presented innovative research on crop segmentation from Sentinel-2 imagery and on the relationship between comet activity and seismic events. He actively collaborates with other scholars and has proposed new strategies for slum upgrading using AI-based urban planning approaches. His interdisciplinary expertise, spanning deep learning, computer vision, remote sensing, and environmental data modeling, reflects a strong commitment to advancing scientific knowledge and its applications for sustainable development.

Abdelhadi Fennan is a senior researcher and professor at the Faculty of Sciences and Techniques, Abdelmalek Essaâdi University, Tangier, Morocco. His work spans several areas in computer science, with a strong focus on artificial intelligence, fuzzy logic, machine learning, and soft computing. He has published extensively in reputable international journals and conferences, contributing to fields such as fuzzy systems, knowledge-based systems, and intelligent decision support. Prof. Fennan also supervises postgraduate research and plays a key role in advancing interdisciplinary approaches that combine AI with real-world applications, particularly in information processing and decision-making systems.

Ikram Gouri is a Ph.D. researcher in Artificial Intelligence at Hassan II University in Casablanca, Morocco. Her research focuses on the application of deep learning and large language models (LLMs) in the medical field, particularly in radiology. She is also involved in projects that bridge AI, natural language processing, and clinical workflows, aiming to enhance the reliability and interpretability of AI-generated outputs in healthcare contexts. Beyond her academic work, she has hands-on experience in data science, software development, and business intelligence. She is passionate about responsible AI innovation and its impact on medical decision-making.

Shital Gupta is a seasoned academician with over 20 years of experience in academia and administration. She currently serves as Professor at the Bansal Group of Institutions, where she also leads as Nodal Center Coordinator for the Virtual Lab initiative (Ministry of Education & IIT Delhi) and the IIRS ISRO Outreach Program, fostering innovation in online and space education. Dr. Gupta has published extensively in SCOPUS and WoS-indexed journals, guided numerous student projects, and has been honored as Best Teacher for her dedication to education and research excellence.

Najlae Idrissi is a senior researcher and Head of the Computer Science Department at Université Sultan Moulay Slimane in Beni Mellal, Morocco. With degrees in Applied Statistics and Computer Science from Mohammed V University and a joint program with Nantes University, she has built a solid foundation in data-driven methodologies and artificial intelligence. Her core research area is medical image processing, with a special emphasis on early detection of cancers such as breast and brain tumors. Idrissi has published over 55 papers, applying both classical probabilistic techniques (Hidden Markov Models and Triplet Markov Chains) and modern deep learning architectures like UNet, ResNet50, and EfficientNet to segmentation and classification tasks. Many of her studies rely on quantitative evaluation metrics such as PSNR, SSIM, and DICE, highlighting her methodical approach to performance validation. Beyond healthcare-related image analysis, she has also worked on driver fatigue detection using recurrent neural networks, pathological voice detection via spectrogram-based learning, and energy-aware routing protocols for wireless sensor networks. More recently, she has begun investigating recommender systems, reflecting her continued evolution in the broader field of AI. Idrissi's academic impact is evident through her significant number of reads and citations on platforms like ResearchGate and Google Scholar. Her combination of technical rigor, applied focus, and interdisciplinary reach makes her one of the prominent AI researchers in the Moroccan academic landscape.

Kirti Jain holds a Ph.D., M.Tech, and B.E. degree in Computer Science & Engineering from Rajiv Gandhi Proudyogiki Vishwavidyalaya (RGPV), Bhopal, India. Presently she is working as Professor at Sage University,Bhopal. She has had the privilege of teaching a range of subjects, including Data Structures, Analysis and Design of Algorithms, Programming Languages (C, Python), Machine Learning, and Data Science. Her research expertise has led to numerous publications in esteemed international journals such as Scopus, Springer, and IEEE conferences. Additionally, she has successfully filed and published five patents and copyrights, with several more in progress, and has authored two books. As a passionate educator and researcher, she is committed to shaping the next generation of innovators and thought leaders in Computer Science and Engineering. She has also earned several NPTEL certificates and received the Srijan and Atmamanthan awards.

Balusamy Nachiappan Experienced IT professional with a strong background in object-oriented Software Development, Design, and Architecture. Certified as a Salesforce System Architect and Salesforce Application Architect. Specialized in Banking, including Investment Banking and Core Banking, with international exposure. Extensive experience in the Travel Domain encompassing Airlines, Ship & Cargo industries, along with proficiency in Supply Chain Management and Real Estate. A solid track record of over a decade in Product Development across various sectors. Proficient in Waterfall, V Model, and Agile-Scrum methodologies. Holds extensive onsite exposure in the US, Japan, the UK, and Qatar.

Soukaina Nai is a IT Engineer and a research student at Department of Computer Science, Faculty of Sciences, Ibn Tofail University (Kenitra Morocco). Her research interests include machine learning, integrated management systems, decision-making systems, evolutionary algorithms and education systems. She has published numerous articles in several journals.

Najat Rafalia, she has obtained three doctorates in Computer Sciences at Mohammed V University, Rabat, Morocco by colaboration with ENSEEIHT, Toulouse, France, and at Ibn Tofail University, Kenitra, Morocco. Currently she is a professor at Ibn Tofail University, Department of Computer Sciences, Kénitra, Morocco. Her research interests are in distributed systems, multi agent systems, concurrent and parallel programming, communication, Security, Big data and Cloud Computing.

Krutika Patre, is an aspiring programmer and technology enthusiast, currently pursuing Engineering in Artificial Intelligence and Data Science. With a passion for learning, she is building experience in a variety of programming languages and technologies, including C, C++, Python, Data Structures (DS), HTML, CSS, and JavaScript, DBMS (My SQL). After learning this programming language, she has created interest in Full Stack Development. She had also attended an Arduino-Based Automation course at Dolphin Labs to improve my software knowledge. There, she learned how to work with sensors, microcontrollers, and circuit design. She has written review paper on Sustainable engineering on build environment. She is doing researching and learning many topics related to AI, Policy and governance and related to my interest. She has taken part in hackathons, workshops, and tech events to explore many fields. She is also working with a group on Hyperloop. Being part of this project has really helped her grow, especially in areas like teamwork, innovation, and systems thinking.

Rajkumar N is an Associate Professor in the Department of Computer Science and Engineering. He earned his Ph.D. in Information and Communication Engineering from Anna University, Chennai. With a rich experience of 15 years in the realm of technical education, he has made substantial contributions to the academic arena. His research background is highly commendable, encompassing over 20 publications in esteemed international journals, coupled with numerous presentations at both international and national conferences. Moreover, he actively engages as a member of prestigious professional societies such as ISTE, IAENG, and CSTA. His primary areas of interest comprise Software Engineering, Computer Networks, Internet of Things, and Machine Learning.

Sunil Sankathala is pursuing B. Tech Computer Science and Engineering at Ajeenkya DY Patil University, with a diverse range of interests that bridge technology, sustainability, and innovation. His academic focus lies in computer science fundamentals like programming, data structures, algorithms, and software development. He actively supplements this with hands-on experience in web development and robotics. Beyond the core curriculum, He has a strong research inclination in emerging and impactful fields. His current research interests include Artificial Intelligence in Healthcare, bioplastics, nano bioplastics, e-waste management, and solid waste management—areas where he believes technology can make a meaningful difference in solving real-world problems. He has been publishing research articles and book chapters in reputed national and international journals and books. He is also part of an ambitious Hyperloop project, which involves interdisciplinary collaboration and cutting-edge engineering aimed at revolutionizing transportation. Working on this project has enhanced his skills in teamwork, innovation, and systems thinking. In the tech domain, he has developed proficiency in web development using technologies such as HTML, CSS, JavaScript, and React. His interests in robotics further reflect building smart, responsive systems that interact with the physical world. Throughout his course, he has helped strengthen problem-solving and collaborative skills. He is proficient in languages such as Python, C, C++, MySQL, Ubuntu, Machine Learning and familiar with frameworks and tools like React, Git. He actively participates in hackathons, coding competitions, and tech events to challenge himself and learn from peers. He is also a quick learner and highly adaptable, with an eagerness to stay updated with the latest trends in the tech world. He aspires to become a skilled software engineer and contribute to building innovative solutions that have a positive impact on society. The long-term goal is to work in a dynamic environment where knowledge, grow professionally, and make meaningful contributions to the field of technology. Driven by a spirit of exploration and sustainability, he aims to contribute to technological solutions that address both human and environmental needs. The long-term goal is to become a versatile engineer and researcher, working at the intersection of computer science, environmental innovation, and human well-being.

Atharva Saraf is currently pursuing a B. Tech degree in Computer Science Engineering at Ajeenkya D Y Patil University. Throughout his academic journey, he has developed a strong foundation in various programming languages, including C, C++, and Python. His interests and focus areas lie in algorithm-based programs, artificial intelligence (with a special emphasis on neural networks), and cybersecurity. His has successfully undertaken several projects that reflect my proficiency and passion in these domains. For instance, he developed a PC-Tuner application aimed at optimizing system performance by employing various methods such as defragmentation. Additionally, he created an automated backup utility capable of securely backing up selected files, folders, and stores them in compressed backup folder in system itself it can also store backups on external hard disk and cloud storages. Beyond project work, he has contributed to the academic community through research articles and book chapters. Notable among these is my co-authored chapter on federated learning techniques, exploring their applications and advancements in the field of machine learning. Moreover, he is currently working on writing a book chapter focusing on federated learning, delving deeper into its methodologies and practical implementations. His academic experiences have honed his skills in problem-solving, critical thinking, and collaborative teamwork. He is eager to further expand His knowledge and expertise in computer science, particularly in areas that intersect with his interests in algorithms, artificial intelligence, and their practical applications.

Aditya Shrivastav is an aspiring technologist currently pursuing a Bachelor of Technology (B. Tech) in Computer Science and Engineering at Ajeenkya D. Y. Patil University. He holds solid programming expertise in C, C++, and Python, alongside strong command over data and business tools such as Microsoft Excel and Tally software. Aditya is a member of Team Vac-Vectoor Hyperloop and participated with the team in the Global Hyperloop Competition organized by IIT Madras, contributing to cutting-edge transportation solutions. He actively engages in hackathons and various technical events to expand his skills and contribute to innovative problem-solving. He has authored and co-authored book chapters in the domains of solid waste management, bioplastics, nanotechnology applications, and artificial intelligence, showcasing his multidisciplinary approach and research acumen. Aditya is also working on an innovative project on predictive e-waste management. The project is targeted toward IT departments, schools, and colleges, aiming to support sustainable practices and resource optimization. In parallel with his academic journey, Aditya is serving as a faculty intern at Disha Computer Institute, where he teaches C, C++, basic Python, basic Java, Excel formulas, and Tally software. His dedication and teaching proficiency earned him a Letter of Appreciation and the opportunity to conduct a workshop on Advanced Excel at G. H. Raisoni College of Arts, Commerce and Science. With a strong foundation in technology, a passion for sustainability, and hands-on experience in both teaching and project development, Aditya Shrivastav is committed to driving impact through research, education, and innovation.

Viji C holds the position of Associate Professor in the Department of Computer Science and Engineering. She accomplished her Ph.D. in Information and Communication Engineering from Anna University, Chennai. Dr. C. Viji's expertise in the realm of technical education has resulted in noteworthy contributions to the academic sphere. Her research background is indeed impressive, encompassing over 10 publications in esteemed international journals, along with numerous presentations at both international and national conferences. Furthermore, she actively engages as a member of renowned professional societies such as IAENG and CSTA.

Index

A

C

D

E

F

G

H

T

W

Z

www.ingramcontent.com/pod-product-compliance
Lightning Source LLC
LaVergne TN
LVHW081538300926
849161LV00006B/1484
9798337380117